AD

STAGED

ARCHITECTURE FOR PERFORMANCE, EXHIBITION, AND FICTION

Edited by Neil Spiller and Ashley Simone

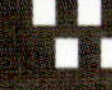
01 | 95 | 2025

STAGED: ARCHITECTURE FOR PERFORMANCE, EXHIBITION, AND FICTION

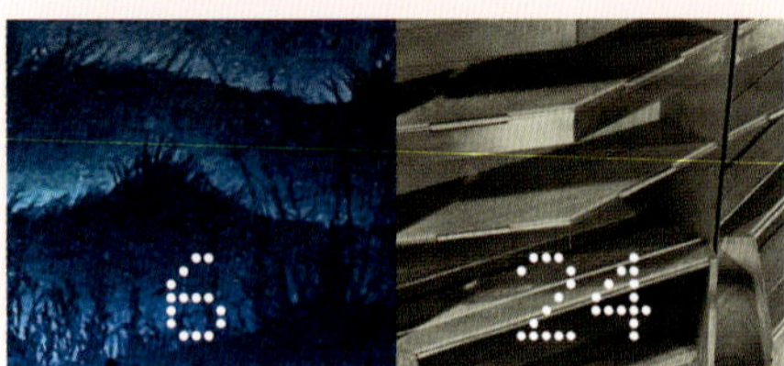

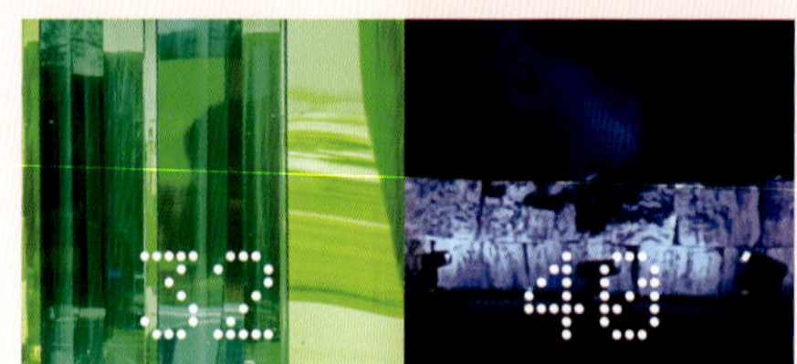

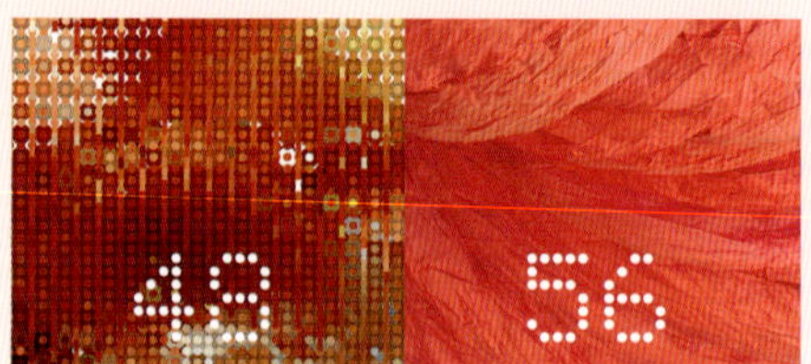

ISSN 0003-8504

ISBN 978-1-961856-98-1

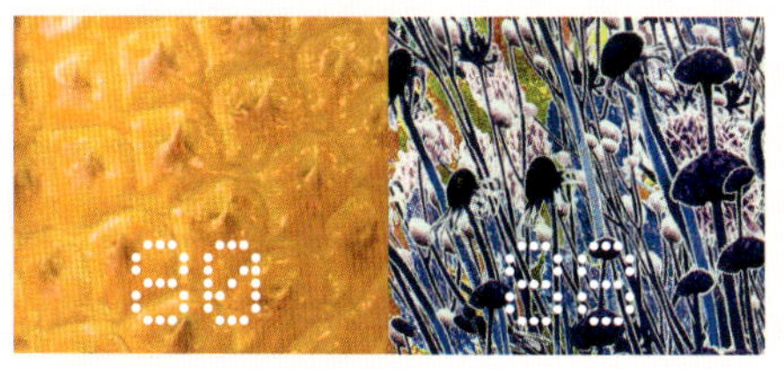

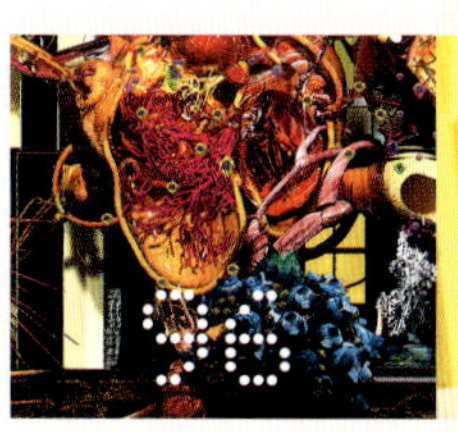

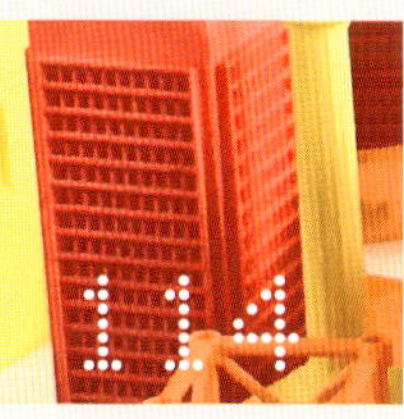

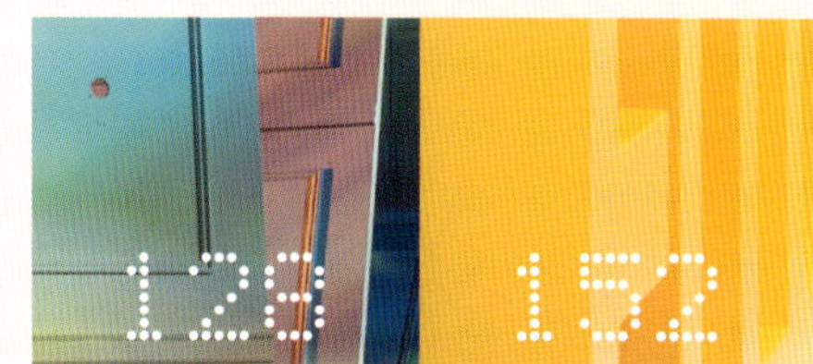

ARCHITECTURAL DESIGN JUNE 2025 VOLUME 95 | ISSUE 01

Editorial Offices
Axiomatic Editions, an imprint of ORO Editions
250 Hudson Street, Ste. 702
New York, New York 10013, USA

Editorial Director
Ashley Simone

Editor
Neil Spiller

Managing Editor
Caroline Ellerby

Contributing Editor
Abigail Grater

Publisher
Gordon Goff

Assistant Production Editor
Sarah Fingerhood

Design
Artmedia Ltd, London

Front cover
Sir John Akomfrah (artist) and vPPR Architects (exhibition design), "Listening All Night to the Rain" exhibition, British Pavilion, 60th Venice Art Biennale, Italy, 2024.
© British Council, photo Tarun Wilkhu

Frontispiece
Atelier Manferdini, *Living Pictures*, Kaida Center of Science and Design, Dongguan, China, 2019. Image courtesy of UAP

Page 1
New Affiliates, Beaux Arts Ball installation, Brooklyn Navy Yard, New York, 2022.
© Michael Vahrenwald/Esto

EDITORIAL BOARD

Journal Customer Services
For ordering information, claims, and any enquiry concerning your journal subscription please go to www.archdesignjournal.com

Print ISBN: 978-1-961856-98-1
Print ISSN: 0003-8504
Online ISSN: 1554-2769

Institutional
$950 print and online
$850 print only
$850 online only

Individual
$190 print and online
$160 print only
$120 online only

Individual issues
$40

All prices are subject to change without notice.

ABOUT THE EDITORS

NEIL SPILLER AND ASHLEY SIMONE

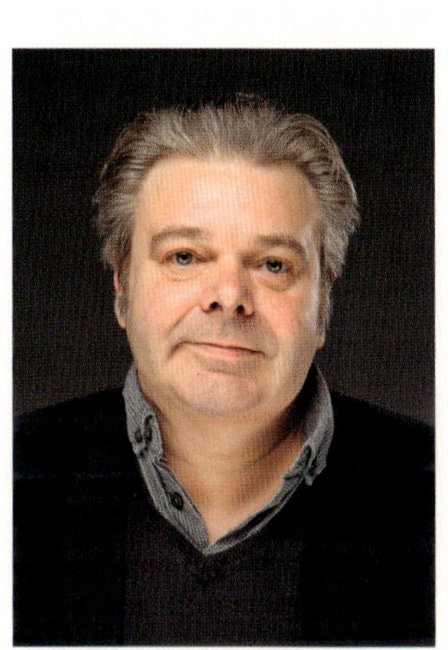

Architect and Editor of AD **Neil Spiller** is based in London. He was Visiting Professor of Architecture at Carleton University in Ottawa, Canada (2020–22) and Visiting Professor at IAUV Venice in 2021. He was previously Hawksmoor Chair of Architecture and Landscape and Deputy Pro Vice-Chancellor of the University of Greenwich, London. Prior to this, he was Dean of the School of Architecture, Design and Construction and Professor of Architecture and Digital Theory at Greenwich, and Vice-Dean and Graduate Director of Design at the Bartlett School of Architecture, University College London (UCL).

His architectural design work has been published and exhibited worldwide.

He has guest-edited eight AD issues, including *Architects in Cyberspace I* and *II* (1995 and 1998), and *Drawing Architecture* (2013), and more recently edited the issues *Emerging Talents: Training Architects* (2021), *Radical Architectural Drawing* (2022), *California Dreaming* (2023), and, with Aleksandra Wagner, *Lebbeus Woods: Exquisite Experiments, Early Years* (2024). His books include *Visionary Architecture: Blueprints of the Modern Imagination* (2006), *Architecture and Surrealism* (2016), and *Educating Architects* (2014), all published by Thames & Hudson. He is also the author of *How to Thrive in Architecture School: A Student Guide* (RIBA, 2020).

He is the founding director of the Advanced Virtual and Technological Architectural Research (AVATAR) group, which conducts research into the impact of advanced technologies such as virtuality and biotechnology on 21st-century design.

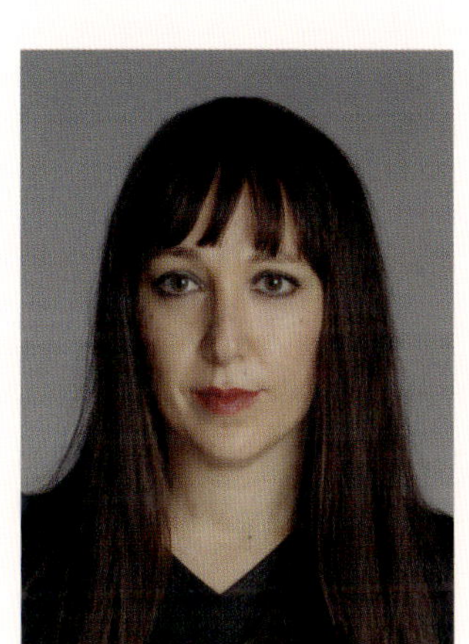

Educator and Editorial Director of Axiomatic Editions **Ashley Simone** is based in New York City, where she teaches and works on books and other publications about architecture and design.

Ashley is an Associate Professor at the Pratt Institute School of Architecture and a Lecturer at the College of Architecture, Planning and Landscape Architecture at the University of Arizona.

Her writing has appeared in numerous books and journals published by AD, Actar, *BOMB Magazine*, Lars Müller, ORO Editions, and Thames & Hudson. Select essays include "Polymorphic Matters" in AD *Lebbeus Woods: Exquisite Experiments, Early Years* (2024), and "Value and the Metaphor of Phenomenology" in the anthology *Modern Architecture and the Lifeworld* (Thames & Hudson, 2020), edited by Karla Britton and Robert McCarter.

Among other books on architecture and design, she is the editor of Kenneth Frampton's *A Genealogy of Modern Architecture* (2015), Allan Wexler's *Absurd Thinking Between Art and Design* (2017), and *Michael Webb: Two Journeys* (2018), all published by Lars Müller, and *Frank Gehry Catalogue Raisonné, Volume One, 1954–1978* by Jean-Louis Cohen (Cahiers d'Art, 2020), and *The Other Modern Movement* by Kenneth Frampton (Yale University Press, 2021). AD

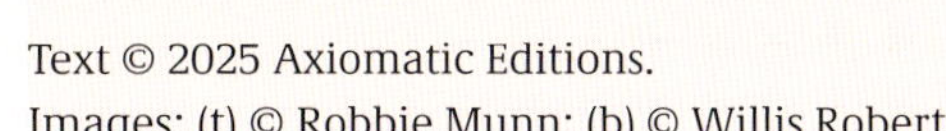

Neil Spiller

INTRODUCTION

Preparing the Stage

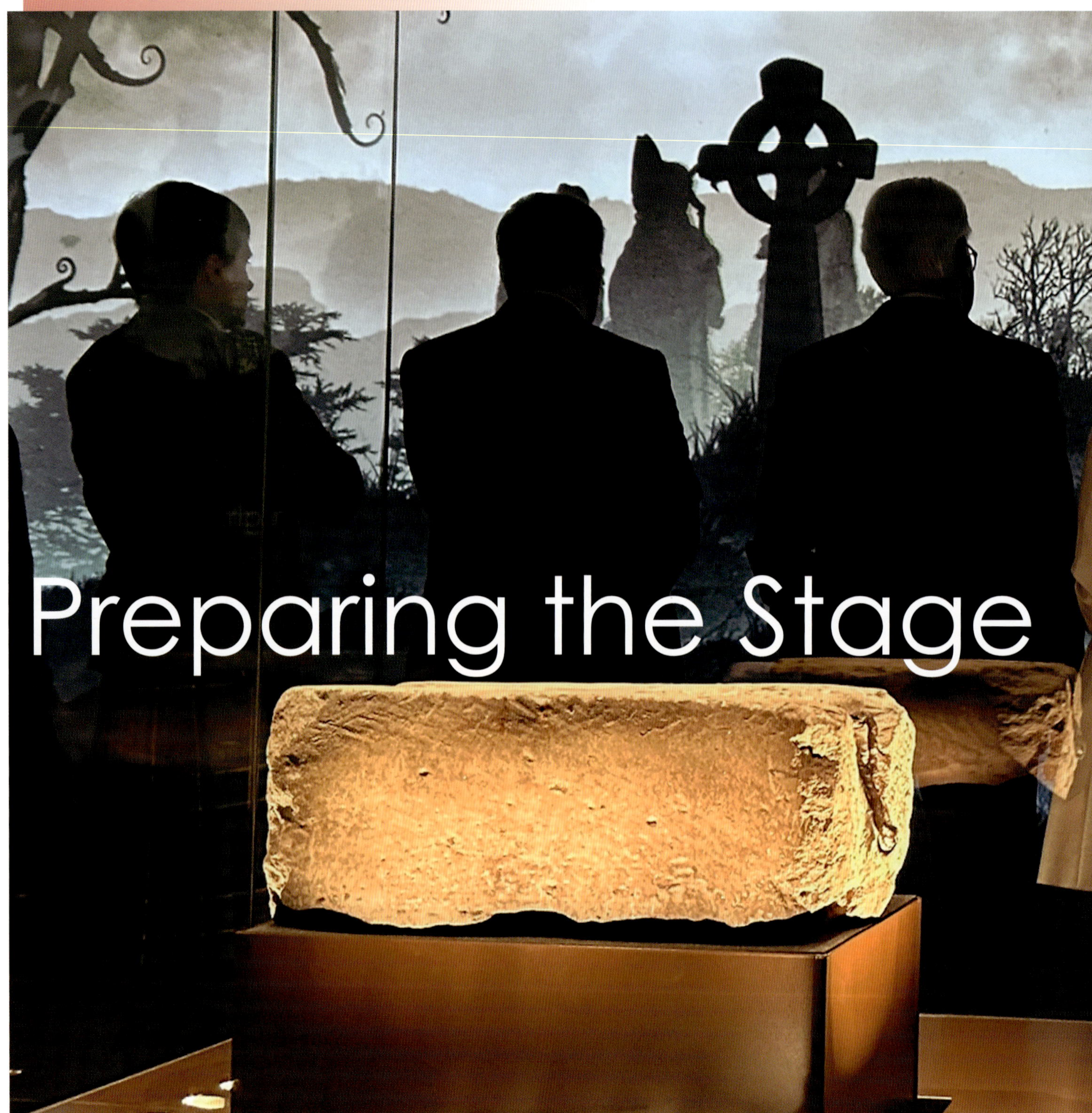

Metaphor,
Perth Museum,
Perth, Scotland,
2024

The newly refurbished museum is home to the Stone of Destiny, otherwise known as the Stone of Scone. A powerful symbol of Scotland, it is wreathed in myths linking Bible heroes, Ancient Egyptian royalty, and Irish High Kings to the Scottish and British thrones. Metaphor designed its staging.

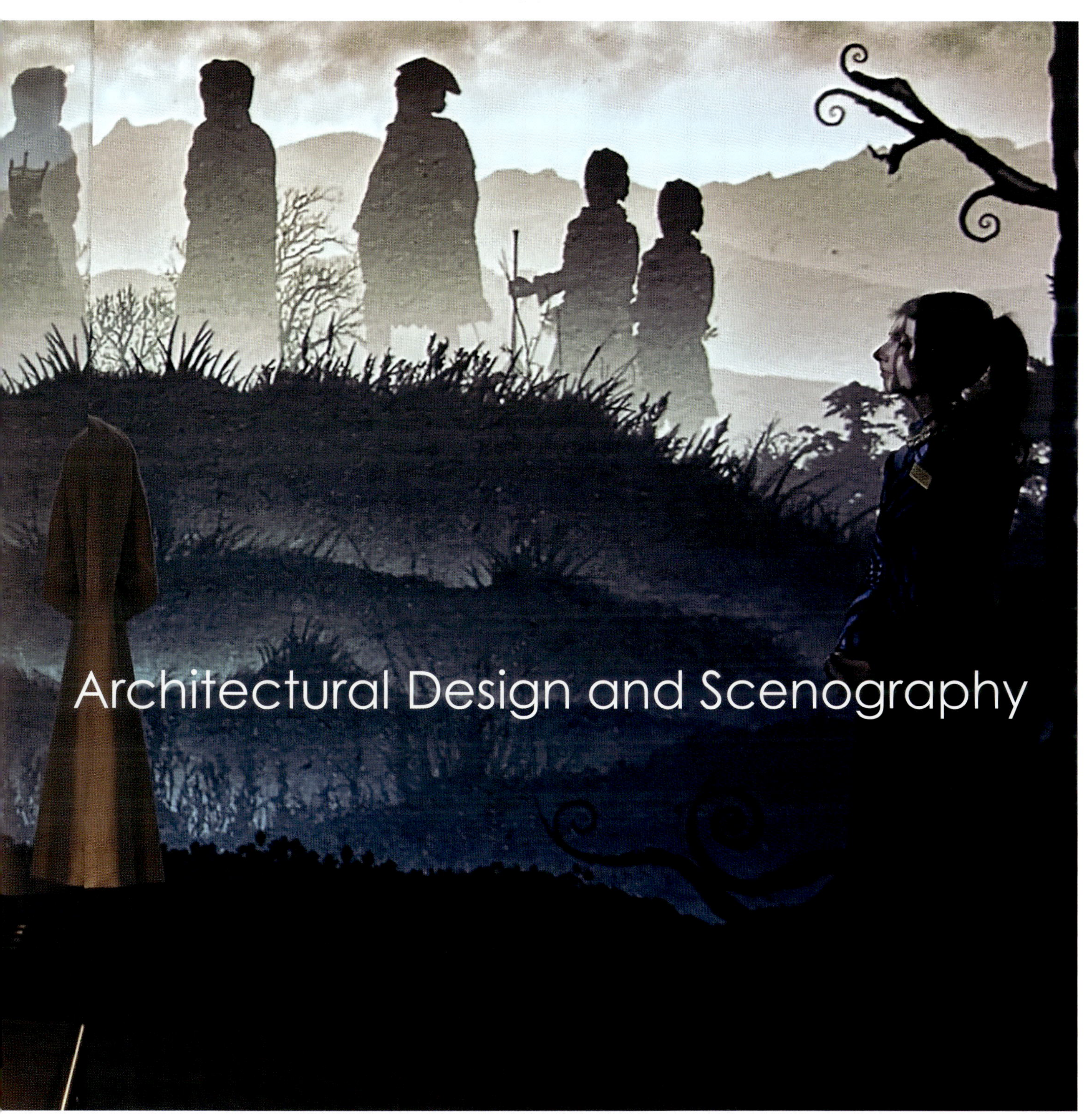

Architectural Design and Scenography

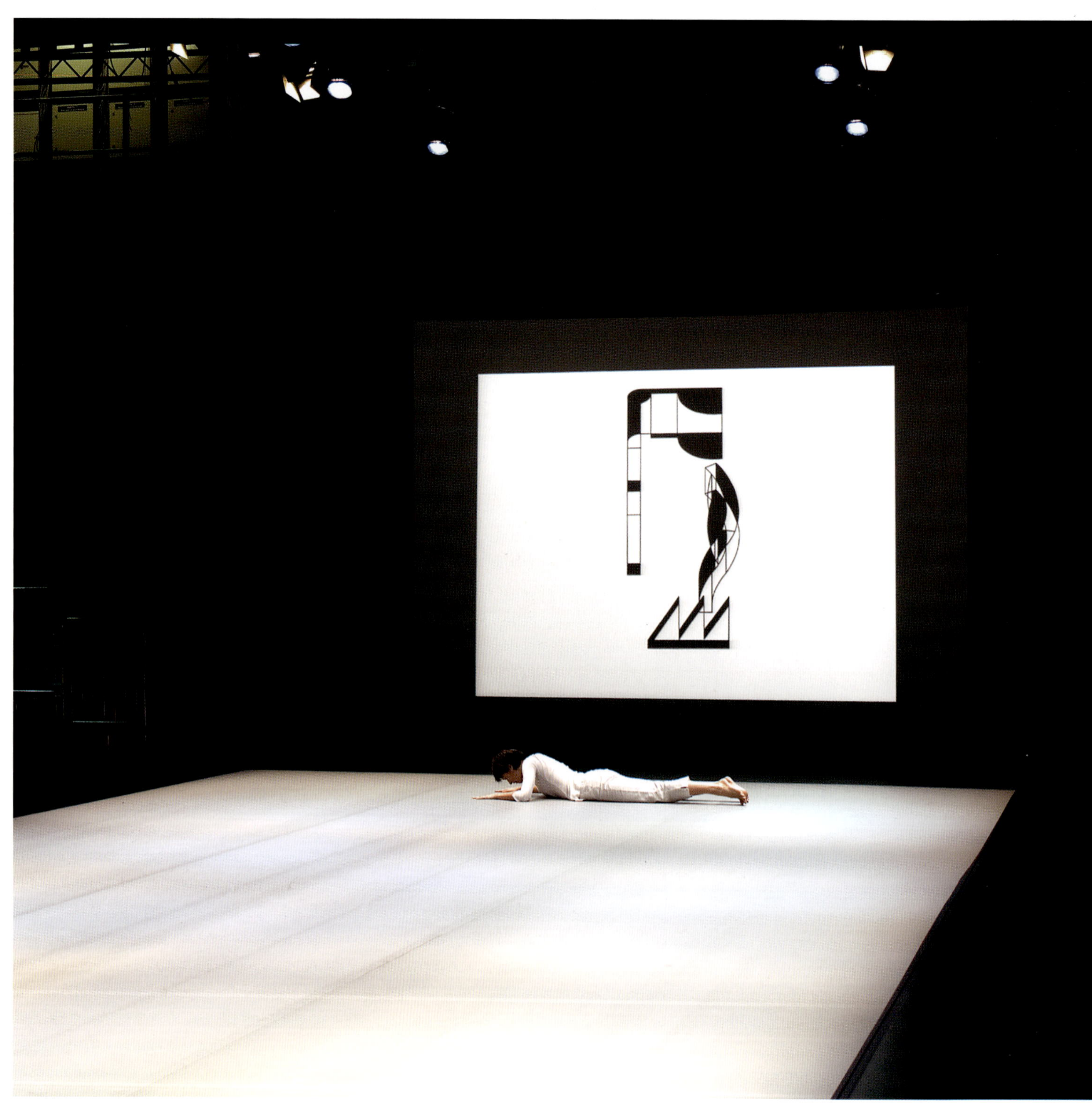

Choreographer: Rosemary Butcher; Designers: Matthew Butcher and Melissa Appleton; Dancer: Elena Gianotti, *Episodes of Flight*, 2008

The reflexive and symbiotic relationship between dancer, music, notations, and viewer traverses the line between controlled choreography and the viewer completing the work.

All the world's a stage,
And all the men and women merely players
—William Shakespeare, *As You Like It*, *c.* 1598[1]

One might suggest that architects are more akin to performers and scenographers than many other professions. They are trained to be performative (spatially and verbally), weaving visually seductive stories and getting their potential clients to suspend disbelief, particularly at the genesis of a pitch and at the beginning of a project. Some architects develop huge egos and become stars; some might believe they are stars even if they are not; other lone architectural minstrels practice from the kitchen table, and others at all scales in between—all playing their parts. Architectural tutors can become impresarios, curating architecture schools, nurturing other bit-part players, and mentoring the young actors. It is not unreasonable to consider the various scenarios within which this play-acting takes place and some of the design outcomes it has recently propagated.

This AD concentrates on how architectural performative skills are deployed in entertainment, communicating design and framing the backdrop in which narratives play out. These architectonic imperatives connect with all aspects of human culture—visual arts (including theater), literature, humor, spatial choreography, technology, and memorialization.

Four overarching themes unite and permeate the issue: curation, performance, fiction, and transience.

Curation and Performance

We begin with a historical account by architect, educator, and expert in the history and typologies of museums Stephen Rustow, who asks for whom and for what purpose the museum typology, exhibitions, and art exist. This is a contemporarily relevant question explored through historical means. Rustow illustrates this by examining American inventor and artist Samuel F.B. Morse's paintings, particularly his most celebrated picture: *Gallery of the Louvre* (1831–3). The painting and his career were a project of transatlantic communication designed to connect the new world with the old.

Another more recent act of exhibition design and curation involved the staging of the "Frederick Kiesler: Vision Machines" exhibition at the Jewish Museum in New York (2024). Leah Kelly, a neuroscientist at the Rockefeller University in Manhattan, examines the work produced by Kiesler in the 1930s and 1940s while he was resident in his Laboratory for Design Correlation at Columbia University, focusing in particular on two works: the Mobile Home Library and the Vision Machine.

The act of looking and interpreting what we are gazing at is part and parcel of New York design studio SOFTlab's architectural output. Michael Szivos, the practice's director and founder, explains how it straddles the fine line between a passive experience and freedom for users/viewers to conduct an open-ended relationship with the work—interactive staging conditioned by technologies, materiality, and observers creating a multiplicity of dialogues.

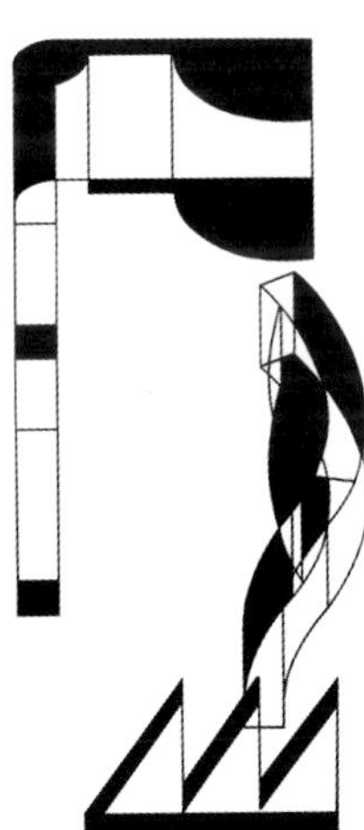

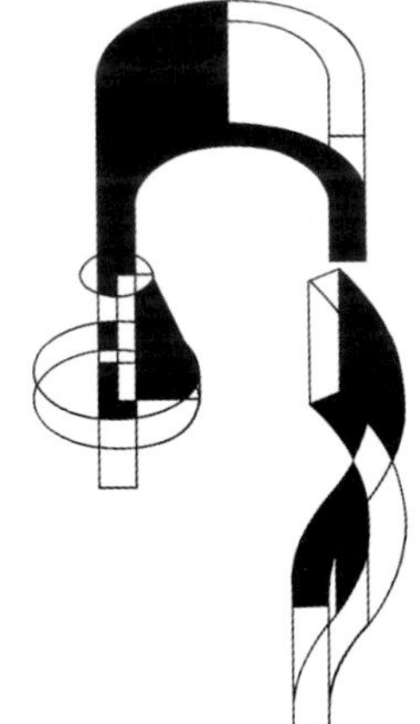

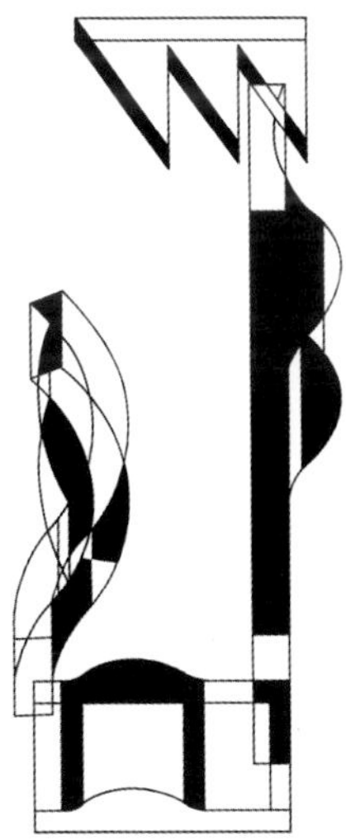

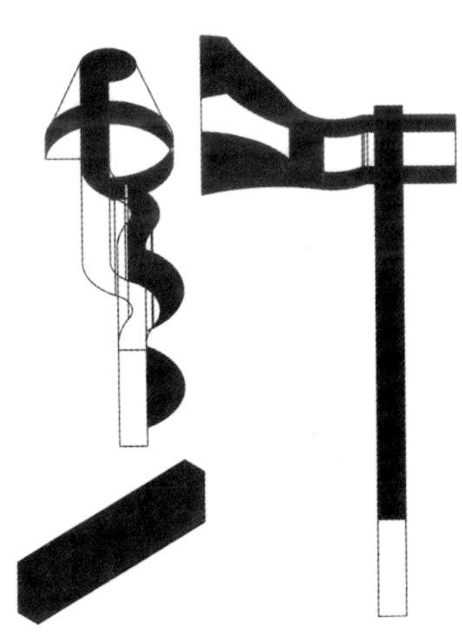

Matthew Butcher and Melissa Appleton, Notations created for the set design of Rosemary Butcher's *Episodes of Flight*, 2008

Butcher and Appleton's dance notations are inspired by American architect Bernard Tschumi's notational approach to "event architecture" from the 1970s onwards.

STUFISH Entertainment Architects,
Stage set for U2's "PopMart Tour," 1997-8

right: U2 toured the world with this breathtaking stage, including a large state-of-the-art (for then) LED screen, to promote the band's 1997 album *Pop*—a lavish production.

STUFISH Entertainment Architects,
Stage set for "Andrea Bocelli 30: The Celebration,"
Teatro del Silenzio,
Lajatico, Tuscany, Italy,
July 2024

opposite: STUFISH has a long history of stage design for musicians, circuses, award ceremonies, and royal celebrations. They are also known as the architects of the transient ABBA Arena where the virtual ABBAtars perform in London.

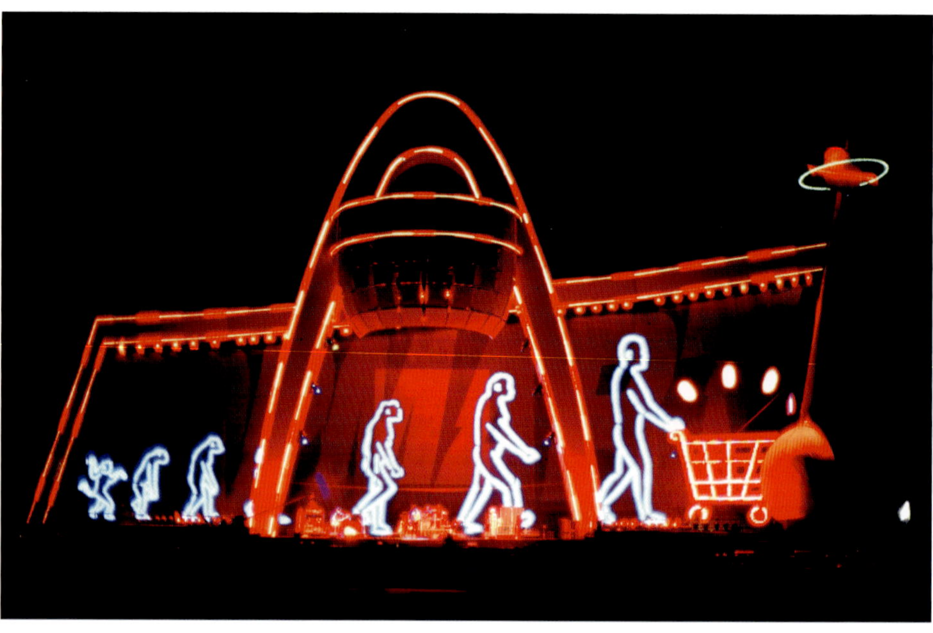

It is such multiplicity of views and uniqueness of experience that conditions the recent spectacular stage designs of entertainment architects STUFISH, who have been responsible for some of the most iconic, dynamic, awe-inspiring music show-sets the world has ever seen. Architect and writer Eva Menuhin examines some of their contemporary output that has presented to the world Adele, Lenny Kravitz, AC/DC, the Rolling Stones, and Andrea Bocelli.

Staged personas are not limited to music stars. Elena Manferdini, director of the MArch program at the Southern California Institute of Architecture (SCI-Arc) in Los Angeles, discusses the Atelier Manferdini exhibition "FLORA" at the city's Italian Cultural Institute (2024). The exhibition sought to engage visitors on questions of personal identity in the face of burgeoning virtual selves, artificial intelligences, and avatars: How do we present ourselves to various worlds at various times? What parts do we play and when? Similarly, Owen Hopkins, Director of the Farrell Centre in Newcastle, England, describes the center's recent experiments in creating architecture and urban salon exhibitions that attempt to move beyond traditional modes of audience co-curation toward performative construction and curation, actively engaging and encouraging skills development in their participants.

Fictions

Mark Morris, Senior Curator of Architecture and Design at the Victoria and Albert Museum in London, describes the architectural content of his novel *Cliffhanger* that is situated against a half-true, half-fictional backdrop of a never-constructed Frank Lloyd Wright building in Ithaca, upstate New York. He explains the narrative link in his novel and its inspiration, drawing from a variety of sources, both literary and architectural. Another example of a building being used as a central character in fiction is discussed and further developed by Mark Burry and his team at Swinburne University in Melbourne, Australia, who have been researching the codings of the descriptions of the library and cloisters in author Mervyn Peake's *Gormenghast Trilogy* of novels. Developing differing parametric models of these spaces defined by different interpretations of their textural descriptions, they have staged a series of new architectural backdrops to Peake's epic story.

Can architecture tell stories? Do spaces speak? Are interiors articulate? What role does fiction play in exhibition design? Charles Holland, whose practice Charles Holland Architects is based in Dover, UK, explains the capacity of architecture to spatialize and fabricate historical narratives in relation to two London exhibitions he designed—"Radical Rooms" at the Royal Institute of British Architects (RIBA) and "Origins" at the Royal Academy of Arts.

Recent projects by London-based vPPR architects are covered by founding partner Jessica Reynolds, offering a new reading on the definition of staging transparency, subverting architectural opposites (inside and outside, void and mass). The practice's collaborations with artists include a sensory dimension with an emphasis on materiality, the sonic, and immersiveness to communicate meaning and narrative.

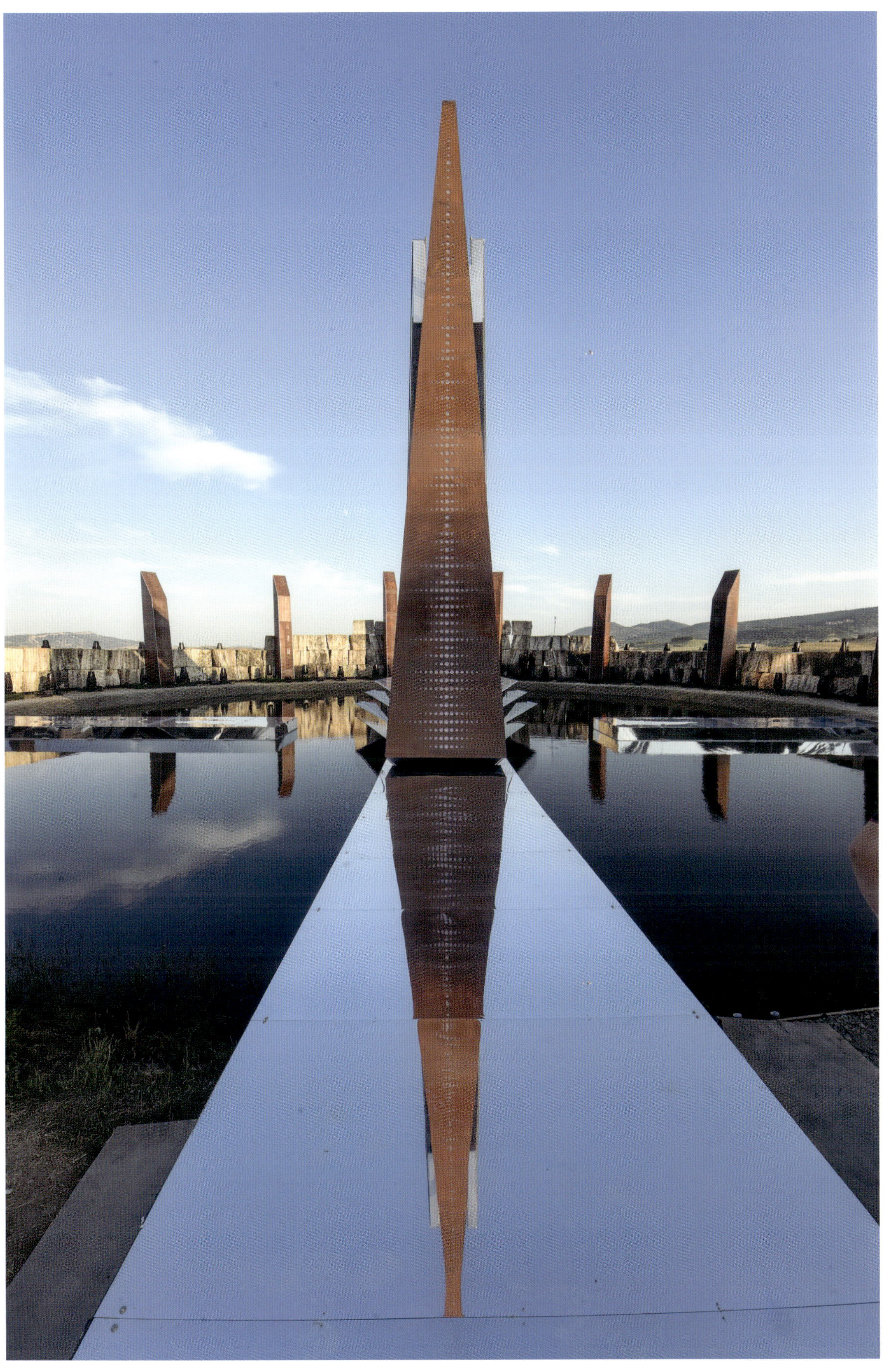

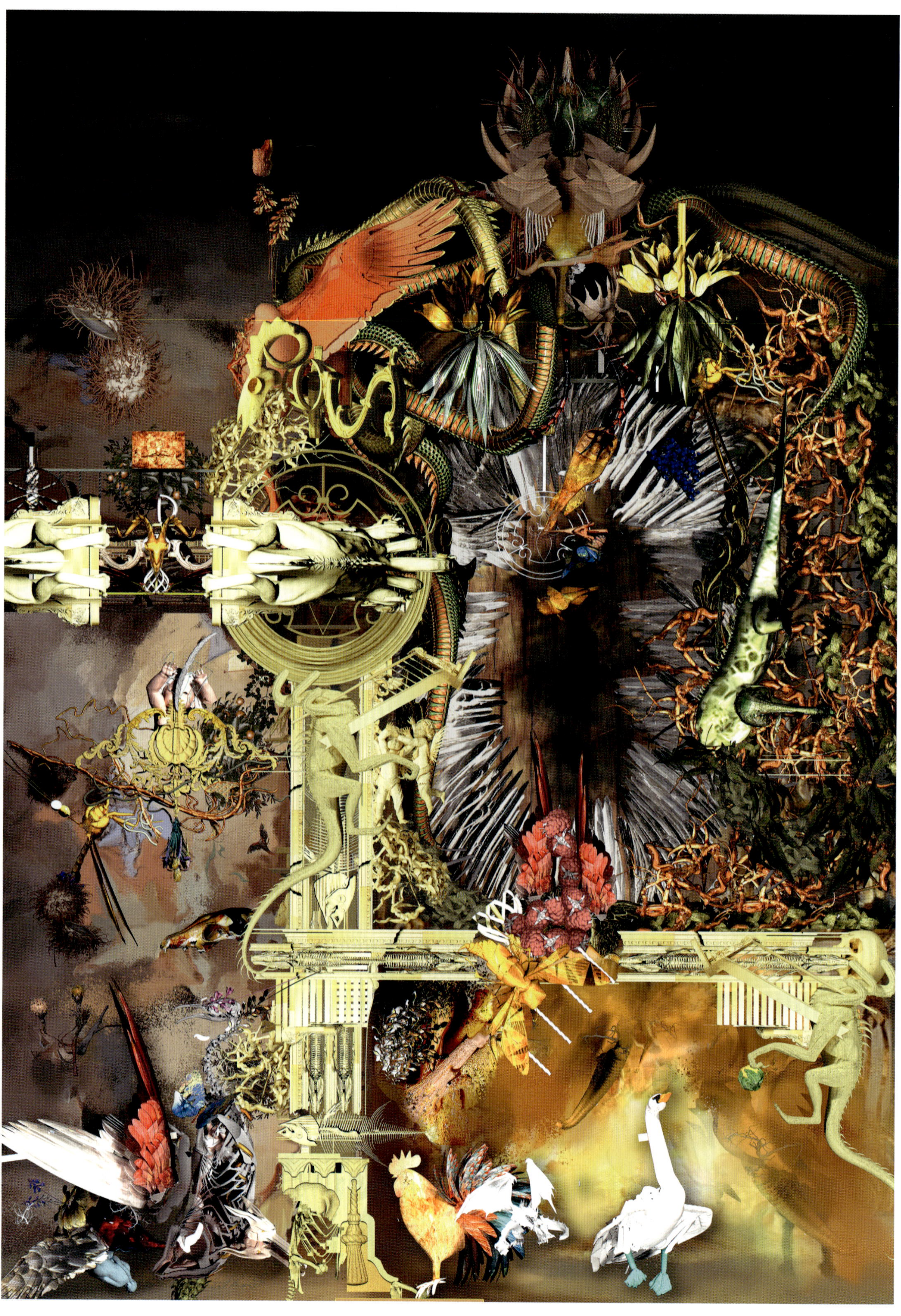

Daniela Yaneva,
Violation of Darwin's House: The Fireplaces,
Down House 2099,
Ideal Villa for Morphogenesis Man project,
Masters in Architecture,
University of Greenwich, London,
2019

Like the *Bestiary of Past, Present and Future Animals* imagined by Peter Greenaway for his 1991 film *Prospero's Books*, inspired by Shakespeare's *The Tempest*, this project also speculates about the future of organisms, evolving in conjunction with biological technologies. This is one of many moments when Yaneva's experiment to grow an Ideal Villa for Morphogenesis Man (a home that is genetically modified and is a sentient being) goes wrong and starts to violate its site—evolutionist Charles Darwin's house.

The works oscillate between stories of science and stories of the imagination, weaving a vertigo of association and blurring the boundaries between fact and fiction, time and space

Unearthly Delights

The speculative fictive future portrayed by MArch student Daniela Yaneva is presented next, by her tutor Rahesh Ram, Head of Architecture at London's University of Greenwich, who explains its strange rationale, its narrative, and its chimeric architectural ambiance and characters, plus the pedagogic process that helped develop this Garden of Unearthly Delights—metamorphosis out of control. Yaneva's project, while not explicitly referencing it, reminds one of another of Shakespeare's multifaceted worlds, in his *The Tempest* (first performed 1611), and of the world based on it that Peter Greenaway designed—and wrote about—for his 1991 film *Prospero's Books*.[2] In *The Tempest*, Prospero, a powerful magician and Duke of Milan, is usurped by his brother, Antonio, who exiles him to a remote island with Prospero's daughter, Miranda. Gonzalo, a Neapolitan aristocrat, is recruited to kill them on the sea journey. Still, he doesn't, taking pity on them and providing them with the essentials to keep them alive; importantly, Gonzalo knows of Prospero's love of books and the contents of his library, and throws many books from it into the boat. Shakespeare does not articulate their titles, but Greenaway does, and these books become a crucial part of the magical epistemological narrative arc of his film. As he writes in his introduction to his book on the film, "These would need perhaps to be books on navigation and survival … how to colonize an island, farm it, subjugate its inhabitants, identify its plants and husband its wild beasts."[3] Among the 24 titles of such volumes that he imagines are *A Bestiary of Past, Present and Future Animals*, *A Harsh Book of Geometry*, and *The Ninety-Two Conceits of the Minotaur.* Once on the island, with the aid of these books, his rage, and sorcery, Prospero creates a magic "kingdom" in which he is the omnipotent ruler of real and conjured figures as he plots his revenge. Yaneva's world could well fit into Greenaway's imaginary *Bestiary of Past, Present and Future Animals*.

The editorial director of Axiomatic Editions, Ashley Simone—who is also Adjunct Associate Professor at Pratt Institute, New York—examines the site-specific installation of narrative dioramas and rendered drawings by Pamela Phatsimo Sunstrum that was exhibited in The Curve gallery at London's Barbican Centre in 2024 under the title *It Will End in Tears*. The work and the liminal space within which it appeared are tied together through Michel Foucault's concept of the heterotopia, first elaborated in 1966.[4] Sunstrum's collection of images creates an immersive environment using analog media that alludes to inspiration from film noir and negotiates existential themes, including identity and cross-cultural strangeness.

Continuing in this vein and evoking virtual and shifting personalities, Sandra Youkhana and Luke Caspar Pearson, founders of architectural design studio You+Pea and tutors at the Bartlett School of Architecture, University College London (UCL), take us into the surreal world of gaming. They show how architectural methodologies and epistemologies also work in parallel with and within game-space, which can be seen as a *bona fide* series of nested, architecturally dynamic staged spaces.

Morris, Burry, Holland, Reynolds, Yaneva, Simone, and You+Pea, all in different ways, examine their subject's fictive presence; and, out of its saturated nuances, architecture is born. The works oscillate between stories of science and stories of the imagination, weaving a vertigo of association and blurring the boundaries between fact and fiction, time and space, as all good productions do. Architectural appearance is carefully choreographed in set pieces, as is the case with all good theatrical events, creating webs of associations to be interpreted by the viewer as new conglomerations of thoughts and connections, as all quality stories do.

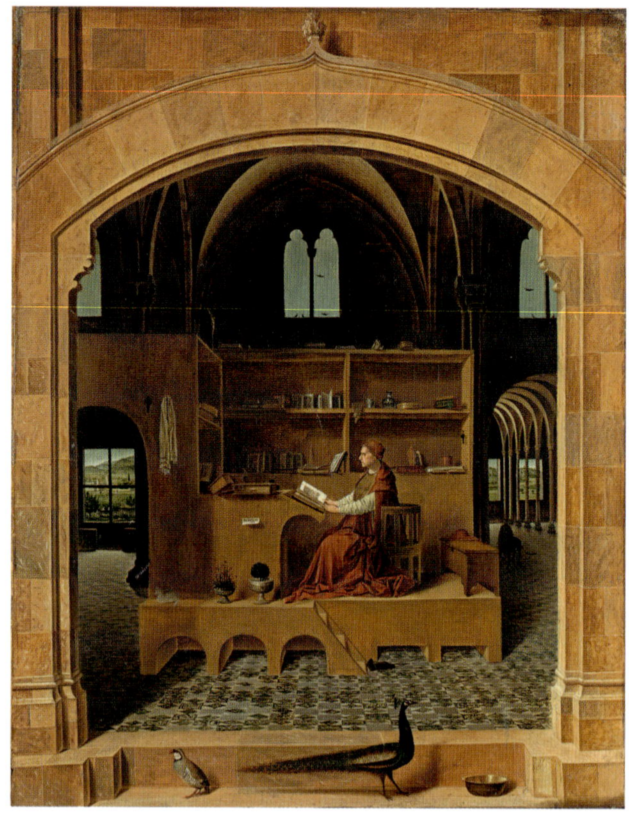

Antonello da Messina,
Saint Jerome in his Study,
c. 1475

right: Peter Greenaway's interpretation of Antonello's painting to envision Prospero's study in his film *Prospero's Books* is one of having mobility and therefore the potential of transience and likewise the ability to facilitate numerous performative locational arrangements and configurations—notions crucial to staging in the past and today.

Neil Spiller with Sixteen*(makers),
Design drawing and image during set-up,
"Landscape Matters" exhibition,
The Landscape Institute at the
Building Centre,
London,
1996

opposite: The exhibition was curated by the Landscape Institute as a showcase for its members' talents. It was prefabricated to be erected and struck swiftly, its leitmotif being the spiky pollen grain.

Lasting Legacies: A Precarious End

Returning to Greenaway's *Tempest*-inspired film, architecturally, the theme of transience is evoked in his description of Prospero's study, which in itself is inspired by the setting depicted in Antonello da Messina's painting of *Saint Jerome in his Study* (*c.* 1475). Greenaway states: "It could in fact be anywhere ... in a palace, seminary, library ... anywhere in fact in 1611. It is a wooden structure with a writing desk, there are shelves, cupboards, pen racks, a chair, a bench, a lectern ... . It is a structure which can be dismantled and reconstructed—sometimes with other parts ... sometimes in a different arrangement. When dismantled, it is portable and can be assembled anywhere ... on the beach, in a forest, among rocks, on board a ship, beside a volcano."[5] A kit of parts, of movable and rearticulated pieces, as all staged productions are. The following articles exploit the precariousness of our lives and worlds in their staging.

Bart-Jan Polman, Director of Exhibitions at Columbia University's Graduate School of Architecture, Planning and Preservation (GSAPP), discusses recent work of Barcelona and New York-based architects TAKK. Their work considers how the architecture of domesticity might be reconfigured in the context of contemporary radical instability. It seems that all manner of human concepts, politics, climate, society, architecture, materiality, and ideas generally are in precarious flux. TAKK designs architecture that seeks to conceive of a post-carbon domesticity that uses their research lab/home as the setting for a series of adaptable, transient micro-houses—like Greenaway's notion of Prospero's study.

The transient nature of staging necessitates a variety of jointing methods and supports. With reference to these protocols, New Affiliates created a design for the setting of the Architectural League of New York's 2022 Beaux Arts Ball. Jaffer Kolb, one of the firm's two principals, describes their design, which also incorporated melting ice joints, thereby introducing a precariousness into the installation—a time-based degradation. Likewise, over time, the human body becomes weaker and less structurally sturdy until, ultimately, we die.

How do we want to commemorate our lifetime's achievements, performances, and staging, leaving our mark for posterity? Art, architecture, and urbanism atelier Metis, through the writing of joint partner Adrian Hawker, introduce us to their *Northroom* installation, conceived in relation to Edinburgh's Calton Hill, a

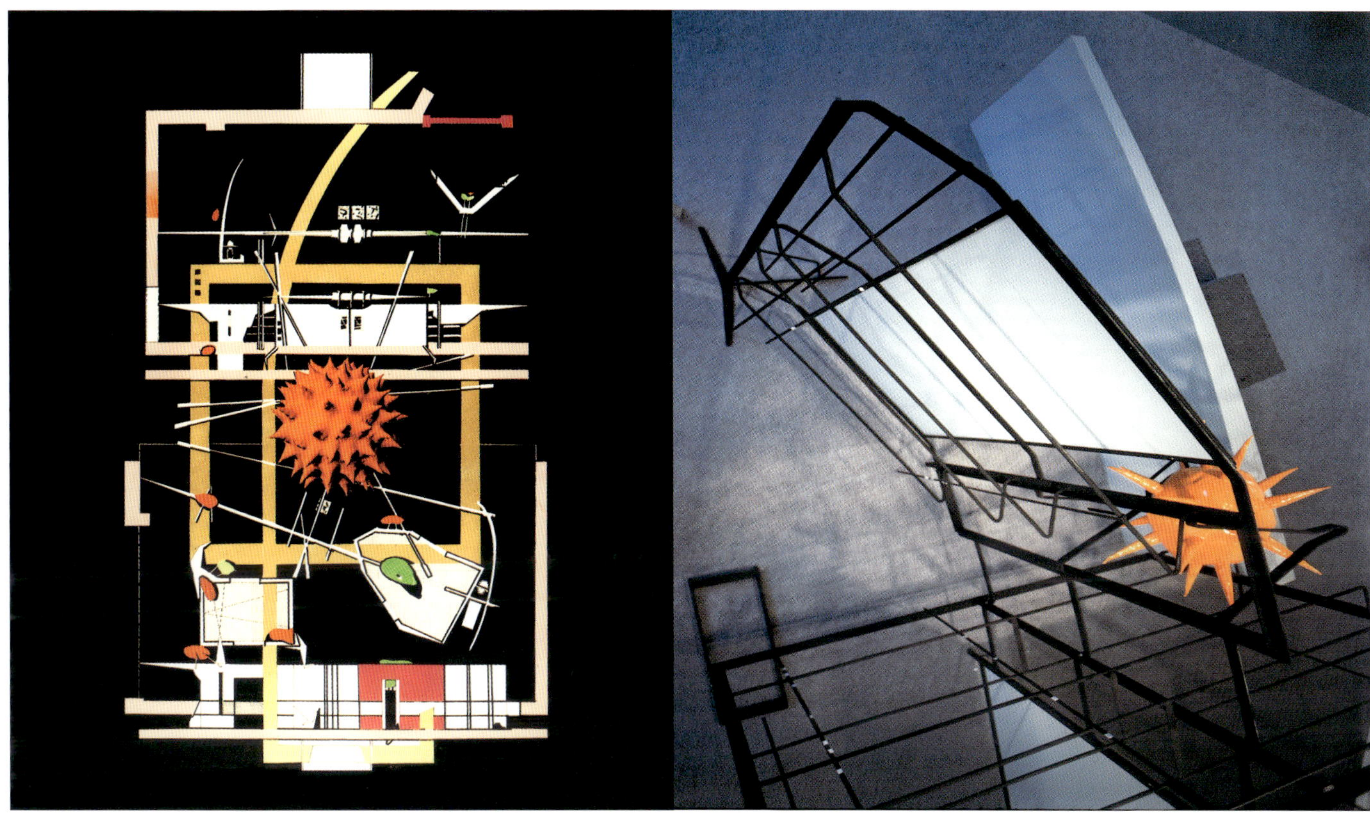

theatrical locus of optical experimentation and the birthplace of the panorama. *Northroom* is a re-staging of 18th-century neoclassical architect Robert Adam's cylindrical monument to philosopher David Hume, an Enlightenment oculus to a shifting sky that re-performs the panorama, switching its distant visuality to one that becomes about the close scrutiny of the monument's surface. Then architectural tutor and writer Peter J. Baldwin explores how architects, over the years, have chosen to stage their own memorials and mausoleums, presenting themselves to the world in another cloak of skins for perpetuity.

Finally, my own *From Another Perspective* focuses on the recent theatrical exhibition spaces wittily created in London by Sam Jacob Studio—the Cartoon Museum, "The Horror Show!" and "Barbie."

This AD has been curated to provide an overview of the differing types of staged productions and technologies used involving architects in a variety of arenas in the recent past—each offering new ways to look at the world as, indeed, do Prospero's 24 books. AD

Notes

1. William Shakespeare, *As You Like It*, Act 2, Scene 7, *c.* 1598, first published 1623.
2. Peter Greenaway (director), *Prospero's Books*, Palace Pictures, 1991; Peter Greenaway, *Prospero's Books: A Film of Shakespeare's The Tempest*, Chatto & Windus (London), 1991.
3. Ibid., p. 9.
4. Michel Foucault, preface to *Les mots et les choses*, Gallimard (Paris), 1966, translated into English as *The Order of Things: An Archaeology of the Human Sciences*, Pantheon Books (New York), 1970.
5. Greenaway, *Prospero's Books*, p. 50.

Portrait of the Gallery

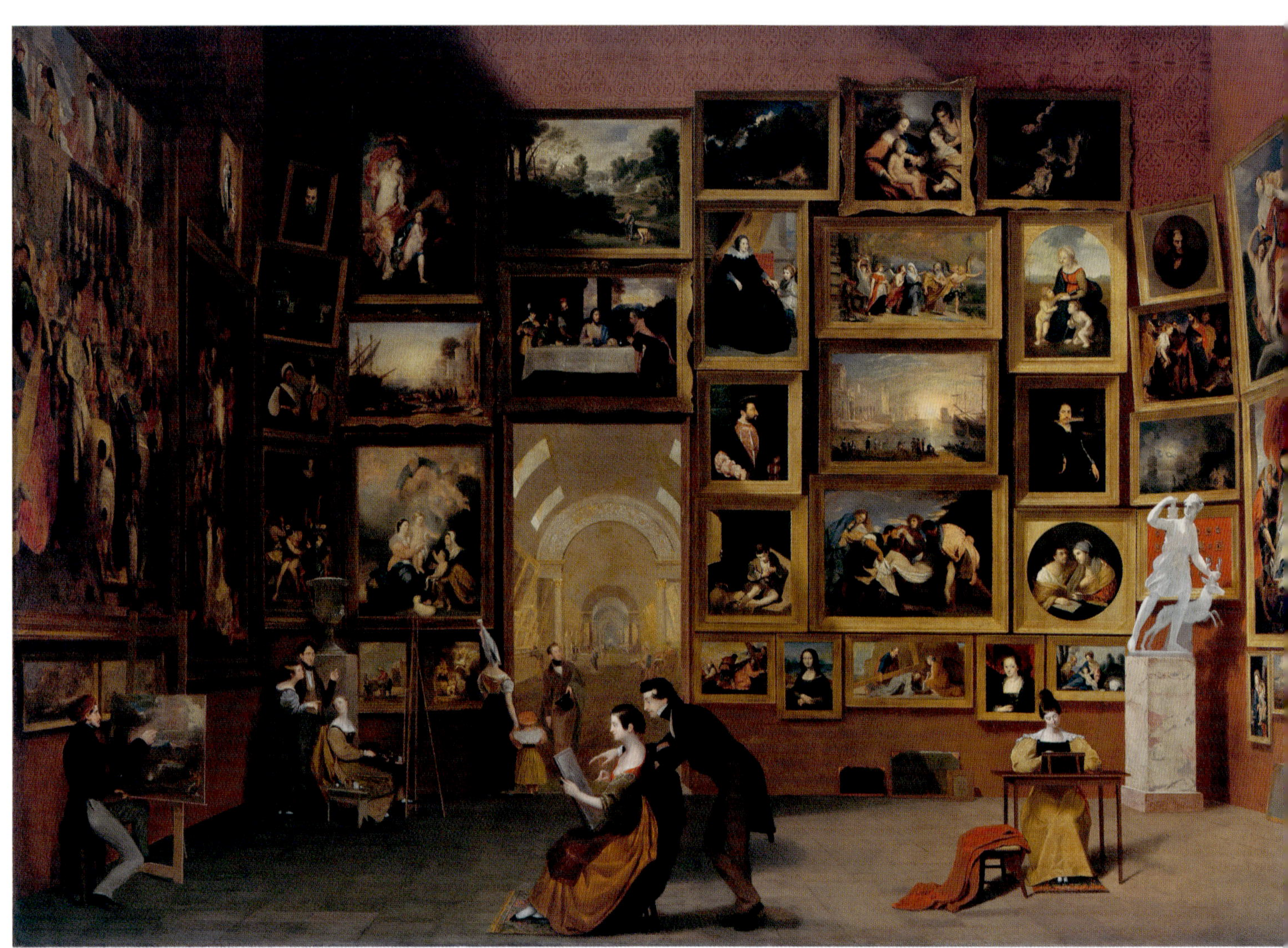

Stephen Rustow

As a Young Museum

Modern museums are always trying to strike a balance between pleasure and teaching, democratic outreach to those with prior knowledge of their collections, and those without. Historical depictions of the gallery illustrate a great deal about how art was presented and to whom. Architect and educator **Stephen Rustow** examines one particular representation of the museum in its infancy and the complex intentions of its creator, Samuel F.B. Morse.

Samuel F.B. Morse,
Gallery of the Louvre,
1831-33

Americans in Paris: the cast of characters in Morse's gallery includes family members and ex-pats in his Parisian circle: the author James Fennimore Cooper and the artists Richard W. Habersham and Horatio Greenough.

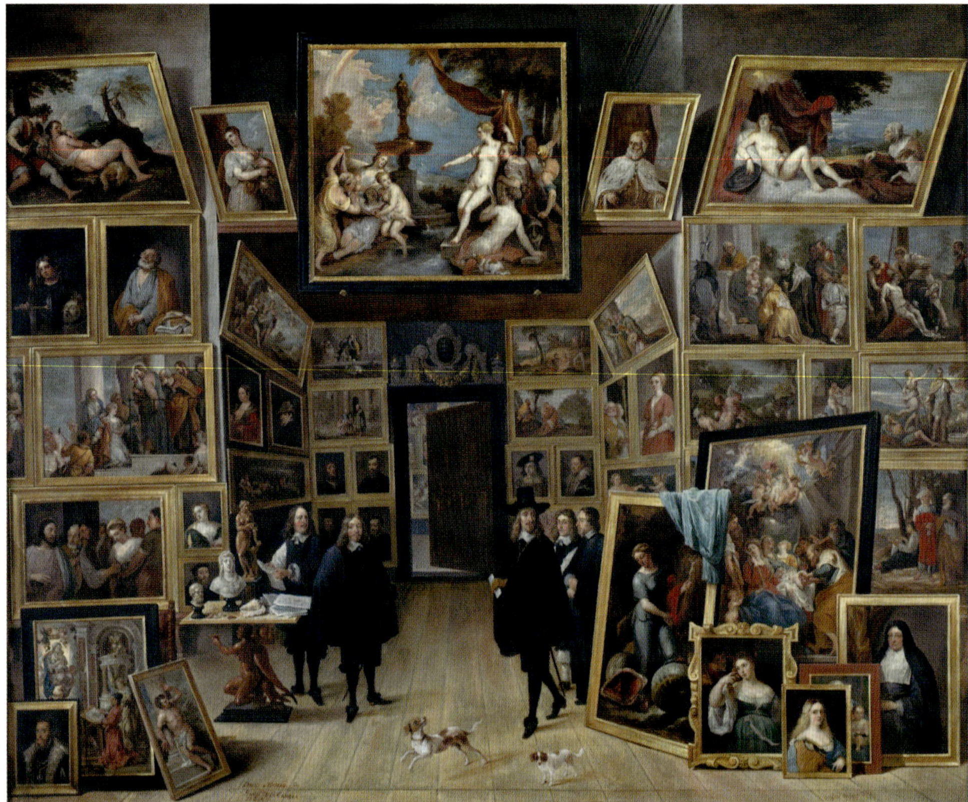

David Teniers (the Younger), *The Archduke Leopold Wilhelm in his Picture Gallery in Brussels*, *c.* 1651

Teniers made several "gallery portraits" for Leopold Wilhelm, the foremost collector of Italian art of his day. The painter later assembled the catalog of the Archduke's entire collection, considered the first such document of its kind.

The Flemish and Italian "gallery portraits" of the 17th and 18th centuries anticipate the modern museum of art before either the institution or its architectural typology was firmly established. These highly staged paintings about paintings prompt a wealth of questions about how art should be shown, and to whom. But it is a quintessentially American, 19th-century example that most clearly lays out the issues that still discomfit the contemporary museum of art: the origins of its collections; the diversity of its audiences; and an underlying tension between pedagogy and pleasure.

Americans in Paris

In 1830 Samuel F.B. Morse traveled to Paris. He was not yet the famous inventor of the telegraph nor of the eponymous code that would make it work, and he had yet to become the conservative pamphleteer and apologist for slavery whose radical politicking on the wrong side of history shadows any contemporary appraisal of his accomplishments. But he was, arguably—and certainly in his own estimation—the most promising American painter of his generation, even though artistic recognition and financial success had thus far eluded him.[1]

Morse went to Paris to deepen his acquaintance with continental art, and while there he began work on his most celebrated picture: *Gallery of the Louvre*. Painted between 1831 and 1833, the monumental canvas was conceived as an art lesson for America that would stimulate cultural interests and native creativity. Morse intended it to travel throughout the States for paid public display, to assure the widest possible viewing and secure his fortune.

One can read in this ambitious project themes that would preoccupy Morse throughout his life: transatlantic communication, and connections between the new world and the old. The painting conjures metaphorically the ocean-floor telegraph cables he would invest in some decades later. But the content of that communication also mattered deeply to Morse. What should the new world take from the old? How should past ideals influence contemporary cultural production, and how should a young nation be instructed in those influences? How might America forge its own vibrant and original artistic culture? Morse's painting was intended to suggest answers to those questions.

The canvas is large, just over 6 feet tall by 9 feet wide. A single-point perspective pulls the viewer into a grand room, which those familiar with the Louvre would recognize as the Salon Carré; beyond one sees the neighboring Grande Galerie, framed by a tall door. The general rust-red hue of the painting evokes the brocade with which the Salon walls were covered. Those walls, one directly before us and two partially visible to each side, are hung with a remarkable collection of framed masterworks, 38 paintings in all; an urn and a lone Classical sculpture occupy the corners of the room.

Precisely in the middle of the canvas stands Morse himself, leaning over the shoulder of a young woman copying a work, and gesturing as if instructing her on some point of composition. We recognize Morse from his profile, a close copy of an earlier self-portrait of 1812.[2] In addition to this central couple there are eight other figures, clearly privileged visitors of a certain class, all engaged in some form of close looking.

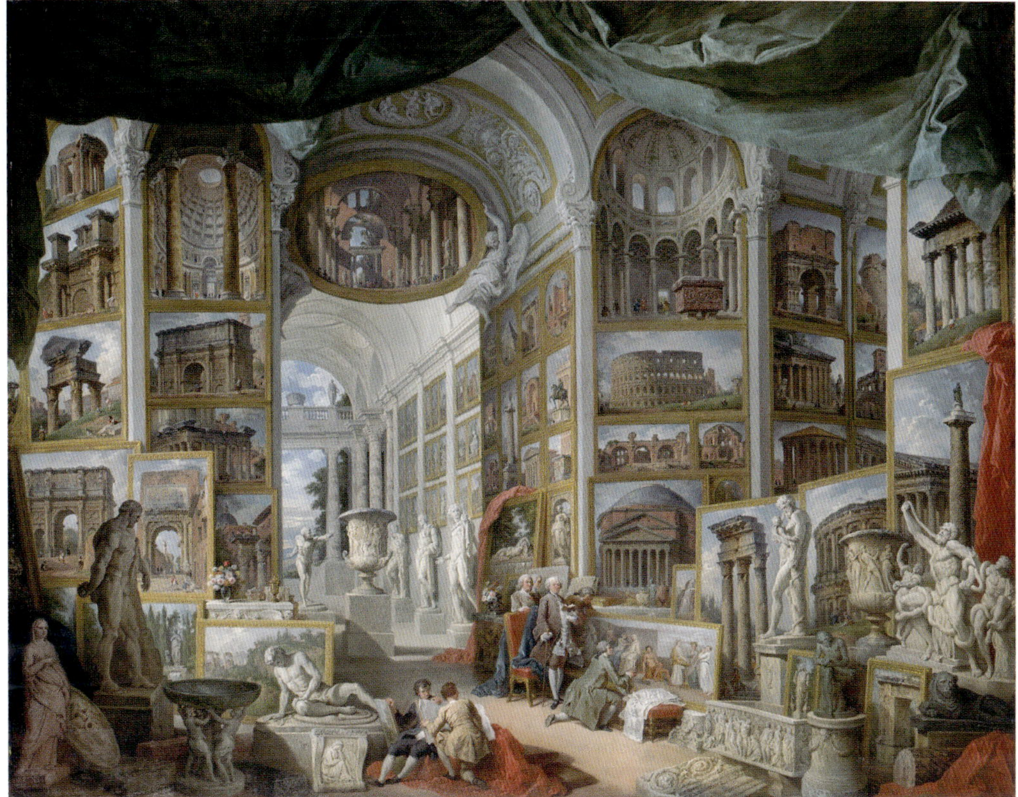

Giovanni Paolo Panini, *Ancient Rome*, 1757

One of three nearly identical paintings into which Panini inserted the particular patron who had commissioned the work. This version, in the collection of the Metropolitan Museum of Art, New York, presents an invented architecture, warehousing a collection of paintings of antique ruins, many copies of Panini's own *vedute*; a luxurious city guidebook.

These are Americans in Paris, here to learn by emulation and to take cultural instruction from the assembled riches on display; the scene before us documents that instruction. The objects of their study are the Renaissance and Baroque collections of the museum, spanning three centuries, a broad mix of genres and including the foremost artists of each "national school": a sampler of the very best the Louvre has to offer.[3]

Morse's claim to virtuosity as a painter lies precisely in this compilation of diverse images. All of the masterworks have been meticulously reproduced by Morse, working as just the kind of copyist he is here portraying, then assembled together in a uniform light that allows us not just to recognize the identity of each painting but its particular palette and compositional subtleties. Morse's canvas can be read as a flamboyant boast that he has mastered the styles of these artists and can bring their achievements into a composition of his own. It is a convincing illustration of the larger project the painting is meant to exemplify: assimilating historical precedent and reusing it to new ends.

Gallery Portraits

But Morse was also working within a well-established genre: the "portrait of the gallery." The history of such images can be traced back at least 150 years earlier to the works of the Flemish painters Jan Breughel (the Younger) and David Teniers (the Younger), especially the latter's portrayals of the collection of the Archduke Leopold in Brussels. A comparable virtuosity is deployed in those paintings, conceived as a kind of double portrait of collectors and their collections, showing their subjects as enlightened cognoscenti among the works that vouchsafed their claim to such status.

The tradition of such gallery portraits reached its apex in the middle of the 18th century with Giovanni Paolo Panini. Trained as an architect, Panini became one of the most renowned of the *vedutisti* ("view-painters") who specialized in creating depictions of Rome for a growing market of connoisseurs. Panini typically painted two kinds of views: *vedute prese da i luoghi* (accurate renderings of actual places) and *vedute ideate* (imaginary views or those that combined elements from several sources into an original composition). But in his two most famous canvasses he devised the new conceit of a collection of collectable views, displayed within galleries that were themselves architectural inventions. These paintings create twin inventories, one of antique and one of modern Rome, each a veritable checklist of the major sites to be visited. Panini made several versions of both pictures and the final renditions of each are in the Louvre;[4] they directly anticipate Morse's painting and may have served as a model for it.

In *Ancient Rome* of 1757 Panini paints over two dozen monuments visible as ruins in the Rome of his day, interspersed with the greatest surviving examples of Classical sculpture. The scene is set in barrel-vaulted galleries that support a dome, partially hidden by a theatrical taffeta curtain. The visitors in attendance include copyists, an expert inspecting a panel, various assistants, and the Duc de Choiseul, Panini's patron. The pendant picture, *Modern Rome* of 1759, shifts the scene to a series of Palladian-inspired triumphal arches; each bay forms a room, the walls of which are again lined with framed paintings of the major palaces, piazzas, churches, and papal works of the preceding century. The statuary is by Bernini and Michelangelo.

Panini's theatrical capriccios assembled real views displayed as paintings to create a tourist's portrait of Rome

These earlier works were certainly known to Morse, and in dozens of details in his *Gallery of the Louvre* one can discern their influence: the attitudes of the copyists; and the piling up of flat images on walls with the occasional punctuation provided by sculpture. Yet there is a clear shift in the purpose of the paintings: Teniers' canvasses for the Archduke documented an actual collection and its real owner; Panini's theatrical capriccios assembled real views displayed as paintings to create a tourist's portrait of Rome. Morse gives us a portrayal of the museum itself. He also broadens the audience depicted; whereas the figures in the paintings of Teniers and Panini are invariably men, Morse has seemingly gone out of his way to include women, both among the copyists training as artists and among the visitors. The earlier works depict ownership and the accompanying privilege of connoisseurship; Morse's scene shows us something quite different: the reception of art among a cross-section of well-to-do but otherwise unexceptional American citizens.

There is another precedent among such "portraits" that tightens the links between Panini and Morse. Hubert Robert, a noted French painter of archeological ruins, came to Rome in 1754 and stayed 11 years. He worked as an assistant in Panini's studio during the time Panini painted his *Rome* canvases and was in the circle of the Duc de Choiseul, Panini's patron for the original versions. Years later, after his return to Paris, he began a series of paintings that projected the transformation of the Grande Galerie of the Louvre into a public museum. Robert painted the long gallery many times, in its existing state and in several variations that proposed solutions for illuminating the space; in one of his most famous canvasses, he painted it as a Roman ruin. But the version of 1796, softly lit by skylights that were only added to the real gallery many years later, assembles the same tropes that Panini had exploited four decades earlier: the elegant group of visitors (including female citizens of the new revolutionary state), some copying works, some in conversation, some simply lost in admiration. And the central device of the genre: the imagined rehanging of the gallery with a compilation of masterworks, each skillfully evoked by the copyist's hand.

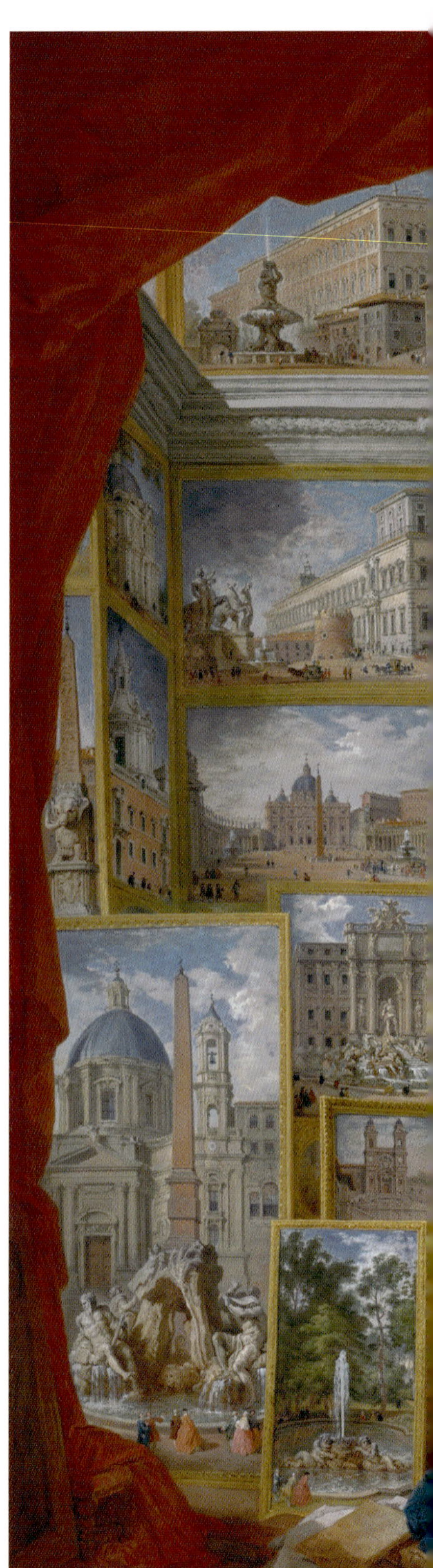

Giovanni Paolo Panini,
Modern Rome,
1757

A pendant composition to *Ancient Rome*, here focused on the city's Baroque monuments, presented as a collection of individual portraits or a lavish album of postcards of the Grand Tour. This version is at the Metropolitan Museum of Art.

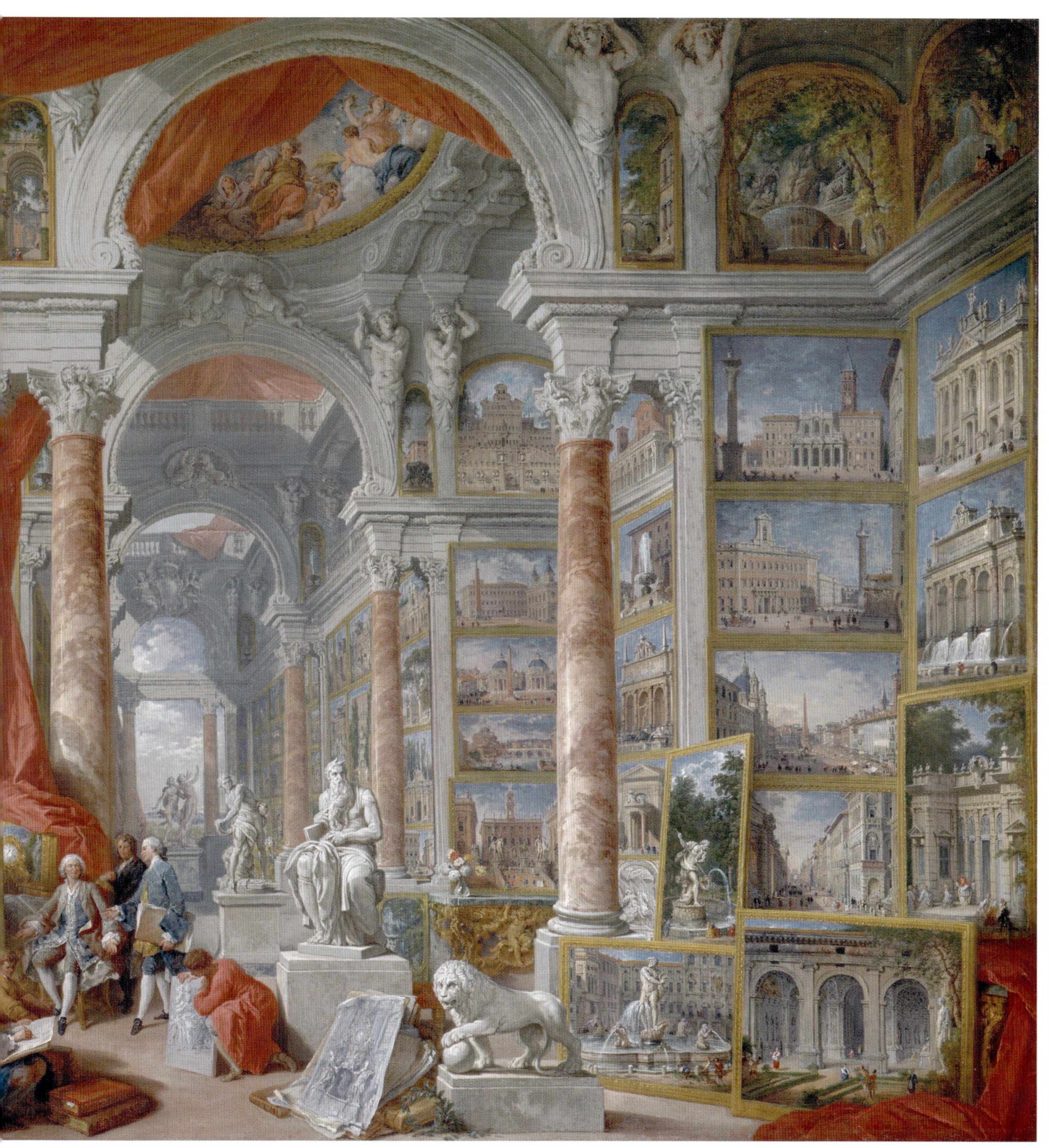

Hubert Robert,
Projet d'amenagement de la Grande Galerie,
1796

Robert's studies for transforming the Louvre's Grande Galerie into a public museum included this proposal for a zenithal or top-lighting solution that maximized wall space for paintings. The mix of visitors corresponds closely to Morse's painting, especially the presence of women among the copyists.

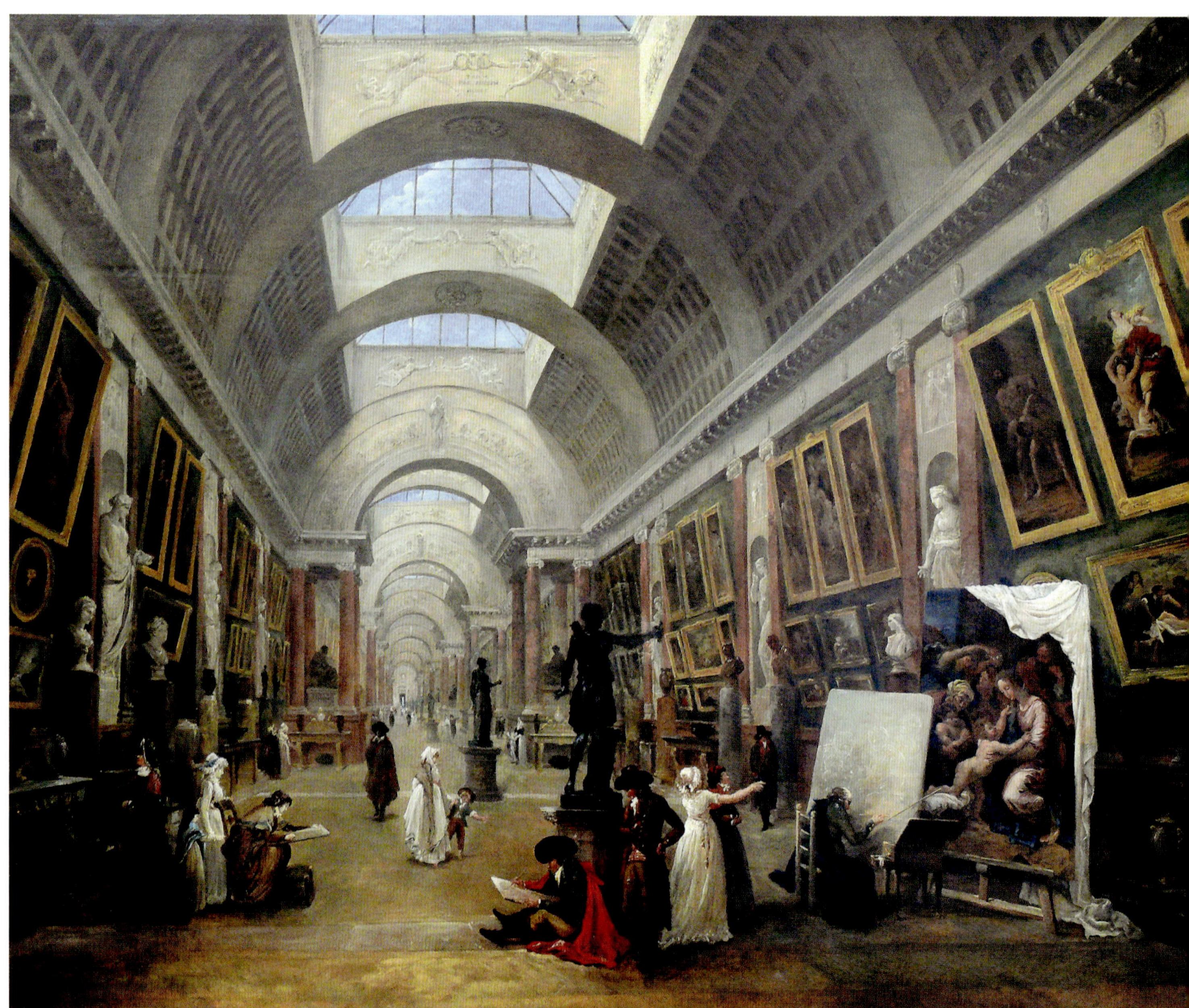

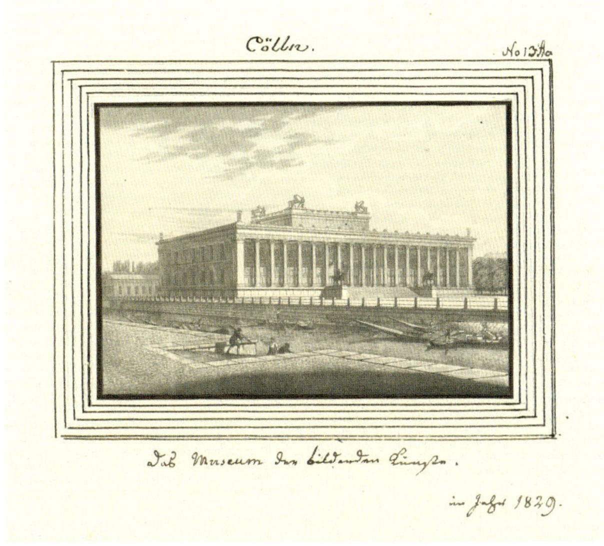

Karl Friedrich Schinkel, *Das Museum de bildenden Künste. Im jahr 1829 (The Museum of Fine Arts in 1829)*, before 1839

A lithograph based on a plate from Schinkel's *Sammlung Architektonischer Entwürfe* (1820–40). His Altes Museum was the first full statement of a new building type, and would dominate museum design for a century to come. The collection it was built to house—works of the Prussian monarchy, pillaged by Napoleon for the Louvre and returned from Paris—anticipates contemporary debates on restitution.

Pleasure and Pedagogy

Thus by 1830 Morse had a choice of models on which to base his own study of the museum just a few steps away from the Salon Carré. Although his composition is clearly connected to this long tradition of making art about displaying art, Morse reworked the tradition to new ends. Painting the picture on his return to the US, he brought the best of European art to an audience that could not travel to Paris to see it. One can interpret his project as he did: a democratizing gesture, intended to instruct and improve American taste and spur artistic creativity. There is a subtle tension, however, for both the picture and Morse's commercial ambitions for it to make clear his wish to flatter an elite audience while still attracting the masses he hoped would make his fortune. And this tension, between the educative value of art for the uninstructed and the appeal of art to an elite versed in its aesthetics, goes to the heart of artistic culture in America.

The dichotomy between a museum for education and a museum for aesthetics—between art as an instrument and art as an end in itself—has long characterized the American debate about "what the museum is for." Though the distinction may seem contrived, it still resonates and influences nearly every aspect of the museum's presentation of its collections. It is ultimately a debate about what the museum is supposed to do and what kind of an institution it should be. And, inevitably, a debate about whom the museum is for.

Panini and Morse give different answers to this question. The privileged figures in Panini's gallery portraits are habitués of these kinds of scenes, the central figure often the patron who has commissioned the very painting we are admiring. Painter and patron are part of a closed knowledge system; the scene at hand memorializes that system and the highly limited audience for which it was intended. Morse's cast of characters speaks to a completely different understanding of the gallery, and shows us a moment of instruction, with all of the social and cultural insecurities that accompany such moments. And in Morse's painting the central figure is the artist, the individual whose talent and sensibility entitles him to present these artifacts and interpret their significance to his countrymen (and women).

One of the ironies of Morse's painting is that the Louvre he depicts is a considerably diminished version of its former Revolutionary self. In the treaties of 1815 that concluded the Napoleonic Wars, an enormous quantity of art seized in conquest to fill the palace museum was returned to the nations from which it had been pillaged. Indeed 1830 is noteworthy for another reason, for it marked the opening in Berlin of the pre-eminent Prussian architect Karl Friedrich Schinkel's Altes Museum to display the plundered collection of the Hohenzollern monarchy, which had been finally repatriated from Paris. Schinkel's project, widely disseminated in his *Sammlung Architektonischer Entwürfe* (1820–40),[5] is arguably the first museum to have been expressly designed as such and the kernel from which the modern museum typology would grow. Within fifty years it would spur the great wave of American museum building, in which the questions first posed in Morse's painting would ultimately be debated.

Notes

1. See Samuel F.B. Morse "Biography": www.nga.gov/collection/artist-info.1737.html.
2. Samuel F.B. Morse, *Self-Portrait*, National Portrait Gallery, Smithsonian Institution, Washington, DC, 1812: www.si.edu/object/samuel-f-b-morse-self-portrait:npg_NPG.80.208.
3. See, for example, "A New Look: Samuel F.B. Morse's Gallery of the Louvre," National Gallery of Art, Washington, DC, 2012: www.nga.gov/content/dam/ngaweb/exhibitions/pdfs/morseinfo.pdf.
4. See https://collections.louvre.fr/en/ark:/53355/cl010059877 and https://collections.louvre.fr/en/ark:/53355/cl010059876.
5. The title is usually translated as "Collection of Architectural Works"; it was published in several versions between 1820 and 1840 and then reprinted by various publishers after Schinkel's death in 1841. See, for example, the version in the collection of ETH Zürich: Karl Friedrich Schinkel, *Sammlung Architektonischer Entwürfe*, Wittich (Berlin), 1820–40: www.e-rara.ch/zut/doi/10.3931/e-rara-8961.

In the

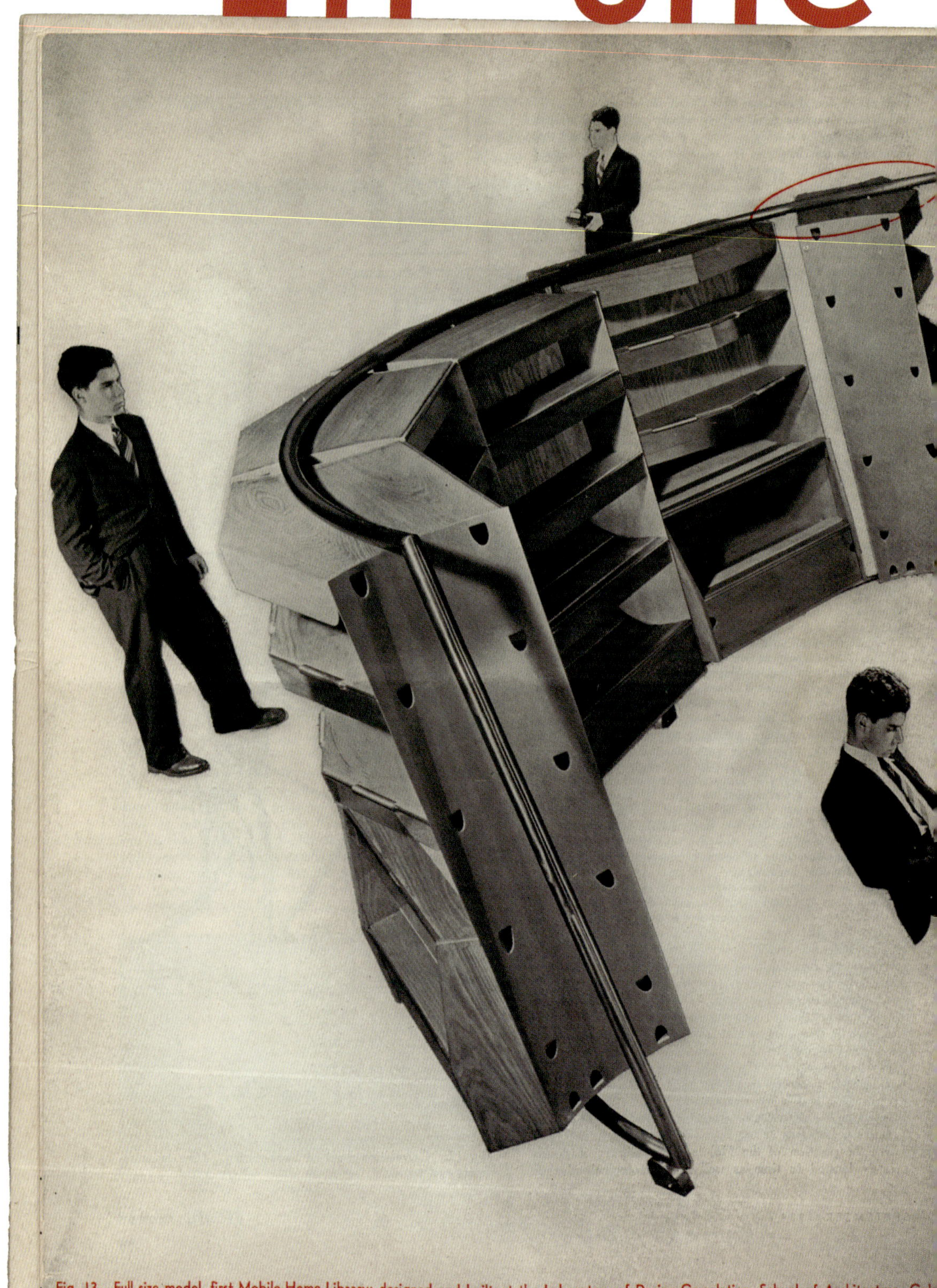

Realizing Frederick

Frederick Kiesler, "On Correalism and Biotechnique," 1939

Spread showing the collage of the Mobile Home Library based on Ezra Stoller's photographs of the test unit. Both the collage and photographs were starting points for construction of the library. The library was reconstructed for the "Frederick Kiesler: Vision Machines" exhibition at the Jewish Museum, New York, 2024.

Round

Leah Kelly

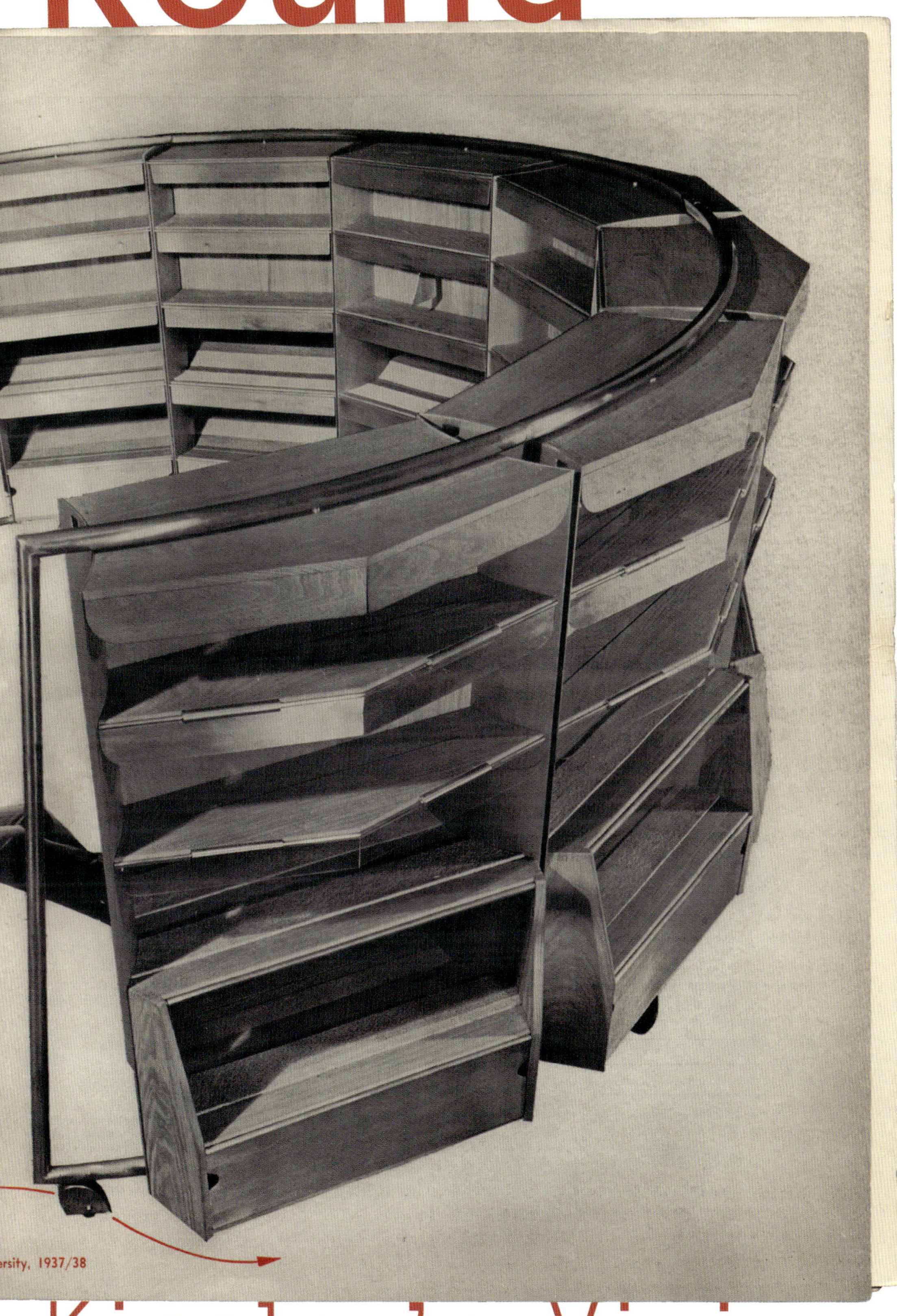

Kiesler's Vision

Austrian-American visionary architect Frederick Kiesler is often referenced in discussions in relation to the Surrealists and in terms of his classic architectural project the "Endless House" of 1953–9. He was fundamentally interested in seeing

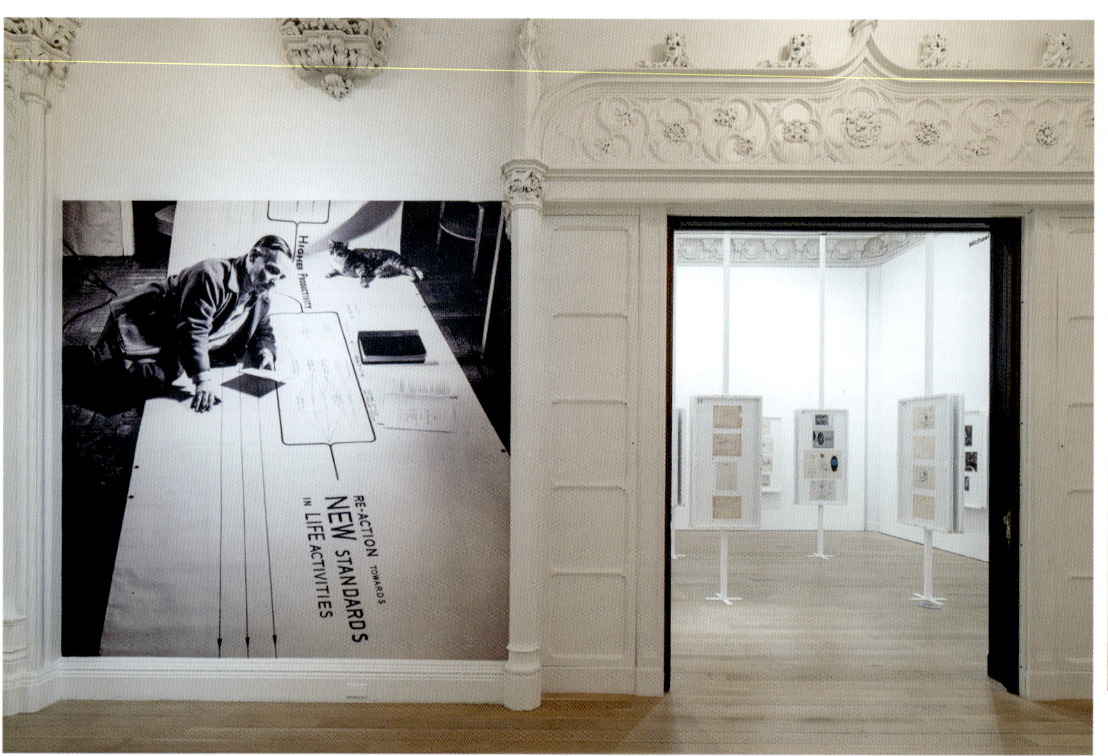

If the world is our stage then architects are our set designers. Frederick Kiesler was both and more. The exhibition "Frederick Kiesler: Vision Machines" at the Jewish Museum in New York ran from April to July 2024 and focused on two of the Austrian-American architect's overshadowed works: the Mobile Home Library and the Vision Machine (1938–1941). Both represent Kiesler's lifetime of thinking and making. They were created during his time as director of the Laboratory for Design Correlation at Columbia University, which fused science and humanities, theory and practice—a synecdoche for his unifying belief, embodied in all he did, in the endless, interconnectedness of all things visible and invisible.

Designing for the Designer

It was in his "electromechanical" set designs for Karel Čapek's play *R.U.R. (Rossum's Universal Robots)*[1] at the Kurfürstendamm Theater Berlin in 1923 that the public would first witness the results of Kiesler's thinking about perception, display devices, and dynamic interaction with the body. The next year he went on to design the set for *Kaiser Jones*[2] at the Lustspielhaus in Berlin, and it was at the "International Exhibition of New Theatre Techniques" for the Music and Theater Festival of the City of Vienna in 1924 where he assembled 600 works including drawings, paintings, and films using his Leger- und Trägersystem (L+T) system.

Leger and Trager described the two main types of wood components that were screwed together to form asymmetric horizontal and vertical lines for the display of the exhibits, to enable and "encourage novel experiences of the objects both individually and as a group."[3] Kiesler had wanted the wooden floor to be covered with linoleum, cork, or sheets of rubber to quieten the sound of footsteps, and the hall to be darkened with the works lit with spotlights—a bleed-through of his multisensorial stage-thinking—but was met with budgetary and institutional constraints. The L+T units were arranged, labyrinth-like, such that the exhibition had no beginning or end and no one work took precedence over another. His vision was already endless.

and the interconnection of all things. Here, neuroscientist **Leah Kelly** writes about the exhibition “Frederick Kiesler: Vision Machines” held in New York in 2024, in which two of his lesser-known projects, the Mobile Home Library and the Vision Machine (1938–41), were realized.

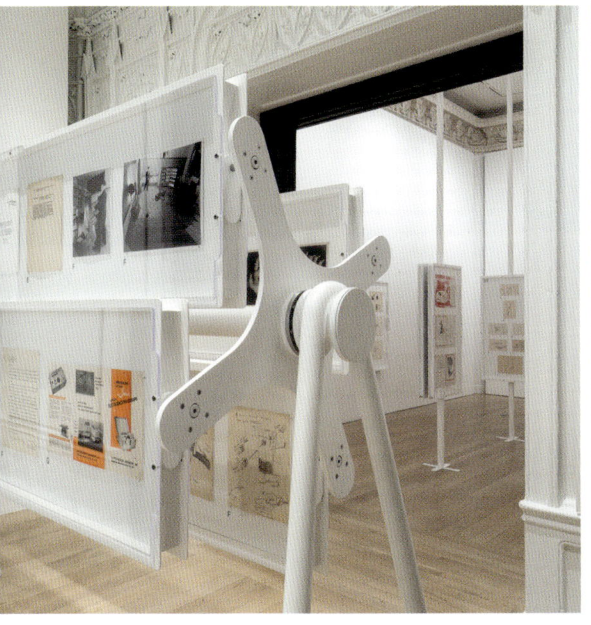

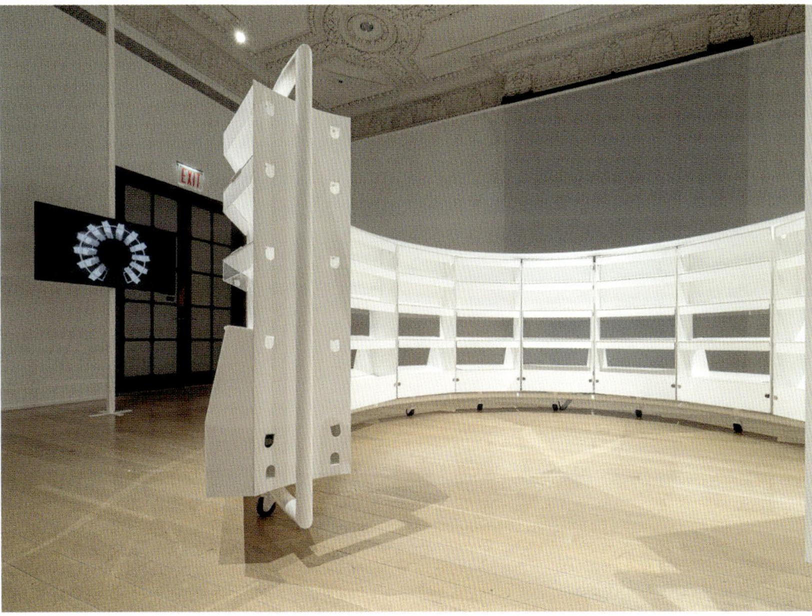

“Frederick Kiesler: Vision Machines” engaged another elegant, more uniform labyrinth that partly shunned the gallery walls as Kiesler would have. The exhibition contained 149 works, including recognized drawings and more obscure artifacts such as doodles on calendars and reports of field trips to scientific departments at Columbia. The exhibition designers, Mark Wasiuta, Farah Alkhoury, and Tigran Kostandyan, formulated a rotating display case that encouraged interaction with the viewers, and realized the Mobile Home Library (“not model, replica, nor sculpture”), which was choreographed with code, echoing Kiesler’s Berlin theater days and his desire to “fill the stage with life.”[4]

Mark Wasiuta, Farah Alkhoury, and Tigran Kostandyan, "Frederick Kiesler: Vision Machines" exhibition, Jewish Museum, New York, 2024

opposite: The perpendicular vitrines of the exhibition design gave a nod to Kiesler without mimicking him.

above left: The rotating display case highlighted interaction of the body with the environment and its role in perception—key ideas in Kiesler’s treatise “On Correalism and Biotechnique” (1939).

above right: The realization of the Mobile Home Library, one of the two main projects developed in Kiesler’s Laboratory for Design Correlation at Columbia University.

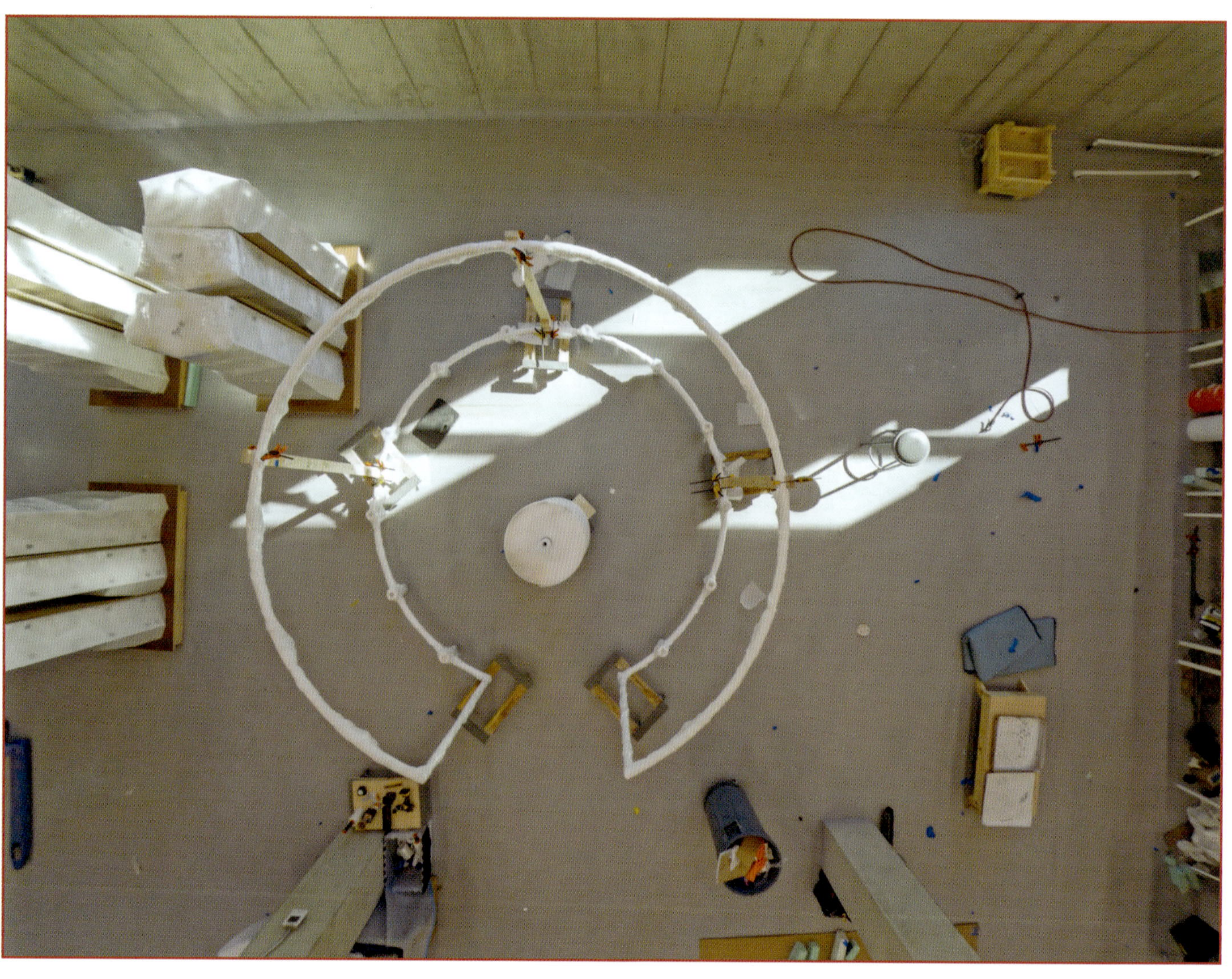

Mark Wasiuta, Farah Alkhoury, and Tigran Kostandyan,
"Frederick Kiesler: Vision Machines" exhibition,
Jewish Museum,
New York,
2024

Still from a movie documenting the fabrication of the Mobile Home Library. The modern version was made with aluminum and acrylic.

Lectures on the evolution of form and function both in nature and technology were structured around laboratory experiments

Giving Life to the Library

> I chose [this] theme because everyone is familiar with it, and by that have probably lost perspective of it.[5]

The Mobile Home Library is a proof of principle for many of Kiesler's ideas about vision, movement, habit, energy, interaction with the body, and pedagogy. After Berlin, these developed, spiral-like, during his time teaching at the Brooklyn International Theater Arts Institute (1926–7) where he built "a laboratory of the modern stage,"[6] creating window displays for the city's Saks department store (1928) and through designing sets at the Juilliard music school (from 1934). They flourished in the Laboratory for Design Correlation and were crystallized in his treatise "On Correalism and Biotechnique" (1939), which focused on "the dynamic of continual interaction between man and his natural and technological environments."[7]

The lab at Columbia was multidisciplinary and open to all students. Lectures on the evolution of form and function both in nature and technology were structured around laboratory experiments. In the case of the Mobile Home Library, students studied the "psycho-physiological succession" from "optical tactilism to manual tactilism" needed to establish contact with books, and engaged in "contact-cycle" studies to dissect the efficient, habitual movement of bodies.[8] The exhibition at the Jewish Museum featured an original sketch for the library as well as photographs of the fabrication of three original panels, built during the laboratory's second year, which formed the basis of the famous collage that was printed alongside Kiesler's "On Correalism" treatise. Using these for reference, Wasiuta, Alkhoury, and Kostandyan constructed the library using modern materials and methods to make shelves that spin.

Experiencing this iteration was paradoxical, as the ideas contained within the Mobile Home Library, concerning the accelerated efficiency in the way we have come to display, engage with, and consume information and the multisensory, multimedia nature of it—flitting between multiple open tabs of prosthetic thought and memory—were so prescient. Yet encountering this very physical container of such ideas confronts us with what we often forget today—that our brains are contained in bodies that move.

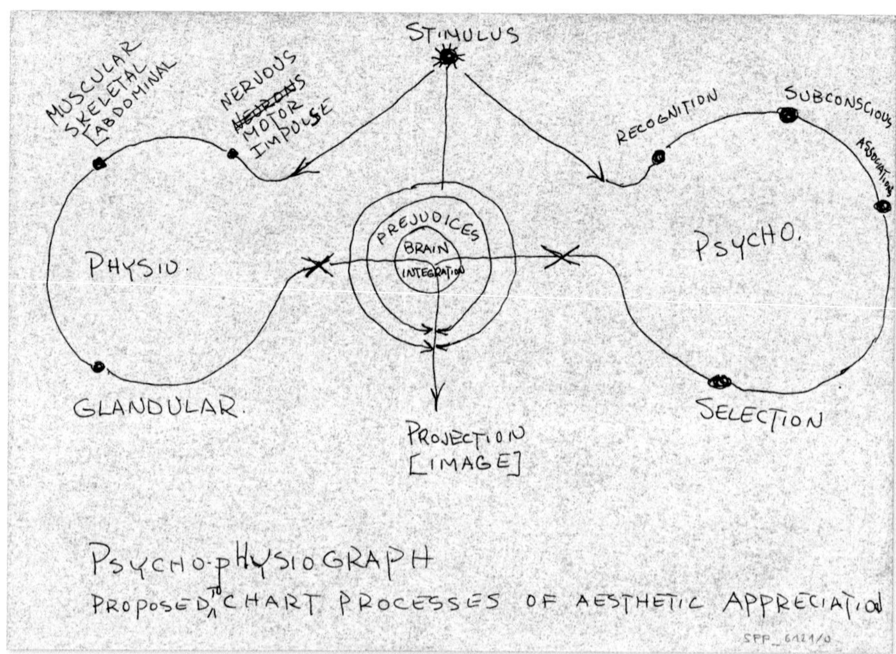

Frederick Kiesler,
Psychophysiograph Correalistic diagram for the Vision Machine,
1930s

right: Students in the Laboratory for Design Correlation were exposed to ideas in both physiology and psychology, and considered how previous experiences altered perception.

Frederick Kiesler,
"Do We See in a Two-Way System?" study of human cognition for the Vision Machine,
1938

opposite: Kiesler's ideas about vision were formed from his studies of biophysics and Gestalt psychology. This drawing hints at his understanding of the interaction between light and bioelectricity of the nervous system, and his idea that all vision is illusion.

Vision and the Visionary

Kiesler was obsessed with vision and perception, and key among his work in the Laboratory for Design Correlation were his sketches for a machine that would demonstrate how we construct them—the Vision Machine. Selig Hecht from the biophysics department at Columbia came to lecture on the eye, and cathode ray tubes and retinas were studied. The machine was to be fabricated using an electrostatic generator, brass balls, blown-glass tubes, colored gases, and electric wires to represent the confluence of physiological and psychological processes that contribute to vision. Reflected light was to be focused by an ocular aperture and projected. Film images provided a depository of associations that simulated recognition, the subconscious, and previous experiences. "From among the array of dreamlike images recollected and presented in accord with bodily affect and environmental conditions, a unified image would be created from a selection, and then reflected back."[9]

It is tempting to write-off Kiesler's ideas as eccentric. From a neuroscientific perspective, however, his thinking is again correct in many ways. Perception is an act of creation. It relies not only on detection of shape and form but on comparison to all previous experience. Object recognition relies on the activation of an entire hierarchy of neurons, a miniscule proportion of which are responding to light.[10] The rest are dedicated to recognition, allocating categories and subcategories to objects. Every visual memory is represented in the brain through a specific pattern of neuronal activity. Activity evoked from seeing an image for the first time and recalling it from memory might not be so physiologically different.

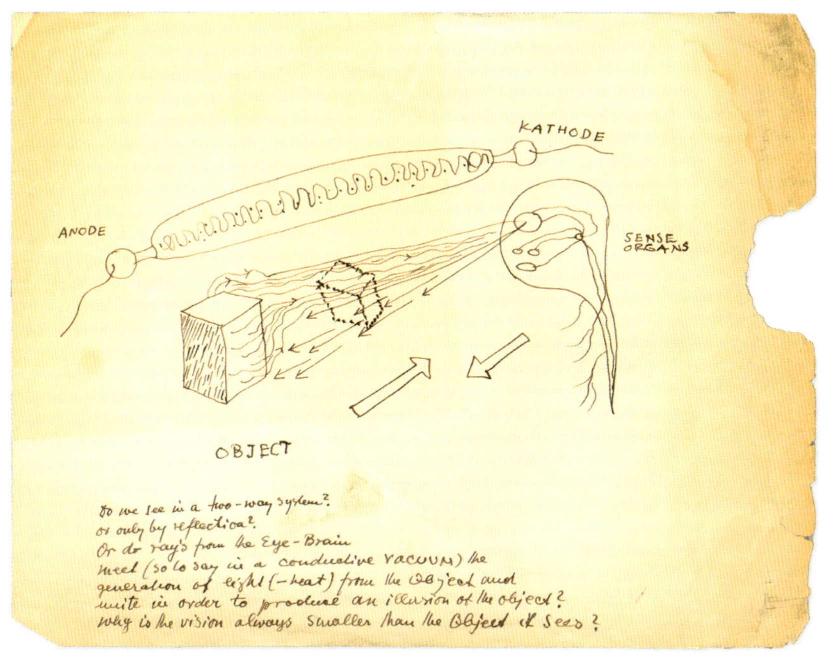

Object recognition relies on the activation of an entire hierarchy of neurons, a miniscule proportion of which are responding to light

In the 1940s, psychologists Fritz Heider and Marianne Simmel made a short animation of geometric shapes and asked people to describe what was happening. The results showed that we project causality, personality, and motivation onto animated squares, circles, and triangles.[11] As visitors ambulated among the vitrines of the "Vision Machines" exhibition, they experienced the endless juxtaposition of ideas that transposed in association with each other depending on their field of view and shifted in perspective, appearing endless and alinear were it not for the numbered panels. With the rotating display unit, similar shifts were experienced with acute agency, highlighting the role of the body in perception. This combination of material *on* and material *of* display created a continuous loop of seeing oneself seeing—the exhibition as Vision Machine. ꝺ

Notes

1. Karel Čapek, *R.U.R. (Rossum's Universal Robots)*, Penguin Books (London and New York), 2004.
2. Eugene O'Neill, *The Emperor Jones*, Stewart Kidd company (Cincinnati, OH), 1921.
3. Laura McGuire, "The Exhibition Display System Leger + Träger," in Peter Bogner and Gerd Zillner, *Wien 1924: Station Der Avantgarde*, Frederick and Lillian Kiesler Foundation (Vienna), 2018, p. 36
4. Frederick Kiesler, "De la Nature morte vivante," *Internationale Ausstellung neuer Theatretechnik*, exh. cat., Vienna, 1924.
5. Frederick Kiesler, "First Report on the Laboratory for Design Correlation," 1937, 3–4, in LDC, REC 03 Box, Activities/Reports, Reports on the LDC Folder, Kiesler Archive, Vienna. See also Frederick Kiesler to Wells Bennett, 1 May 1940, LDC, REC 10 Box, Unmarked Folder, Kiesler Archive, Vienna.
6. Stephen Phillips, "Toward a Research Practice: Frederick Kiesler's Design-Correlation Laboratory," *Grey Room*, 38, 2020, p. 93. See also "Plans Laboratory of Modern Stage: Former Vienna Director Says He Will Develop 'Fourth-Dimensional Theatre' to Exemplify Democracy—'Psychological, Scientific, and Artistic' Instruction Will Be Given," *New York Times*, March 15, 1926, in Frederick Kiesler Papers, microfilm reel 127, Archives of American Art, Smithsonian Institution, Washington, DC.
7. Frederick Kiesler, "On Correalism and Biotechnique: A Definition and the New Approach to Building Design," *Architectural Record*, 86, September 1939, p. 67.
8. See "Multiple Unification, a Study by: Ideographic Disintegration," Student Report, n.d., 2, in LDC Files, Box 8, Series 11, Kiesler Archive, Vienna.
9. Phillips, "Toward a Research Practice", p. 109.
10. Charles D. Gilbert and Wu Li, "Top-down Influences on Visual Processing," *Nature Reviews Neuroscience*, 14, 2013, pp. 350–63.
11. Fritz Heider and Marianne Simmel, "An Experimental Study of Apparent Behavior," *The American Journal of Psychology*, 57, 1944, pp. 243–9.

RULES OF
Interactions between Materials,

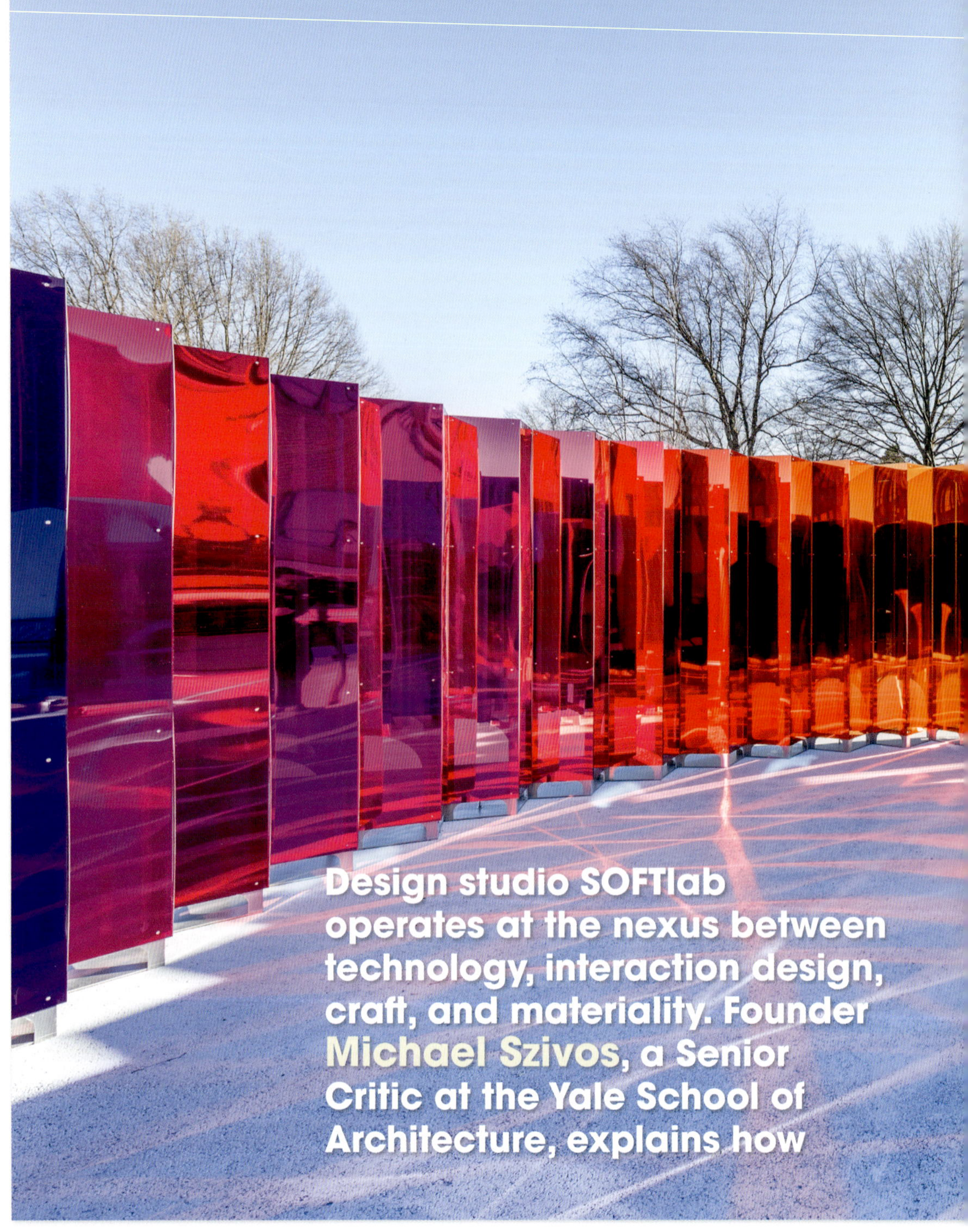

Design studio SOFTlab operates at the nexus between technology, interaction design, craft, and materiality. Founder Michael Szivos, a Senior Critic at the Yale School of Architecture, explains how

ENGAGEMENT
Media, and Code

Michael Szivos

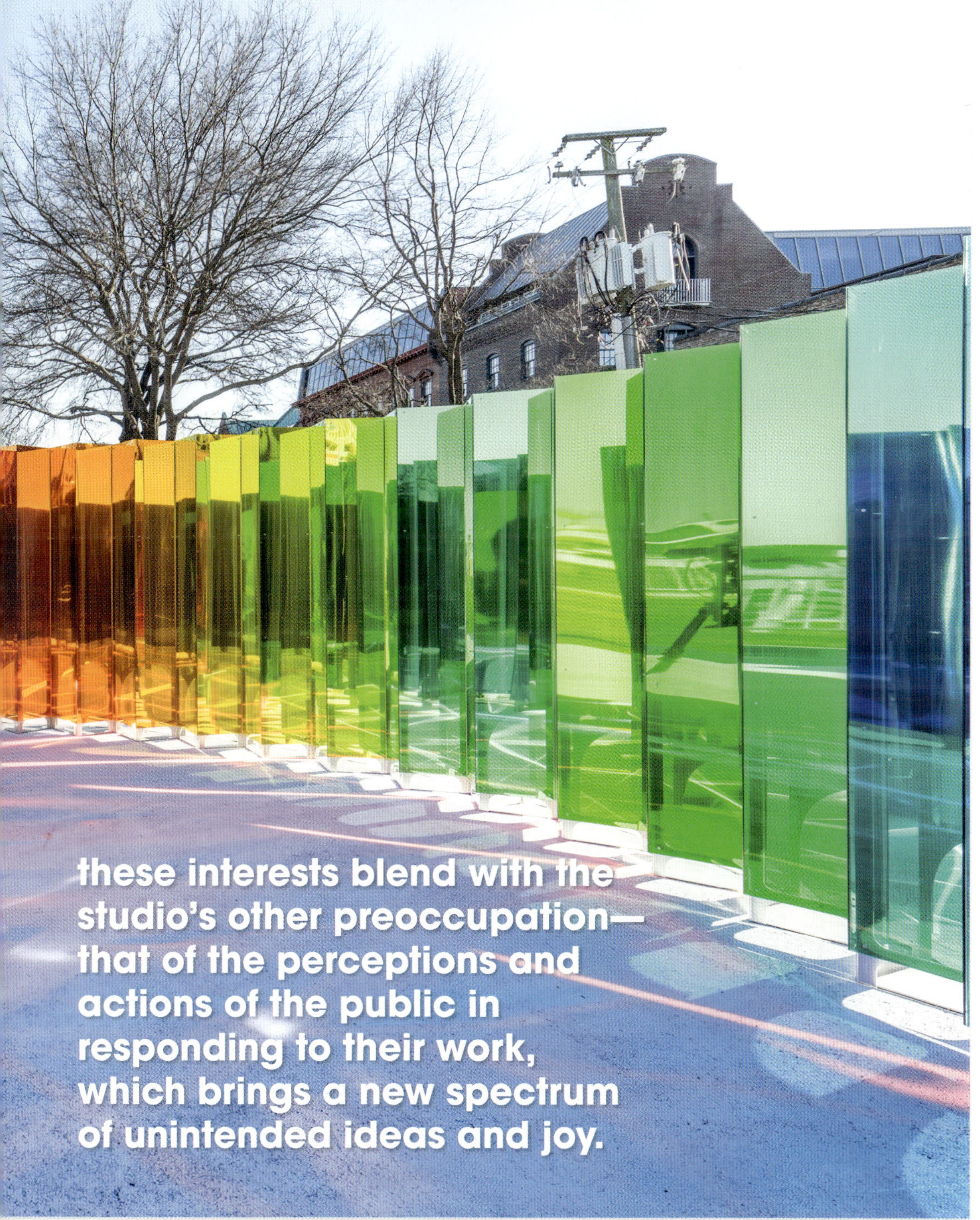

these interests blend with the studio's other preoccupation—that of the perceptions and actions of the public in responding to their work, which brings a new spectrum of unintended ideas and joy.

SOFTlab, *Mirror Mirror*, Alexandria, Virginia, 2019

The lenticular exterior and interior mirrored surfaces of *Mirror Mirror* became inverted when the internal LED fixtures were activated by sound, becoming transparent infinity boxes.

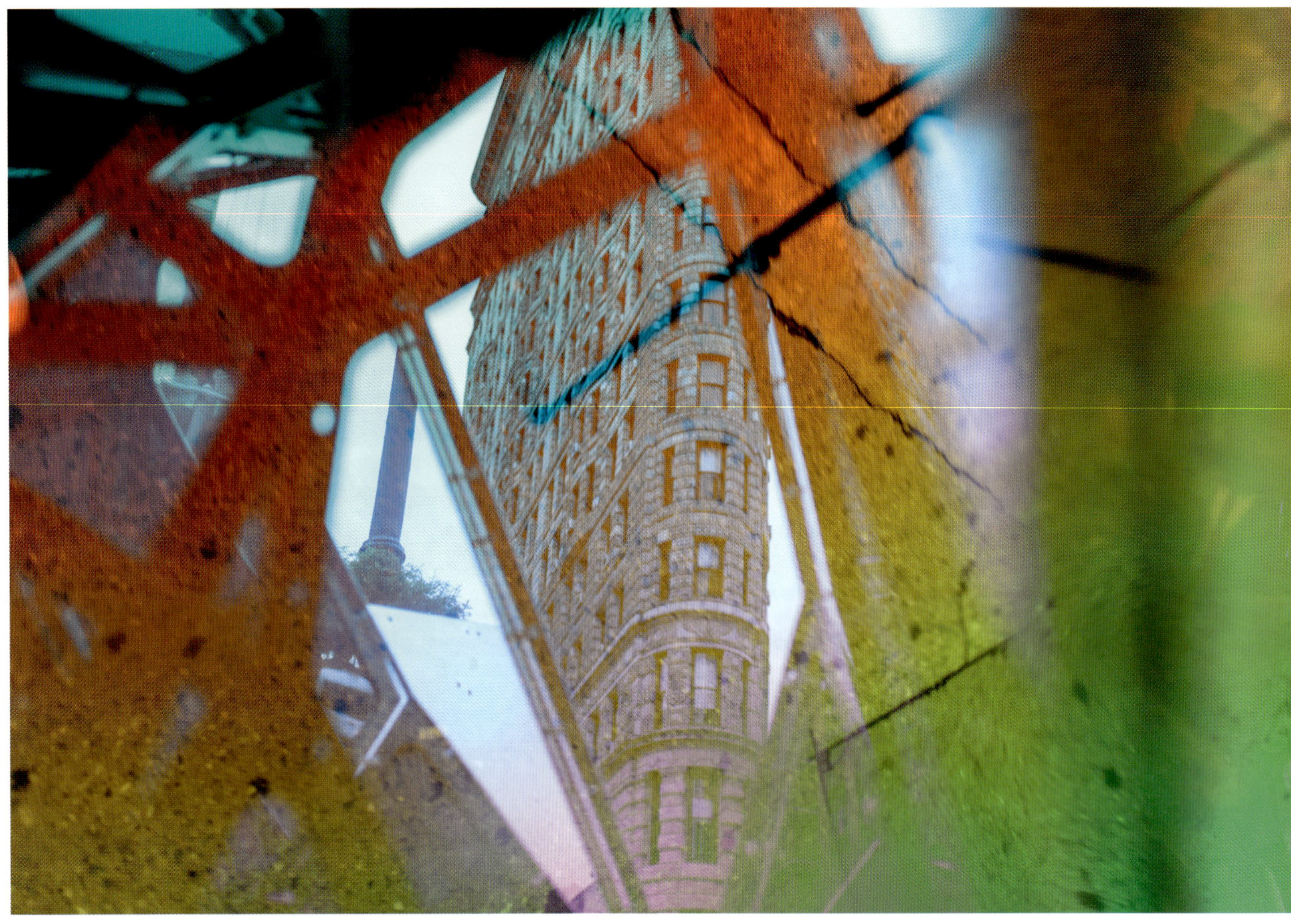

Based in New York, the SOFTlab design studio combines a research-based design practice with an interest in how technology, craft, and materials come together in ways that explore the boundaries between art, architecture, interaction design, other disciplines, and the public.

The projects designed by SOFTlab are scripted in two distinct ways. One way is through the customization of the software-based tools the studio uses to automate the production of its work. The other is through the design of projects as the studio thinks through how they unfold when the public engages and interacts with them. The first method of scripting is very discrete and geared towards specific outcomes, while the latter is much more open-ended and acts more as a framework that allows the public to become co-authors as they contribute to and create their own interpretations of the studio's work.

Beyond the discreteness of their outcomes, the way the studio approaches these two methods of scripting is very different. The scripting the studio does for production is fairly straightforward. It helps automate production of complex assemblies and makes production pipelines more efficient. For example, the studio would use scripting to customize software like Rhino to rationalize a complex three-dimensional geometry into two-dimensional cut files and labels for parts used for fabrication and construction. Beyond automation and efficiency, these processes also remove the element of human error that would be inevitable if someone were to draw thousands of custom parts.

The second type of scripting is much more experiential, sequentially based, and plans for human idiosyncrasies rather than removing them. The first step in this process is looking for dynamic conditions on the site that may not be readily apparent, and then reframing them through a composite of form and materials. This creates what the studio calls an experiential contextualism rather than a literal one. While a project might appear to be distinct from its surroundings, its connections to the site and appropriateness unfold as visitors approach and engage with it.

Experiential Contextualism

Nova (2015), installed at Flatiron Plaza in Manhattan, New York, and facing the Flatiron Building (1902), is a good example of how the studio creates a project that unfolds. The project was part of an annual competition held by the Van Alen Institute to design a pavilion for the beginning of the holiday season. The studio's selected proposal reframed the site's rich historical context of the buildings and landmarks as a constellation to be viewed much like a star map. The primitive form of the pavilion was inspired by a gazebo with seven sides that was meant to offer panoramic views of the surroundings. A strategy of gazing along with the constellation of landmarks surrounding the site led the studio to extend the seven sides of the pavilion into simple four-sided "scopes" in a radial arrangement. Those scopes were individually rotated in plan and section so they were aimed at various landmarks that could be seen from the plaza, such as the Flatiron and Empire State buildings, giving what was previously a self-similar form a shape that not only looked different from all sides, but also implied a registration with the site's context.

The outside of the pavilion was clad in aluminum composite panels with a mirrored finish facing the interior, while the exterior was given the neutral finish of untreated aluminum. While the material is neutral, the oddly noncontextual form piqued the curiosity of pedestrians from around the high-traffic plaza. Rather than use a stick-frame structure for the construction, the studio used a cellular soap-bubble-like structural system. This was lightweight, but also acted as a three-dimensional arch made of aluminum-framed "stones." When exposed in the interior they created a crystalline dome in the pavilion that was clad with dichroic acrylic panels. Dichroic is an optical film made by 3M that dynamically filters spectrums of light depending on the angle of view. It appears to change color and reflectivity as it is viewed from different angles.

As visitors entered the pavilion they were surprised by the multifaceted crystalline interior. The combination of the dichroic acrylic, interior-facing mirrored composite panels, and the cellular structure, created a pedestrian-scale kaleidoscope. As visitors explored the framed views of local landmarks, they discovered that while the pavilion was a playful mix of form and materials, it was also a new way to view their surroundings. Because the dichroic shifts between reflective and transparent, images of visitors were also cast into the remixed images of the city, becoming a part of the context.

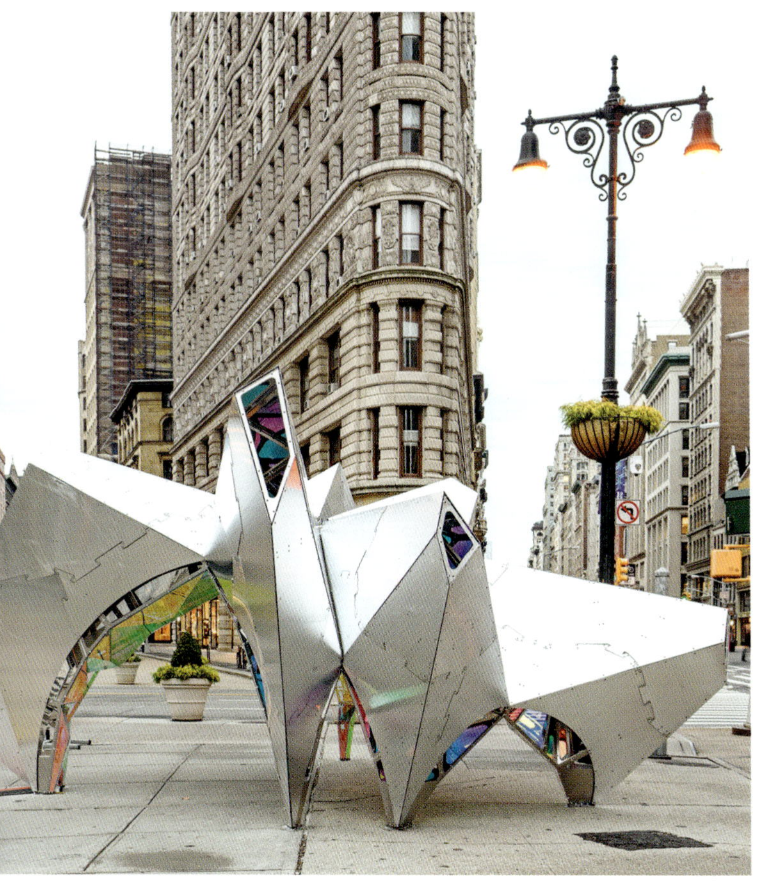

SOFTlab,
Nova,
New York City,
2015

left: At first glance the temporary installation's aluminum-clad form appeared out of context, but the seven scopes aimed at various buildings and landmarks offered a secondary mapped registration of the context that could only be experienced from the interior.

opposite: The crystalline interior created a pedestrian-scale kaleidoscope, fragmenting and remixing the rich context, structure of the pavilion, and people.

Inside Out

Halo (2023) is a permanent artwork designed by SOFTlab in the public space surrounding Google's new headquarters in Mountain View, California. The project uses similar materials and assemblies as *Nova*, but in a very different formal strategy and relationship to the site. In this case the context is a large landscaped public area. The landscaping is loosely reminiscent of the informal nature of English gardens. *Halo* was designed as a pavilion in the round that acts as a landmark within the public space. Lacking the traditional ornament of garden pavilions, it is a perfect cylinder clad in matte anodized aluminum tubes. At 22 feet (6.7 meters) tall, the cylinder is visible from a distance just above the tree line as the same on all sides.

As visitors approach *Halo* they discover five arches at various scales subtracted from the cylinder in a stereotomic fashion. The intersection of the arches with the cylinder creates large, curved, cantilevered thresholds. Beyond the arches are hints of the crystalline cladding of the interior. This structure and cladding are similar to the interior of *Nova*, but the effect is much more like entering a geode, given the form's stereotomic quality. Once inside the cylinder, visitors are completely immersed in another world made of faceted crystalline geometry and reflected light, as sunlight entering from above is recast in unexpected ways.

At night, LED fixtures integrated into the aluminum tubes shine light through perforated holes facing inward. The lighting is programmed to create a generative cloud-like animation that gives the sense of wind blowing through the structure. Dichroic filters out spectrums of light based on the direction it is cast and viewed. The color of the dichroic-clad interior is inverted, as the light is now coming from behind the acrylic rather than sunlight passing through the front. From a distance, the cylinder which appeared solid during the day appears to dematerialize as the lighting now exposes the shadows of the structure behind the tubes in an X-ray-like fashion. This inversion happens on many levels, from the approach during the day to the way the lighting reverses the solidity of the massing at night.

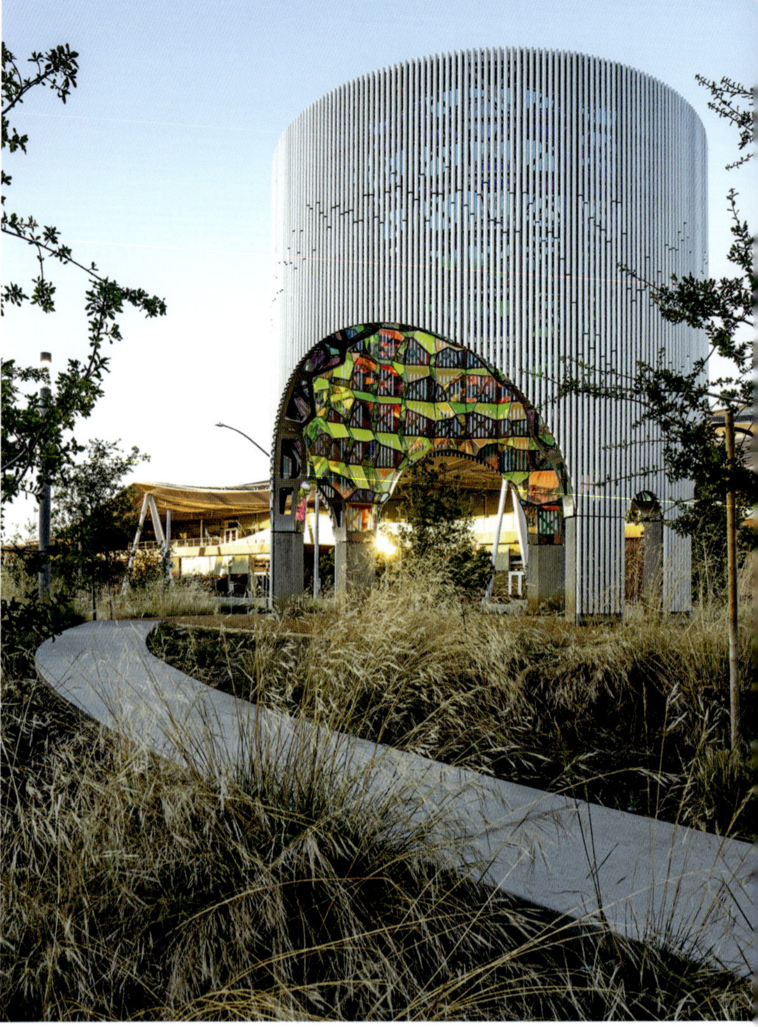

SOFTlab,
Halo,
Mountain View, California,
2023

As visitors approach, the simple shape of the cylinder above recedes through five different-sized arches that offer glimpses of the crystalline interior.

Coded Behavior

The software-based scripting that went into the design and production of the *Nova* and *Halo* projects is evident in their complexity, highly customized parts, and digitally aided fabrication methods. These projects were also designed with curated but indeterminate experiences in mind. These two types of scripting are typically exclusive to one another and have very different goals. But another type of project has emerged within SOFTlab's body of work, one where the lines between the coded scripting and the narrative-based scripting is very much blurred. These are interactive projects where the coded nature of the production continues through into the scripted narrative, behavior, and experience of the project.

The scripting the studio does during the design and production process is really about managing complexity, and this continues into the coded behaviors of its interactive projects. The same coding for discrete systems management in the studio's static projects transitions into an interactive control system that manages similar attributes, but now as a response to real-time dynamic conditions based on how the public engages with each project. The following projects showcase how the merging of software scripting and experiential scripting has enabled the studio to rethink how it approaches its projects.

Curious Signaling

One of the first concerns with any of SOFTlab's interactive projects is how visitors discover that interactivity. The studio makes a big effort to avoid using a call to action or didactic instructions for how to interact with the work. Just as with the studio's static projects, it should unfold through discovery and surprise. This requires simple but highly calibrated responsive behaviors. The studio's temporary interactive installation *Iris* (2018), located in the Klementinum Mirror Chapel in the center of Prague, Czech Republic, used sound-responsive lighting and motion tracking to create an interactive experience that was easily discovered. The installation was made of a series of two-sided mirror assemblies that sandwiched programmable LEDs on either side and were individually mounted on a base containing a computer-controlled servo that allowed for the precise control of the mirror assembly's rotation. The installation almost disappeared as the Baroque architecture and patterned floor tiles were repeated in the mirrors. As visitors approached, any noise or echo in the chapel activated the circular array of LEDs. A depth camera above tracked people's motion when they entered the installation, causing the mirrors to rotate to face the nearest person. The speed and rotation were highly calibrated so the mirrors were seen less as an interactive mechanism, and more as a set of strange characters in the space. Visitors were meant to feel a sense of gaze and curiosity, rather than sensors and mechanics. Avoiding calls to action has enabled the studio to think about projects as not just tectonic assemblies, but as new occupants in a space that can even incite new emotional or empathic responses.

The lighting is programmed to create a generative cloud-like animation that gives the sense of wind blowing through the structure

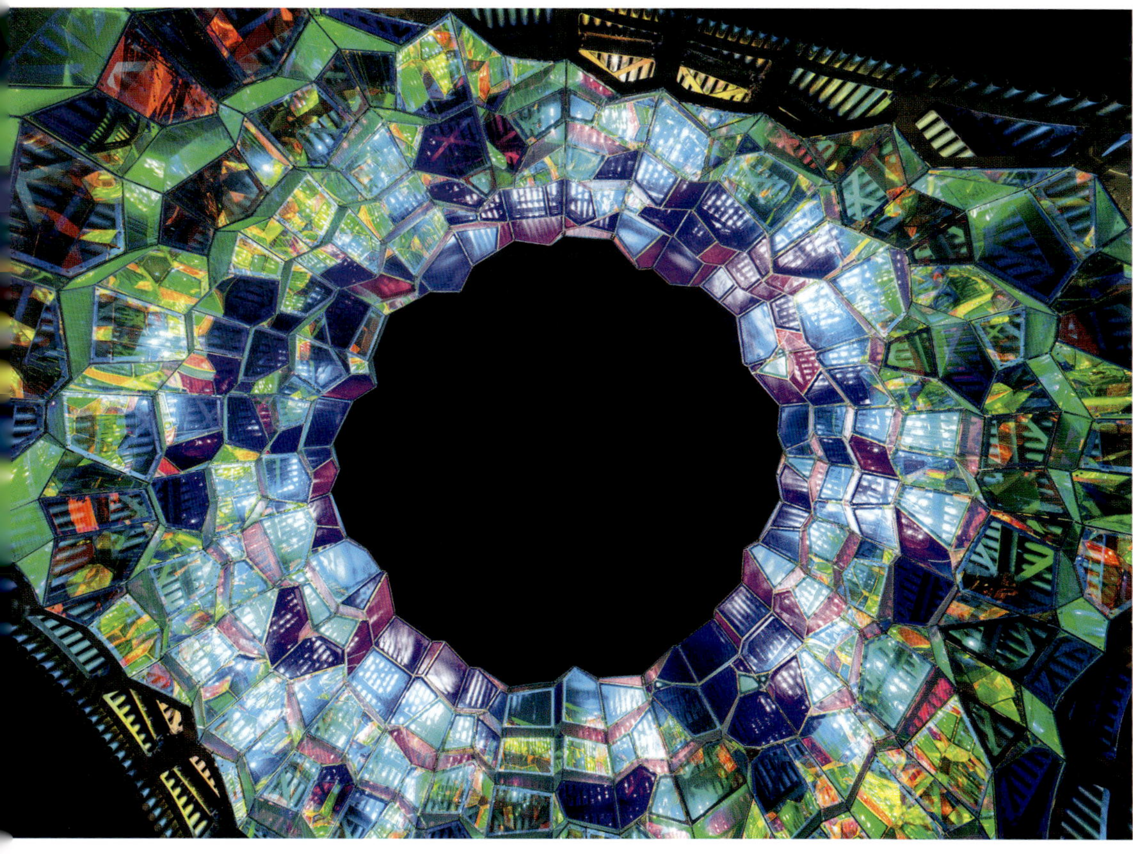

At night, LED fixtures integrated into the aluminum tubes cladding the exterior backlight the faceted interior with an atmospheric animation that activates the materials' optical qualities.

SOFTlab,
Iris,
Prague, Czech Republic,
2018

right: As visitors interacted with *Iris*, there was a breakdown in the distinction of who (or what) was responding to whom. The installation became a new kind of character in the space as a playful exchange emerged between the people, the environment, and the installation.

below: The circular array of the installation's rotating mirrors responded to the movement of people, while the LEDs on the edge of each mirror assembly responded to sound. As the lights and the Baroque architecture were reflected in the mirrors, they created unpredictable switches of reciprocity between people, space, light, and sound.

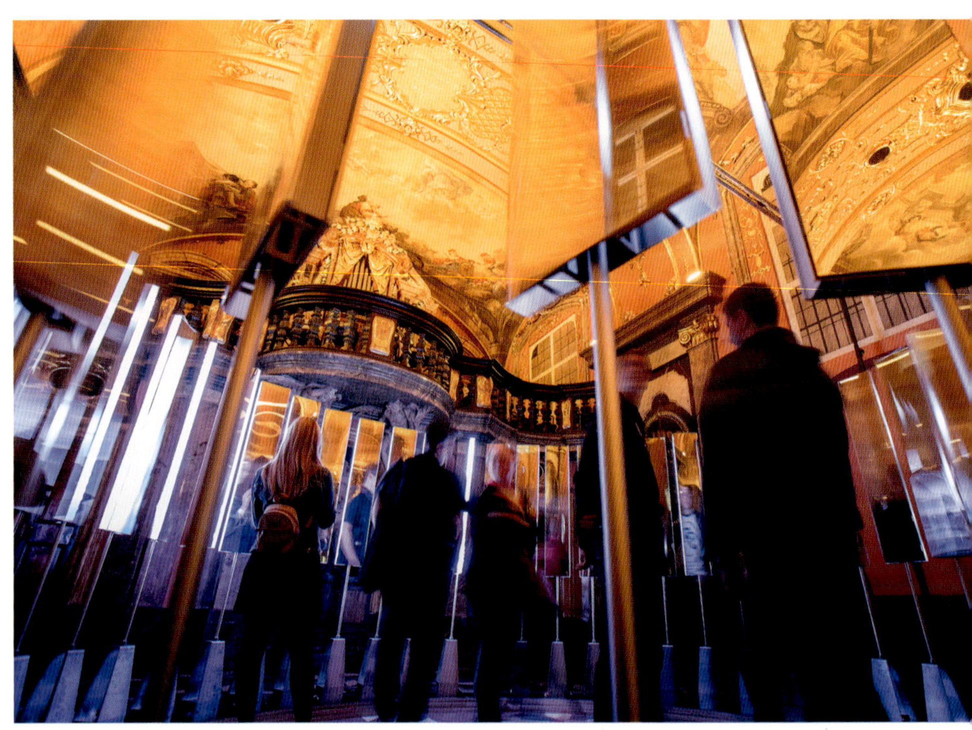

Interactive Composites

Just as SOFTlab approaches static projects through a composite of form, structure, and materials to create an integrated experience, any interactive elements are designed in a way so that they are perceived as part of a material assembly rather than a standalone element. The studio's temporary public installation *Mirror Mirror* (2019) for Waterfront Park in the Old Town neighborhood of the city of Alexandria, Virginia is a good example of this. Custom LED fixtures that respond to sound were integrated into a circular set of chambers. These chambers were clad with two-way mirror acrylic on the exterior and on the interior with the mirrored surface also laminated with a full spectrum of colored film. The serrated surface on the exterior reflected a panoramic view of the rich historical context, Potomac River, and pedestrians, while the interior was inverted, multiplying reflections of pedestrians as they entered in a full spectrum of color. The interactive lighting was hidden until it was triggered by sound. Once activated, the lighting made the inside of the chambers brighter and the mirrored surfaces became transparent, while the opposite surface became reflective, turning the chamber into an infinity box. The 36 linear fixtures became an infinite forest of light. This assembly of optical material and lighting created an atmospheric material composite where the interactive elements and the materials worked so closely together to craft the experience that it was hard to see them as separate systems.

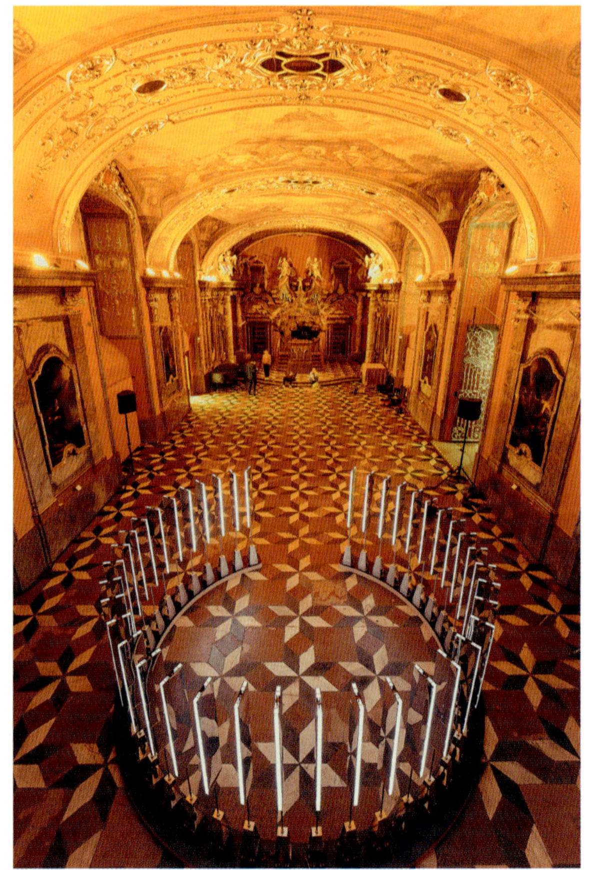

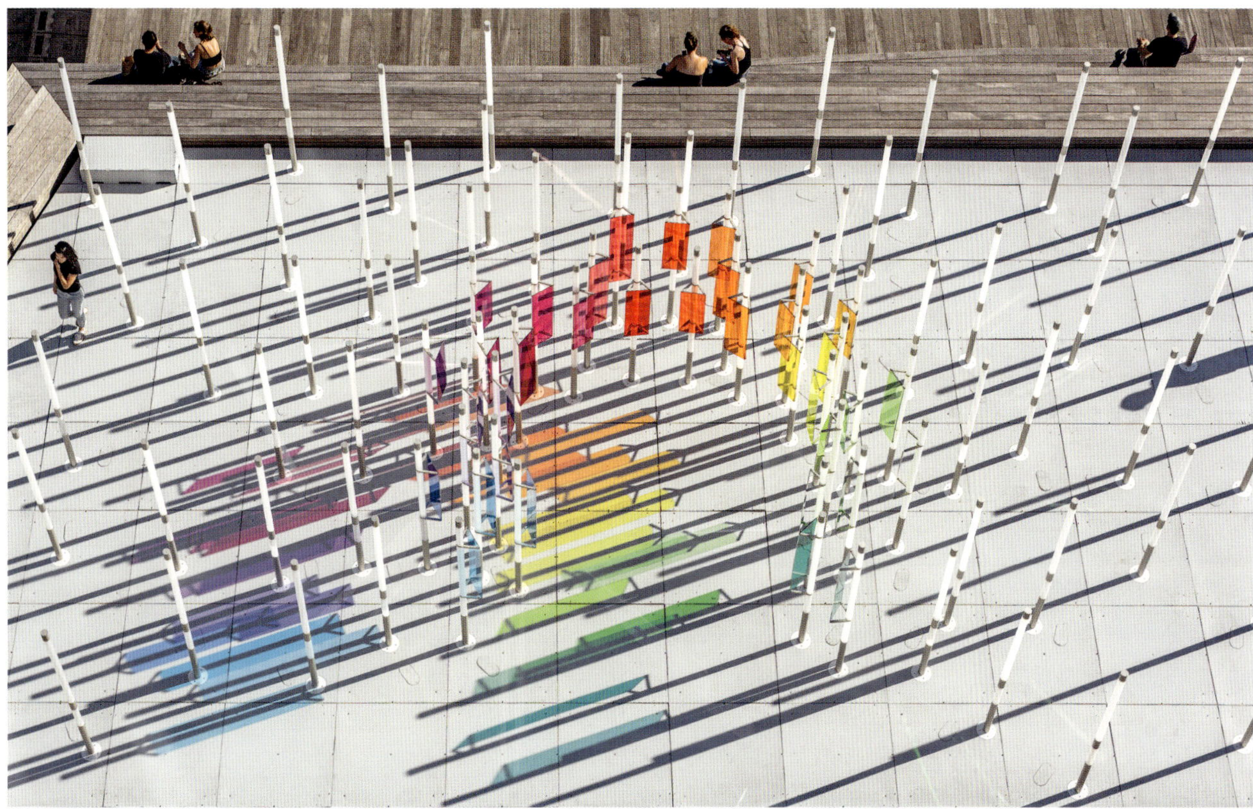

Touch Me

Similar to the tactile nature of materials in architecture, interactivity can be activated by touch through the use of capacitive sensors. These can detect anything with a conductive capacity different from air, such as human touch. SOFTlab's immersive interactive installation *Nautilus* (2019), installed in Manhattan's Seaport District, integrated them into a vertical light assembly of 96 vertical poles installed in a field. Each of these poles was made of anodized aluminum and translucent acrylic tubes. The tubes contained programmable LEDs, speakers, and a portion of aluminum tube in the middle that held a capacitive sensor and a microprocessor. The installation acted as a touch-interactive environment that allowed people to come together to produce an unexpected symphony of light and sound. As a person touched the capacitive portion of a pole, it activated a tone based on metrics of their touch. As that tone was played, lights in the surrounding poles reacted with a pulse emanating from that pole. While a single touch produced one melody, simultaneous interactions by various people created a complex, layered chorus. Rather than a button or touchscreen, the material of the installation became the mode of interaction. While the formal arrangement of the installation was quite simple, it acted as a large network where the distinction between material, light, and sound was blurred.

Off Script

By extending the same software programming that it uses in the production of its work into the experience, SOFTlab has fostered not only inventive and pragmatic solutions, but new ways for it to consider the nature of its work and how a composite of static material systems can be transformed into an interactive assembly. While these projects are highly technical, perceiving the experience through the lens of more narrative-based scripting has allowed the studio to think of their projects as characters in a performance, set in a particular context, and that they have a transactional relationship with people. The studio's projects do not simply respond, but a curious exchange occurs as people react to them and they react back. In a sense, part of the human experience is learning how to communicate in the syntax of something which is new or different, here in a playful setting.

SOFTlab,
Nautilus,
New York City,
2019

above: The field of 96 touch-responsive poles that made up this installation in Manhattan's Seaport District acted as a spatial sound and light sequencer. While a single touch produced one melody, simultaneous interactions with the installation created a complex, layered chorus.

Live Performance

Where Entertainment

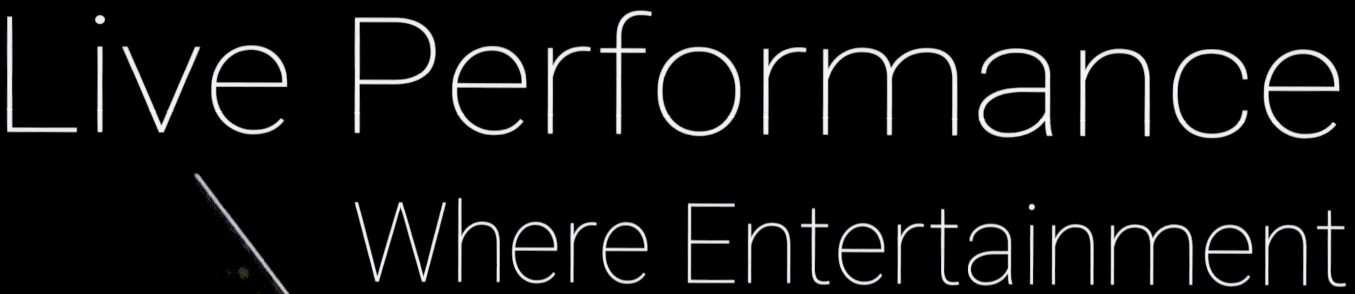

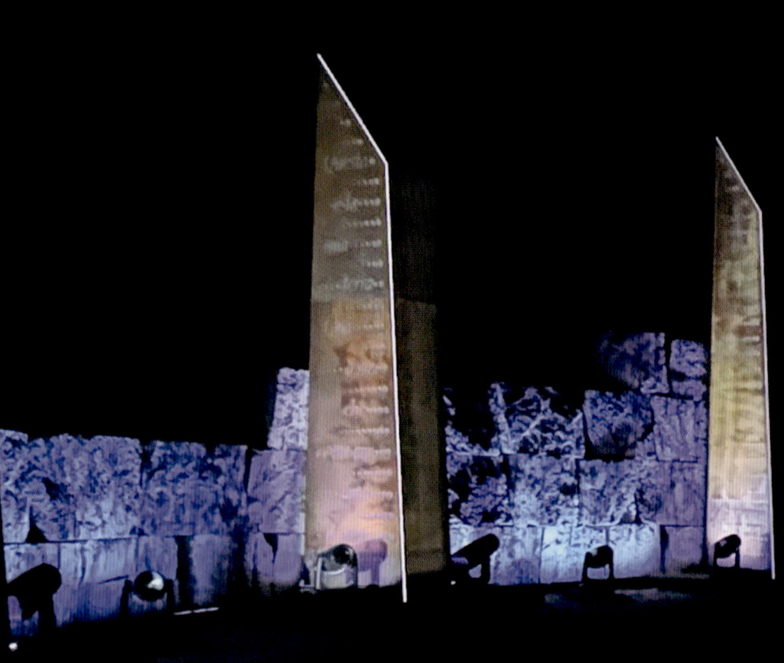

STUFISH,
Stage set for "Andrea Bocelli 30: The Celebration,"
Teatro del Silenzio,
Lajatico, Tuscany, Italy,
July 2024

The existing stone wall and the angular pillars positioned around the reflecting pool were lit to create a dramatic, changing, otherworldly backdrop for the performers. Their massive aspect is reminiscent of ancient monuments, linking past and present landscapes.

Architecture Meets Audience

STUFISH Entertainment Architects has a long history of designing stage sets and musical experiences that have been enjoyed by billions of people around the world. Exploring new ways to inspire and push the boundaries of audience expectation, many of the designers at STUFISH are trained architects. Art and architecture writer and editor **Eva Menuhin** focuses on some of their recent stagings for the Rolling Stones, Adele, Andrea Bocelli, AC/DC, and Lenny Kravitz.

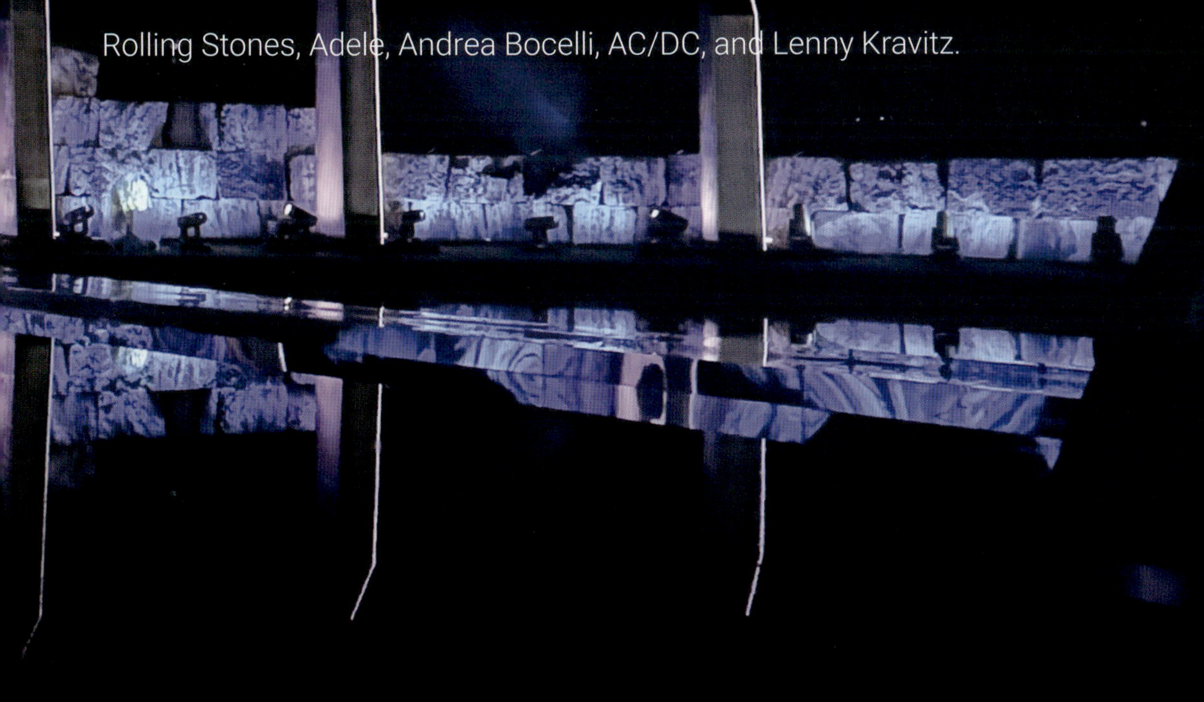

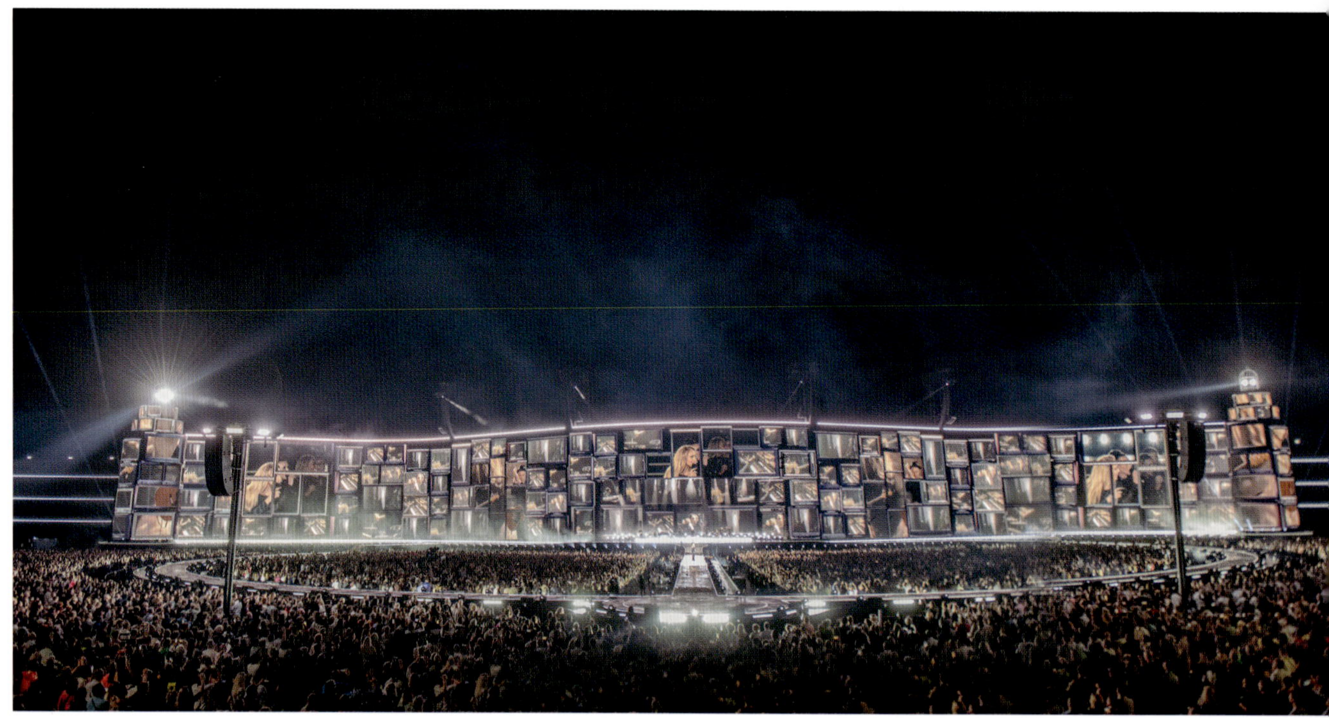

Entertainment architects have the luxury of being able to let their imaginations run free. They can explore new materials and technology in ways impossible for other architects, because the structures and scenography they design are usually temporary, and although they must be functional, are specifically created to facilitate enjoyment. Perhaps simple envy of this freedom explains why entertainment architecture is so often discounted as frivolous by the traditional architectural profession.

Over the years, the team at STUFISH Entertainment Architects have exhibited highly creative imaginations and have done a lot of exploring. As a consequence, they have been redefining the boundaries of live performance design since the company was founded, and their combination of multidisciplinary expertise and creativity means they understand the potential of technological advances better than most in the profession. They currently lead the industry in manipulating current technology to create a synergy between the physicality of architecture and computer-generated virtuality, delighting audiences of the world-famous clients whose award-winning, spectacular stage sets STUFISH has designed and produced for more than 30 years.

The Intimate Crowd

"Adele in Munich" took place over a 10-night period in August 2024, in the world's largest purpose-built temporary outdoor arena, situated in the grounds of the Neue Messe München, an exhibition and trade fair center on the site of the former Munich-Reim Airport. The event had been more than three years in the planning, and required the international collaboration and flawless coordination of dozens of industry experts and hundreds of technicians and crew. STUFISH's scenography for the show was developed to create an intimate embrace of the 80,000-strong audiences for each performance.

Notwithstanding the vast scale of the production, the term "embrace" was not simply conceived of as a metaphor. STUFISH's 200-meter (656-foot) main stage wrapped around the concertgoers, reimagining the interaction between audience and performer to create intimacy even within the expansive space. To allow Adele to get even closer to her fans, two semicircular runways, each approximately 130 meters (430 feet) long, sprang from the sides of the main stage in two great arcs, curving around and enclosing parts of the audience before meeting the B stage, which ran out at 90 degrees from the main stage's center. For the stage background, STUFISH conceived a 220-meter (720-foot) wide by 19-meter (62-foot) high curved LED wall–4,800 square meters (5,170 square feet) of panoramic, dynamic, digital imagery. Its shape mimicked that of an unfurling scroll, representing both the flow of Adele's life and her songwriting career, with curled-up edges that bookended the stage perimeter.

STUFISH's main stage wrapped around the concertgoers, reimagining the interaction between audience and performer to create intimacy even within the expansive space

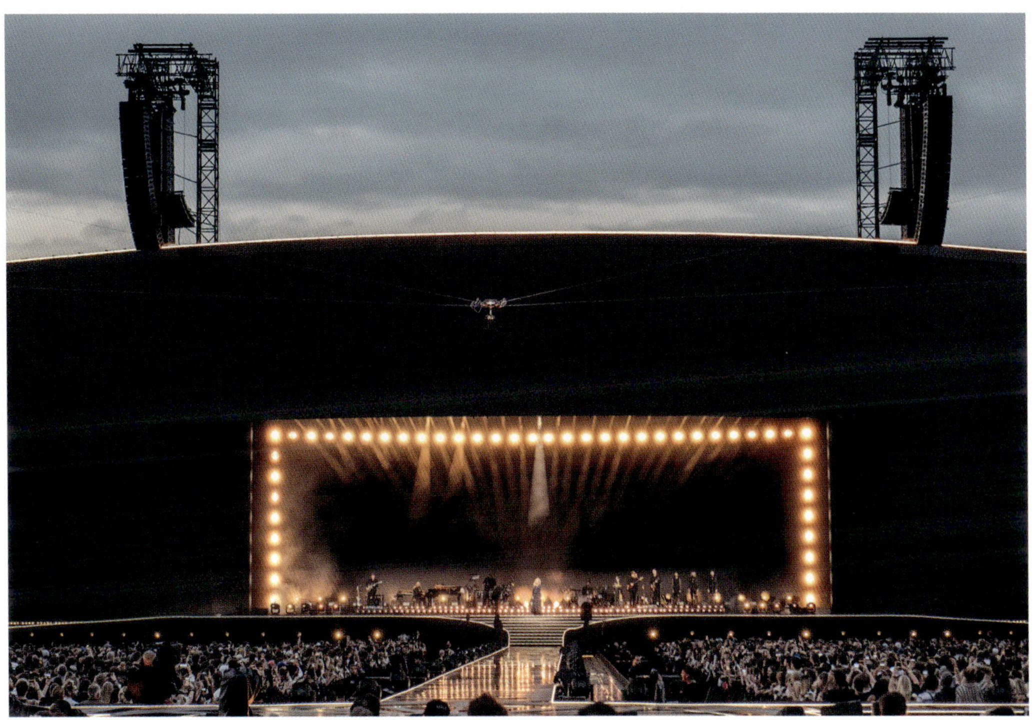

STUFISH had designed the world's first portable large-scale LED video-display screen for U2's 1997/98 "PopMart Tour." At the time, it had been groundbreaking technology and the invention forever changed the way live concerts were presented. So, it is not surprising that 25 years later the screen for Adele's Munich residency set a new Guinness World Record for size, although that had not been the intent. The screen's colossal size developed during the design phase of the project to be in keeping with that of the stadium, and its wave-like form enabled Adele's desired proximity to her huge audience. The internal layout of the venue, coupled with the scale of the screen and stage architecture, immersive lighting, pyrotechnics, and sound design all coalesced to create a breathtaking sensory and auditory experience for the audience, once again redefining what a live concert could feel and sound like.

STUFISH,
Stage set for "Adele in Munich,"
Neue Messe München,
Munich, Germany,
August 2024

above: The lighting altered to shift the scale and mood of the stadium from the expansive to the intimate and back again. A string orchestra was concealed within the encircling runways, rising up behind Adele to accompany the singer to heighten the dramatic impact of her music.

opposite: The curving screen was flanked by two "lighthouses" shaped like the curling ends of an unrolled scroll. These functioned as part of the panoramic LED wall for the dynamic lighting landscape, on occasion casting beams of light from their apex across the arena and beyond.

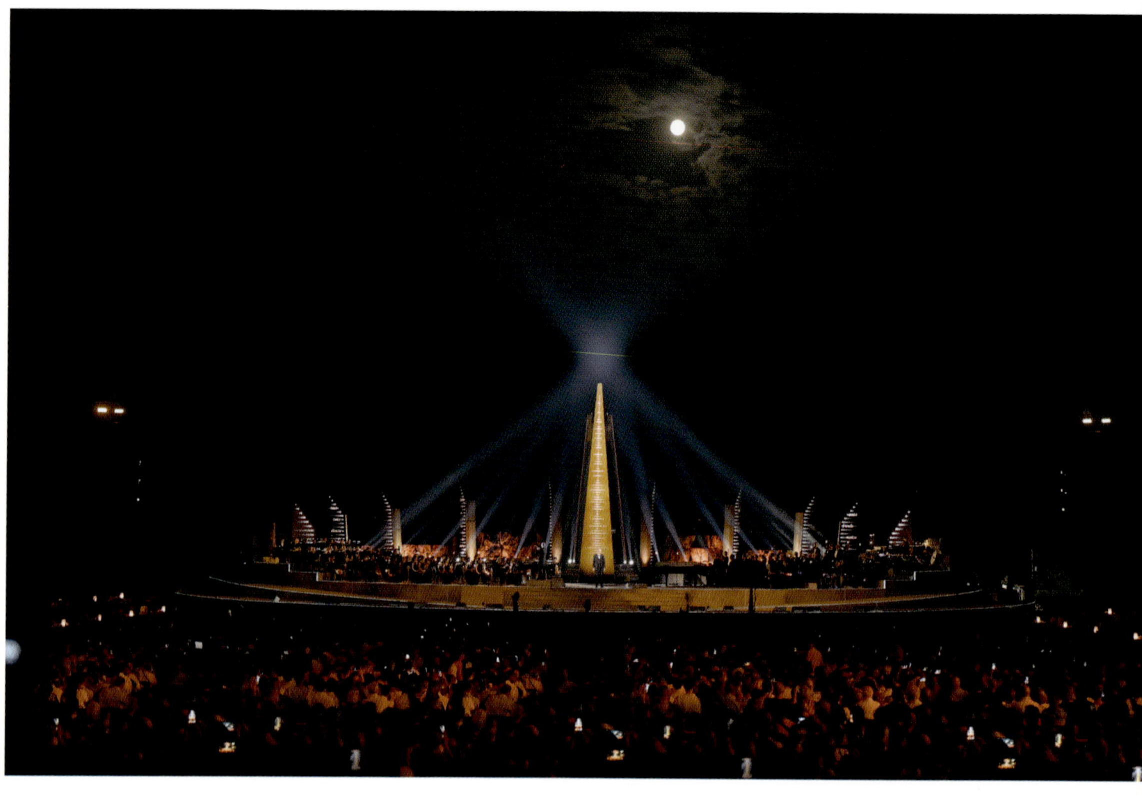

STUFISH,
Stage set for "Andrea Bocelli 30: The Celebration,"
Teatro del Silenzio,
Lajatico, Tuscany, Italy,
July 2024

above: The gnomon at the center of the stage functioned as a scenic element in the set design as well as a piece of art in its own right. Here it connects the land to the sky, like a pathway to the moon, while focusing audience attention on Bocelli.

STUFISH,
Stage set for the Rolling Stones "Hackney Diamonds" studio album tour,
US,
April–July 2024

opposite top: Digital media and images embellished the stage around the band in a choreographed fusion of sound, light, and architecture. The Stones' iconic logo was displayed and decorated with graphics reminiscent of neon graffiti on a wall.

opposite bottom: The minimalist, slab-like LED screen provided a clean, contemporary silhouette for the ever-shifting light display that mirrored each of the band's numbers in real time. The live footage integrated with the content on the screens, creating a unique performance experience for each show.

Music, Time, and Landscape

The Neue Messe München had been agreed as the location for Adele's pop-up arena by the concert developers in consultation with the artist herself because of its proximity to a major freeway and efficient, high-volume public transport and freight facilities. The location for "Andrea Bocelli 30: The Celebration"—a series of filmed concerts in July 2024 celebrating his 30 years as a performer— could hardly have been more different: a beautiful, isolated, natural amphitheater in Lajatico, Bocelli's home town in Tuscany. The Teatro del Silenzio (Theater of Silence) was built in 2006 at Bocelli's instigation and with his support, and each year he gives a concert there. Otherwise, the small lake at the center of the rough, semicircular marble wall lies silent, reflecting nothing but the sky and stars.

Transforming the isolated site into a world-class performance space for an international line-up of entertainment superstars and suitable for audiences of 10,800 presented interesting and decidedly physical challenges for STUFISH. Everything, including construction machinery, had to be trucked in through the countryside along narrow, winding roads. The asymmetrical natural terrain had to be mapped and a 3D model made to ensure STUFISH's stage design would function properly, while the lake's wildlife and surrounding environment also had to be respected. There were additional complex structural and technical logistics to be solved, not least a complete absence of Wi-Fi, electricity, and bathrooms.

STUFISH's sculptural scenography became a continuation of the theater's existing wall, embracing the lake from all sides, and staging elements were clad in stone-colored materials that blended with the environment. For the lake's center, STUFISH designed a revolving sculpture inspired by the shape of a sundial to express the passage of time, sound, and landscape. The rotating gnomon functioned as a metronome, staircase, performers' riser, and as a revolving screen for projections. Ten tall "milestones," like ancient megaliths, stood in a circle around the multilevel stage, decorated with graphics of soundwaves and text that symbolized aspects of Bocelli's life and different times of day. As Bocelli, guest stars, and an orchestra of over a hundred musicians performed in this outdoor opera house overlooking the Tuscan hills, 500 drones created a celestial landscape of stars in the evening sky above.

Like the massive architecture constructed for Adele's concerts, once the celebration of Bocelli's career had finished, the stage and its ancillary structures were dismantled and removed without trace, leaving the lake to its silent reflections for another year.

Getting What You Need

In contrast, STUFISH's set design for the Rolling Stones' US "Hackney Diamonds" studio album tour, from April to July 2024, was sleekly contemporary, sophisticated, and entirely digital. This was a first for the notably progressive band, with whom STUFISH have been working since 2000, and who were interested in doing something they hadn't done before.

STUFISH's production concept was to create a simple architectural geometry to support a virtual stage set that could adapt as the tour progressed. A massive LED screen spanning the full width of a standard stage and wrapped around the sides was configured to allow real perspective. It provided an immersive digital canvas on which ever-evolving, overlaid visuals could be linked to the band's real-time action, mirroring the pace and narrative of each song and varying from performance to performance, almost like a series of TikTok videos.

STUFISH's particularly architectural approach to designing productions includes the principle that technical advancements are no guarantee for a better experience and should be used for good reasons rather than for their own sake. The team use their creativity and heterogeneous expertise to adapt every available resource and technology—ancient, modern, digital, virtual, or otherwise—to their purpose. Tools and materials are "misused" in unexpected and interesting ways for which they weren't developed, and they appropriate useful concepts from what would seem to be unrelated fields. Their approach is both playful and rigorous, and requires close work and communication with the artists and creative experts in related professions, many of whom are long-time and trusted collaborators

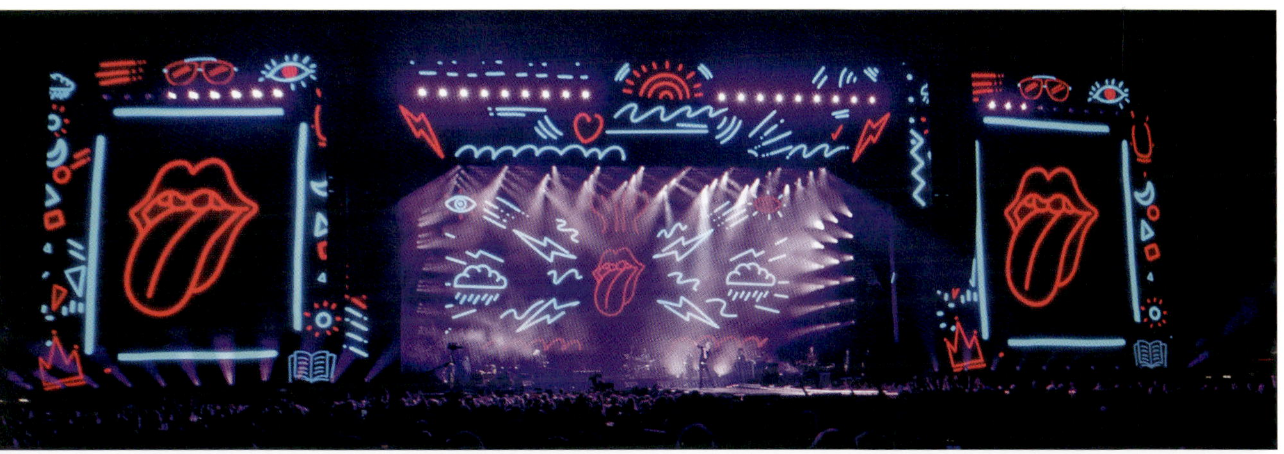

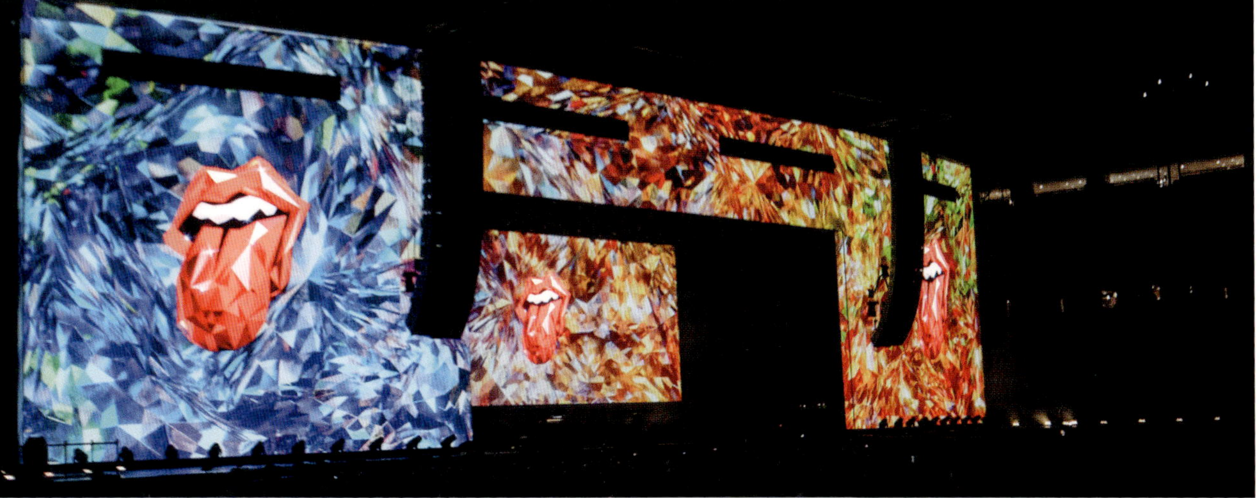

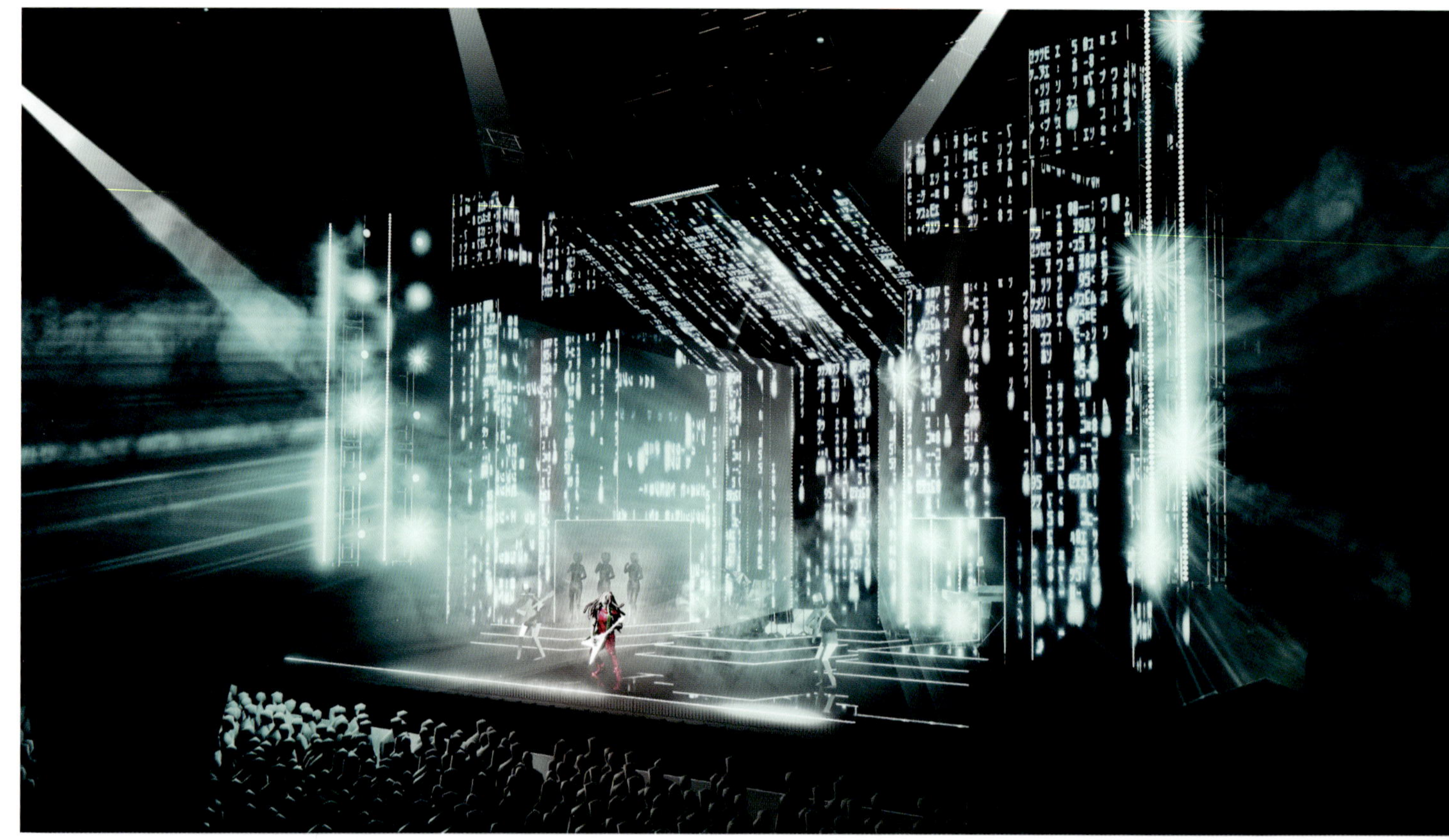

Because ultimately it is the audience who determines whether or not a show is successful, it follows that the audience is also STUFISH's client— perhaps even more than the artist—since a good part of the studio's job is to convince people it is worth spending their time and money to experience a live performance when so many other alternatives are available. Inevitably, as audiences and technology have evolved, so have the factors that need to be taken into account when creating a scenography.

The inherent tension between the parallel worlds of social media and real life underpins much of STUFISH's design process. Whereas the concert photographs released for public consumption and publicity were once carefully curated by the artists and producers, every member of an audience with a smartphone is now their own photographic curator. The large-scale immersive experience for the live audience must now also translate effectively into images for social media. That is to say, productions must look good in photographs snapped in seconds, by any member of a live audience, from any angle, and uploaded onto Instagram or TikTok. This means STUFISH now designs not only for live audiences of thousands in a stadium, but for potential audiences of millions looking at phone screens a few inches from their faces, experiencing the concert vicariously and judging it by the images they see.

Electrifying Performances

Lenny Kravitz's worldwide 2024 "Blue Electric Light" arena tour and AC/DC's "PWR UP" European stadium tour from May to August 2024, were classic album-linked tours. STUFISH used giant LED screens as key elements of these set designs, which, like all touring architecture, were informed by the need to move sets efficiently, economically, and quickly between venues.

The "PWR UP" tour was the fourth time STUFISH and AC/DC had worked together to create a stage design that enhanced the band's unique combination of music, audience participation, and interaction between the performers and fans—many of them now second-generation.

Architecturally, the set was a minimalist yet powerful backdrop to the band's performance. Three LED video screens slid apart into multiple configurations to create a canvas for the dynamic visual experience, while LED video tiles above and to either side of the band formed an expansive display blending context and content. AC/DC's iconic stage elements were central to the design but, except for the descending bell that tolls slowly at the beginning of their song "Hell's Bells," the famous props of previous years were transformed into visual effects linked to each song, shifting the audience's attention onto the band and their performance.

STUFISH,
Stage set for Lenny Kravitz
"Blue Electric Light"
world tour,
2024

opposite: The modular stage design explicitly referenced architectural Brutalism and the cuboid volumes and massing that define it, to stunning effect. These also provided the flexibility that allowed the show to be performed at a wide range of festival sites and venues.

STUFISH,
Stage set for AC/DC "PWR UP"
European stadium tour,
May-August 2024

below: The stage set consisted of LED screens that framed the stage, tracking open to reveal additional lighting. Their architectural simplicity, combined with theatrical lighting, gave the band's performance a fresh, modern look that is still familiar to its fans.

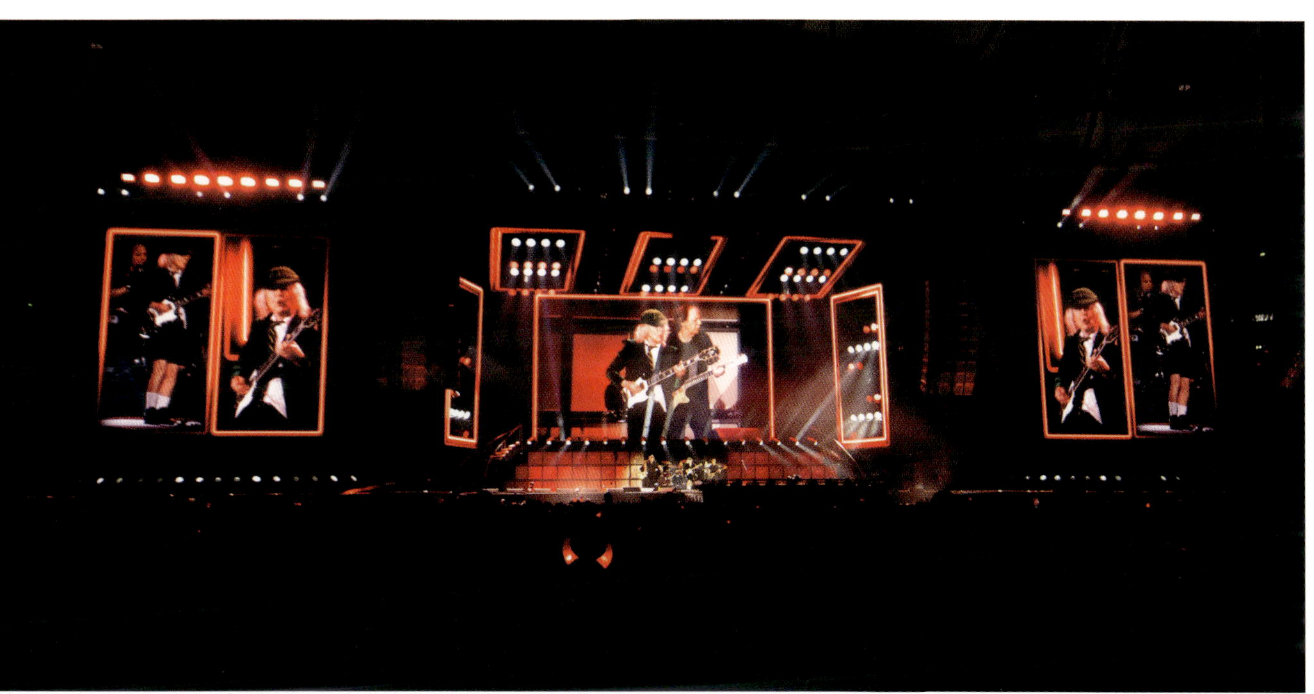

For Lenny Kravitz's "Blue Electric Light" tour, STUFISH created a scenography that incorporated the volumetric qualities of architectural Brutalism to help develop a strong energy that complemented the narrative of Kravitz's show. Towers and cubes flanked the stage and acted as three-dimensional screens for digital 3D content, while retreating in height to create a false perspective. Lights were woven into the fabric of the screens to blur the boundaries between the lighting and scenic and three-dimensional video surfaces. The lighting landscape was dynamic, changing depending on the music and surrounding action to help connect the concertgoers to the artist's performance, as did the multilevel steps and platforms that allowed Kravitz to approach his audience.

Entertainment is a Feeling

Although digital technology and internet connectivity are radically changing the way human beings interact with each other, we still want and need to share stories and experiences in the real world. The desire for shared experience, and the intimate yet ephemeral emotional bond created between artists and their audiences, is the essence of live performance. It is what transforms a crowd of individuals from many different classes and backgrounds into that one collective organism: the audience —held on one breath, hearts beating in unison. Trying to achieve this magic is STUFISH'S raison d'être, and the goal that drives the entire live entertainment industry.

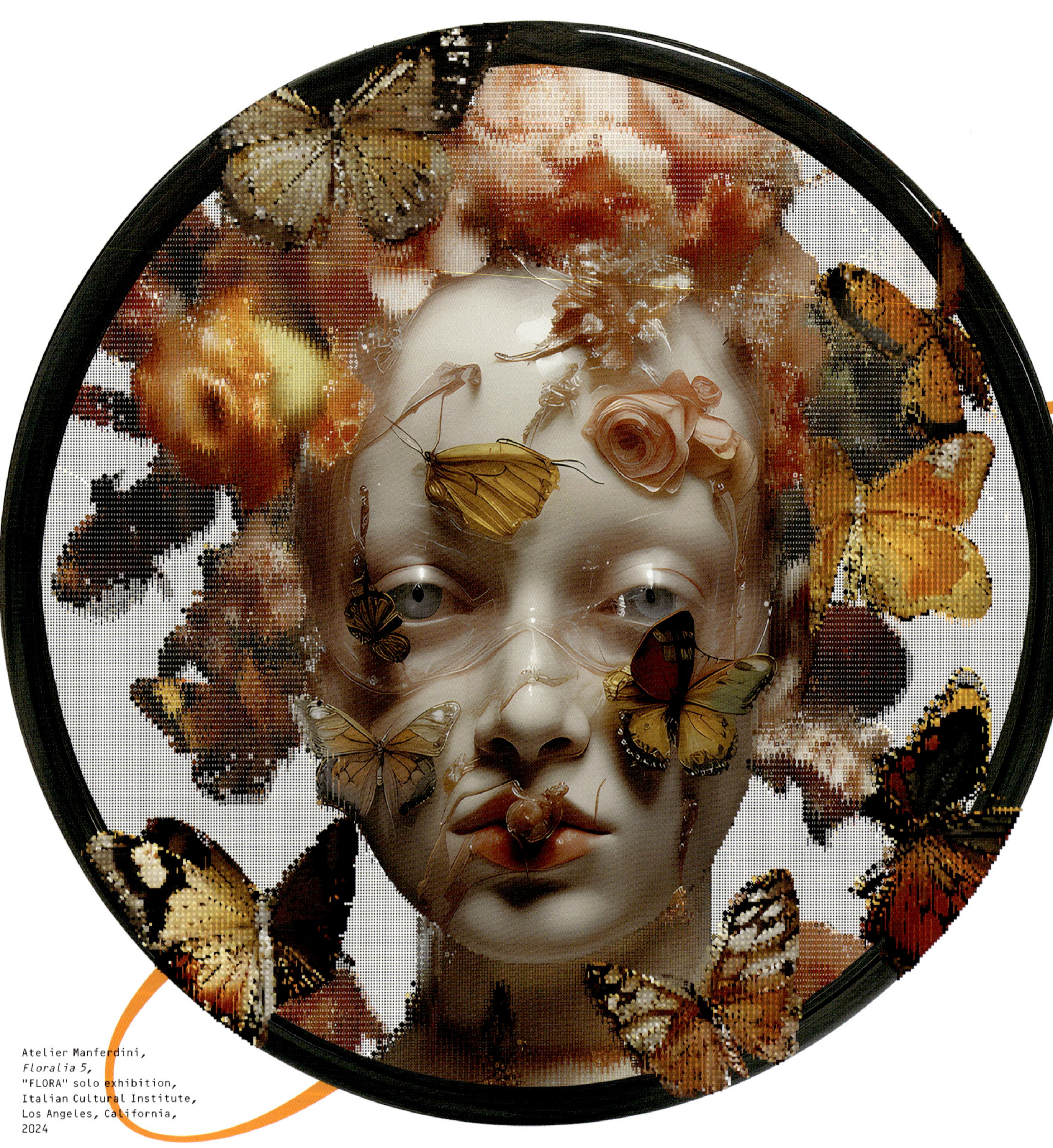

Atelier Manferdini,
Floralia 5,
"FLORA" solo exhibition,
Italian Cultural Institute,
Los Angeles, California,
2024

above: The *Floralia* series of works were created using Midjourney, and printed on mirrored surfaces. Exhibition visitors could scan a QR code next to the mirror to unlock an augmented-reality experience, where the artwork came to life in a new dimension.

opposite: The interactive piece invited viewers to engage with the fantastical world of reimagined nature. The exhibition showcased the fusion of natural and synthetic forms, offering a reflection on human emotion and the emerging aesthetic identities of contemporary culture.

Elena Manferdini

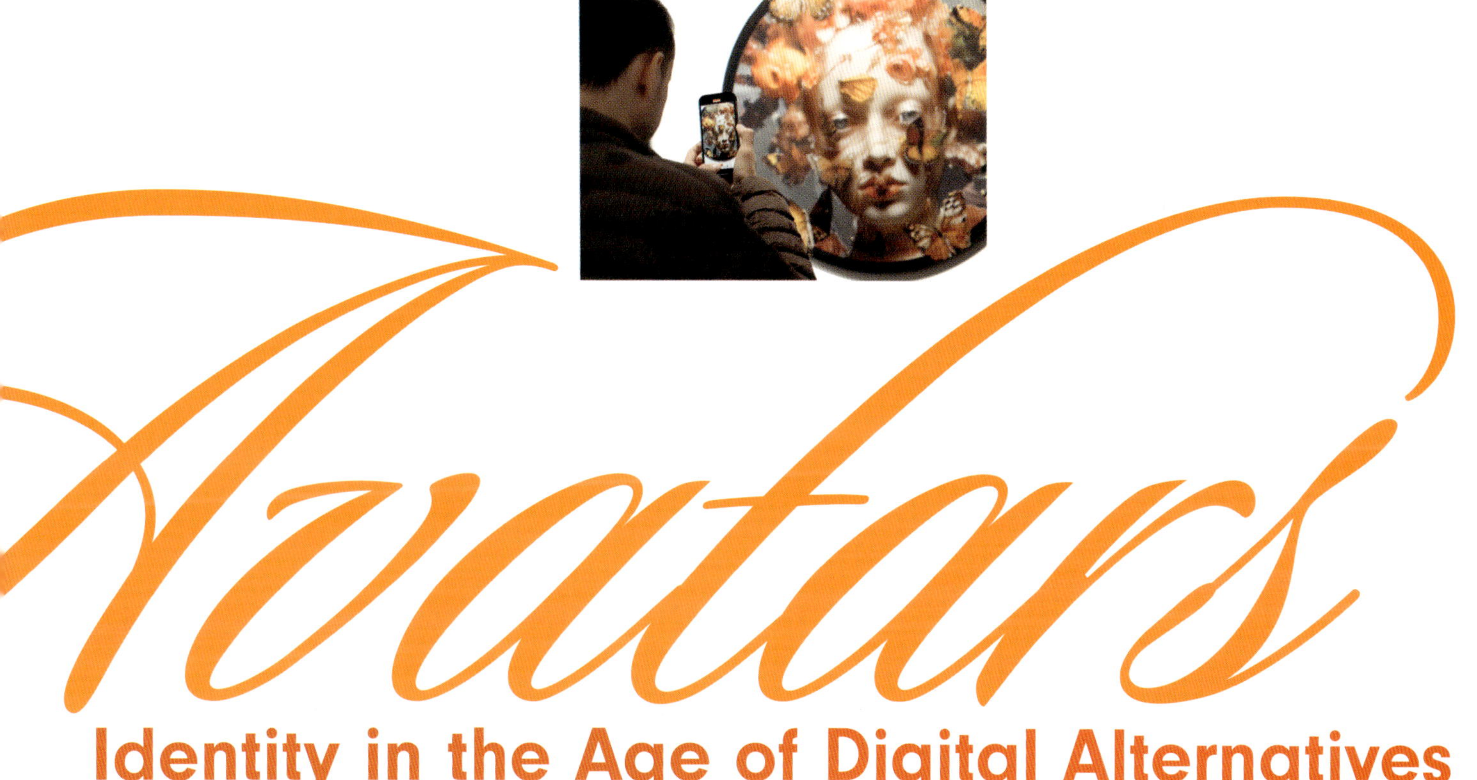

Avatars: Identity in the Age of Digital Alternatives

Elena Manferdini, principal and owner of Atelier Manferdini, has more than two decades of professional experience in design, placemaking, education, and creative leadership. She currently teaches at the Southern California Institute of Architecture (SCI-Arc), where she is the Graduate Programs Chair. The "FLORA" exhibition at the Italian Cultural Institute in Los Angeles explored the shifting nature of identity in the digital age. Featuring AI-generated imagery and sculptures, the show raised questions about beauty, transformation, and the boundaries between life and death. In this increasingly virtual world, how do we define who we are, and how do these digital extensions shape our sense of self?

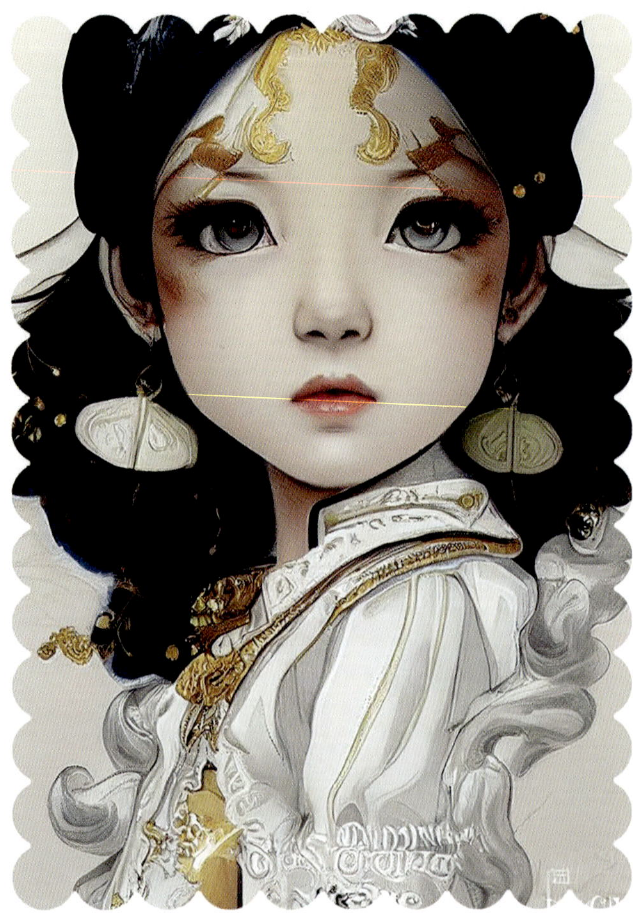

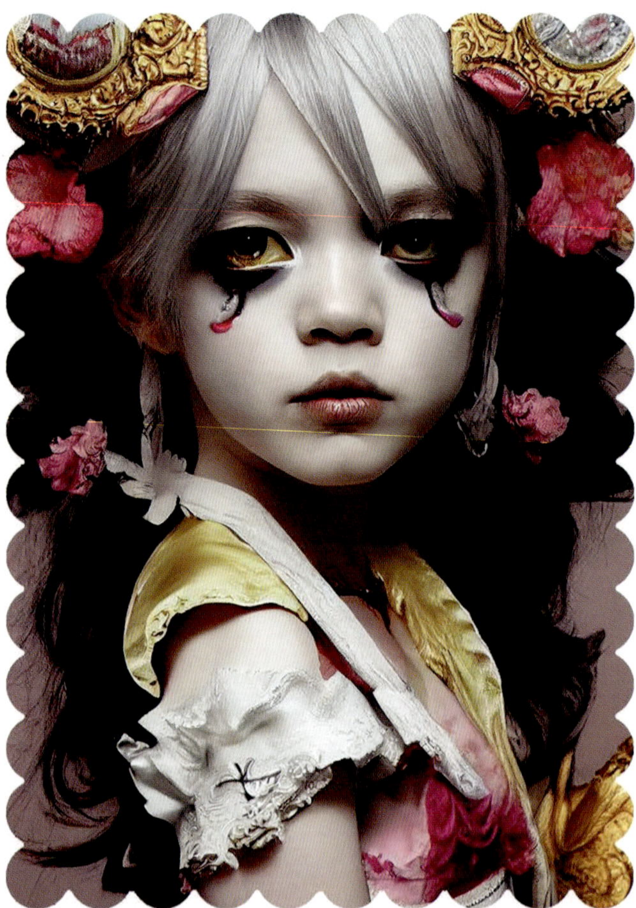

In today's jungle of avatars and filters, we cannot help but ask: What does

Every virtual influencer's tale begins in the same way: she is beautiful, possesses a shallow yet addictive personality, and has millions of followers. Designed to resemble an alluring human without being offputting, she has realistic features—like freckles—combined with an impossible body. And yes, you guessed it, she is the product of digital advertising.

In the past few years, virtual influencers have emerged as the forefront of commerce, revolutionizing our notion of human identity in the digital age. The most notable example is Lil Miquela @lilmiquela, the effortlessly hip, forever-19-year-old who appeared on Instagram in 2016, sparking various theories about her origin, ranging from a marketing gimmick to a disturbing social experiment. Created by Trevor McFedries and Sara DeCou, the Los Angeles-based creators of the first computer-generated social media influencers, she swiftly made her mark in the ever-evolving landscape of digital innovations that dominate today's feeds, becoming an inevitable Angeleno celebrity.[1]

Lil Miquela, a CGI creation, embodies the pinnacle of unrealistic beauty standards while simultaneously using her platform to advocate for important causes like Black Lives Matter and LGBTQ+ rights—all while sporting trendy branded swag. This juxtaposition of perfection and activism highlights the complex nature of digital influencers as they navigate the fine line between promoting consumerism and championing social change.

Lil is not an isolated example; others like her exist, such as Imma @imma.gram, a Japanese fashion and lifestyle influencer. Her talent manager, Sara Giusto, has spoken at TED Conferences, highlighting that, despite being "unreal," Imma has collaborated with major brands, built a connection with her audience, and actively engaged in discussions on global issues.[2]

In today's jungle of avatars and filters, we cannot help but ask: What does identity truly mean in this digital age? How do our experiences weave into the narratives we craft and ultimately believe?

Role-playing

Concepts of alternative personas span a multitude of artistic forms, from painting and photography to contemporary CGI and AI. In 2014, the Argentine-Spanish artist Amalia Ulman harnessed the then-nascent platform of Instagram to launch her five-month *Excellences & Perfections* project.[3] During this

Atelier Manferdini,
Pick Me,
Modest Common Gallery,
Los Angeles, California,
2023

Pick Me reflected on the effects of contemporary aesthetic judgments on female self-worth, and how media stereotypes are connected to aesthetic pleasure with violence. The piece displayed the ways AI tools subtly amplify dominant ideas within powerfully beautiful images.

time, she staged selfies of herself sneaking into hotels and restaurants in Los Angeles, presenting them as authentic snapshots of her life. Once the project concluded, Ulman revealed that these images were part of an artistic performance.[4] By leveraging stereotypical representations, she prompted audiences to question how we shape our perceptions of reality.

Long before the rise of social media, the artist Cindy Sherman began exploring identity through her photographic self-portraits in the late 1970s and early 1980s. In her iconic *Untitled Film Stills* series (1977–80),[5] she embodied a wide range of characters, from femme fatales to vulnerable women, challenging viewers to question the boundaries between authenticity and performance, and the narratives we construct around our true selves.

become so accustomed to a world where staged pictures blur the lines of reality that we find ourselves drawn to these curated personas. Maybe we are willing to embrace a fake influencer because, deep down, we all crave acceptance in our own digital lives. In a world where likes and followers often feel like currency, it is easier to connect with a robot that embodies the perfection we chase. After all, if we can buy into Imma's curated reality, perhaps we can convince ourselves that our own carefully crafted Instagram profiles are equally valid. It is a delicate dance of desire and validation, where even the most artificial representations can mirror our aspirations, allowing us to feel seen in a world where the real and the imagined are now often indistinguishable.

depicting the artist's alter ego as women's faces staged between life and death. These heads, resting on mirrored plates amid images of insects and flowers, represented themes of desire and consumption.

The AI-generated avatars in *Floralia* capture feminine beauty standards, oscillating between allure and repulsion and challenging viewers to confront the commodification of female bodies. The work critiques how women's identities have historically been shaped by societal perceptions, revealing the underlying tension between the appeal of beauty and the inevitable decay that accompanies it.

As viewers engage with the artwork by scanning a QR code, the static images transform into a dynamic 3D experience, paralleling how our digital selves transcend physical boundaries and expand into virtual realms.

identity truly mean in this digital age?

From 1998 to 2001, Japanese photographer Tomoko Sawada created *ID400*, 400 different ID-card-style self-portraits exposing the growing gaps between personal identity and state-sanctioned identification.[6] In front of her work, spectators often find themselves uncertain whether the images depict one woman or many, highlighting the risk of racial generalizations. These catalogs provoke important questions about personal expression and self-image for women in a society that values conformity.

Today the line between real and fake is so blurred that Lil Miquela's followers inquire about her skincare routine. One follower posted: "I know this is crazy, but I believe you. Even though you are a robot physically, everything else is human."

Why are we so eager to embrace what we know is fake? We have

The Possibility of Being Reimagined

Today, communities exist online, where likes, shares, and comments act as new forms of validation. Our sense of self is therefore split between who we are in real life and how we represent ourselves online. Phone apps, filters, alter egos, and deepfakes? They are just the opening act in this grand performance of identity shifting into the cloud. The digital turn has granted all of us the possibility of being reimagined, and contemporary identity is filled with the new risks and potentials that come with role-playing.

The tension between real and artificial is embodied in works like Atelier Manferdini's *Floralia* (2024), which featured in the solo exhibition "FLORA" at the Italian Cultural Institute in Los Angeles. Through augmented reality, *Floralia* brought a thousand AI-generated self-portraits to life,

The mirrors in *Floralia* encourage viewers to see themselves within the work, much like how our digital identities reflect curated versions of who we are. Just as the artwork shifts through augmented reality, our digital personas continuously evolve with technology. The project raises questions about the authenticity of self-representation, exploring how AI influences both human creativity and our place in the world.

By pushing the boundaries of self-representation in the digital era, *Floralia* is like that new filter we can't resist—it gives us an alternate version of ourselves, but no matter how flawless it looks it is still tethered to the same old questions we have been asking forever: What is beauty? How do we deal with our own mortality? And, most importantly, in this pixel-perfect world, how do we stay connected to each other?

Complicit AI Aesthetics
AI-generated imagery provides a platform for reimagining identity, raising essential questions about whether algorithms can foster diverse representation or simply echo cultural norms. It challenges us to consider how our aesthetic preferences reflect societal values, highlighting the intersection of technology and culture. Atelier Manferdini's artwork *Pick Me* (2023) exemplified this by considering the complexities of identity amid the rise of AI-generated imagery. Although the images resembled self-portraits, they transcended traditional methods like collage or photography as all were produced by Midjourney from a single text input. This series presented a temporal evolution of faces. The progression moved from cute, cartoonish faces inspired by Japanese manga to beauty pageant-like headshots, shifting from childhood to womanhood, and gradually incorporated themes of disenchantment, sadism, and substance abuse. The work highlighted how cuteness is commodified and associated with powerlessness in our culture.

Pick Me critiqued contemporary beauty standards and their impact on self-worth, illustrating how media stereotypes intertwine aesthetic pleasure with violence. This piece exposed how AI tools can perpetuate dominant cultural narratives through strikingly beautiful images. These biases are not just incidental; they reflect long-standing societal norms that dictate how one should look and behave. Ultimately, the work challenged us to consider the implications of our aesthetic preferences and the societal values they reflect, urging a deeper examination of the intersection between technology and dominant culture.

Image Trafficking
It is undeniable that our level of connectivity has reached unprecedented heights, and our reliance on social media is at an all-time high. Our online feeds have fundamentally transformed our perception of the world around us. Our attention span has drastically shortened, and our brains have been quickly trained to posts, likes, and shares. Social media thrives on positive reinforcement, and this pursuit of pleasure has inevitably seeped into how we consume architectural imagery. Social media has redefined the digital and physical presence of buildings, turning architecture into a backdrop for selfies and fueling the economy of image consumption. As we scroll through endless feeds of stunning-colored backdrops, one cannot help wondering how this obsession with visual appeal influences the way architects create

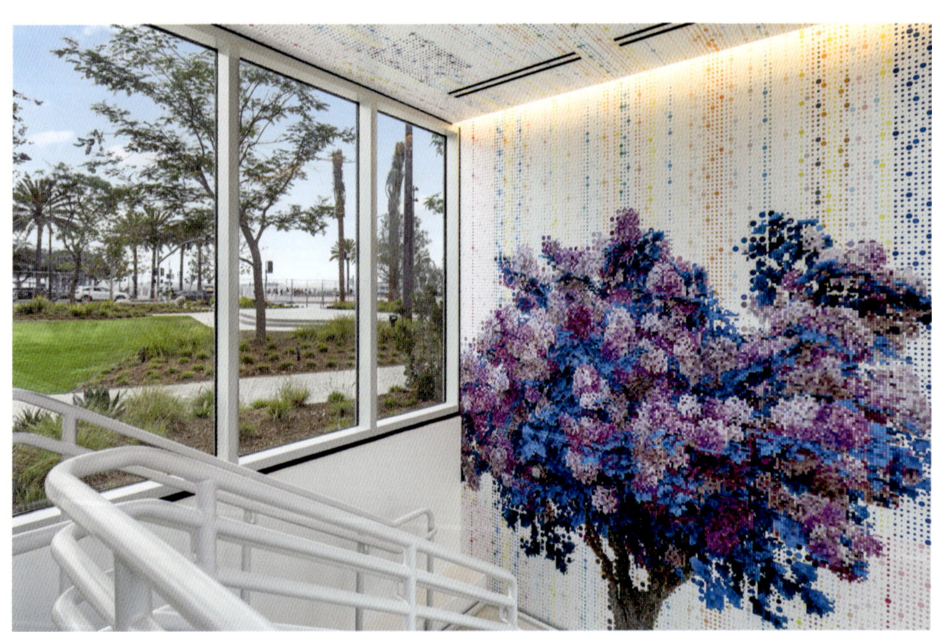

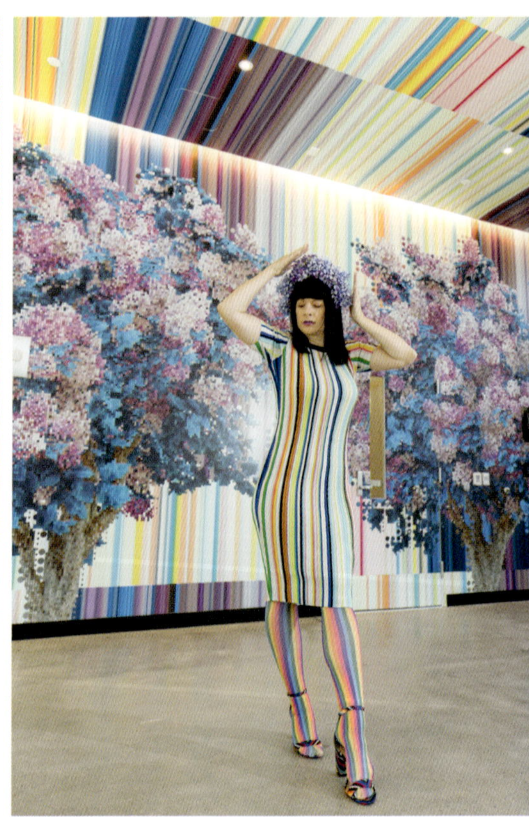

Atelier Manferdini,
Purple Haze,
Integrated Quest for Human Quality Research and Development District (IQHQ-RaDD),
San Diego, California,
2024

above: The large digital landscape of *Purple Haze* envelops the two IQHQ-RaDD garage exits, seamlessly blending the structures with the surrounding environment.

right: *Purple Haze* serves as a stage for a photo-taking experience created by @polychromist, blending real and man-made elements in an architectural-scale interpretation of landscape painting.

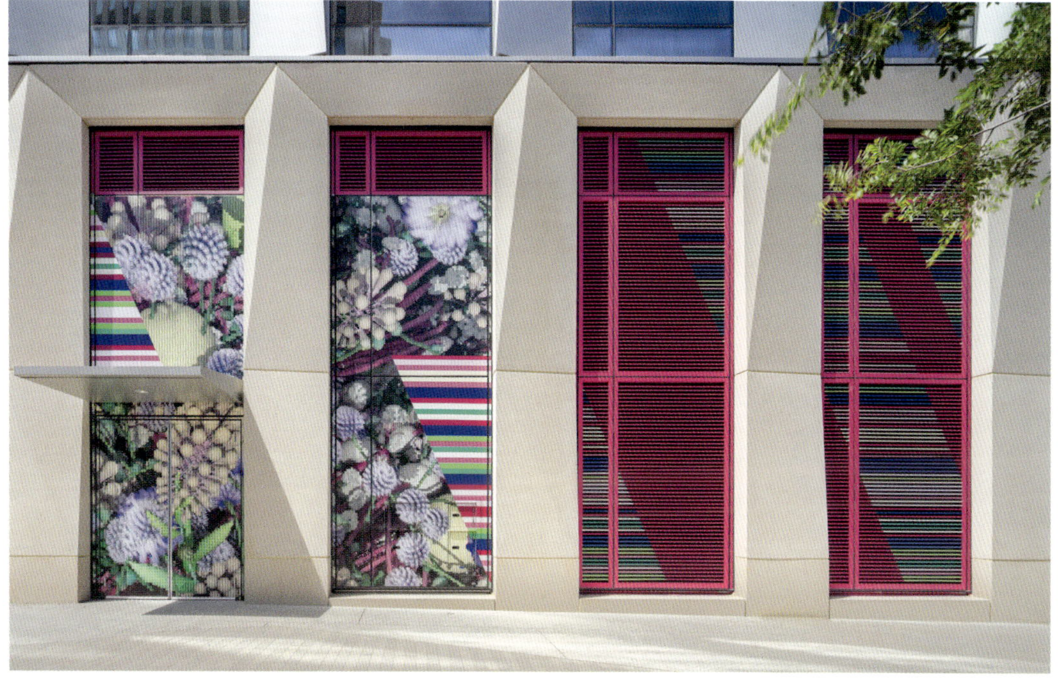

Atelier Manferdini,
Purple Rain,
Integrated Quest for Human Quality Research and Development District (IQHQ-RaDD), San Diego, California, 2024

Purple Rain highlights nature's beauty with vibrant purple flowers emerging from the interplay of natural and man-made elements. Inspired by San Diego's springtime jacaranda blossoms, the artwork invites viewers into a contemplative dialogue with the natural world.

spaces. In a world where every angle is considered for its Instagram potential, what does it mean for the future of architecture?

Purple Haze and *Purple Rain* (2024) explore the intersection between public interaction and the growing influence of shared digital images. Drawing inspiration from San Diego's iconic jacaranda trees, these large-scale digital landscapes merge natural elements with digitally printed imagery and painted components. They challenge viewers to reflect on how digital tools shape our perception of the world. *Purple Haze* has transformed the parking garage exits of the Integrated Quest for Human Quality Research and Development District (IQHQ-RaDD) into immersive environments, while *Purple Rain* reimagines its building's façade as a canvas for public participation. These works mirror the performative nature of CGI-generated influencers like Lil Miquela, whose identities are reshaped by public perception.

In today's social media-driven world, transforming physical spaces into "Instagrammable" backdrops raises critical questions about how architecture and audience interact. Social media feeds create an appetite for encountering these backdrops in reality, leading to the digital colors of the screens being printed and applied to surfaces to enhance their visual impact. The aesthetic allure presented in *Purple Haze* and *Purple Rain* fuels an economy of image consumption, prompting architects to consider how their designs will be photographed and curated online.

The integration of digital elements extends beyond mere visuals. In *Purple Rain*, viewers can scan a QR code to access animations and sounds, enriching their experience. The audience in these hybrid spaces is not just a passive observer but an active participant, interacting with environments that blend digital creation and physical architecture.

Just as *Purple Haze* and *Purple Rain* invite public interaction and transform spaces into immersive environments, Atelier Manferdini's *Living Pictures* (2019) explores the relationship between reality and digital representation. Situated in the lush ecosystem of Dongguan, China, this project transforms a connective corridor into an engaging environment through a 5.5-meter-tall art wall. The upper portion features a fixed metal tile mosaic illustrating a colorful landscape, while the lower section comprises 1,700 rotating blocks that encourage viewers to engage with the artwork physically. As participants manipulate these blocks, they contribute to a transformative play of color, embodying the project's theme of participation.

Atelier Manferdini,
Living Pictures,
Kaida Center of Science and Design,
Dongguan, China,
2019

right: The mirror insert of the *Living Pictures* interactive wall allows viewers to see themselves within the piece, fostering deeper connections to both the artwork and the surrounding environment.

below: Illustrative of Atelier Manferdini's "Living Picture" concept, the project treats viewers as active participants in a transformative play of color.

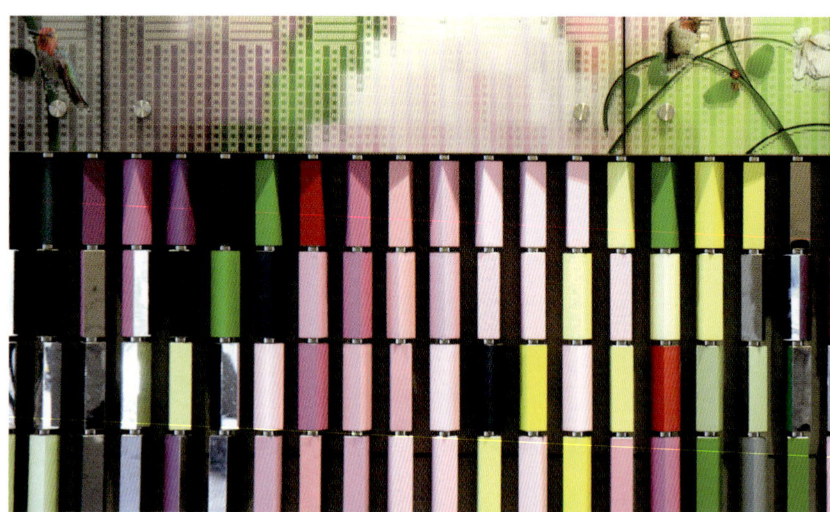

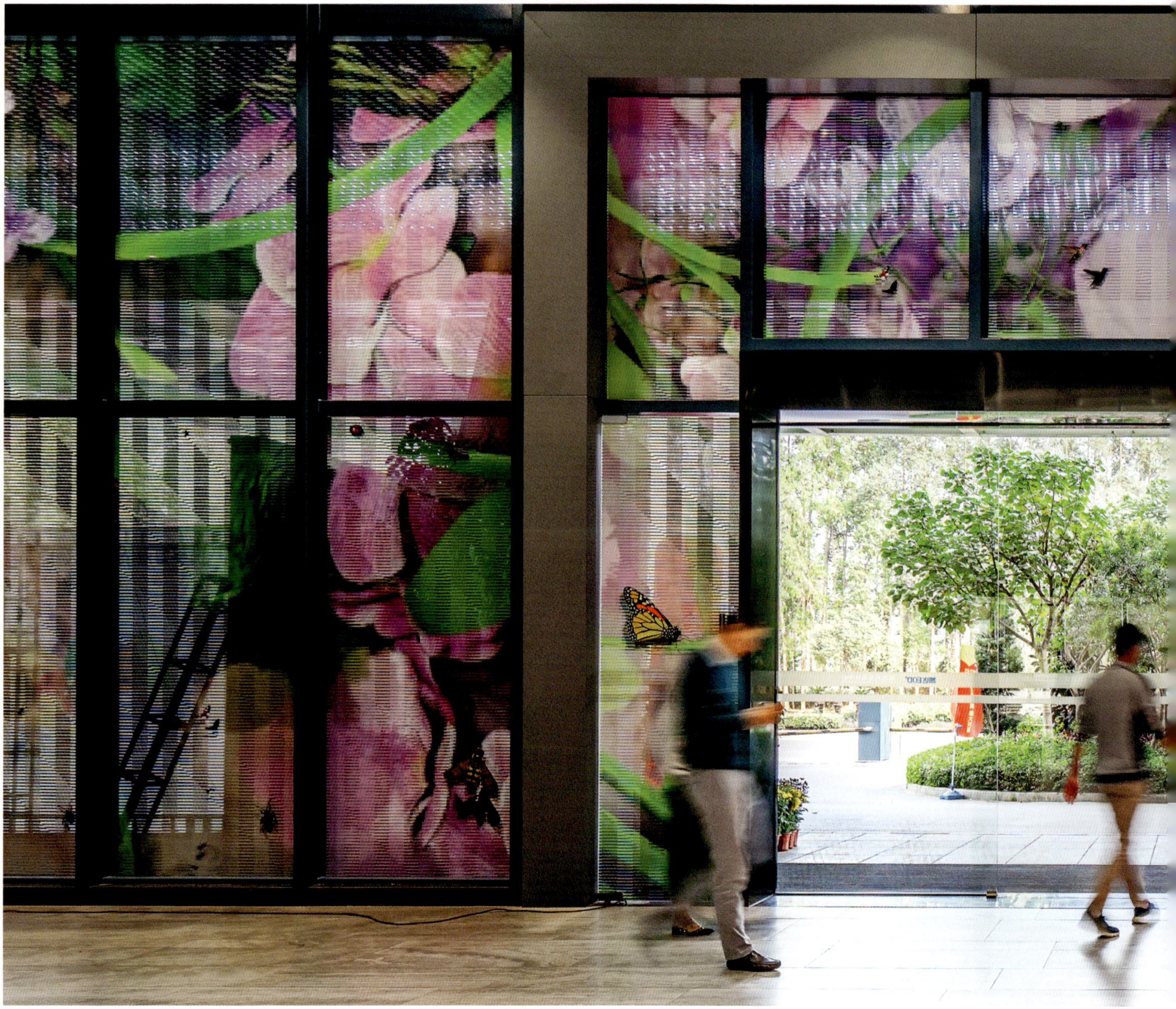

The vivid colors and prints in *Living Pictures* bridge the gap between the digital and physical worlds, making online aesthetics visible within the physical environment. Mirror inserts reflect viewers, deepening their connection to the artwork and their surroundings. This interactive aspect allows individuals to create unique backdrops, emphasizing how architecture and art today foster participation. The project transcends its geographical boundaries, encouraging viewers to share their experiences online. It highlights architecture's potential to foster connection and build community.

Ultimately, architects must rethink how audiences interact with their environments. The future of design may depend on our ability to seamlessly integrate the digital and physical worlds to resonate with our new forms of social engagement. But how do we ensure this integration enhances genuine connection rather than creating further detachment? If we fail to address this concern, we risk designing environments that alienate individuals, reducing human interaction to mere digital exchanges.

Notes

1. Matt Klein, "The Problematic Fakery of Lil Miquela Explained—An Exploration of Virtual Influencers and Realness," Forbes, November 18, 2020: www.forbes.com/sites/mattklein/2020/11/17/the-problematic-fakery-of-lil-miquela-explained-an-exploration-of-virtual-influencers-and-realness/.
2. Sara Gusto, "The Rise of Virtual Humans—and What They Mean for the Future," TED Talk, April 2024: www.ted.com/talks/sara_giusto_the_rise_of_virtual_humans_and_what_they_mean_for_the_future?subtitle=en.
3. See https://artsandculture.google.com/story/excellences-perfections-preserving-social-media-with-webrecorder-rhizome/owVRTPJVh-JgJw?hl=en.
4. Amalia Ulman, *Excellences & Perfections*, Prestel Publishing (Munich, London, and New York), 2018.
5. See https://artlead.net/journal/modern-classics-cindy-sherman-untitled-film-stills/.
6. See https://global.canon/en/newcosmos/gallery/selected-artists/tomoko-sawada/.

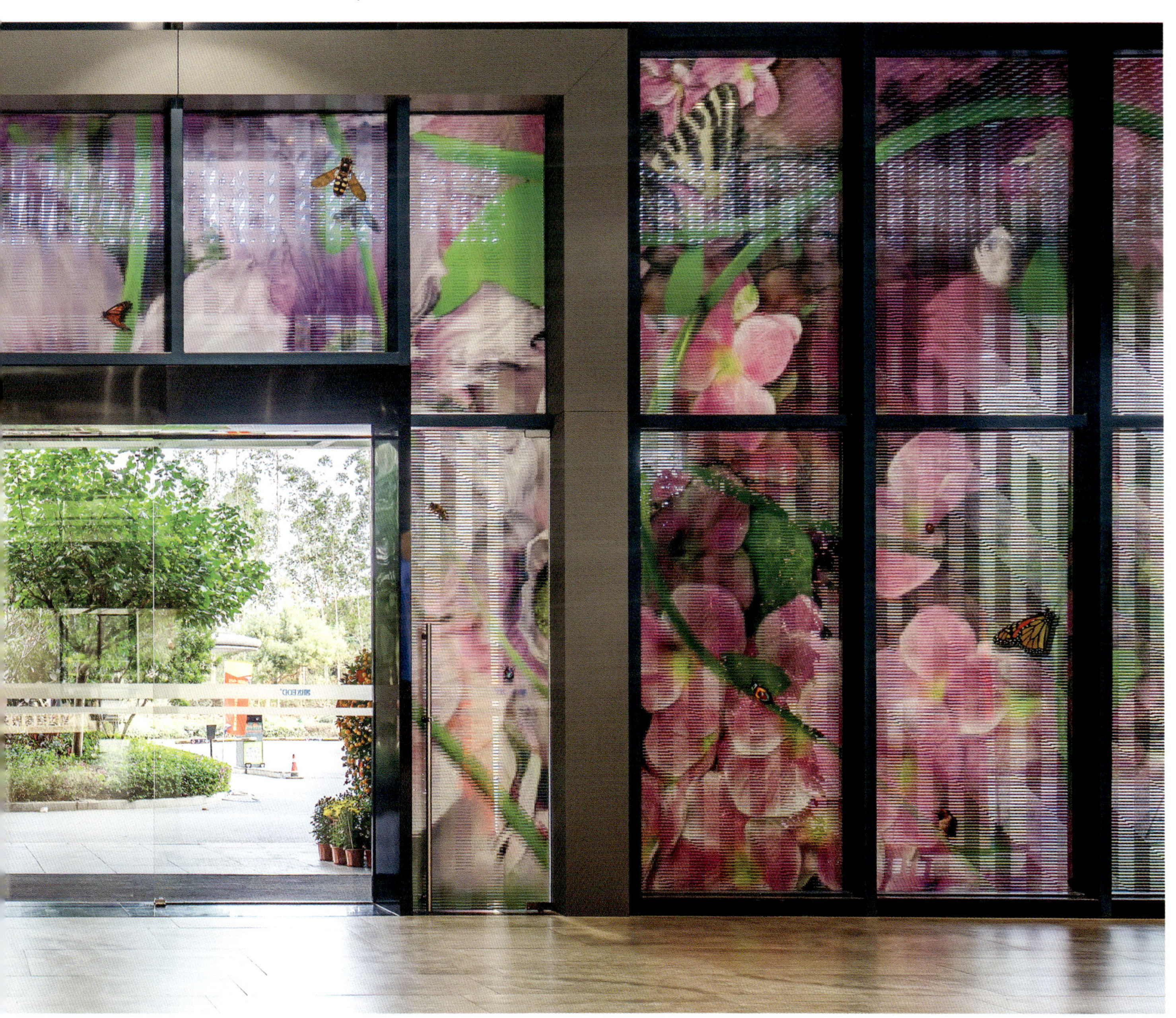

Owen Hopkins and Lorna Burn

BUILDING ... An Exhibition

When buildings are built, the public is often kept isolated from them until they open. So often the act of building in all its manifestations is obscured. **Owen Hopkins**, Director of the Farrell Centre at Newcastle University, and Assistant

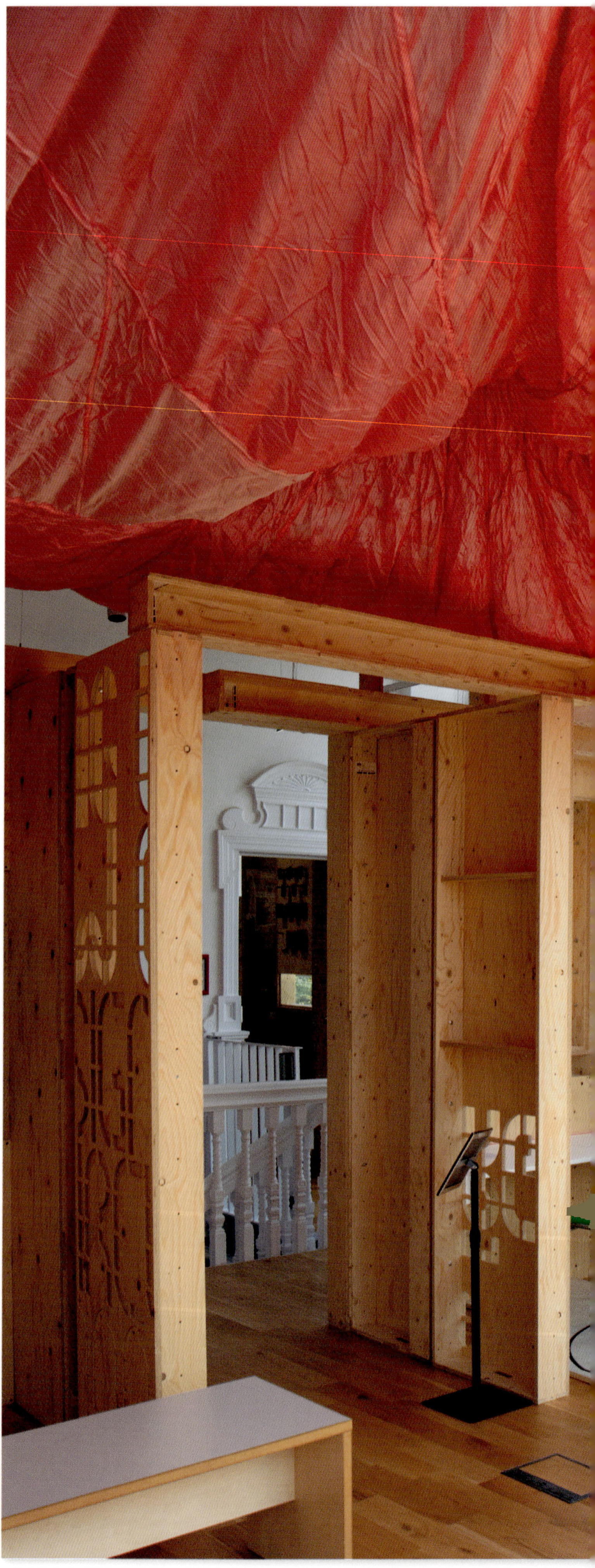

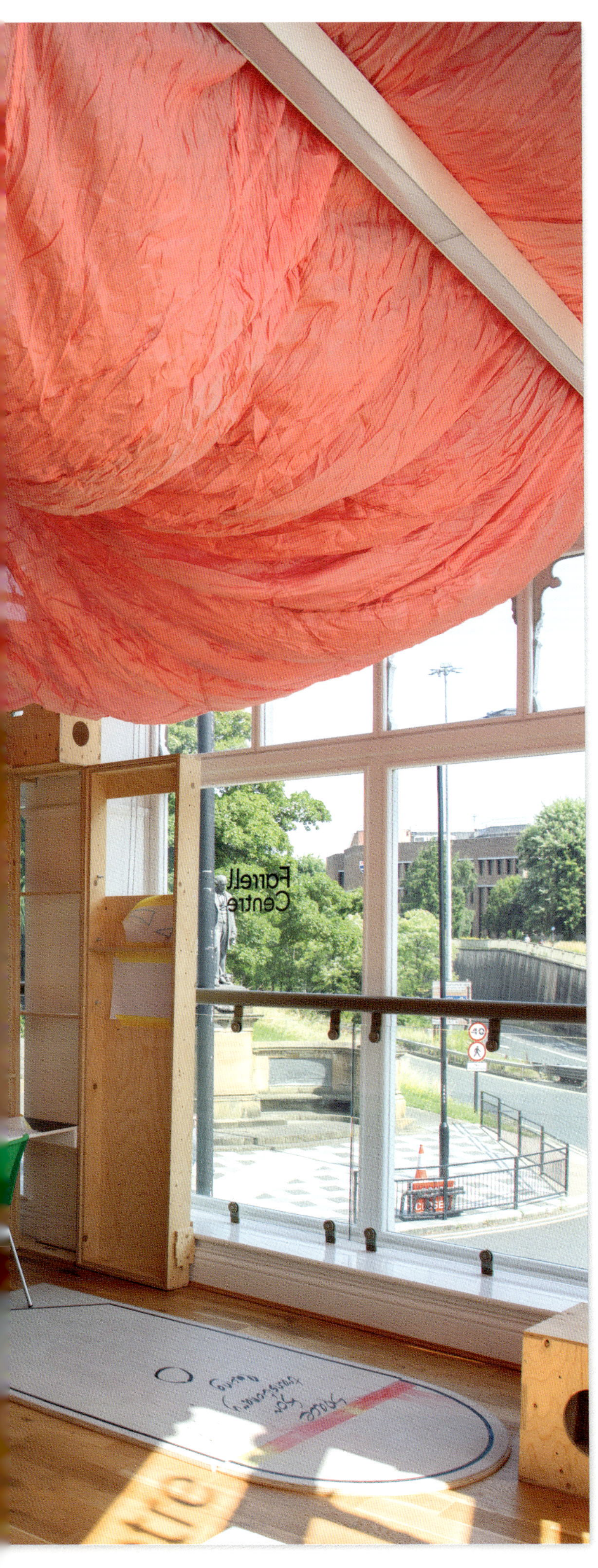

Experiments in Collaboration

Curator Lorna Burn, explain a 2024 initiative that brought this world of construction into the center's exhibition space, and allowed visitors and participants to build their own show, becoming its designers, builders, and curators.

Andjeas Ejiksson and
Joanna Zawieja,
Stage Directions,
"BUILDING: An Exhibition
Under Construction,"
Farrell Centre,
Newcastle University,
Newcastle, England,
2024

Local multidisciplinary artist, carpenter, and technician Peter J. Evans was given the "Stage Directions" brief written by Andjeas Ejiksson and Joanna Zawieja. He conceived and built a waiting room using the U-Build modular construction system, timber recycled from previous exhibitions, and a pink tarpaulin canopy.

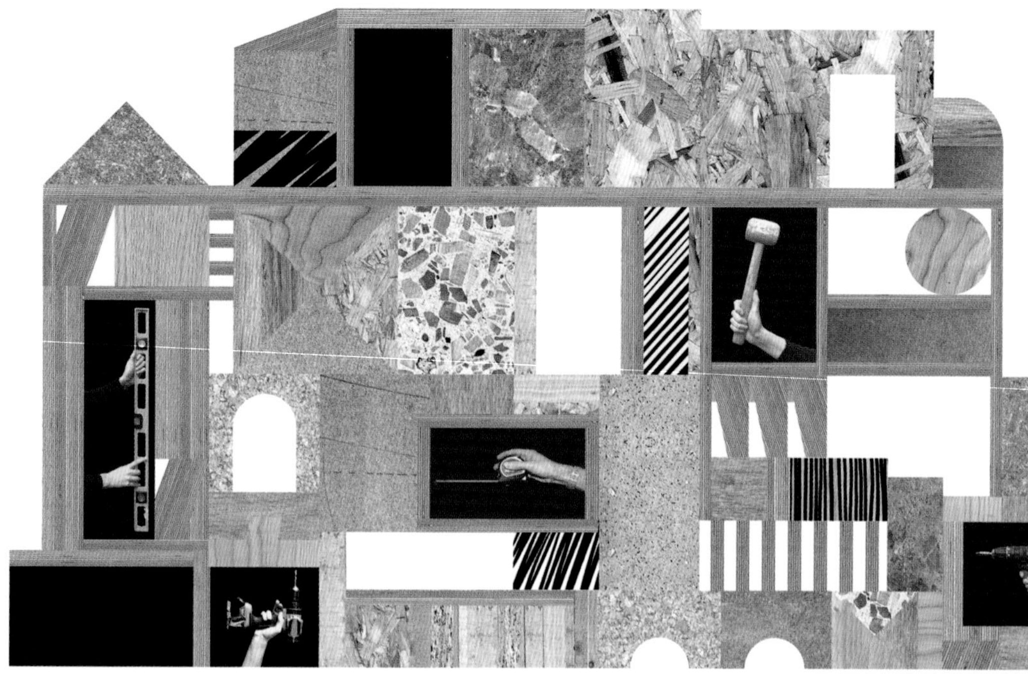

Foundation Press, Graphic identity for "BUILDING: An Exhibition Under Construction," Farrell Centre, Newcastle University, Newcastle, England, 2024

left: Foundation Press conceived the graphic identity of the exhibition, creating a design that expressed the collaborative and provisional nature of the project, which was also modular and able to be applied to its various constituent activities.

Building sites are ever-present in our cities. Yet we are always separated from them, experiencing them at a distance and from behind hoardings. There are, of course, important practical and health and safety reasons for this—building sites can often be dangerous. But this separation has the effect of disconnecting us from the construction process, which exists almost in another world, where questions about how buildings are made and who they are ultimately for can struggle to get heard.

"BUILDING: An Exhibition Under Construction," which ran at the Farrell Centre, Newcastle University, England, from April 3 to August 18, 2024, aimed to help change this. It recast building not as object, but as action. When you do this, everything the hoardings serve to obscure comes into view: who builds our buildings, the conditions they work in, the tools they use, and the skills they employ; the materials buildings are made from and their environmental impacts both locally and further afield; the money that funds buildings, where it comes from, and what it wants in return.

Rather than opening in fully realized form, this exhibition was conceived to take shape over several months, shining a light on the process of making not just buildings, but exhibitions too. With the galleries transformed into live making spaces, the exhibition proceeded as a series of live build projects, installations created by students and apprentices, visitor participation, and a program of workshops and events for all audiences. In this way, it offered new models not just for architectural curating, but for reimagining the built environment as something we can all positively shape.

Seeing Architecture from Below

The starting point for the exhibition was the work of Brazilian architect, painter, and theorist Sérgio Ferro. Born in 1938, Ferro has long been concerned with the separation that has emerged over centuries of architectural development between the design and the building processes. From this separation, he observes, has emanated the widespread degradation of workers' conditions within the building industry in Brazil and beyond.

These ideas were shaped by Ferro's experience working as a student in the late 1950s on the building site of the new Brazilian capital of Brasília. There, Ferro witnessed a terrible contradiction between the democratic intentions and soaring Modernist concrete designs by Oscar Niemeyer and Lúcio Costa and the brutal conditions and exploitation of the building workers pouring concrete in the sun. Ferro would devote himself to understanding how this came about, putting these issues in the forefront of architects' minds, and seeking alternative ways of building.

While researching the historical evolution of this separation between design and building, Ferro began to conceive architectural projects that considered the conditions of workers during the construction process. In one such example, working with fellow architects Flávio Império and Rodrigo Lefèvre, he created a small number of arched structures that provided shade to workers as they were built. They also sought to challenge the deskilling of the workforce and looked at ways of encouraging cooperation between trades, both of which Ferro saw as having been eroded in order to increase control over workers and maximize profits.

Ferro's unique and challenging body of work remains little known in the English-speaking world. The ambition of changing this and introducing Ferro's ideas to an international audience lay at the core of a four-year research project involving collaborations between Newcastle University and the University of São Paulo. Entitled "Translating Ferro / Transforming Knowledges of Architecture, Art and Labour for the New Field of Production Studies" (TF/TK), the project translated three of Ferro's books into English while creating opportunities for cross-disciplinary research and dialogue.[1]

"BUILDING: An Exhibition Under Construction," Farrell Centre, Newcastle University, Newcastle, England, 2024

below: And+ Studios devised an exhibition environment using U-Build, making use of the possibilities of the system, while playfully subverting it. Here we see the small materials library and various interactive activities for children as well as older visitors.

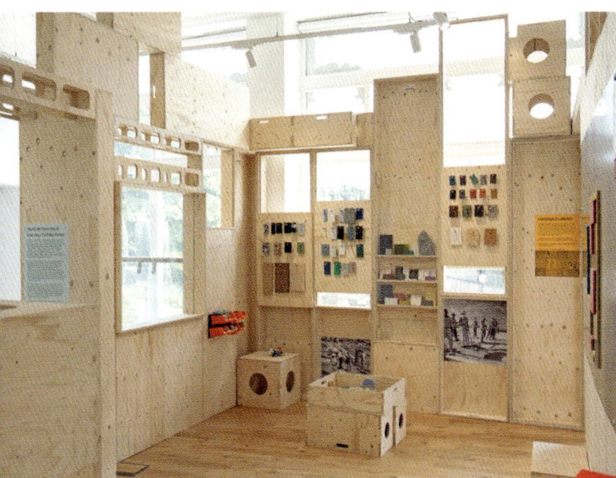

below: For part of the exhibition's run, Gallery 3 was used as workshop space for a range of programs and activities. These included The Sunday Builder—a free workshop where technicians took participants through some common DIY tasks such as preparing a wall for painting, tiling, and bathroom resealing.

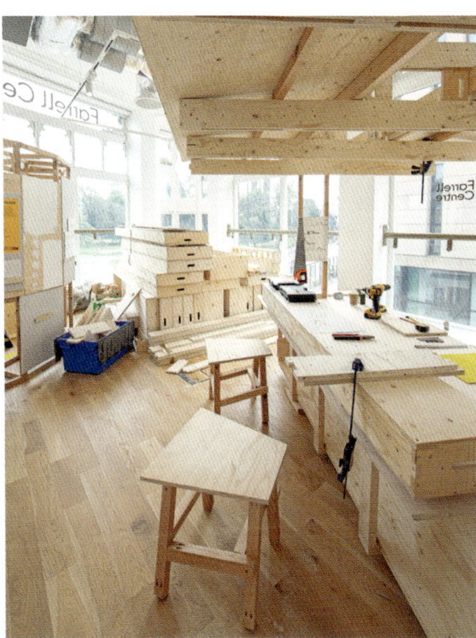

below: Alongside the graphic design, Foundation Press conceived various activities to involve visitors in the making of the exhibition. These included pipework printmaking, where visitors could use stamps to create their print which they could then join up with the evolving pipework on the gallery wall.

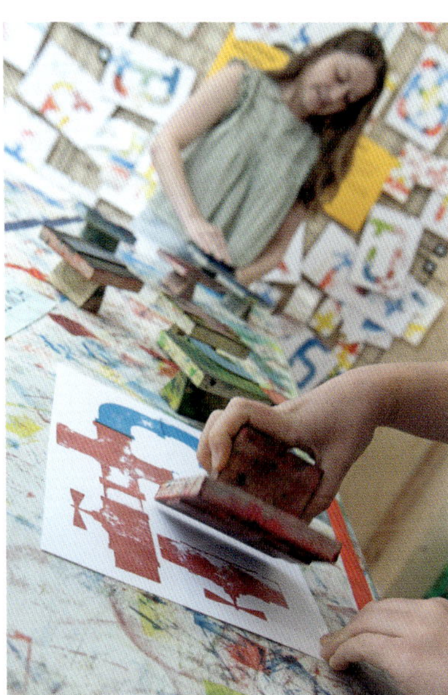

Reflecting the ethos of that project, the exhibition was conceived during 2022 and 2023 through a collaborative curatorial process involving Katie Lloyd Thomas, Professor of Architectural Theory and History at Newcastle University (and Principal Investigator UK of TF/TK); Will Thomson, TF/TK Research Associate in the School of Architecture, Planning and Landscape at Newcastle University; Lorna Burn and Hannah Christy, Assistant Curators, Farrell Centre; and myself as Director of the Farrell Centre.

With Head and Hand

Architects design buildings, but they don't actually build them—or at least that is the way it has been for the last five hundred years or so. Of course, this distinction between intellectual and manual work is not confined to buildings. Even in today's post-industrial era, we still refer to white-collar and blue-collar jobs to distinguish those who work in offices and those who do not—and as shorthand, or code, for middle-class professions and working-class occupations. One of the results of all this is the comparative lack of value that society places on manual skills and trades, not least in building construction.

How do we change this? One place to start is to overturn that old distinction between the intellectual and the manual and instead find ways to work with both head and hand. The result would not only empower those who build our buildings, and attract more people to the industry, but would help create a fairer, more inclusive built environment—and perhaps even society as well.

To put this into practice, the curatorial team for "BUILDING" approached 3D designers And+ Studios and graphic designers Foundation Press with an unusual brief. Rather than a list of specific requirements, the brief was left open, with the scope of their respective roles emerging during discussion and several meetings. Central to this was the intention that their involvement would not cease with the exhibition's opening, but would continue through it.

For the exhibition design, And+ Studios arrived at the task of creating an environment that could sustain change and adaptation over several months. They made use of a large existing stock of U-Build—a building system created by architects Studio Bark with structural engineering from Structure Workshop and testing from Cut and Construct, which aims to transform the way buildings are made—and how we think about them—by simplifying the construction process. The system itself is highly flexible, made from strong and lightweight modular boxes that connect together. It can be used on a small scale to build storage or internal walls, but has also been designed to construct more substantial spaces such as garden rooms and even houses.

And+ Studios modeled various versions of their design, which included spaces for display, making, and play, before building it themselves, improvising in response to ideas that occurred during construction. The spatial requirements were specified not just by the curators, but by Foundation Press whose role extended from the exhibition's visual identity and standard graphic elements, to devising interactive activities that allowed visitors of all ages to play a role in the exhibition creation. This included print-making to create a collaborative wallpaper and a Heras fence template that visitors were invited to fill in directly on the gallery wall. The result was an exhibition environment that felt open, accessible, and provisional.

Sunderland College students,
Apprentice(ship) Piece,
"BUILDING: An Exhibition Under Construction,"
Farrell Centre, Newcastle University,
Newcastle, England,
2024

right: Technicians from Sunderland College installing the students' work in the Farrell Centre shop window. The installation showcased an array of materials, techniques, and technologies, including heat pumps and solar panels, which are central to retrofitting buildings of all ages and types.

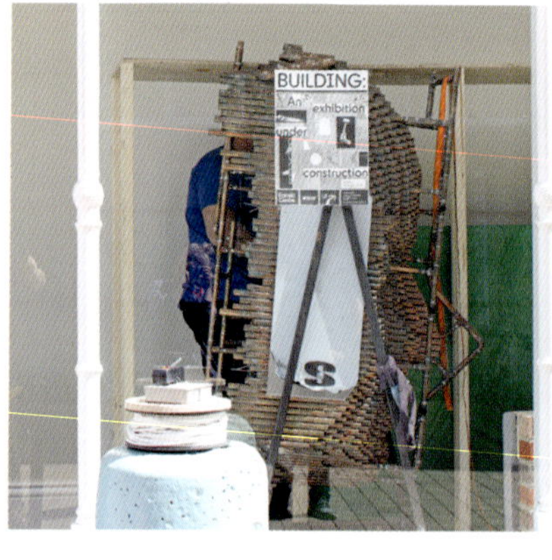

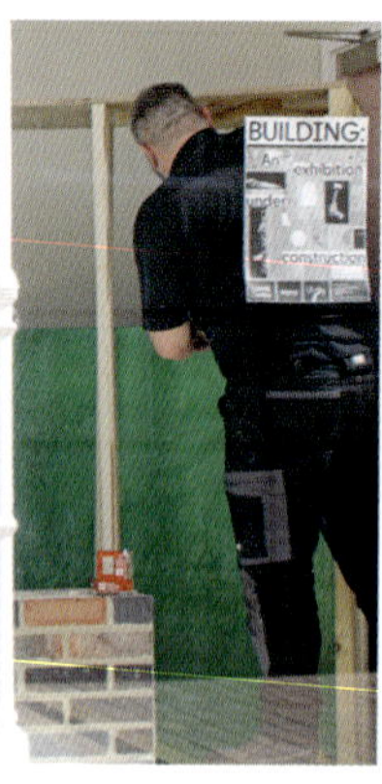

Sharing Know-how

Historically, building skills and trades were handed down in families, from father to son. In the medieval period, guilds were established to protect and control access to that specialist knowledge. And then in the 19th and 20th centuries, professional bodies were instituted to regulate and promote the interests of professions and disciplines.

While there are many positives to this—from improving building safety to increasing efficiency—a major downside is that for most people construction has become an almost mystical process, relying on skills and knowledge that are unseen and inaccessible to anyone outside the industry. As the built environment becomes ever more complex, the ways it is constructed and maintained are becoming ever more inaccessible, and ultimately out of our control.

Specialist expertise will always be necessary to ensure buildings at the very least stand up—and hopefully much else besides. Yet, sharing know-how so we can all get involved on some level is vital to creating a built environment that works for everyone.

This idea of democratizing knowledge and expertise is at the heart of the mission of Sunderland College, a leading further-education college and technical school in the northeast of England. For "BUILDING," Level 2 and 3 apprentices from the college worked alongside local architecture practice MawsonKerr to create an installation that explores the potential of retrofitting existing buildings and the impact of modern construction on the environment.

At the center of the installation—entitled *Apprentice(ship) Piece*—is a work directly inspired by the "apprentice pieces" that, historically, aspiring craftsmen would make to showcase their proficiency. Taking the form of a human head in profile, the intricate copper pipe construction stands as a celebration of the skills of students and staff and expertise that goes into the installation of even the most functional piece of pipework, while its abstracted human form points to the broader possibilities of our creative exploration and human ingenuity, and the impacts we have on the planet.

The underlying theme of the installation was around retrofit, which is of course central to the future of construction, reducing the need for wasteful, unnecessary demolition of existing buildings while improving their energy efficiency. However, for retrofit to be harnessed in everyday construction, new skills and processes need to be developed and taught—with the ongoing work of institutions like Sunderland College playing a vital role in leading the way.

Working Together

We used to think of the architect as the conductor of the orchestra—writing the score and ensuring the various professions and trades involved in constructing a building work together in harmony. Today, however, the architect is rarely the conductor, but—to use a different analogy—is a small cog in a large and complex machine. That is when an architect is even present. For all the attention the profession still attracts—positive and negative—nowadays the vast majority of building projects do not actually involve an architect at all.

Instead of vainly attempting to reclaim the architect's pre-eminent position, this situation provides an opportunity to rethink the role of the architect entirely, helping alleviate the disconnection that many people feel with how the built environment is produced. To do this, we no longer need architects to aspire to work as conductors, but instead to operate as facilitators, using their skills and expertise to find ways of connecting designer, maker, and user—and, ultimately, of working together.

To explore this idea, a group of Newcastle University architecture students worked with the architect Lee Ivett on a project called "Care and Repair," to design and build a mobile bike-repair workshop inside the exhibition galleries. Ivett's background is as an academic (as Head of the Grenfell-Baines Institute of Architecture at the University of Central Lancashire, England) and as founder of the architecture and design practice Baxendale, which empowers people to be actively part of the architectural and building process. Reflecting that ethos, he worked with the students to create the design from an initial idea through to technical detail, and then on to fabrication using the materials assembled in the gallery.

Although Ivett played a role in guiding the group through this process, he was clear that ownership over what was created sat with the students. They would leave the process with skills and experience that they can use in the future, enabling them to instigate their own projects and develop participative ways of working with different communities. When complete, the bike workshop was put on display in the exhibition before being disassembled at its close to be reused as an actual workshop.

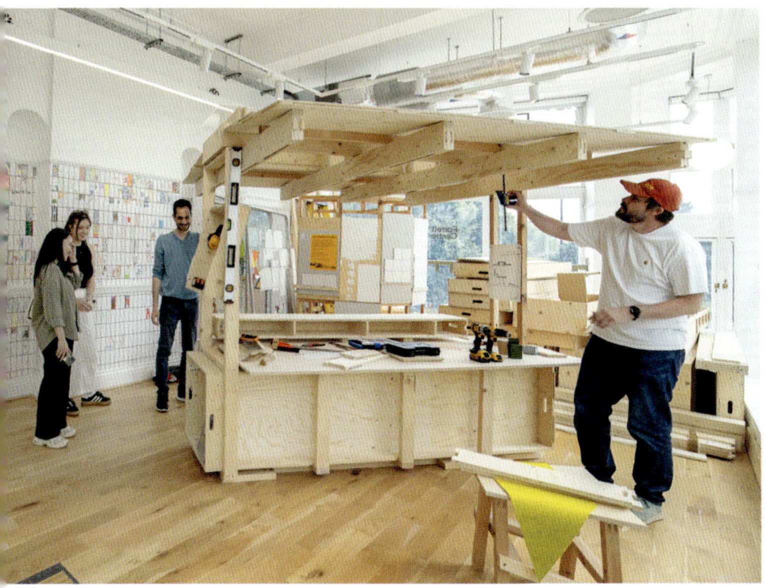

Lee Ivett and Newcastle University students, Care and Repair, "BUILDING: An Exhibition Under Construction," Farrell Centre, Newcastle University, Newcastle, England, 2024

left: Ivett worked with the students in Gallery 3 of the exhibition, which had previously been used as a workshop space for visitors. Visitors were able to see the bike-repair workshop structure take shape from adjacent galleries.

Andjeas Ejiksson and Joanna Zawieja, Stage Directions, "BUILDING: An Exhibition Under Construction," Farrell Centre, Newcastle University, Newcastle, England, 2024

below: During the construction of the waiting room, Peter J. Evans transformed the gallery into a workshop space, giving visitors a chance to look literally behind the hoarding and see—as well as interact with—the processes through which an exhibition installation is fabricated.

Space for Uncertainty

Today, building construction is governed, above all, by risk management. We see it in the way designs are fixed early on, with little scope for flexibility as projects evolve. And it is also there in the prevalence of only the most familiar, tried and tested building methods and materials, and in the way workers are treated like machines, dutifully following ever more detailed instructions.

While ostensibly about safety, risk management's refusal of the unexpected is arguably really about controlling costs. Either way, the result is a building culture that has become deeply conservative, that shuns the unusual let alone the original; a culture where "fit for purpose" is the highest we can aspire to.

If we want to change this, a good way to start is by empowering building workers and finding ways to better utilize their expertise and experience. If we set the financial aspects of risk management to one side, we can create space for workers to take the initiative, to deploy their skills, even to improvise—with benefits for all of us in creating a richer, more inclusive built environment.

Stage Directions—a collaboration between artist, writer, and researcher Andjeas Ejiksson and architect, critic, and curator Joanna Zawieja—has uncertainty at its core. Having started as a letter correspondence between Ejiksson and Zawieja, the project has been ongoing since 2013, inviting a fabricator, armed only with scant written design rules, to design and build a waiting room. No visual references, guidance, or technical drawings are provided. It is the process of design through making that is important rather than what is built; so as long as the rules are adhered to, the maker has complete design autonomy.

For the sixth iteration of Stage Directions as part of "BUILDING," the brief was given to local multidisciplinary artist, carpenter, and technician Peter J. Evans. Over the course of several weeks, visitors to the exhibition saw Evans create his own version of the waiting room. When complete, the public were able to experience it for themselves and examine the build process through documentary images and a written design narrative that Evans typed in the space during the making of the room.

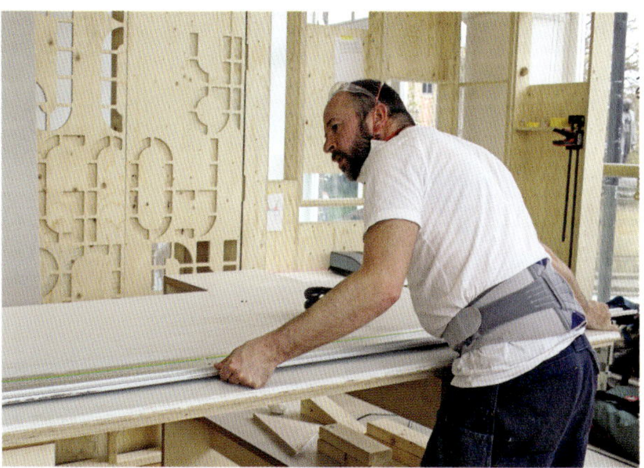

It has become commonplace for exhibitions and the institutions that produce them to seek to involve their audiences in the curatorial process via "co-curation" and "co-production." While important, this leaves the relationship between curators and fabricators largely intact. In contrast, "BUILDING" sought to unpick this power dynamic. Rather than the curators being the authorial figures, with fabricators, designers, and technicians charged with delivering their "vision," this project instead sought to empower these highly skilled and experienced collaborators to take a creative role in shaping the exhibition. The insights gleaned over the course of the project offer new models not just for architectural curating, but, more broadly, for reimagining architecture itself as an inherently collaborative practice.

Note

1. These books by Sérgio Ferro are: *Architecture from Below: An Anthology*, MACK (London), 2024; *Design and the Building Site and Complementary Essays*, MACK (London), 2025; and *Construction of Classical Design*, MACK (London), forthcoming.

Constructing a

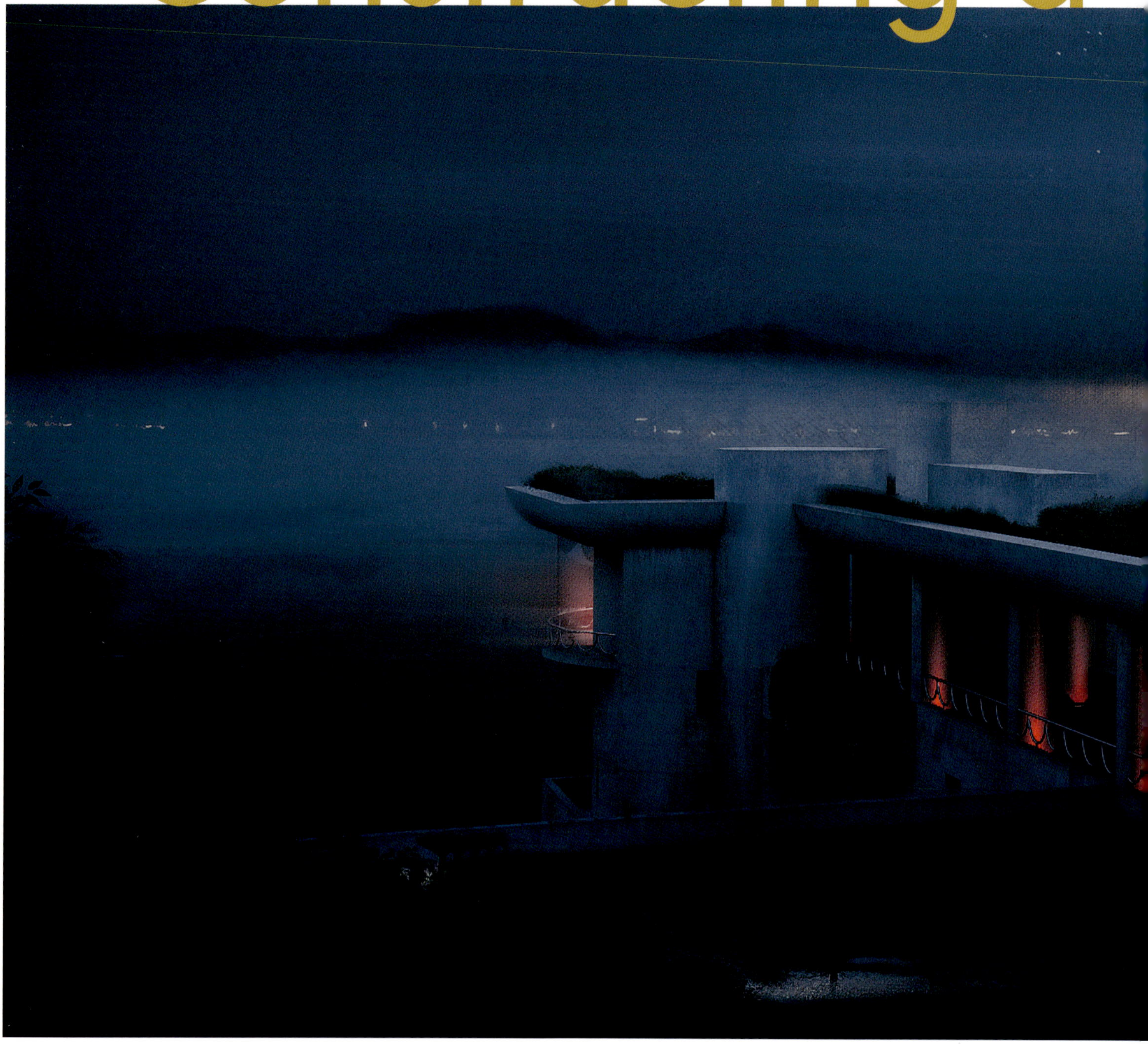

Martin Loureiro,
The Morris House, A Story in Six Shots: Quiet Night,
2018

The approach to Seacliff from the road was intended to be meek compared with its presentation from the bottom of the slope

Mark Morris

Cliffhanger

An Architectural Fiction Built on Half-Truths

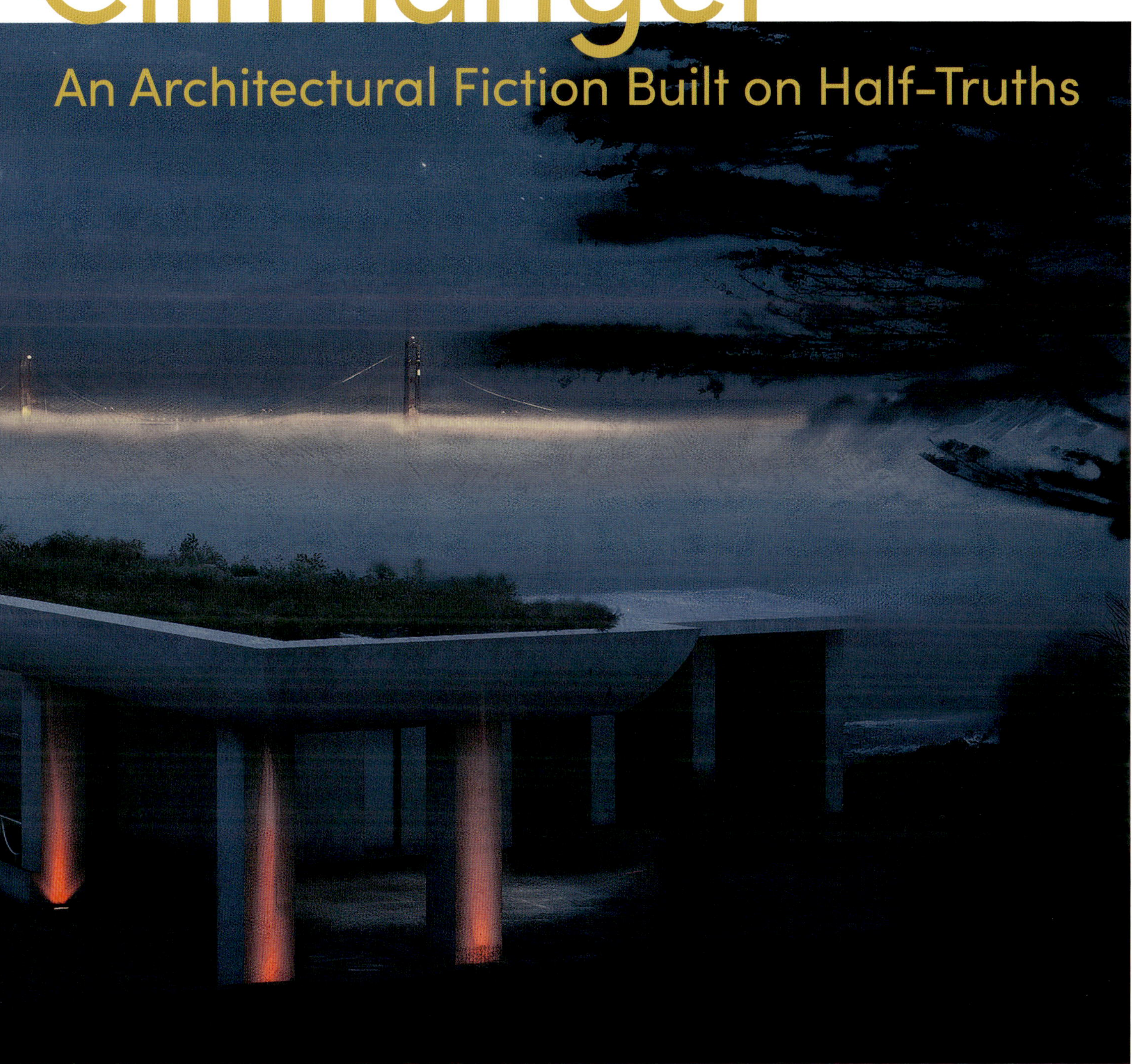

below. A carport and entry loggia are capped by a long slab of roof garden that extends along the full length of the house.

As the backdrop to a work-in-progress architectural novel, **Mark Morris**, Senior Curator of Architecture and Design at London's Victoria and Albert Museum, alights on a Frank Lloyd Wright house designed but not built for a craggy cliff-edge site in San Francisco, California. The house becomes the setting for an enigmatic two-header drama, a cliffhanger on more levels than one, and a curious case of fact meeting fiction. Here he presents a taster of the book and its literary genealogy, alongside some of the history of the house project.

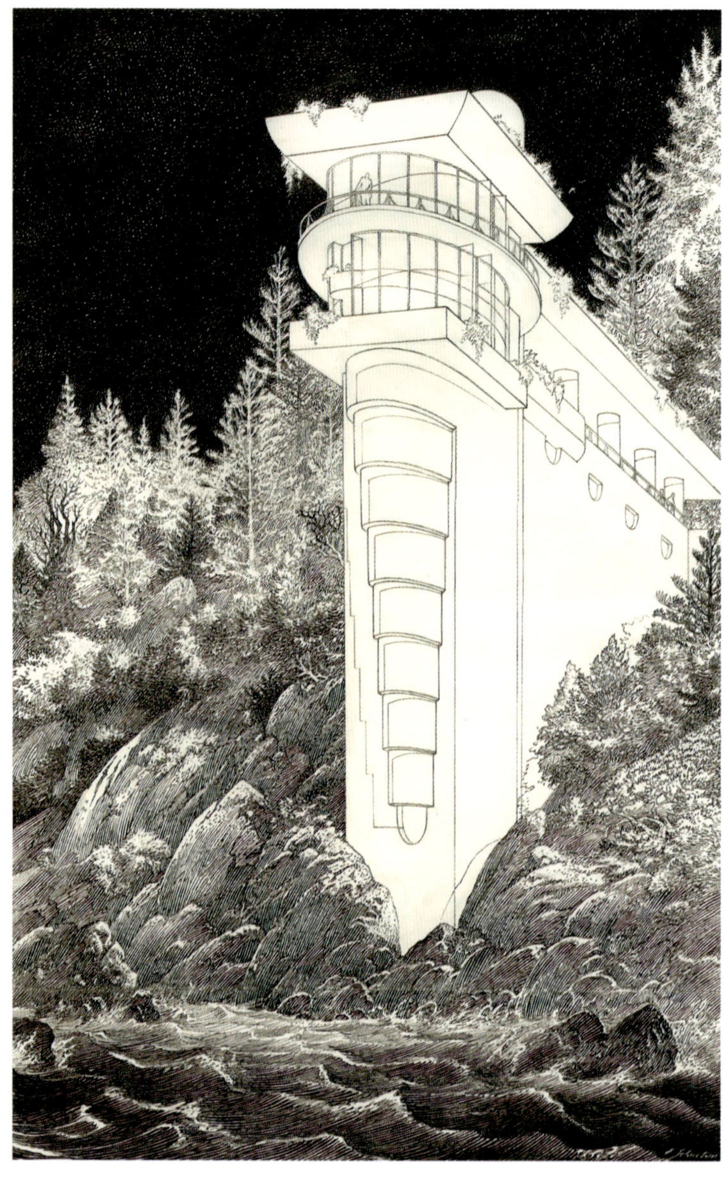

François Schuiten,
Sea Cliff,
2020

above: The graphic artist of the lauded *Les Cités obscures* series, first published in 1983, created this compelling drawing of the Frank Lloyd Wright-designed Morris House (1945; unexecuted) in 2020. The building itself is rendered as if in negative with its environment—the water, rocks, and sky—flooded with inky details. This image, more than Wright's well-known published perspectives of the house, inspired Mark Morris's novel.

Frank Lloyd Wright,
V. C. Morris house (San Francisco, California), Seacliff, Scheme 1, Unbuilt Project,
1945

opposite left: Though delighted with Wright's 1948 design for their gift shop built in San Francisco, V.C. and Lillian Morris would never give final approval for Wright's various iterations of a house intended for their bayside site on El Camino Del Mar with views of the Golden Gate Bridge.

Title page to the first edition of Thomas Hardy's *A Laodicean*, vol. 1,
1881

opposite right: Hardy's architectural novel broke new ground with doctored telegrams and photographs featuring as false evidence within the narrative. New technology, like new architecture, was not to be fully trusted. Yet the architect seeking to embrace the modern wins the day.

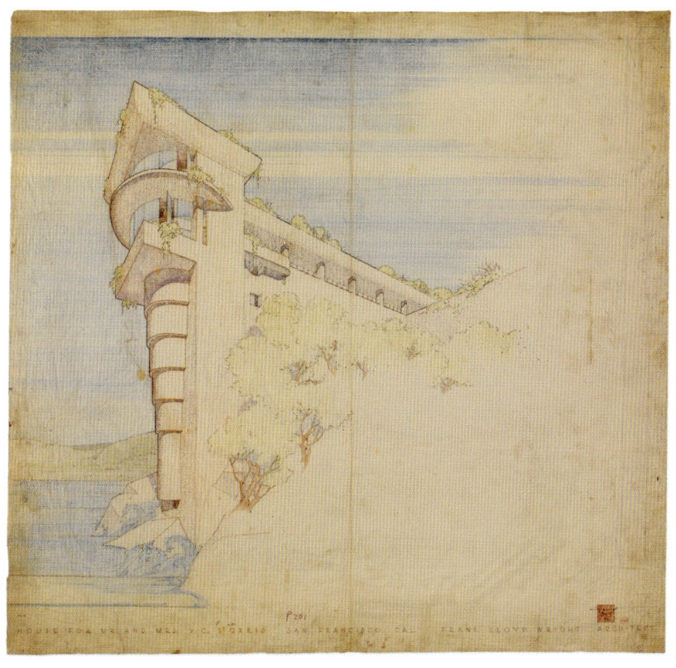

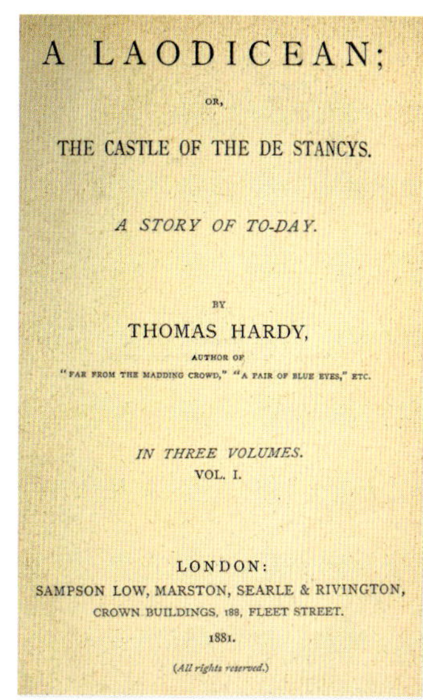

A LAODICEAN;

OR,

THE CASTLE OF THE DE STANCYS.

A STORY OF TO-DAY.

BY

THOMAS HARDY,

AUTHOR OF

"FAR FROM THE MADDING CROWD," "A PAIR OF BLUE EYES," ETC.

IN THREE VOLUMES.

VOL. I.

LONDON:

SAMPSON LOW, MARSTON, SEARLE & RIVINGTON,

CROWN BUILDINGS, 188, FLEET STREET.

1881.

(All rights reserved.)

The English poet and novelist Thomas Hardy, author of *Far from the Madding Crowd* (1874)[1] and *Tess of the d'Ubervilles* (1891),[2] had trained to be an architect, winning prizes from the Royal Institute of British Architects and the Architectural Association in London, as well as building his own house, before leaving the profession in favor of writing full-time. *A Laodicean; or, The Castle of the De Stancys: A Story of Today,*[3] a novel dictated during a protracted illness in 1880, saw Hardy raiding his architectural past, making the hero a trail-blazing architect, and architecture central to the plot.

After a strong start with an intriguing premise—inheriting a castle that needs attention, Paula Power hires two architects, one a local romantic fascinated by medievalism, the other an architect from London focused on the future, and an inevitable love triangle ensues—the second half of the novel stumbles around with subplots and literary clichés. Paula ends up with the Londoner, but remains on the fence regarding her preference for historicism versus Modernism.

Such equivocation mirrored Hardy's own feelings. He would eventually decide on restoring old churches and joining the Society for the Preservation of Ancient Buildings, founded in 1877 by William Morris and Philip Webb, both leaders of the Arts and Crafts movement. Sensitivity to architecture and landscape suffused several of Hardy's novels. Wessex, the imaginary English county where so many of his novels take place, might be viewed as a career-spanning world-building project. But for all of that, writing about architects and architecture head-on was a struggle for Hardy. *A Laodicean* is held to be his most autobiographical work, yet one flawed in terms of narrative structure.

Wright or Not

A commercially successful recent architectural novel, and one inspired by actual events, *Loving Frank* (2007)[4] by historical fiction author Nancy Horan is written from the perspective of American architect Frank Lloyd Wright's doomed lover, the feminist intellectual Mamah Borthwick. Double triangles this time: two painful divorces, two families fractured, and all for fleeting happiness squelched by a madman and a terrible fire at Wright's house-studio complex Taliesin in Wisconsin. Horan grew up in Oak Park, Illinois, the neighborhood where Wright built many of his early homes from 1889 to 1909, including one of his own alongside his studio.

Attempting my own as-yet unpublished architectural novel, tentatively titled *Cliffhanger*, in 2024, I could not shake Hardy or Horan as forebears. Like Horan, I grew up in proximity to what I thought were Frank Lloyd Wright houses. Rush Creek Village, the largest Frank Lloyd Wright-inspired collection of houses after Oak Park, was built by Wright acolyte Theodore Van Fossen in the 1950s. My later experience teaching at Cornell University from 2007 to 2017, where the architecture department is situated beside a deep gorge, allowed me to draw on colleagues who became characters, as well as the topography of Ithaca, New York. In contriving a house that may or may not be by Frank Lloyd Wright, as with Rush Creek, a question of provenance is raised that propels my story. A perspective drawing of Seacliff (also known as the Morris House—more doubling), a daring 1945 design that Wright desperately wanted to build, anchors the story as much as it is anchored to its site, not along the San Francisco coastline, but the inland network of gorges and waterfalls that characterize Ithaca.

Theodore Van Fossen,
Usonian home,
Rush Creek, Worthington,
Ohio,
2024

One of 48 houses designed by Theodore Van Fossen starting in 1954 at the behest of Martha and Richard Wakefield, who had visited Wright at Taliesin West, his winter studio-house complex in Scottsdale, Arizona. Mostly designed with flat roofs and set obliquely to the street, the houses featured carports, a Wright invention. While hardly a comparison to the verticality of Seacliff, one can see the same formal architectural gesture in respect to the sloping site; a Seacliff becalmed.

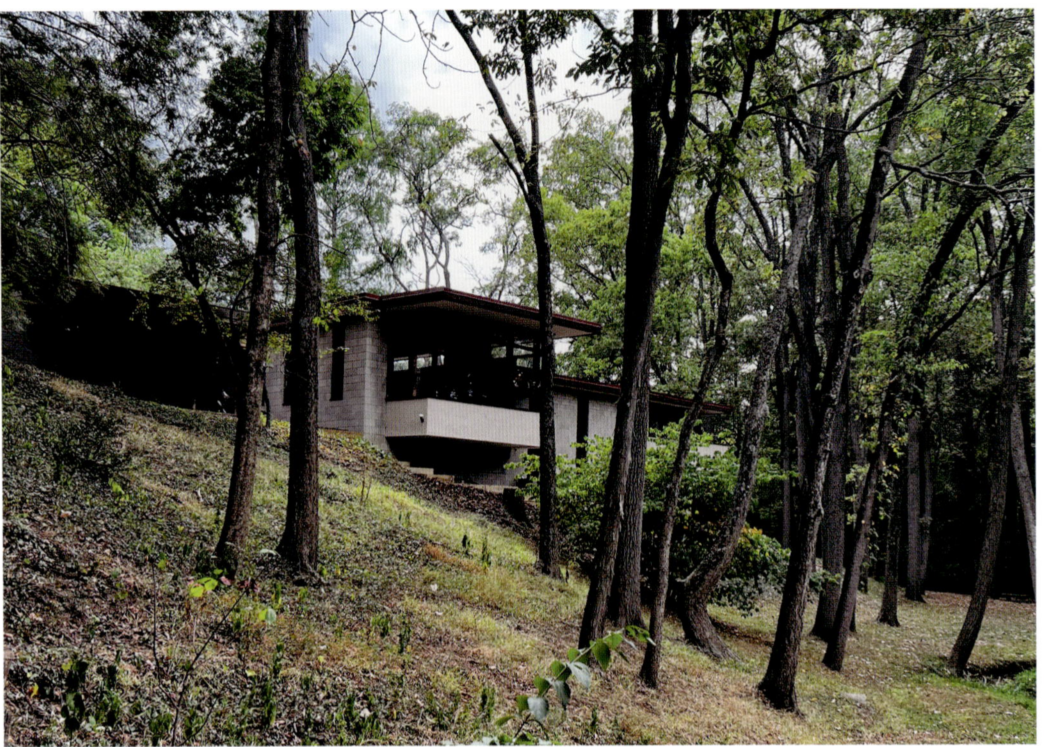

The only problem with my mystery house premise was the seeming improbability that Wright would have ever come to Ithaca to build anything. So it was a happy surprise when I found out he had an old friend in George Robinson Dean, who had been president of the Chicago Architectural Club and a member of The Eighteen, a Steinway Hall supper-club set that included a young Frank Lloyd Wright. In 1900 Dean built a fraternity house in the ground-hugging Prairie School-style on Cornell's campus, later lost in a fire. He could also be a contender as architect of the house in the gorge.

Further research revealed that Cornell's architecture department had invited luminaries to campus as part of its visiting critic program: Walter Gropius, Philip Johnson, Buckminster Fuller, and, in 1952, Wright. Fuller had architecture students build a large geodesic dome on the roof of the architecture building. Why couldn't Wright have had students likewise build a prototype house, the one he so wanted to build in San Francisco but could not? This dose of reality helped sharpen the narrative.

A Few Fragments

To set the stage, I needed to introduce my three principal characters—Lina, Maxfield, and the house itself—at the outset. Lina, an architecture professor, kicks things off with a long walk:

> I was on a hunt to see a particular cascade following a path in the morning sunlight, when something came in to view that seemed impossible. Approaching the structure head-on, it looked like a slender tower emerging from the mist of the cascade below. A glassy cylinder topped a tapering base. As I came nearer, I could see it was less a tower and more a slab that simultaneously grew out of and sliced into the rocky hillside. The top of this structure extended level into the gorge, which highlighted how steep the slope was to either side. My jaw dropped at the sight of it as I reached for my phone to shoot photos of it as if it might disappear.
>
> Maybe it was a secret society lair like the old Sphinx Head Club nearer campus? But the more I looked at it, noting the scale from the handrails of balconies that girdled the topmost rooms lined with windows, it seemed a house. Oh, but what a house! I imagined the view would be spectacular. A strange urge took hold of me, I had to get inside and see for myself, but this required getting to the other side of the gorge.
>
> I descended the slope on my side and crossed over the creek bed where the cascade flattened out. Water splashed around my ankles, I had to be careful not to slip and fall. I found a couple of stepping stones to get me over the last several feet, and then I was there at the base of the house, staring up at the underside of its first balcony. There was a reason why the trail was across the way: this side of the gorge was much steeper. To attempt to climb along either side of the slab would be tricky. So, I lingered there with cold feet.
>
> Looking at it closely, I realised the tapering effect was down to a series of concentric curves projecting from the end of the slab, each stacking bigger than the next, like an

extended telescope balancing a tray, a feat of engineering. Then I noticed the quality of the concrete work; the slab had obviously been poured in stages with imprints from rough formwork, but, from a distance, it just looked like a monolith. Centred under the bottommost curve, I noticed a high window cut into the concrete with a graceful semicircular sill. It had first looked like a shadow cast from the projecting curve above. Yet, coming nearer, I could see glass reflecting the morning light. Then a light switched on behind the glass! I was so startled at this that I nearly fell backwards.

I suddenly felt like the trespasser I was. Architects think they can just go up to any building and prod around, but I was now keenly aware I was on private property. I crouched down below the window. For a moment I imagined holding very still would render me invisible. Then, with a delicate pivot, the window opened, and a voice called out, "Are you stuck?"

This voice belongs to the agoraphobic owner of the misplaced Morris House, who offers a rope ladder from the window after explaining there is no other way up on his side of the gorge.

I was about to scale up a wall and go inside a fortress-like house at the behest of a person I'd never met before. Did my eagerness to see this place eclipse any consideration for my personal safety? Yes, it did. Half-jokingly, I called up, "You're not some kind of reclusive axe murderer, are you?"

Without a moment's hesitation he responded, "I'm a reclusive murder-mystery writer."

"Really? Are you?" I asked incredulously.

"Yes."

"Which one?"

"Maxfield Morris, author and rescuer of noisome architects."

Again, incredulously, "How do you know I'm an architect?"

"It's only architects and hikers who end up in this spot."

"But how do you know I'm not a hiker?"

"Hikers eventually find their way back across."

After Lina becomes a housemate of Maxfield's, and reads some of his books, she tries to draw him out regarding his moodiness. They talk about the perilousness suggested by the design of his house. How the height, the views, the balconies can invite thoughts of self-destruction.

"One of your novel's characters was pushed or jumped from this balcony."

"And another from the balcony above."

"Lots of choices with this house," I reflected.

"Wright was very generous in this," Maxfield smiled.

"I wish you wouldn't joke."

"Joke? This place *is* perilous. That's a big part of its charm. A house jumping down the gorge, its every window and balcony a sublime invitation."

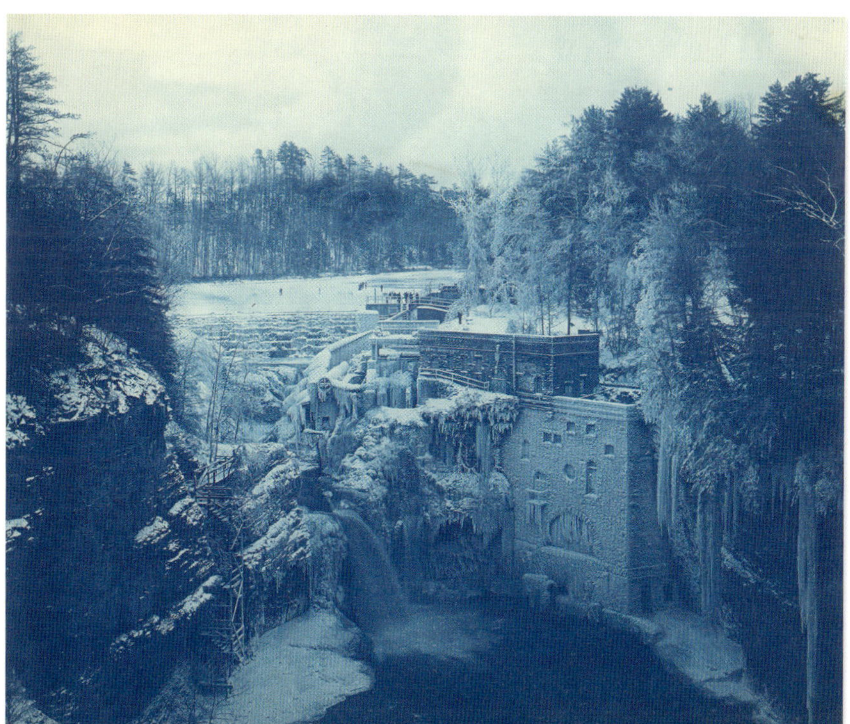

Gardner S. Williams (chief engineer), Hydraulic Laboratory, Cornell University, Ithaca, New York, photographed *c.* 1900

Built in 1898 for Cornell University's Civil Engineering Department, the building was left vacant after a flood in 1963 and collapsed in 2009, leaving an eerie ruin. The lab dances down beside the waterfall and tucks into the gorge by several floors. The version of Seacliff I imagined being realized in Ithaca draws heavily on this local precedent.

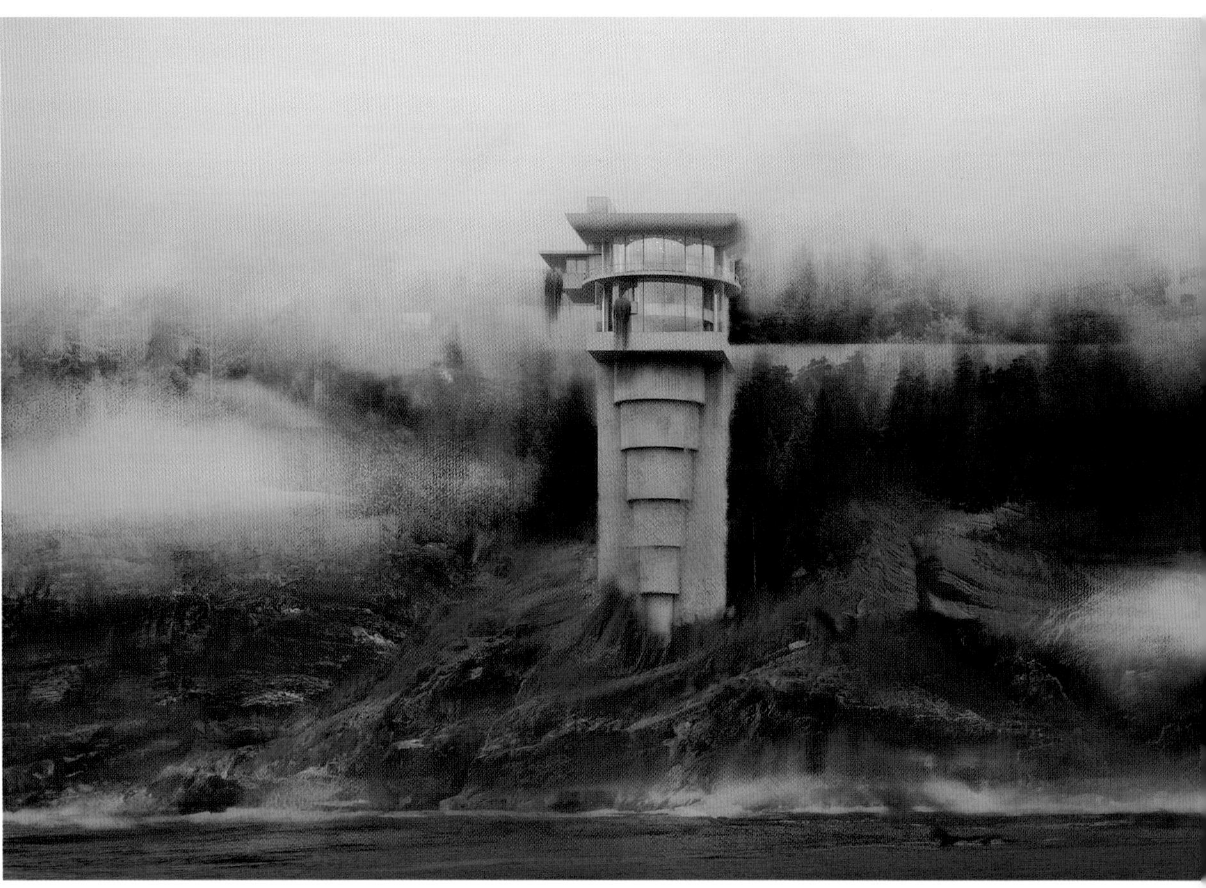

"We had talked about how depression, coupled with a place like this, invites, well, dark imaginings."

"All my books," Maxfield said, "are dark imaginings."

"Yet I've lived here just long enough to know that, equally, this house invites contentment, calm reflection, even joy. The light in the morning streaming in, the stars as your night-time wallpaper. It's like living in an ocean liner some days, the house cutting through the mists and skimming over the trees."

"One can take pleasure in the perilous."

Finally, in an effort to help him combat his phobia, Lina cajoles Maxfield into pacing the loggia just outside his front door, which the wind blows shut when they are halfway down its length. Foreshadowing eventually going up to the roof garden sets up the narrative's climax.

"Thank goodness you have the key," he said.

"It's in my coat hanging in the foyer," I gulped.

"I asked if you had the key."

"I had it, just not on me."

"This is precisely what I did not want to happen. Are you trying to kill me?"

"Calm down. We'll call your folks." I called them. "They'll be over quickly enough."

"Half an hour," Maxfield seethed.

"We'll wait here by the door and talk. Time will fly."

Maxfield closed his eyes and steadied his breathing. He was trying very hard not to lose his composure, "My first stab at exposure therapy and this happens."

"We're still in the house, according to Wright," I assured.

"How do you mean?" Maxfield said, eyes still closed.

"It's just an extension of the foyer pulling out to meet the drive. He deployed the same vocabulary of form you have with the house. It's all one. You don't mind the balconies off the living room or your study for the same reason."

"They finish the rooms they're attached to."

"This space is the same thing, really, just looking the other way."

Maxfield opened his eyes, "Keep talking like that."

I rattled off Wright's signature compression-decompression moves with the entries to most of his houses, and the hidden door game.

"But my door isn't hidden, it's aligned to the loggia."

"Ah, but the loggia acts as a screen from the road, being perpendicular to it. No one driving by has a direct view of your door, the columns visually stack up as a palisade from that vantage point."

His hand was shaking in mine either from cold or fear, "Keep talking."

"Maybe we can try the roof garden tomorrow?" I squeezed his hand.

"You'll probably lock us out there, too."

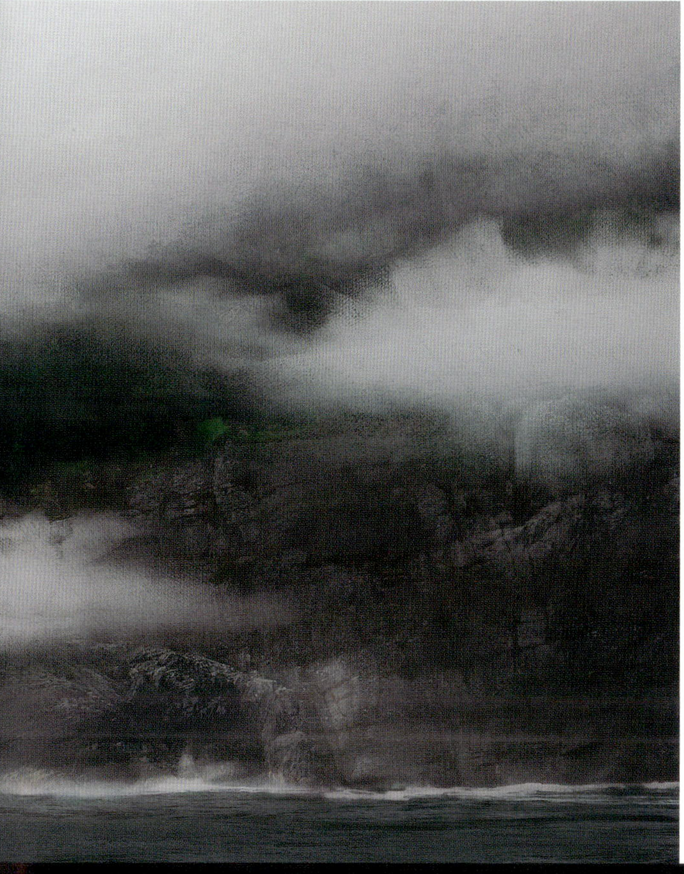

Edging Closer

Mindful of Hardy's problems with *A Laodicean*, I am keen to avoid literary clichés, but one seems essential. Hardy invented the "cliffhanger" in a previously serialized novel, *A Pair of Blue Eyes* (1873),[5] where a character is left literally hanging from a cliff, their life flashing before their eyes, between two instalments. It was the most assertive form of similar devices intended to garner readership. Charles Dickens had deployed various types of cliffhangers, but not with such dramatic effect nor actual cliffs. Something about the De Stancy castle set on its crag in *A Laodicean*, and the upland siting of Taliesin, a Welsh term for the shining brow of a hill, also suggested a cliffhanger in the architectural sense. This duality of literal and figural cliffhangers, alongside the house's provenance conundrum, underpins my novel's narrative structure. The question of whether I can pull off something worthwhile out of all this is, of course, the real cliffhanger.

Notes

1. Thomas Hardy, *Far from the Madding Crowd*, Smith, Elder & Co. (London), 1874.
2. Thomas Hardy, *Tess of the d'Urbervilles: A Pure Woman*, James R. Osgood, McIlvaine & Co. (London), 1891.
3. Thomas Hardy, *A Laodicean; or, The Castle of the De Stancys: A Story of Today*, Sampson Low, Marston, Searle & Rivington (London), 1881.
4. Nancy Horan, *Loving Frank*, Random House (New York), 2007.
5. Thomas Hardy, *A Pair of Blue Eyes*, Tinsley Brothers (London), 1873.

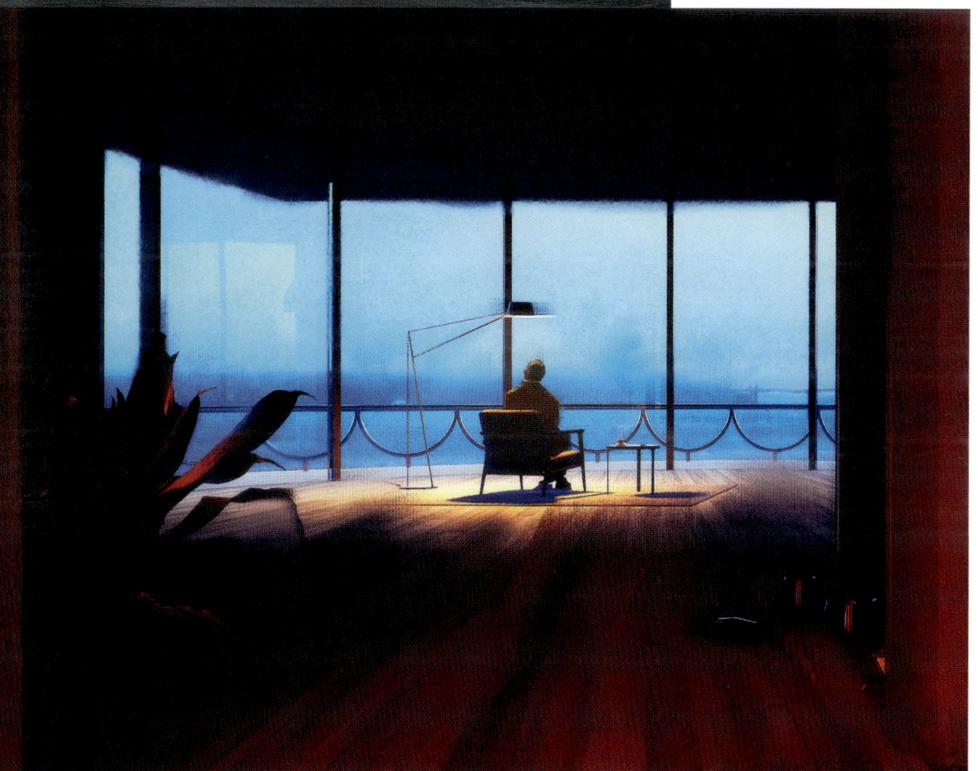

Martin Loureiro, *The Morris House, A Story in Six Shots: Feed the Fish*, 2018

above: One can see a similar architectural vocabulary to Wright's New York Guggenheim Museum in Seacliff, depicted here in Martin Loureiro's visualization. Both were designed roughly in parallel toward the end of Wright's life. There is something of a lighthouse in the design of the house, more appropriate to the San Francisco Bay site than my inland Upstate gorge.

Martin Loureiro, *The Morris House, A Story in Six Shots: It's Just a Job*, 2018

left: Glass fenestration set on a curve was to offer sweeping views from the living room and study below. A balcony railing just beyond plays up the scalloped lines found in certain windows and the telescopic curves on the exterior. My brooding agoraphobic murder-mystery writer lets the world come to him in such a space.

Place and
Lessons from

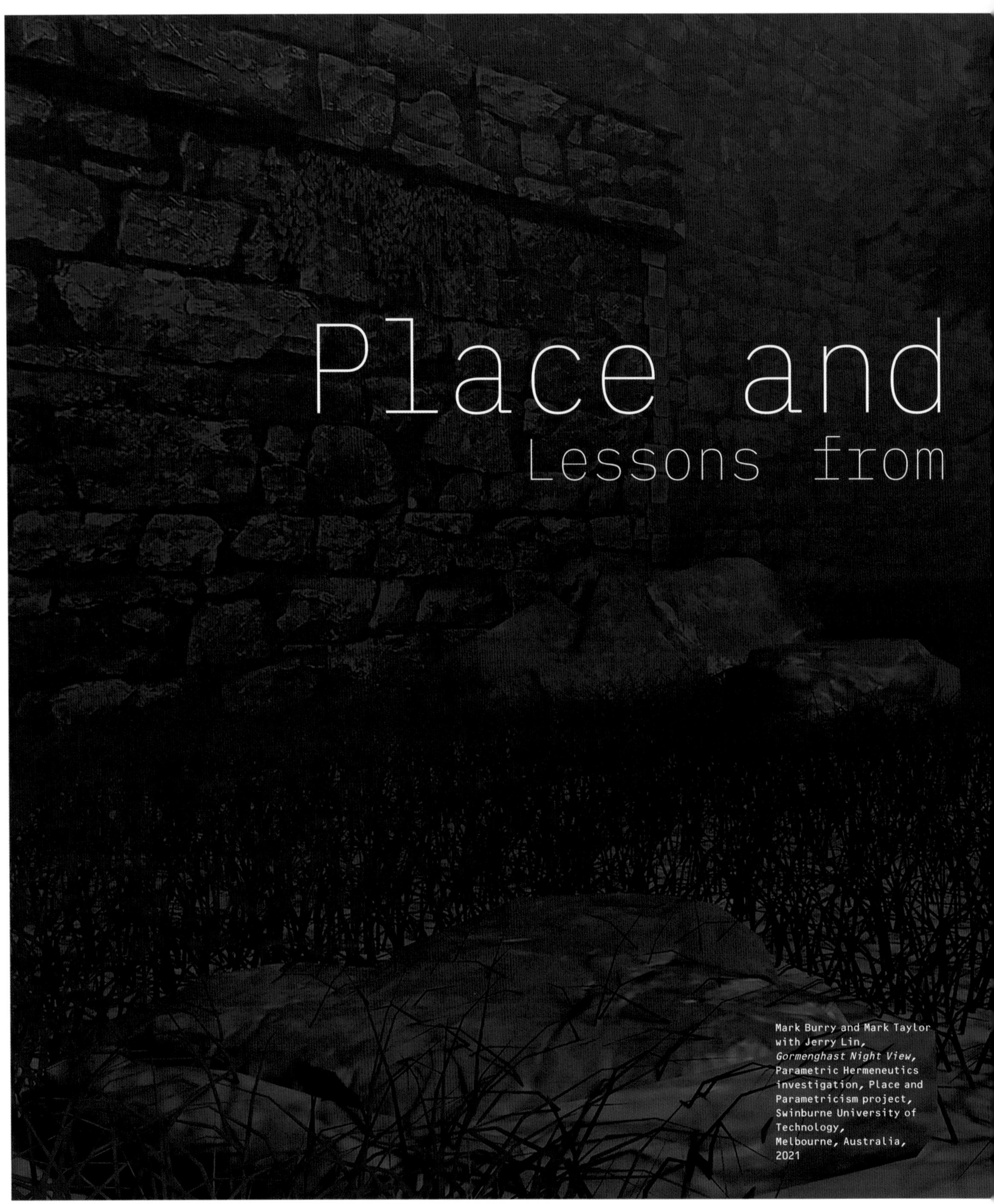

Mark Burry and Mark Taylor with Jerry Lin, *Gormenghast Night View*, Parametric Hermeneutics investigation, Place and Parametricism project, Swinburne University of Technology, Melbourne, Australia, 2021

Mark Burry

Parametricism Mervyn Peake

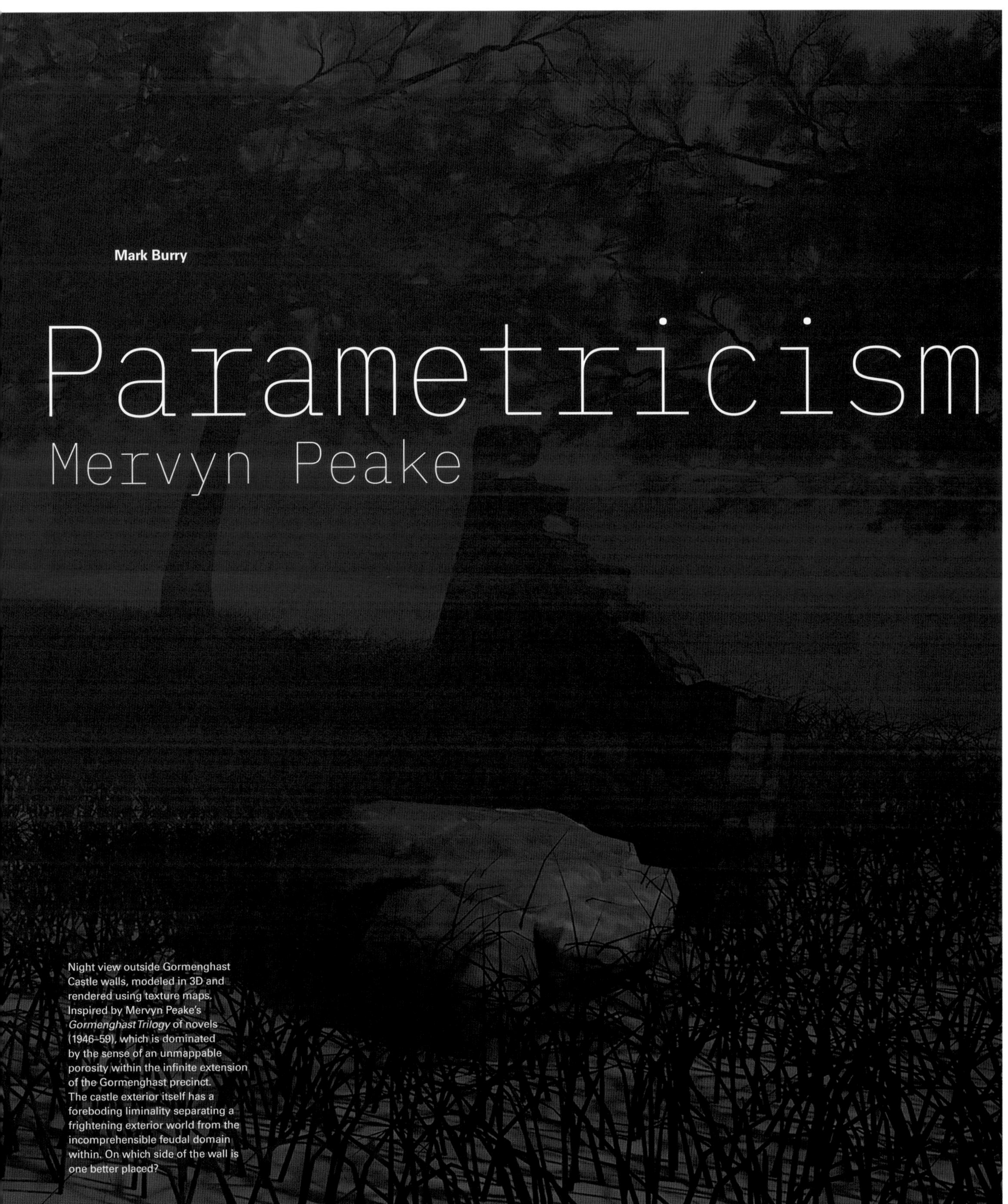

Night view outside Gormenghast Castle walls, modeled in 3D and rendered using texture maps. Inspired by Mervyn Peake's *Gormenghast Trilogy* of novels (1946–59), which is dominated by the sense of an unmappable porosity within the infinite extension of the Gormenghast precinct. The castle exterior itself has a foreboding liminality separating a frightening exterior world from the incomprehensible feudal domain within. On which side of the wall is one better placed?

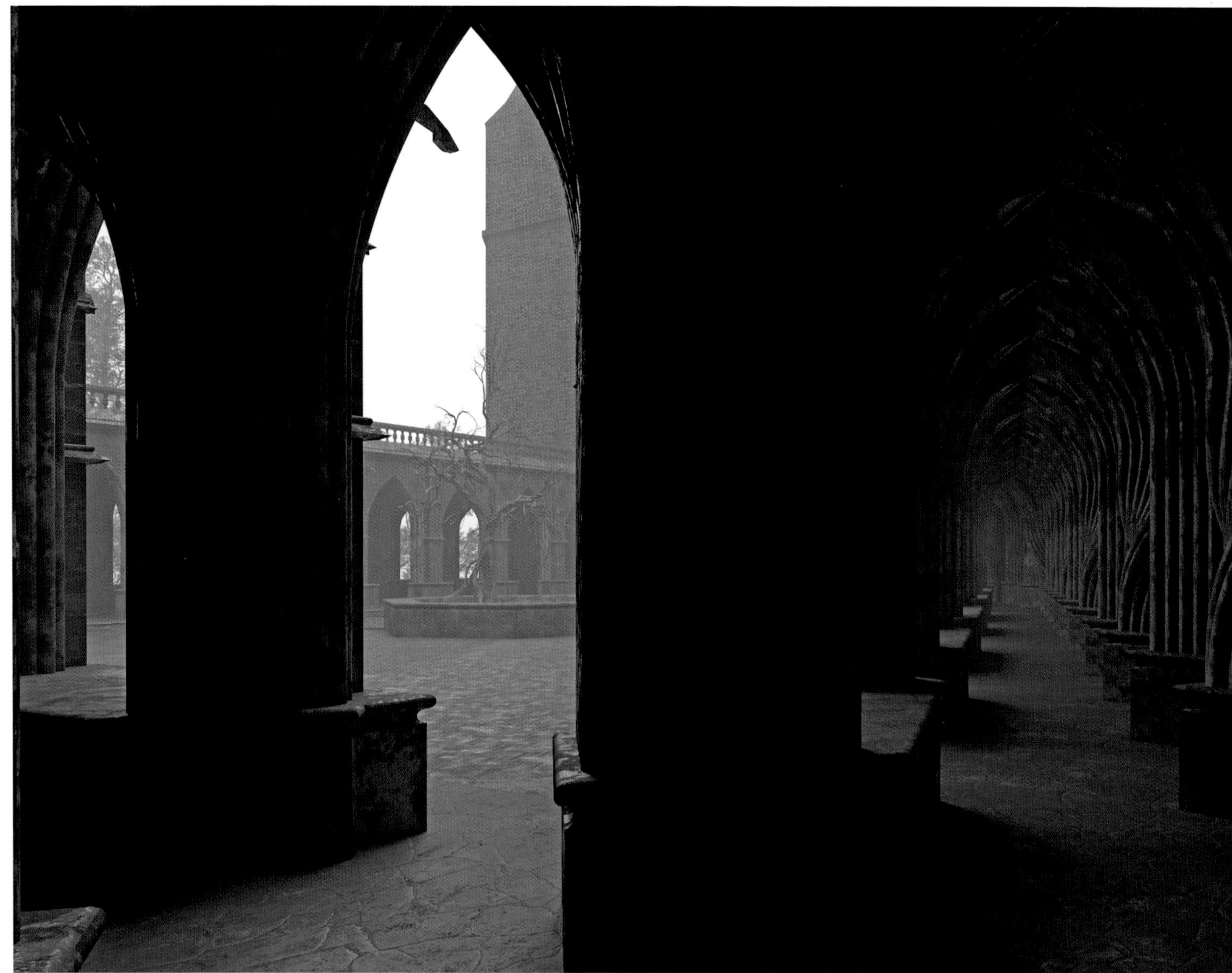

> The shelves that still stood were wrinkled charcoal, and the books were standing side by side upon them, black, grey, and ash white, the corpses of thought. In the centre of the room the discoloured marble table still stood among a heap of charred timber and ashes, and upon the table was the skeleton of Sourdust.
> — Mervyn Peake, *Titus Groan* (vol. 1 of *The Gormenghast Trilogy*), 1946[1]

The aim of the Parametric Hermeneutics investigation (2018–21) was to build parametric digital models as flexible versions of spaces derived from literature. The investigation formed part of a wider Place and Parametricism project (2017–22) involving researchers from Swinburne University of Technology, the University of Melbourne, and the University of Tasmania, all in Australia, to be published as a book of collected essays in 2025.[2]

Age-old questions about place and placemaking were the core challenges for the Parametric Hermeneutics investigation—how might a place be defined parametrically and computationally modeled? While dimensions and physical constraints offer no real challenge, the qualities of a place, especially those that are intrinsically *felt* more than they can be defined physically, elude ready conversion into computational inputs for a digital model. Given literature's powerful evocation of a sense of place through words, might it assist as a creative proxy?

Mervyn Peake's *Gormenghast Trilogy*, a great 20th-century work of fantasist fiction published in sequence between 1946 and 1959, was selected to test this proposition.[3] The Place and Parametricism project's findings affirm the centrality of human interpretive creativity in architectural design, even as AI continues to reshape the way designers design.

What Makes a Place?

Architects act as critical mediators between defining a space and giving it meaningfulness, seeking to balance the material concerns of form, structure, and function with less tangible qualities such as atmosphere and narrative. A physical expanse becomes a place when it is imbued with identity and resonates emotionally with its visitors. The role of culture, memory, and human interaction in transforming space into place are given

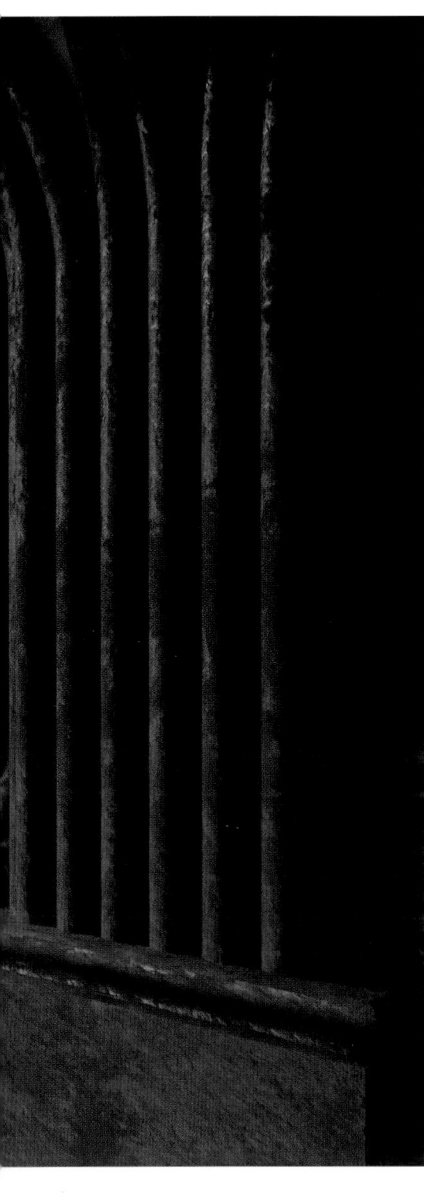

Architect and professorial researcher at Swinburne University of Technology's Smart Cities Research Institute in Melbourne, Australia, Mark Burry has been leading a team examining the textural descriptions of the library and cloisters in Mervin Peake's *Gormenghast* novels. The parametric versions of these spaces were defined by the individual designers' different interpretations of the descriptions of the spaces in the books, resulting in some very atmospheric projections and new architectural backdrops.

theoretical foundations from phenomenology to postmodernism. Mervyn Peake's *Gormenghast Trilogy* is a speculative work of fiction; a unique contribution to 20th-century English literature in the vein of J.R.R. Tolkien and C.S. Lewis. Literary scholars including John Clute, John Grant,[4] and Michael Moorcock[5] regard it as "fantasist" literature due to its richly constructed otherworldly setting and mood, even though it eschews conventional fantasy elements. Other critics debate this classification, viewing it instead as Gothic, Surrealist, or simply genre-defying. Fantasist writing differs from mainstream literary modes, emphasizing constructed otherworlds, mythopoetic symbolism, and narrative frameworks that challenge or blur the boundary between reality and imagination.

Gormenghast Castle, the central setting for the first two novels, is an existential physical entity providing a metaphor for tradition, hierarchy, and decay. Its cloisters, halls, and chambers are extensions of the characters' minds—places of memory, fear, desire, and, in many cases, madness. The novels' focus on ritual and routine highlights an introverted, self-contained world where the past is omnipresent and the future seems an impossibility.

Mark Burry and Mark Taylor with Matija Dolenc, *Gormenghast Cloister*, Parametric Hermeneutics investigation, Place and Parametricism project, Swinburne University of Technology, Melbourne, Australia, 2021

Likewise created using texture maps, this rendering of the cloister captures the sense of Gormenghast's myriad semi-enclosed spaces that offer contemplative pauses within an architectural treatment steeped in ritual and history. Courtyards, cloisters, squares, patios, yards, and quadrangles punctuate Gormenghast Castle's endless mycelium of passages and tunnels.

Creativity as an Emergent Process

Initiating the creative process by facing a blank page often requires a conceptual anchor: the parti pris (the parti). Writer's block is as familiar to designers as it is to the novelists who define the condition. With its capacity to evoke both mood and narrative, literature is a potent analog to architectural design with the power in common to provide a creative spark to initiate something beyond the work in hand—surprise, delight, a sense of doom, for example. The impact of architecture on literature is relatively uncontested: English novelist and playwright Daphne du Maurier's co-option of Venice as moody co-instigator to the tragic narrative of her 1971 short story "Don't Look Now!," for example.[6] The account demonstrates how a real setting, like Venice, can actively inform and shape the literary narrative, saturating it with the city's atmospheric complexity and layered cultural meaning. In contrast, Peake's trilogy is an ideal source for investigating how literature can inspire an architectural response in return. The *Gormenghast Trilogy* creates an invented architectural realm that has inspired architectural imaginations. It is a perfect example of the boundaries between architecture and fiction being blurred. Peake deploys detailed and often borderline surreal imagery to depict the infinite variety of spaces within Gormenghast, from the vast, silent library filled with its ancient tomes to the winding, narrow staircases that seem to lead nowhere.

The Place and Parametricism project homed in on the library in Gormenghast. The way Lord Sepulchrave, 76th Earl of Gormenghast cherishes it symbolizes the weight of tradition and the burden of knowledge. Its destruction by fire, a politically motivated act orchestrated by the kitchen-hand usurper Steerpike, represents the unraveling of the old order and the potential loss of wisdom that travels with it. The fire is a turning point in the narrative signaling the beginning of the end for this stagnant, ritual-bound society. The total devastation of the library is a powerful image of loss—not just of books, but of history, memory, and identity. Like the rest of the account, the description of the fire—its lead-up as well as the aftermath—is redolent with Peake's extraordinary gift with language. Dissected analytically, it provides a rich source of qualitative parameters, extracted from the texts as a set of heuristics and converted hermeneutically into computational variables to update the flexible digital model.

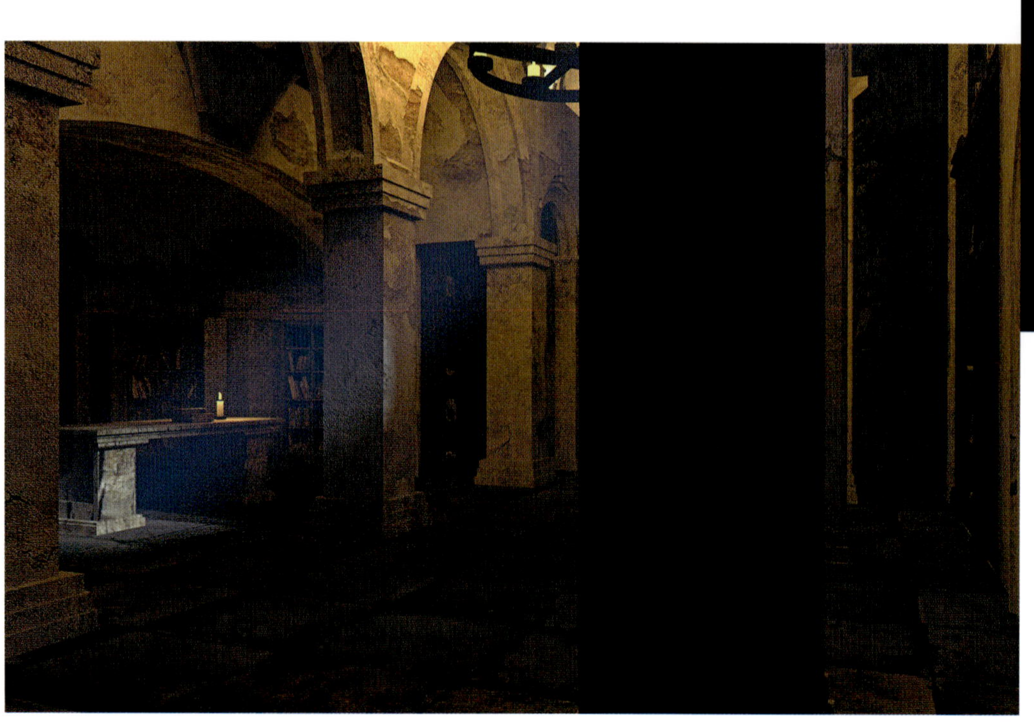

Mark Burry and Mark Taylor with Jerry Lin, *Gormenghast Library Interior*, Parametric Hermeneutics investigation, Place and Parametricism project, Swinburne University of Technology, Melbourne, Australia, 2021

left: Again modeled and rendered using texture maps, the library relies more on the effect of how the interior "feels" through its decrepitude, furnishing, and materiality than spatial configuration and dimension.

Can "Words + Spaces = Places"?

In thinking about parametric hermeneutics or—embracing the receding *zeitgeist*—the hermeneutics of Parametricism, the project questioned whether parametrically variable spatial configurations could yield new interpretive insights for any given literary extract. Parametric hermeneutics implies reliance on description rather than specification: "the space felt extensive" versus "the space measured x, y, z." But if the variable were less specific, such as "dark and foreboding," how would more or less of these qualities be inflected within the flexible digital model?

The project group compiled an extensive library of visual precedents guided by the descriptive force of the trilogy. Using old-school methods and word searches, the core descriptions of the library and all of Gormenghast's exterior spaces including courtyards, cloisters, squares, patios, yards, and quadrangles were extracted as parametric prompts.

Mark Burry and Mark Taylor with Hsin Yeh and Kenneth Wu, *Gormenghast Library Interior*, Parametric Hermeneutics investigation, Place and Parametricism project, Swinburne University of Technology, Melbourne, Australia, 2021

The sense of place envisaged mid-afternoon from Peake's text also relies more immediately on the effect of light and its play on the interior surfaces, which register more immediately than does the library's spatiality.

Mark Burry and Mark Taylor with Matija Dolenc, *Gormenghast Library Interior*, Parametric Hermeneutics investigation, Place and Parametricism project, Swinburne University of Technology, Melbourne, Australia, 2021

below: Games and film industry software give the designer far greater opportunity than architectural software provides for creating atmospheric effects to reinforce a strong sense of place.

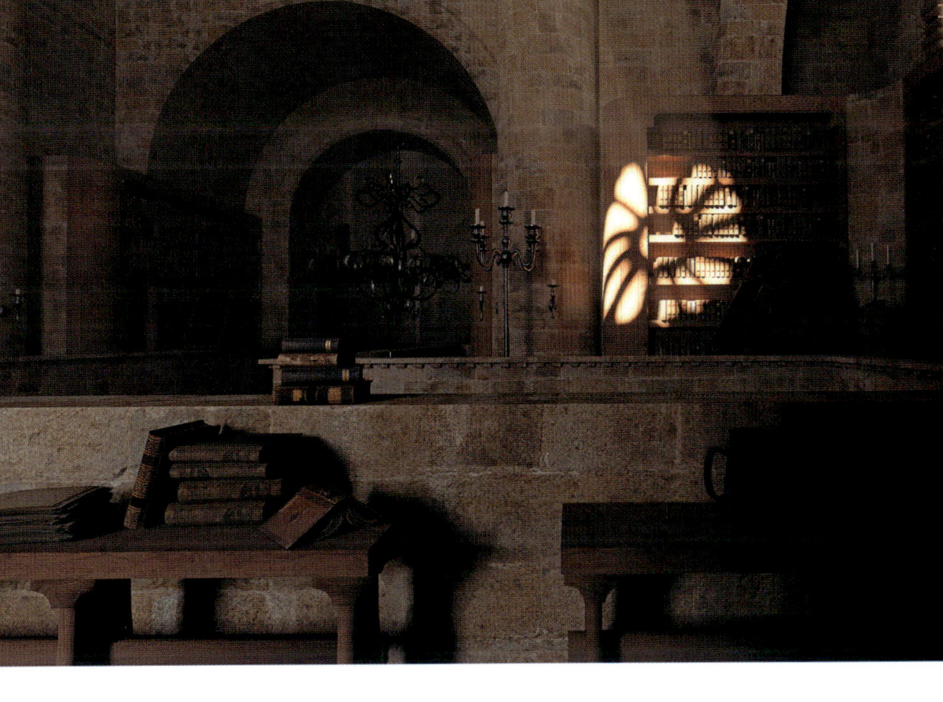

The project questioned whether parametrically variable spatial configurations could yield new interpretive insights for any given literary extract

The trilogy benefits significantly from its ambiguity. It avoids historical specificity or geographical reference and context, and Peake invites his readers to project their own interpretations onto the places featured in the castle's description. This ambiguity provides opportunities for individual creative interpretation, while it challenges the parametric modeler to consider what to extract from the novels that remains faithful to the spirit of the text yet still works architecturally. The insights drawn from the literary samples are the "heuristics" that drive the creative architectural response to the text. Possibilities can be presumed that might yield revised relationships between flexible spatial definitions and placemaking, propositions that are fundamentally different for each reader given their diverse worldviews and prior experience.

As three of the project team members went on to create independently digitally modeled interpretations of the library and associated courtyard, the trilogy proved to be an inspiring parti pris with which to confront the proverbial blank page. Drawing from the same text, each designer produced a unique version of the library and cloister that were similar in some ways but different in others.

The parametric reactivity between text and model offers bidirectionality within the design decision workflow. Selected texts influence the interpretation of spaces as places with different layers of meaning for each visitor, while the parametrically elevated places reveal subtleties of the text otherwise trapped between the lines of the writing. The resulting hermeneutics keep the setting from being easily placed within a specific time or location. This was never going to be an easy task. As noted by China Miéville in his 2011 introduction to the *Illustrated Gormenghast Trilogy*: "Our minds are perpetual hermeneutic engines, and they do not stop attempting to decode, but their gears cannot get traction."[7]

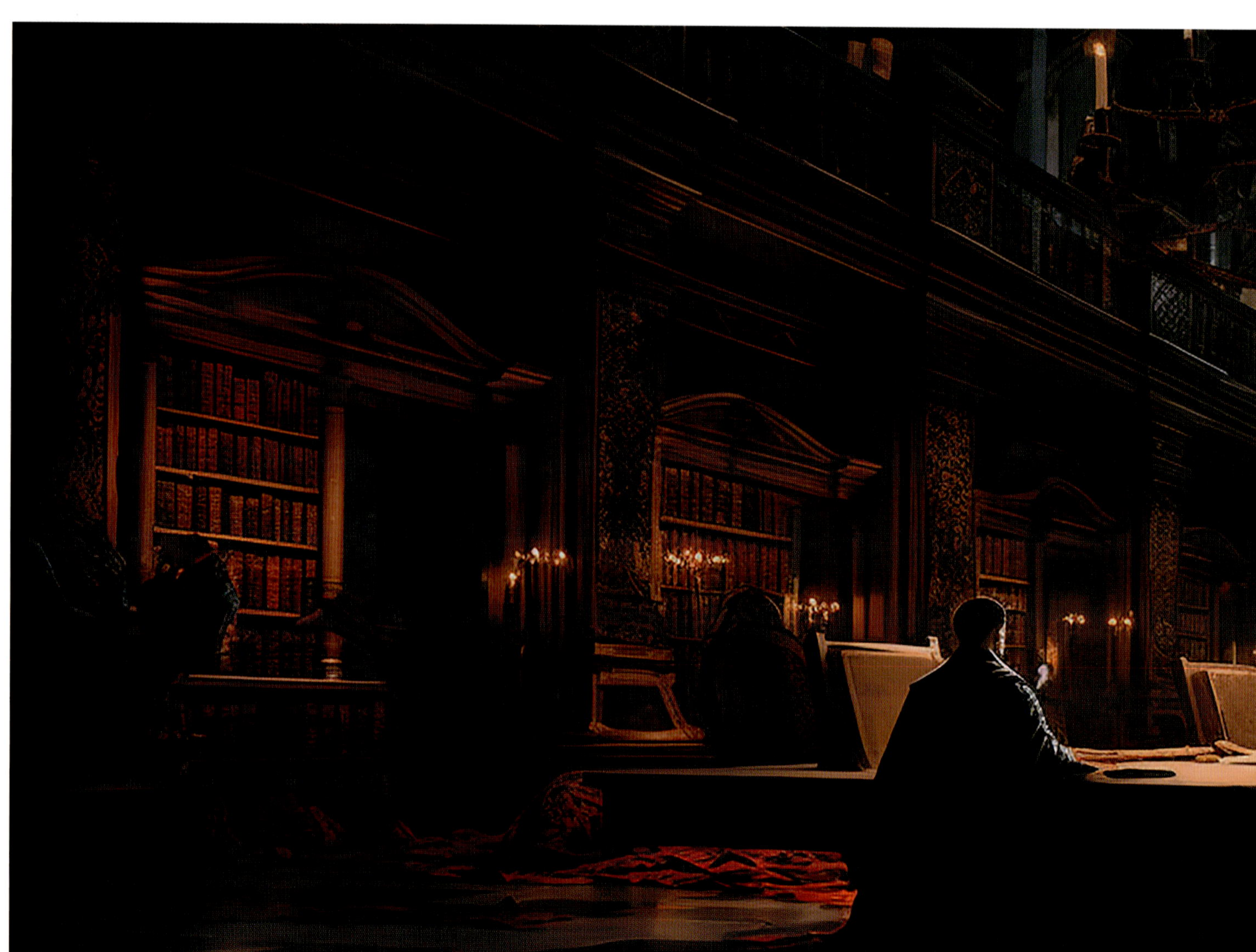

The Place and Parametricism project's research trajectory unexpectedly transformed through computational overreach and the arrival of accessible AI tools. The resulting models were simply too big for parametric reconfiguration. As the project matured, the group concluded that atmosphere, more than dimensions, was the key driver for emotional engagement. While doubling the library ceiling to test accentuated verticality was worth appraisal, critical assessment of this void required each complementary feature to "know what to do" in response to rescaling. Ultimately, to meet the project's ambitions, innumerable constraints, complex rule sets, and sophisticated algorithms would be needed to handle all this. Parametricism, which in this context can be characterized as "designing the design," is a potential can of worms that might be best left firmly closed: such flexibility within the project risked going beyond the original remit to work with the text; reading between the lines was not a license to go beyond them.

Other computational designers who model effect in situations where material actuality and spatial accuracy are not required were investigated, such as the film and games industry. "Imagery" rather than "actuality" spelt out the difference. By diverting to games software with vast digital libraries of digital effects, it was found that different atmospheres within the same explicit digital 3D space would emerge by applying different effects. Reflecting on this, it was realized that testing the narrative effects of digitally parametrizing places had been arrived at via a different route: shifts in effects were easier to achieve than physically altering volume and proportions. Parametrically shifting the sunlight pouring through the library window—from the yellow-orange brilliance of a summer's setting sun to the same scene being illuminated with midwinter frigidity from weak sunlight emanating at a lower angle—produced profound atmospheric changes without any spatial dimension being altered.

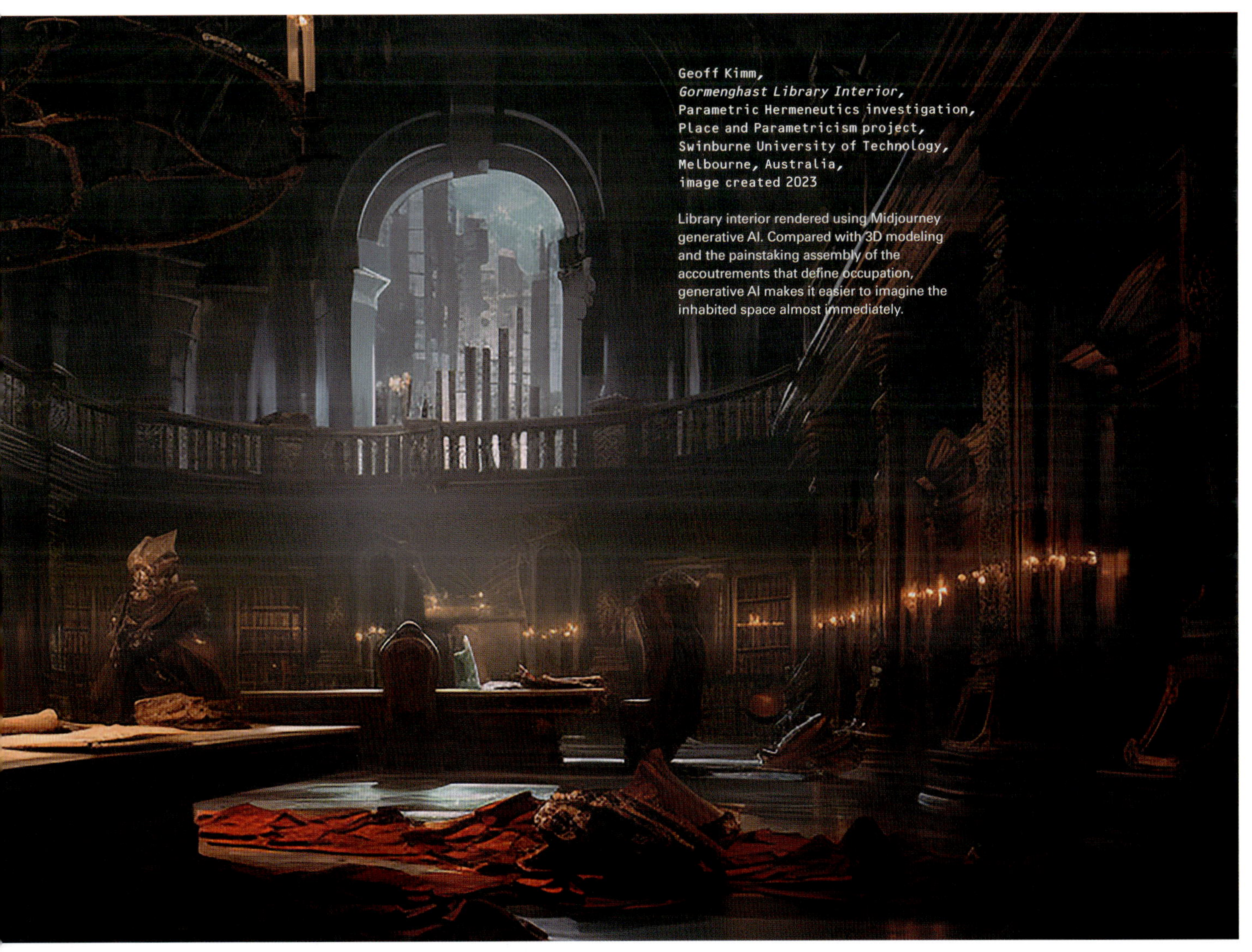

Geoff Kimm,
Gormenghast Library Interior,
Parametric Hermeneutics investigation,
Place and Parametricism project,
Swinburne University of Technology,
Melbourne, Australia,
image created 2023

Library interior rendered using Midjourney generative AI. Compared with 3D modeling and the painstaking assembly of the accoutrements that define occupation, generative AI makes it easier to imagine the inhabited space almost immediately.

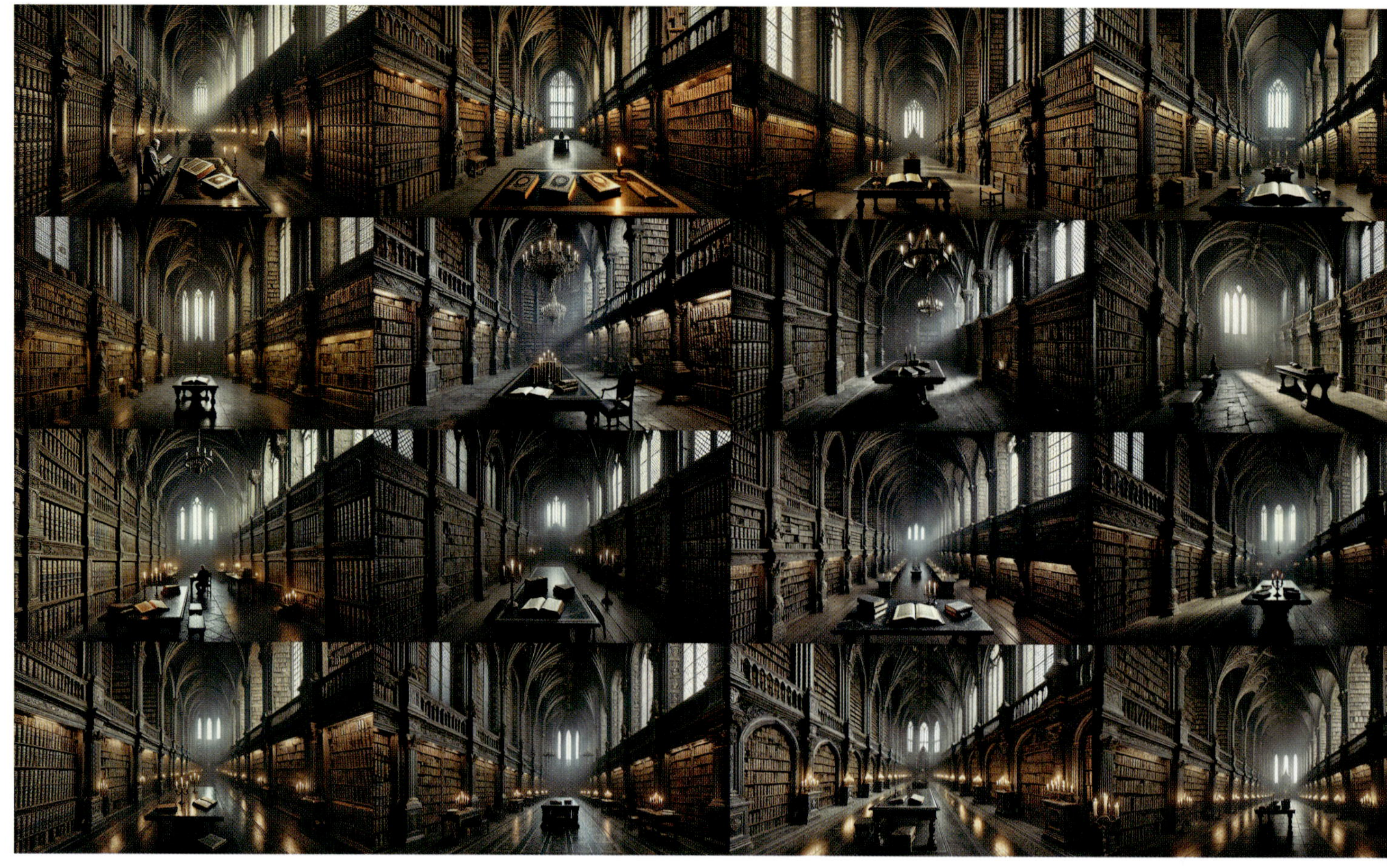

Mark Burry,
Gormenghast Library Interior,
Parametric Hermeneutics investigation, Place and Parametricism project,
Swinburne University of Technology,
Melbourne, Australia,
image created 2024

above: The library interior rendered, using fully licensed DALL-E software, as a matrix of generative AI regurgitations. No matter how patient the coaxing, if the AI engine decides that the Gormenghast library needs lateral windows and electric shelf lighting, it will be given them.

Mark Burry,
Gormenghast Library Interior,
Parametric Hermeneutics investigation, Place and Parametricism project,
Swinburne University of Technology,
Melbourne, Australia,
image created 2024

opposite: The library interior "photo-realistically" rendered using fully licensed openart.ai generative software. Again, regardless of which tool is being used, features such as the windows along the side keep being reintroduced despite explicit instructions not to do so.

Generative AI—Quo Vadis?

The *Gormenghast Trilogy* was an excellent parti pris. Confronting the blank page gave the designers license to pore over thousands of images of castles, palace quarters, monastic libraries, courtyards, and cloisters; a rich training set to help carry Peake's prose toward a spatialized interpretation. Accessible AI landed just after the project concluded. One AI tool composed a brief from the 2,811-word chapter "The Library," from which other generative AI tools spawned impressions of what the library might have looked like. Unique but similar versions appear in seconds, compared to the project's three-year foray into analog and digitally modeled interpretations. But just as Peake would have been astonished by today's technology, unimaginable in his time, it is impossible to imagine what a reader in 50 years' time will make of the current period of technical transition. Society's problem today is not knowing what we are transitioning from and having no clear sense of where we will be landing. It may buoy the reader

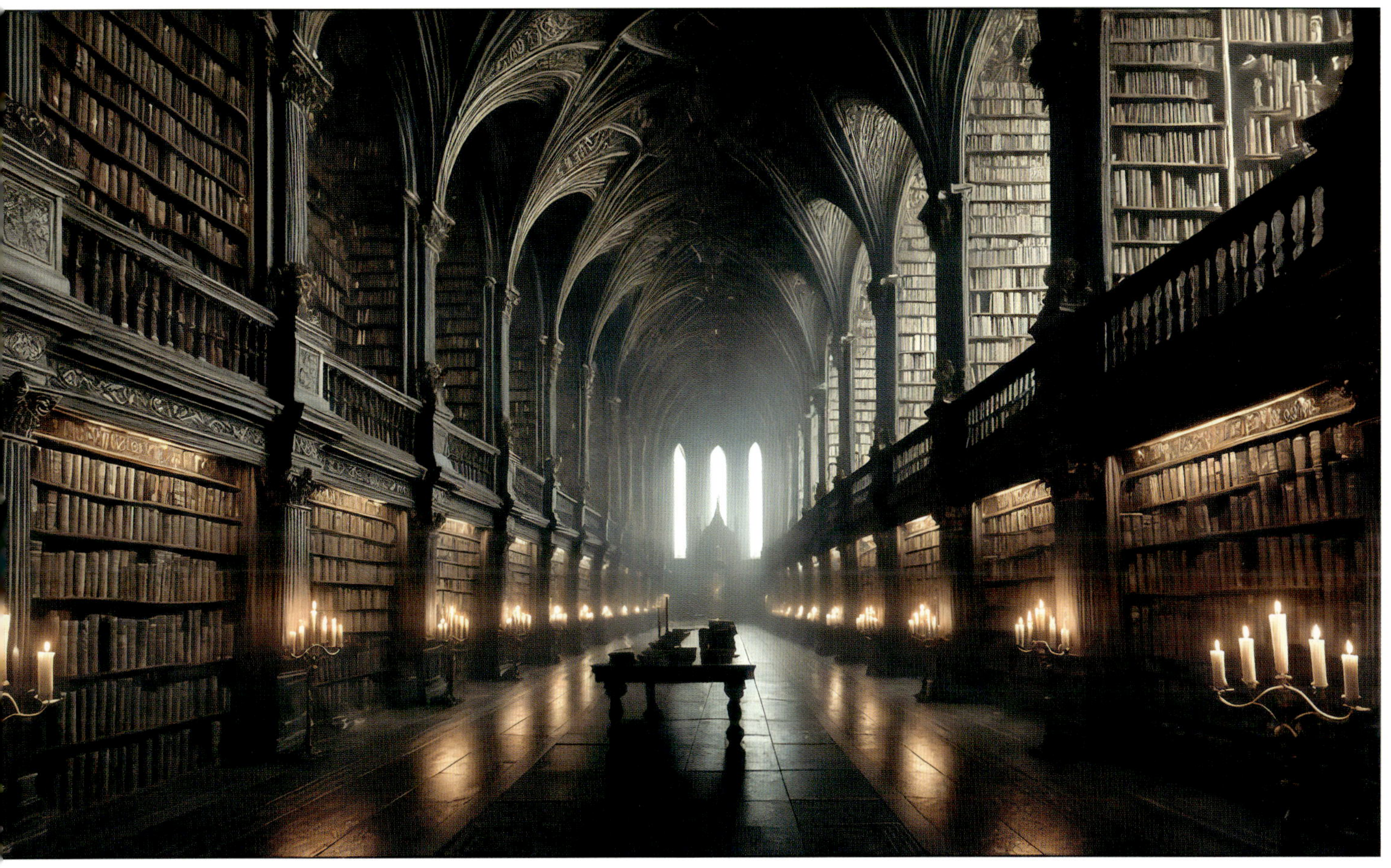

to know that both the project team and the AI software worked from a similar parti pris: training data comprising a vast set of precedents to guide the imagination.

In contrast to AI's agility, the project took the team far deeper than the AI equivalent as they grappled with the tectonic, the material, and the spatial actuality of the novels' many places. All the AI could give in return to the prompts were impressive (for their speed) effects. Peake's description of the remnants of the library's incinerated books, the tidy piles of ashes, as "corpses of thought" ultimately eluded ready definition by the project team as parametric variables for design computation. The evocation in just three words of the burnt-out library as a meaningful place ruined by pure wickedness remains a uniquely human capability, for the time being at least.[8]

Notes

1. Mervyn Peake, *The Illustrated Gormenghast Trilogy*, Kindle Edition, Vintage Digital, 2011, p. 231.
2. Mark Burry, Gini Lee, Jeff Malpas, Stanislav Roudavski, and Mark Taylor (eds), *Place and Parametricism: Critical, Archival and Digital Approaches to Contemporary Design*, Bloomsbury Visual Arts (London), 2025.
3. Peake, *The Illustrated Gormenghast Trilogy*, comprising: *Titus Groan* (first published 1946), *Gormenghast* (1950), and *Titus Alone* (1959).
4. See John Clute and John Grant (eds), *The Encyclopedia of Fantasy*, Orbit Books (London), 1997.
5. See Michael Moorcock, "Preface," in Maeve Gilmore, *A World Away: A Memoir of Mervyn Peake*, Gollancz (London), 1970.
6. See Daphne du Maurier's short story "Don't Look Now" in *Not After Midnight, and other Stories*, Gollancz (London), 1971, pp. 7–58, and Nicolas Roeg's 1973 film adaptation.
7. Peake, *The Illustrated Gormenghast Trilogy*, p. 2.
8. The Place and Parametricism project was generously supported by the Australian Research Council (ARC) from 2018 to 2021.

Until You Realize (It's Just a Story)

Ordinary Architecture,
The Grocer's Order,
"Origins" exhibition,
Royal Academy of Arts,
London,
2016

The exhibition was a series of installations forming a five-part architectural treatise: "Construction," "Space," "Shelter," "Decoration," and "Precedent." *The Grocer's Order* installation was part of the "Precedent" section and offered a contemporary reinterpretation of the origins of the Corinthian capital.

Charles Holland

Fiction and Myth in Architecture

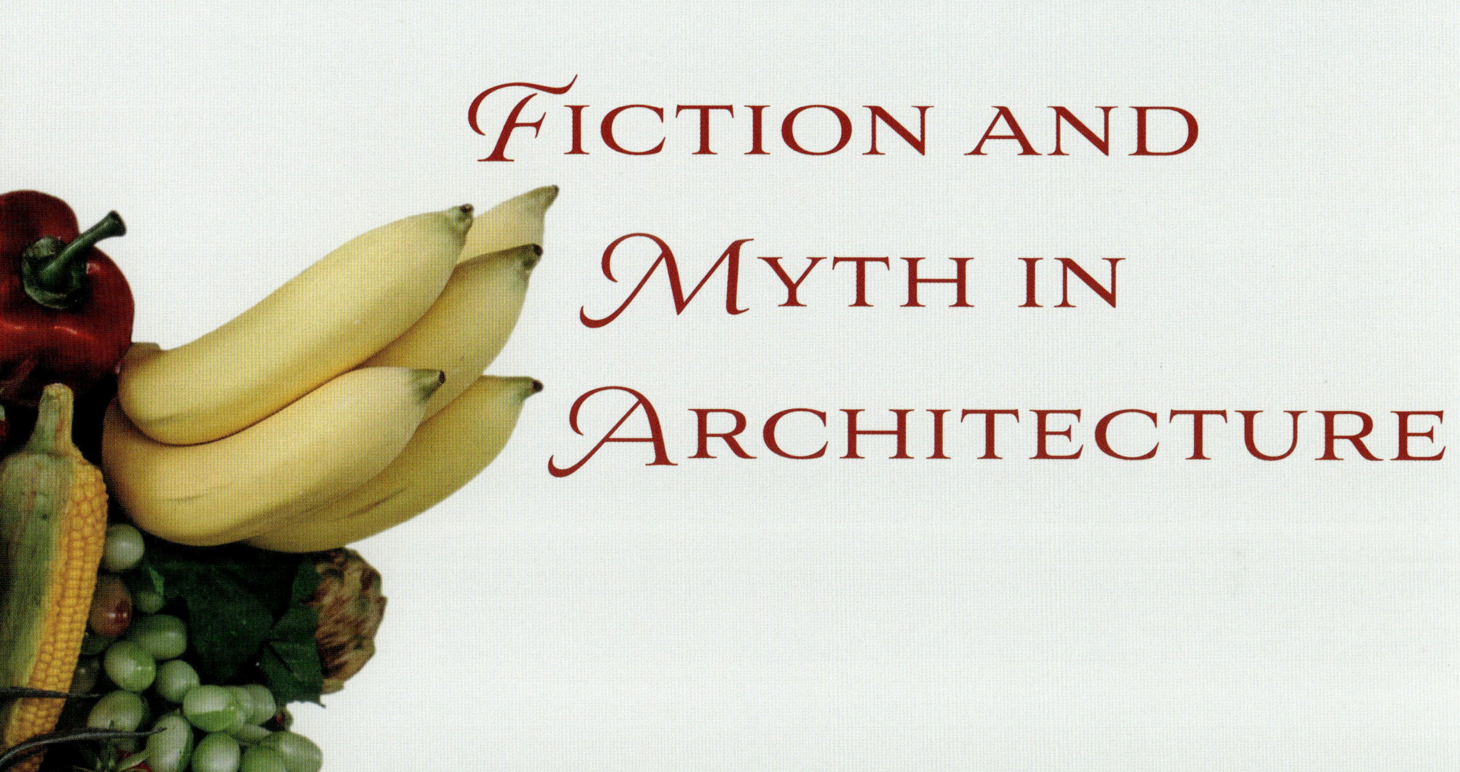

Storytelling and narrative abound in the making, drawing, and staging of architecture at any scale and within its constituent parts. Charles Holland, principal of **Charles Holland** Architects and Professor of Architecture at the University for the Creative Arts in Canterbury, takes us through two of the practice's exhibition designs, at London's Royal Academy of Arts and Royal Institute of British Architects, explaining their stories and how such narratives propelled the work forward.

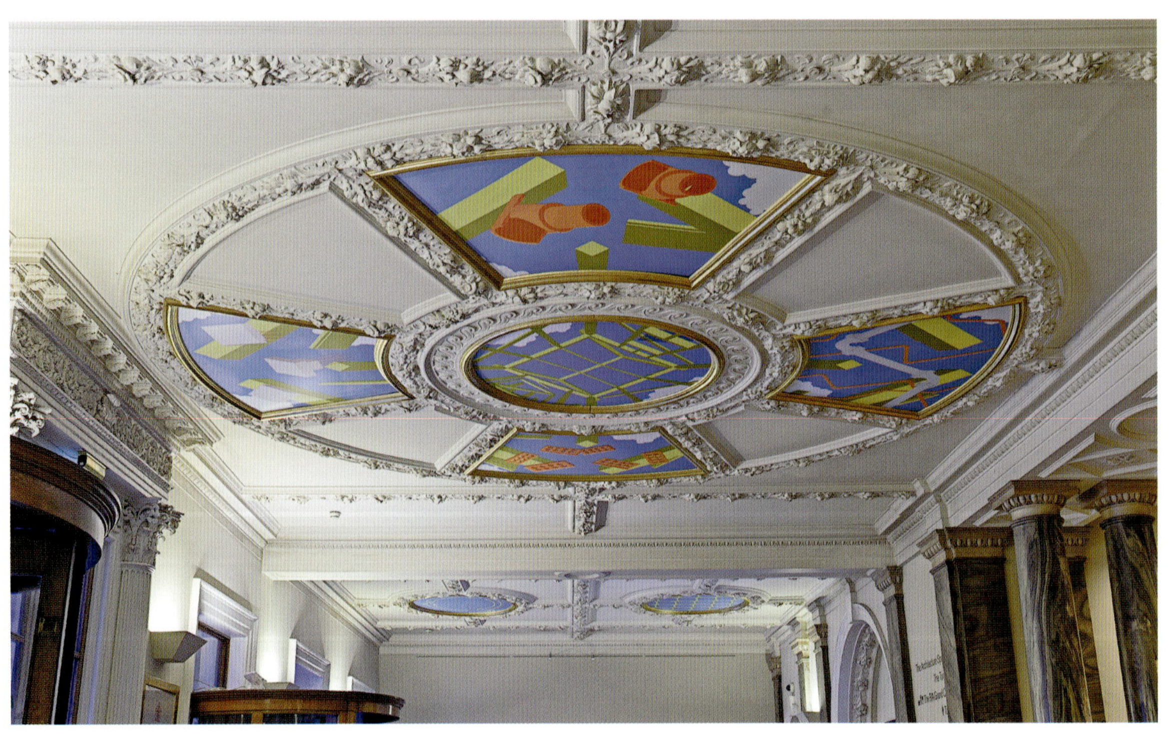

Ordinary Architecture,
Foundations, Ventilation, Fire Safety, and Plumbing,
"Origins" exhibition,
Royal Academy of Arts,
London,
2016

opposite: "Origins" occupied key spaces, offering an episodic experience starting in the main entrance hall with a series of ceiling paintings exploring contemporary "Construction".

Ordinary Architecture,
Endless I Section,
"Origins" exhibition,
Royal Academy of Arts,
London,
2016

below: The "Space" section occupied the main staircase and included a large wall painting depicting columns within an infinite field, and a physical column placed in a mirror-lined niche.

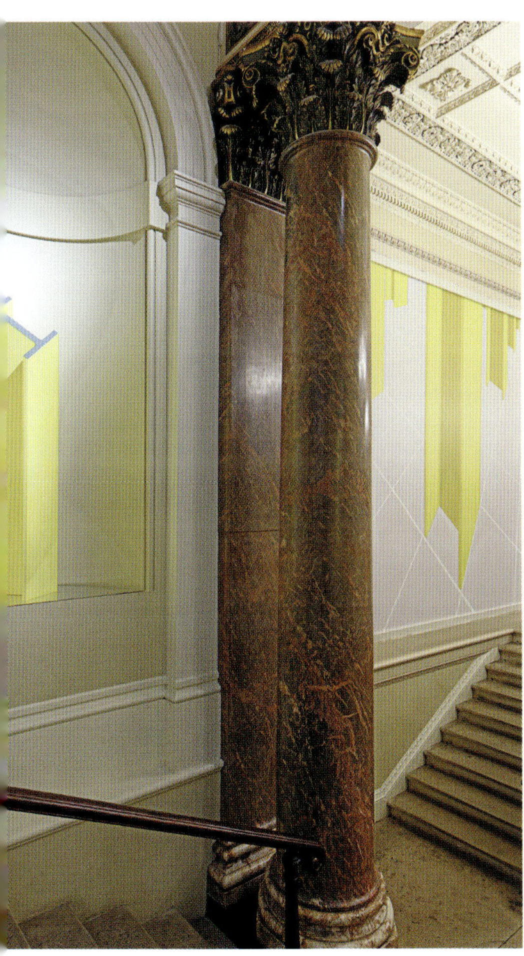

What is the relationship of fiction to architecture and design, both in terms of approach—how we conceptualize design decisions—and language—can architecture express narrative content? As well as informing how we think about design, can narrative also be evident in how it is experienced?

Beyond process, narrative can be said to be part of the way that the organization of spaces is experienced by a building's users. This in turn could be seen as analogous to the sequence of a literary and cinematic plot. Narrative informs aspects of spatial organization through expectation, anticipation, and an unfolding journey. It can also relate to the construction of meanings and associations, particularly through the stories that architects tell themselves about where architecture comes from. Process thus also contains its own narratives.

But buildings are not the same as stories, and fiction—if it exists within architecture—is not necessarily clear or unambiguous in its meaning. Buildings are not always "read" in a particularly conscious way. Instead, they are often experienced in a blur of habit. It is useful here to evoke the French literary theorist Roland Barthes's concept of the "death of the author."[1] If, following Barthes, written texts cannot be reduced to a single meaning intended by their author, then buildings and spaces—with their multiple authors and multiple ways of being used—are even more resistant.

Two exhibitions designed by Ordinary Architecture and Charles Holland Architects (CHA) are good examples of narrative being employed as a way of establishing spatial relationships, as a method for developing content, and as a process of reflection on the myths of architecture itself. Both explore the gap between intended meaning and multiple ways of reading space.

"Origins"

It is language that speaks[2]

The "Origins" exhibition at the Royal Academy of Arts, London, in 2016, explicitly dealt with the narrative basis of architecture. It concerned itself with the persistent "origin myths" that have shaped the discipline, for example that of the "primitive hut." The concept of the primitive hut was developed during the 18th and early 19th centuries by various architectural theorists—most notably Marc-Antoine Laugier in his *Essay on Architecture* (1753)[3]—and grounds classicism within a mythology of natural forms and archetypal construction. Fabricated from trees assembled in a forest, its components are translated directly into Classical elements such as columns, capitals, and porticos.

Burlington House, the Royal Academy's home in London, is a building in which such myths are intrinsically present in the form of paintings, textiles, sculptures, and other artworks, as well as the architecture itself. Within its interior spaces, individual artworks depict stories drawn from a mythology of the origins of Classical art and architecture. For instance, the four ceiling paintings within the entrance—*The Elements of Art* (1778–80) by the neoclassical painter Angelica Kauffman—represent four stages of the artistic process: *Invention*, *Design*, *Composition*, and *Colouring*.

Like other artists of the time. Kauffman drew on Classical iconography to depict the origins of art embedded within antiquity. The inclusion of her work within the fabric of Burlington House—itself a revival of Classical architectural antecedents—helped to establish the Royal Academy's pedagogic role in British art history.

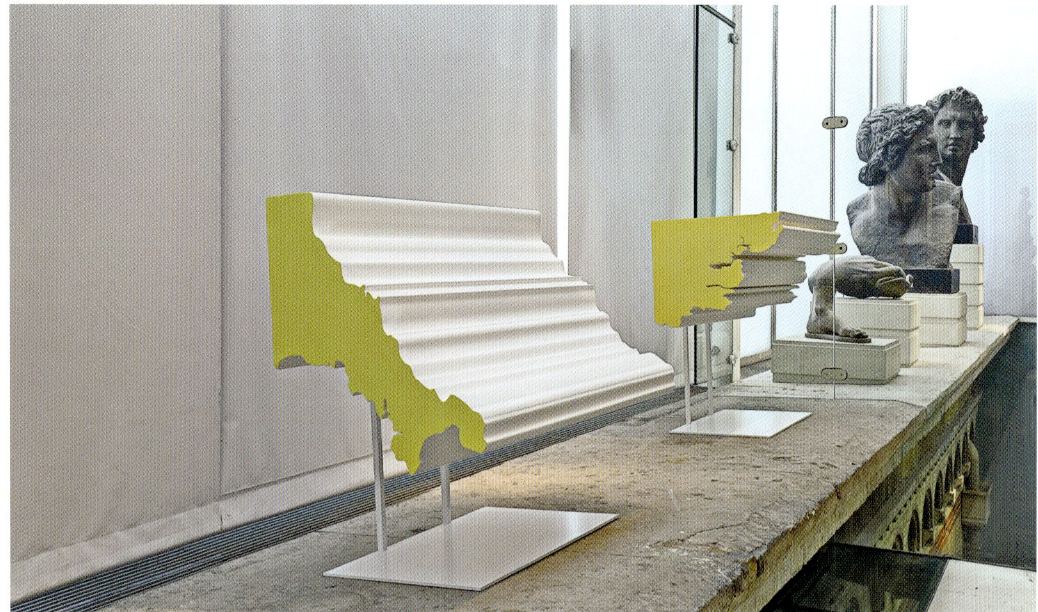

Ordinary Architecture, "Origins" exhibition, Royal Academy of Arts, London, 2016

In the part exploring "Decoration," two architectural cornices based on the profile of specific sections of the UK coastline with biographical associations created a personal origin mythology informing Classical moldings.

"Origins" was a sequential series of installations that inhabited the spaces of the original artworks while they were temporarily removed as part of a wider refurbishment project, in the process offering an alternative series of historical myths. Taking its cue from the original artworks, it was episodic and conceived as a spatial narrative journey that started at the ground-floor entrance and ended in the library on the top floor. It was a form of physical treatise of five chapters—"Construction," "Space," "Shelter," "Decoration," and "Precedent"—which collectively explored the origin myths of contemporary architecture.

"Construction" took the form of a series of ceiling paintings by Ordinary Architecture that replaced those of the British-American artist Benjamin West's *c.* 1779 works depicting the four elements—*Earth*, *Air*, *Fire*, and *Water*—with contemporary equivalents: *Foundations*, *Ventilation*, *Fire Safety*, and *Plumbing*. From here, the exhibition moved to the main staircase in which "Space" was depicted via two giant wall paintings as well as a pair of columns—fabricated as if the result of planometric drafting techniques—placed within a mirrored niche in which they extended into virtual spaces beyond.

"Shelter" revisited the 19th-century German architect Gottfried Semper's concept of cladding—as opposed to structure—as the origin of architecture. Contemporary animal skins (in fact, faux-leather fabric), on which were printed a series of CAD block patterns, were hung from the ceiling. "Decoration" interpreted biographical information—personal origin stories—as architectural profiles and moldings. And finally, "Precedent" raided the Royal Academy's extensive library for the origin myths of Classical architecture enshrined within architectural treatise in order to develop *The Grocer's Order* installation, a high-street version of the origin of the Corinthian capital.

Rendered in a graphically deadpan Pop Art manner, each installation had an impersonal quality while also containing explicit autobiographical information. Drawing on both the abstracting lens of the contemporary diagram and the polemical drawing, personal information was granted the same authority as the architectural treatise. The history presented might have been highly suspect, but it was given authority and legitimacy through the spatial and institutional framing of the Academy.

"Radical Rooms"

> Ordinary things contain the deepest mysteries.[4]

Commissioned by the Royal Institute of British Architects (RIBA), London, in 2022, "Radical Rooms" combined aspects of spatial narrative, fictional worldbuilding, and performance. A collaboration between Charles Holland Architects and artist Di Mainstone, whose work focuses on the body and performance, the exhibition explored ideas of power within the domestic plan, following the late architectural historian Robin Evans's investigations of social relations and historic house layouts in his 1978 essay "Figures, Doors and Passages."[5]

Evans observed that in the typical Palladian villa plan, the house consists of a series of interconnected rooms. There are no corridors or passages and very few doors. Instead, the interiors were laid out on a nine-square grid, with each room connected to at least two others. In such a scenario, Evans argued, the specific functions of each room were left relatively fluid.[6]

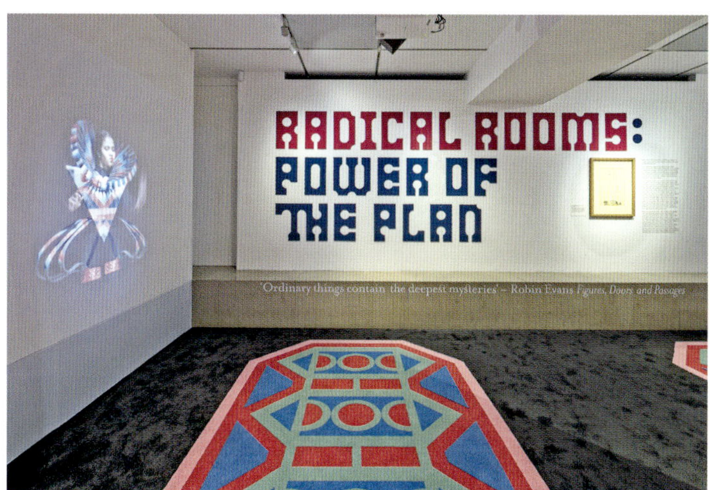

Charles Holland Architects and Di Mainstone, "Radical Rooms" exhibition, Royal Institute of British Architects (RIBA), London, 2022

The exhibition explored an alternative history of domestic design, one in which women played a pivotal role. It combined performance and physical installations with the display of archival material.

Evans compares this with the later evolution of the English country house throughout the 17th, 18th, and 19th centuries,[7] where the insertion of a corridor into Palladio's plan forms allowed for separate circulation systems for family and servants.

"Radical Rooms" presented a history of domestic architecture that escaped from the tyranny and social hierarchy of this corridor. It also focused on the exclusion of women from the emerging profession of architecture. Drawing on a number of houses designed or commissioned by women, it homed in on three in particular: the Elizabethan Hardwick Hall (Chesterfield, Derbyshire, 1590s) commissioned by Bess of Hardwick; A La Ronde (Exmouth, Devon, 1798), a Regency cottage designed and lived in by two female cousins, Jane and Mary Parminter; and the Hopkins House (Hampstead, London, 1976), a high-tech hymn to flexible living designed by architect Patty Hopkins and her husband Michael, also an architect.

The layout of the exhibition was conceived as a Palladian nine-square grid, a sequence of interconnected rooms through which visitors could move in a non-chronological way. The rooms were formed not by walls but by curtains that masked the columns interspersed throughout the L-shaped gallery. As the gallery wasn't square, the grid was partly implied rather than real. What was left was a fragment of a perfect plan which suggested spaces beyond the physical limits of the room.

Drawings, models, and photographs of houses were displayed behind the curtains, which had to be drawn back to reveal a full view of the exhibits. The exhibition layout thus invited a level of physical engagement and interaction through the partial concealment of the objects themselves.

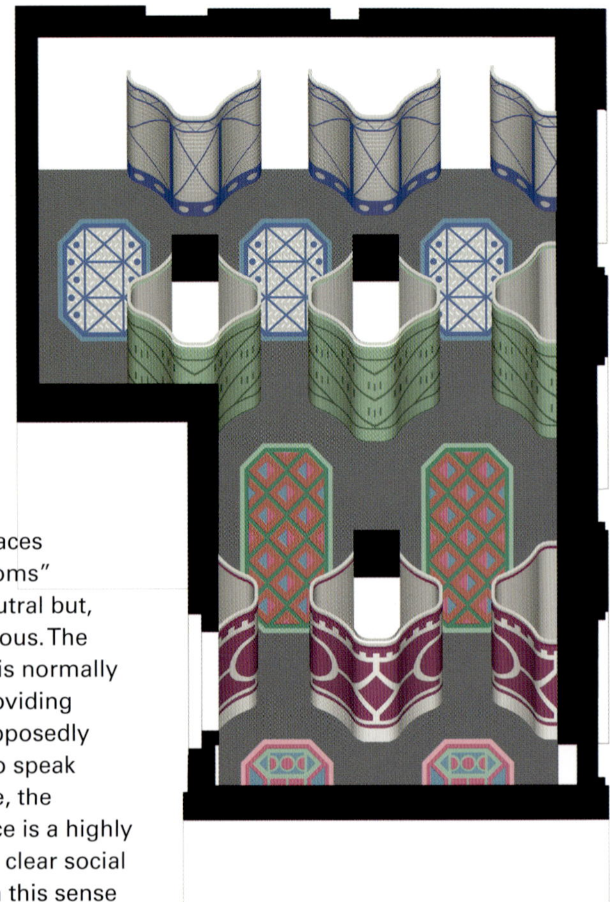

Charles Holland Architects
and Di Mainstone,
"Radical Rooms" exhibition,
Royal Institute of British
Architects (RIBA),
London,
2022

The spatial organization of the exhibition was based on a nine-square grid, which fitted imperfectly into the L-shaped space of RIBA's architecture gallery, suggesting a much larger spatial order beyond the immediate confines of the space.

If the space behind the curtains was full (of information and objects), then the rooms they defined were "empty" in conventional terms. Like the rooms of Palladio's villas, these were spaces waiting to be animated and made sense of by human occupation, in the form of Di Mainstone's projected performances. The four female protagonists—Bess of Hardwick, the Parminter cousins, and Patty Hopkins—appeared as a series of audiovisual performances projected onto the sections of wall between the curtained-off areas. Costumes, soundtracks, and dance became the functions of the spaces, and the gallery became a stage set for human action.

Evans's point in his essay is that the domestic arrangement of space shapes social behavior at the same time that social expectations demand certain kinds of space. The invention of the corridor did not simply enable domestic privacy; it was instrumental in its formation. Spaces are never neutral, but already shaped by patterns of inhabitation. To return to Barthes, the intention of the room is one thing, but our occupation of it is quite another. It is in the slippage between these positions that new forms of behavior are developed and new kinds of architecture emerge.

Similarly, the grid of spaces underpinning "Radical Rooms" was not intended to be neutral but, rather, profoundly ambiguous. The white space of the gallery is normally assumed to be neutral, providing a lack of context which supposedly allows the work within it to speak more clearly. But of course, the contemporary gallery space is a highly codified environment with clear social expectations. Whiteness in this sense is an overwhelming presence.

"Radical Rooms" placed the exhibited work within explicitly contextual settings, using pattern, color, and iconography derived from the exhibited houses as framing devices. "Patty Hopkins" moved through a space in which elements of her house were printed onto diaphanous curtains and carpets. But she also appeared in spaces coded with the Regency decorative scheme of A La Ronde, forming unexpected narrative connections across space and time.

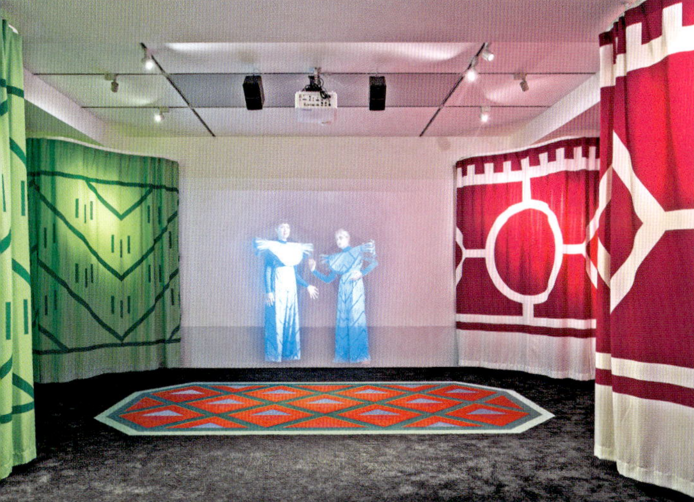

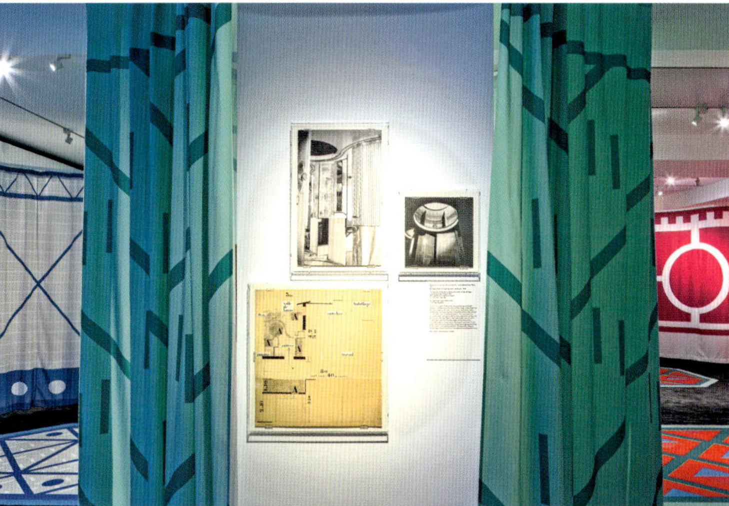

The Swiss architect and writer Bernard Tschumi once claimed that "murder in the street is different from murder in the cathedral,"[8] by which he meant that actions are both independent from and shaped by the spaces in which they occur. Murder is murder, but it takes on different meanings in different places. The "rooms" in "Radical Rooms" were not radical in themselves, but might allow radical things to happen.

True Fiction

The exhibition designs for "Origins" and "Radical Rooms" focused on architectural history, aiming to disturb established narratives and disrupt accepted storylines. In both, "truth" is seen as transient and frequently highly suspect. Less concerned with overturning established truths or even inventing new ones, the exhibitions instead sought to explore the ways in which stories and myths are formed through architecture. Using the actions of performers and of participants, they provided a dynamic interplay of people, plans, and places. Architecture is a stage set. But it is also a character itself, shaping not just the actions but how those actions are subsequently corralled into historical narratives. Instead of a single storyline, or an authoritative version of events, multiple mythologies and a plurality of performances were encouraged with the intention of opening up and once again reinventing the discourse.

Notes

1. Roland Barthes, "Death of the Author" [1967], in *Image Music Text*, tr. Stephen Heath, Fontana (London), 1977, pp. 142–8.
2. Ibid., p. 143.
3. Marc-Antoine Laugier, *Essay on Architecture* [1753], Hennessey + Ingalls (Los Angeles, CA), 1985.
4. Robin Evans, "Figures, Doors and Passages," in *Translations from Drawing to Building and Other Essays*, MIT Press (Cambridge, MA), 1997, p. 56.
5. Ibid., pp. 55–91.
6. Ibid., p. 62.
7. Ibid., pp. 62–91.
8. Bernard Tschumi, *The Manhattan Transcripts*, John Wiley & Sons (London), 1994, p. xx.

above left: The main protagonists of each of the three featured houses from the 17th, 18th and 20th centuries—Hardwick Hall, A La Ronde, and the Hopkins House—appeared as projected performances developed and choreographed by artist Di Mainstone.

above right: Curtains hung from the ceiling suggested a series of implied rooms further defined by patterned areas of carpet. The rooms became stage sets for performance while archival material was displayed behind the curtained-off zones.

Color Fields, Striated Landscapes, and Urban Follies

The Intersection of Architecture and Art

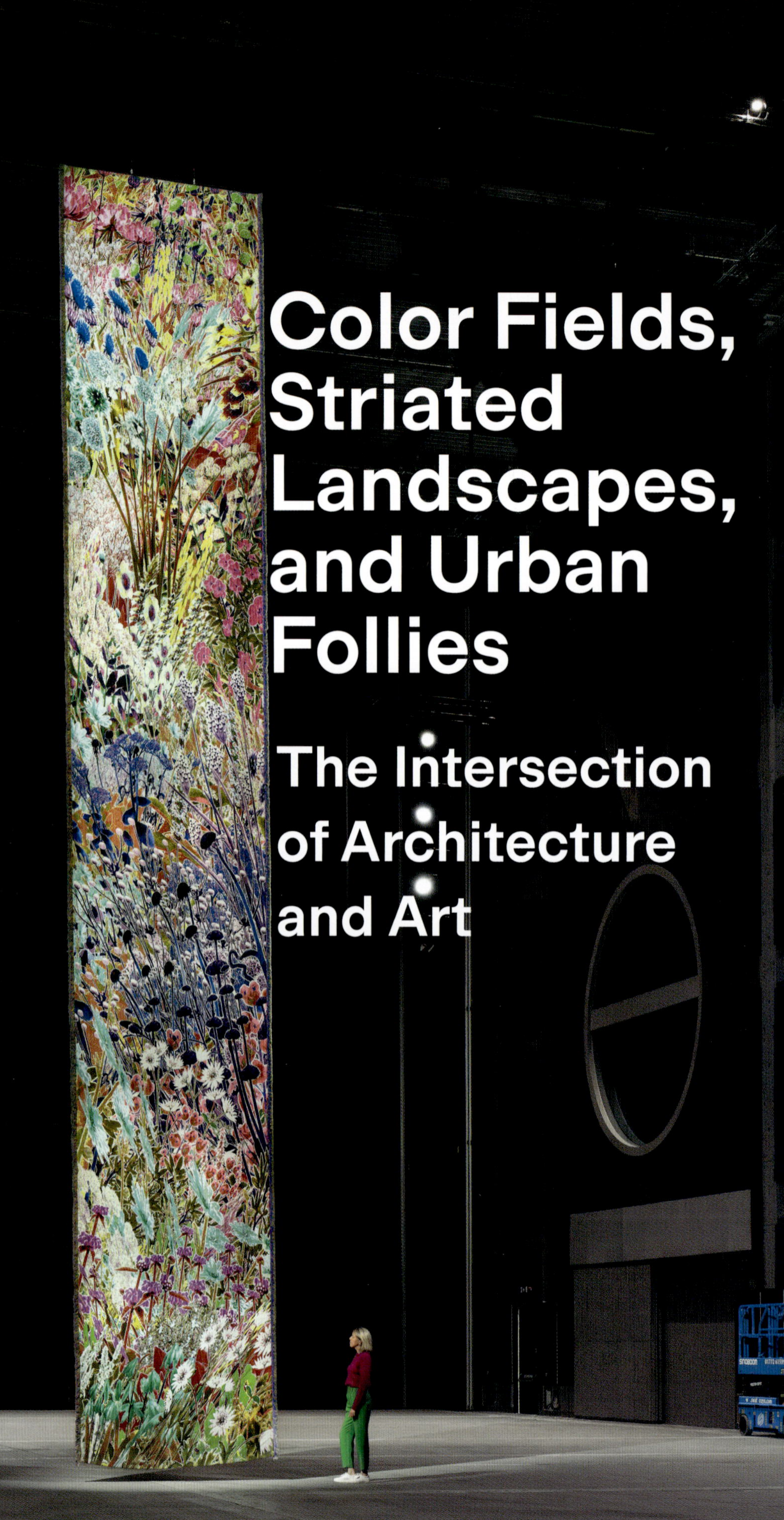

Jessica Reynolds

For all good architects, the combination of art with building is a crucial ingredient in the development of a recognizable aesthetic in their work or a project-by-project originality and sensibility that differs from previous schemes. Jessica Reynolds, a founding partner of vPPR Architects, foregrounds her office's approach, illustrating it at varying scales of design—a workplace, an exhibition, and an urban park, all distinct from each other in content, materiality, and aspirations.

Alexandra Daisy Ginsberg,
Pollinator Pathmaker: Four Epochs of Paradise (Pollinator vision side) for Office Plus,
Birmingham, England,
2024

A 14-meter-long (46-foot) woven double-sided tapestry depicts oversized pollinating flowers, rendering humans to the scale of pollinators. One side captures human vision, the other side pollinator vision. Photographed at Aviva Studios.

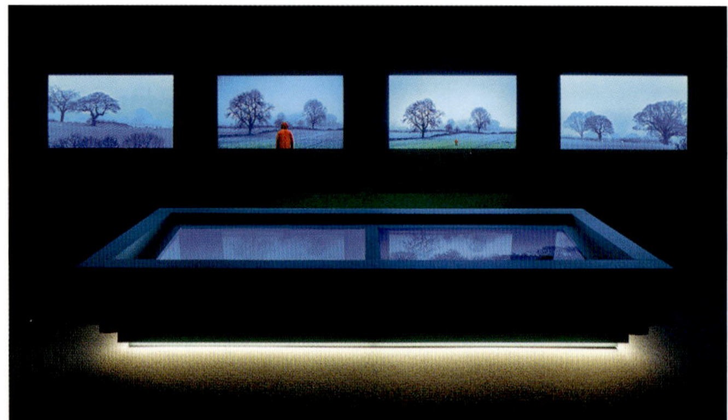

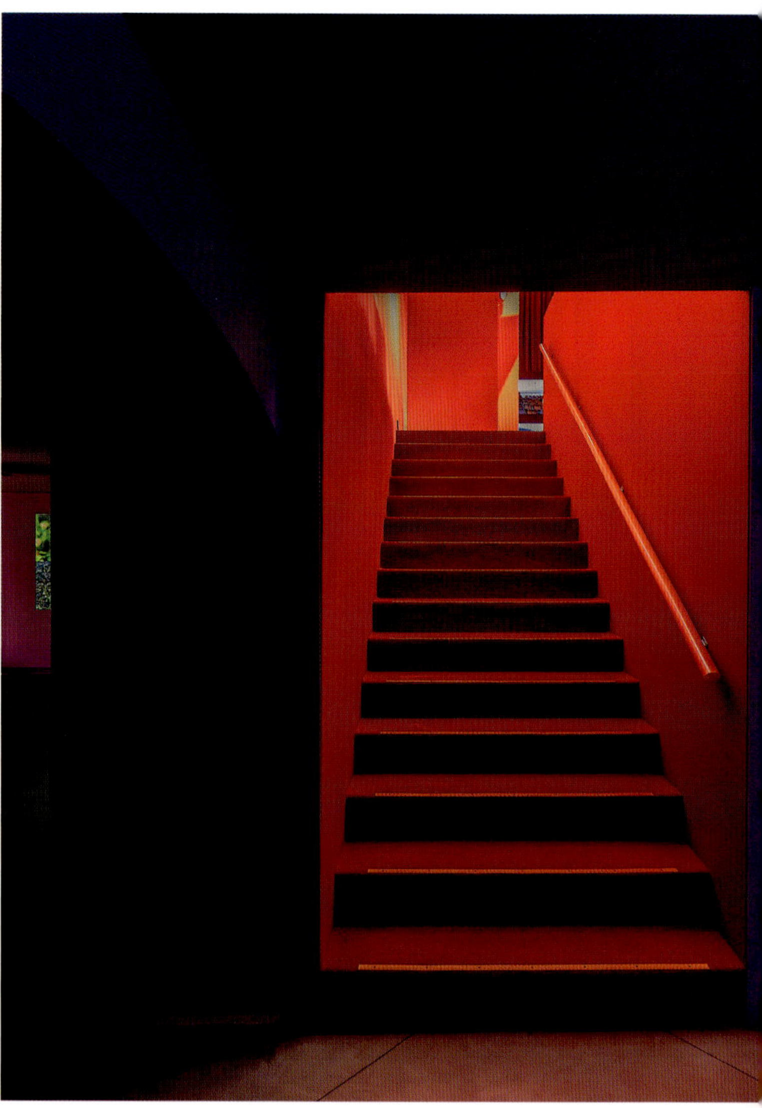

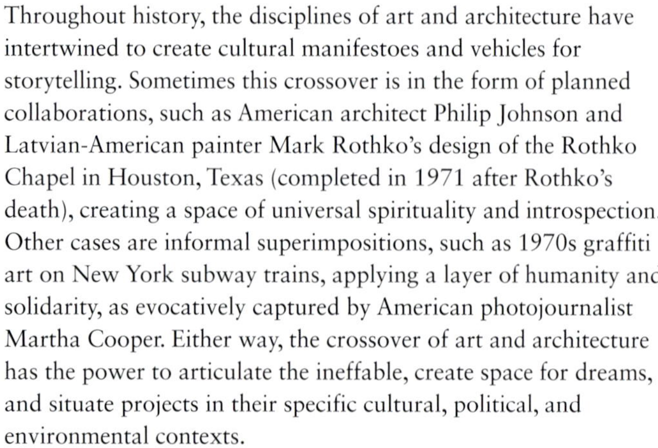

Throughout history, the disciplines of art and architecture have intertwined to create cultural manifestoes and vehicles for storytelling. Sometimes this crossover is in the form of planned collaborations, such as American architect Philip Johnson and Latvian-American painter Mark Rothko's design of the Rothko Chapel in Houston, Texas (completed in 1971 after Rothko's death), creating a space of universal spirituality and introspection. Other cases are informal superimpositions, such as 1970s graffiti art on New York subway trains, applying a layer of humanity and solidarity, as evocatively captured by American photojournalist Martha Cooper. Either way, the crossover of art and architecture has the power to articulate the ineffable, create space for dreams, and situate projects in their specific cultural, political, and environmental contexts.

For vPPR Architects, the intersection of art and architecture is a central focus, fostering a deeply collaborative process where artistic languages are transformed into conceptual frameworks and immersive environments. The practice seeks to combine sculptural spatiality with a sensorial material palette of color, texture, light, and sound, creating inclusive spaces that embody an idea. In some instances, the architecture extends from an artwork; at other times site-specific artworks reinforce the architectural language. Instead of an afterthought, art is a conceptual driver for vPPR from the start. The projects discussed here—an exhibition design, a workplace, and an urban park—demonstrate how artistic collaborations can serve as a catalyst for architectural narratives, transforming spaces into richly layered architectural experiences that communicate complex curatorial themes and provoke critical questions about environments and human experience.

The Elevation of Space

For the British Pavilion at the 60th Venice Art Biennale, in 2024, vPPR collaborated with Ghanaian-British filmmaker Sir John Akomfrah, producer Smoking Dogs Films, curator Tarini Malik, and the British Council to transform the neoclassical building into an immersive journey through diasporic narratives.[1] The exhibition's title, "Listening All Night To The Rain," was inspired by the 11th-century Chinese writer and artist Su Dongpo's poetry, exploring the transitory nature of life during a period of political exile. Its displays consisted of eight sequential multimedia works or "cantos," combining film, sound, and sculptural installations. The films weaved new and archival footage and audio, depicting the stories of migrant communities, with a special emphasis on water—as a reservoir for memory, for its role in migration stories to the UK, and for the impact of rising sea levels on diasporic communities.

The exhibition began by subverting the building's traditional hierarchy. The neoclassical entrance façade was obscured by a suspended triptych of large-format digital screens presenting the first canto and implicitly redirecting visitors to enter at the rear, through the low-ceilinged, back-of-house basement level. This gesture mirrored the exhibition's

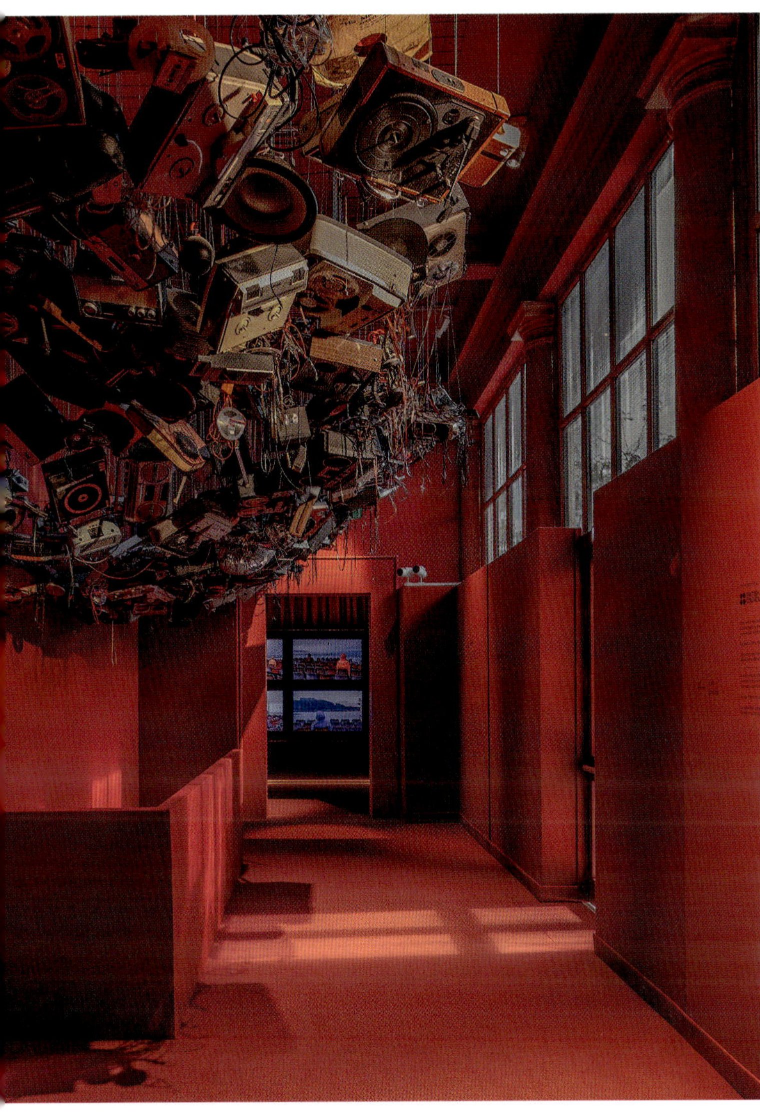

Sir John Akomfrah (artist) and vPPR Architects (exhibition design), "Listening All Night to the Rain" exhibition, British Pavilion, 60th Venice Art Biennale, Italy, 2024

opposite left: The turquoise hues of *Canto VII* and the sculptural encasement recalled a font, alluding to the motif of water, a recurring narrative in the artwork about migration stories to the UK.

opposite right: The immersive colors of each room were inspired by American painter Mark Rothko's canvases. Each room was designed as a complete color field for a specific "canto," framing the next color field at the threshold.

left: In *Canto III*, a cloud-like installation consisting of audio recording devices suspended from the ceiling communicated the significance of the sonic as a political act, set within an immersive red color field.

themes of displacement and marginalization, alluding to journeys of migration. A new stair, installed in a historic opening, invited visitors upstairs, as if making a metaphorical ascent through history, memory, and experiences, circulating in a counter-sequence to the original pavilion, and exiting through the back door at upper-ground-floor level.

Building on Akomfrah's resonance with the color theory that Rothko developed in the 1940s and 1950s, which explored color's potential to evoke deep emotional response,[2] each room of the pavilion was conceived as a complete color field, achieved by lining every interior surface in a coordinated color range. Featuring a sequence of chromatically distinct environments, the rooms progressed through carefully chosen hues of purple, red, crimson, violet, blue, turquoise, and green. Each room color was highlighted within the films themselves, as if the rooms were extensions of the artworks. Thresholds between rooms became pivotal moments where the color in one room framed that in the next, creating layered and interlocking views between the cantos.

The exhibition's materiality was intrinsically linked to its sonic themes. All surfaces were designed to perform acoustically, creating a soundscape that supported Akomfrah's exploration of acoustemology—the study of how sound shapes knowledge—and the concept of listening as a political act. Foregrounding a powerful soundtrack combining audio from protests to club culture, the material palette included acoustic carpeting, fabric backdrops, generous soft seating, and felt structures—the latter made from recycled ocean-sourced plastic bottles, connecting to the exhibition's recurring water motif while addressing environmental concerns. In *Canto III*, a cloud-like formation of audio-recording devices was suspended from the ceiling, creating a dramatic ascent from the basement. In this way, the pavilion's monumental neoclassical architecture was softened by rich sensorial linings communicating the importance of the sonic.

Seeking to create an atmosphere of sacred reflection, as well as referencing the role religion played in migration stories, vPPR designed a series of secular "altarpieces" to display the multi-channel films in each canto. The dramatic lighting at the base of each altar elevated the digital displays and created a spiritual atmosphere. The monolithic forms were symmetrical and sculptural, enhancing the sense of solemnity, significance, and reverence. For *Canto VII*, in a turquoise color field, the display structure included the form of a font where the monitors were displayed horizontally, referencing the reflections and passages of water, while the seating recalled the language of pews.

Through this powerful art and architecture collaboration, the artistic narratives around diasporic journeys and the weight of history that were portrayed in each canto seeped into the spatial and material embodiment of each room. The division between 2D and 3D was dissolved. By interweaving counter-sequences, immersive color, acoustic textures, and religious typologies, vPPR sought to create all-encompassing environments that both served and extended Akomfrah's vision.

(Left) David Cox,
Boys Fishing,
1859,
and
(right) vPPR Architects,
Diagram for Office Plus,
Birmingham, England,
2024

David Cox's painting *Boys Fishing* invited a reflection on the past and future landscapes of the site. The painting was abstracted into layers of nature that became distinct floors in a workplace, connected by a staircase.

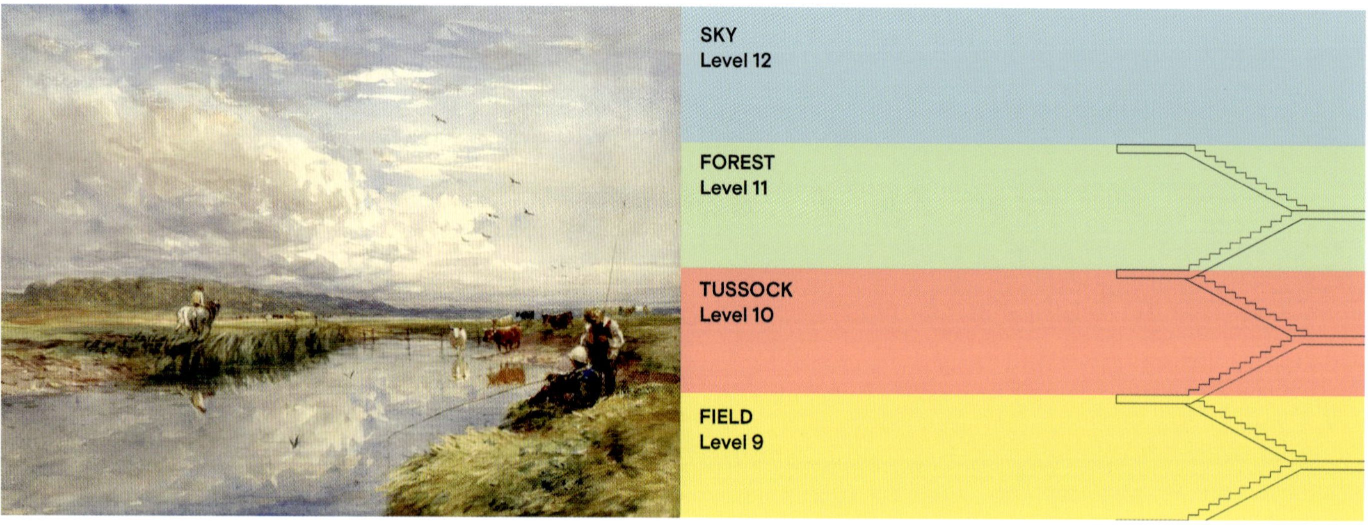

An Ecological Connection

In another project, vPPR's interior design for a leading investment bank, Office Plus, in Birmingham, England, completed in 2024, further demonstrates how art can serve as both a conceptual framework and a spatial catalyst. Transforming the top four floors of a tower into a layered, immersive ecological environment, it challenges users to question their relationship to the natural world through the overlay of art and architecture. Programmatically, Office Plus is open-ended: it is a workplace plus a social hub, a garden, an event venue, a wellness space, and more. Formally, Office Plus uses the Plus motif as a spatial device that is multi-directional and inclusive.

The design's narrative begins with 19th-century English landscape painter David Cox's painting *Boys Fishing* (1859). Cox was one of the most important members of the Birmingham School of landscape artists and an early precursor of Impressionism. Rather than hanging the artwork on a wall, vPPR abstracted the painting's pastoral landscape into four vertically stacked layers of nature—Field, Tussock, Forest, and Sky—each corresponding to a floor of the office. Within this stratification, occupants inhabit different layers of a painted landscape, with each level featuring its own distinctive name, color palette, planting scheme, and environmental character. vPPR connected these layered landscapes by a new internal staircase linking all floors to a terrace.

The architectural interpretation extended beyond simple color coding. A series of pixelated curtains directly sampled from scaled-up details of the artwork create translucent spatial divisions that blur the boundaries between work zones while maintaining visual connectivity. These dynamic, layered elements not only reference local landscape heritage but also provide visual softness and practical acoustic control, demonstrating how artistic inspiration can yield functional design solutions. Reducing the need for signage, color is drawn into key elements such as collaboration carpets, internal columns, amenity lighting, and internal planting, and on the sky floor the soffit is always blue.

vPPR invited contemporary artists Alexandra Daisy Ginsberg and Michael Wang to bring alternative perspectives on the urgency of the climate crisis to the project. Ginsberg's two interconnected artworks, *Pollinator Pathmaker Paradise Edition* and *Pollinator Pathmaker: Four Epochs of Paradise* (both 2024), create a dialogue between interior and exterior, real and represented nature. The first artwork is a living sculpture of pollinating plants on the 12th-floor terrace; the second is a 14-meter (46-foot) double-sided woven tapestry, placed in the middle of the stairwell, depicting plants through seasonal changes, with pollinator-colored vision on one side and human-colored vision on the other. The plants are oversized to invite humans to feel as if they are the scale of pollinators. Conceptually this pair of artworks forms an ecological connection to all the office floors and the terrace. These interventions bring softness, warmth, and criticality to the space, as well as actively contributing to local biodiversity.

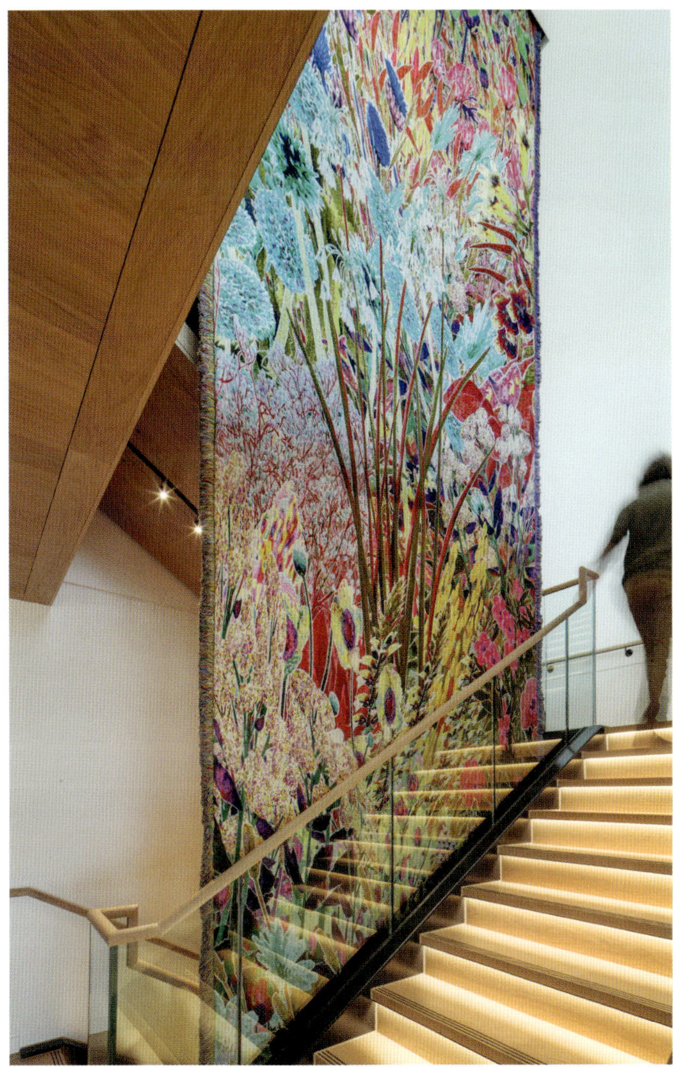

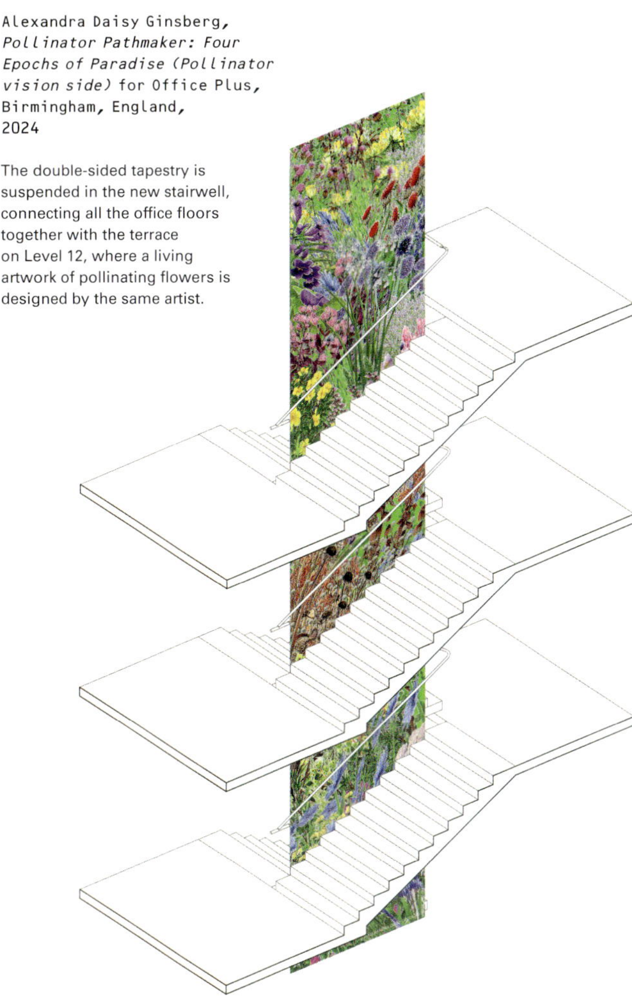

Alexandra Daisy Ginsberg, *Pollinator Pathmaker: Four Epochs of Paradise (Pollinator vision side)* for Office Plus, Birmingham, England, 2024

The double-sided tapestry is suspended in the new stairwell, connecting all the office floors together with the terrace on Level 12, where a living artwork of pollinating flowers is designed by the same artist.

Michael Wang's "Holoflora" series (2024) adds another layer of environmental commentary, using holographic technology—originally invented in nearby Rugby—to resurrect plants that have vanished from Birmingham's landscape. These ghostly botanical apparitions, paired with black-and-white photographs of their last-known locations, serve as powerful reminders of environmental change while connecting the workplace to its regional ecological history. In addition to raising environmental awareness through these interventions, wider environmental strategies in this net-zero office include reuse of landlord lighting and other services, use of 100 percent recycled emulsion paint, and creating two new Environmental Product Declarations, which quantify environmental information about the life cycle of a product.

Having established the overall concept and curated the site-specific artworks, vPPR arranged the workplace according to a "Plus Grid" or a weave, its open-ended geometry enabling multiple perspectives, multiple circulation routes, and potential for multiple reconfigurations. vPPR then designed a series of modular elements for the Plus Grid. These included the "Plus Desk" designed in collaboration with Unifor—a Molteni Group company based in Milan that develops bespoke solutions for modern interior design—which transforms from private to collaborative mode simply by rotating screens and chairs, and can cluster together to form larger chains suited to different-sized teams; "Plus Lighting," which is two-directional following the Plus Grid and enables different desk orientations; "Plus Sofas," which can tile together and create collaborative social seating arrangements; and "Plus Pods" with collaborative interstitial zones defined by colored carpets. This design approach creates human-scale, sensory warmth and promotes collaboration.

Office Plus demonstrates how art can become a fundamental organizing principle for architectural space. Each floor presents a distinct environmental scene, maintaining coherence through the overarching landscape narrative. The design balances the need for flexible, technology-enabled workspaces with a meaningful connection to nature and local cultural heritage. Divisions between interior and exterior are dissolved through the site-specific artworks. By treating art as an integral part of the process, the design creates an environment where occupants engage daily with questions of environmental stewardship and local identity.

James Corner Field Operations and vPPR Architects, Camden Highline, London, 2023–

opposite: The Camden Highline will be a new public park that connects Camden Gardens to York Way in north London, with a live railway running alongside it. The pink vertical connections between the street and the park are designed as urban follies that will stand out in the context but also embrace the bold spirit of Camden.

right: The park will have a distinctive pink porous boundary to the live railway and extraordinary planting by landscape designer Piet Oudolf. There will be spaces for art displays, cultural events, and a permanent artwork by Hew Locke, activating this linear park.

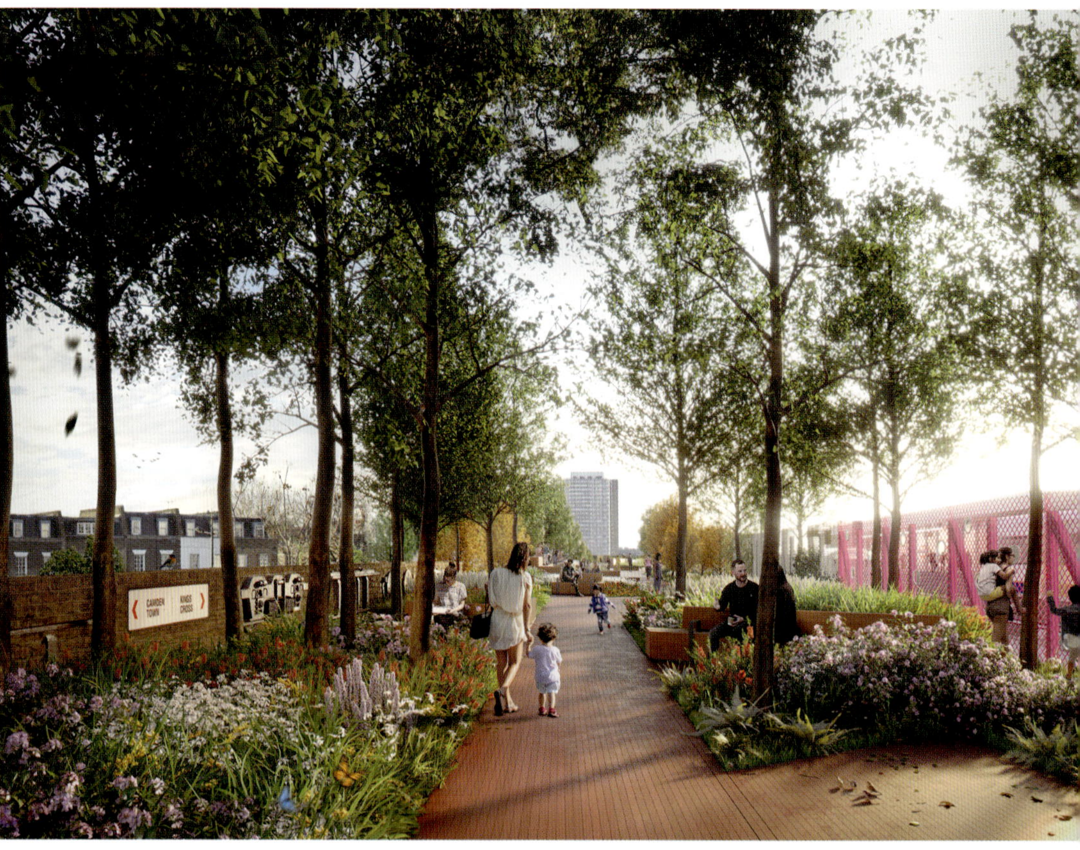

The Art of Ascent

In another project, the Camden Highline in London will transform a Victorian viaduct into a 1.2-kilometer (three-quarter-mile) elevated park, connecting Camden Town to King's Cross. vPPR collaborated with lead consultant James Corner Field Operations from the US and Dutch landscape designer Piet Oudolf, who also both collaborated previously on the New York High Line, as well as British sculptor and contemporary visual artist Hew Locke, among others, on the design of this new piece of cultural infrastructure for the city. The park's width will vary dramatically from an intimate 1.2 meters (4 feet) to an expansive 17 meters (56 feet), creating diverse spatial experiences as it passes through housing, gardens, and light industrial spaces below. This adaptive reuse project will incorporate spaces for cultural events, rotational art displays, and permanent installations by Hew Locke, while preserving the spirit of Camden in the historical graffiti that adorns the viaduct bridges. While planning permission for Phase 1 has been received, construction for this phase is intended to begin in 2026.

vPPR's collaboration focused on the design of four entry points, including stairs and lifts, that will act as the critical interface between the city and the raised park. Drawing inspiration from Hilla and Bernd Becher's typological studies from the late 1950s to 1990s,[3] the access points are conceived as a family of types that function as urban follies—gateways to another world. These circulation cores are designed to transform the act of ascending into a theatrical event, alluding to 19th-century Victorian pleasure gardens.

The distinctive vibrant pink color of these access structures provides a complementary contrast to the context at street level as well as the greenery in the park, enhancing the feeling of immersion in planting on arrival above. With a strong identity, the pink cores, illuminated at night with a matching pink hue through careful lighting design by London-based Speirs Major Light Architecture, will serve as both wayfinding devices and landmarks. These surreal, intriguing structures will become visual markers or signage in the city.

The stair and lift designs respond playfully to each entrance site's historical architecture, treated as ruins. The designs wrap, cantilever, and weave through existing masonry structures and steel girders, embracing historical openings while avoiding unnecessary intervention into the original fabric. At Camden Gardens, the stair sequence will perform an architectural promenade—rising beneath an archway and cantilevering over the park before returning alongside the viaduct and entering through a new opening in metal cladding, rather than penetrating historic brickwork. Similar playfulness will take place at Camden Road station, where the intervention will open up a historic underground station, while at York Way, bricked-up openings will be carefully reopened to create new street connections.

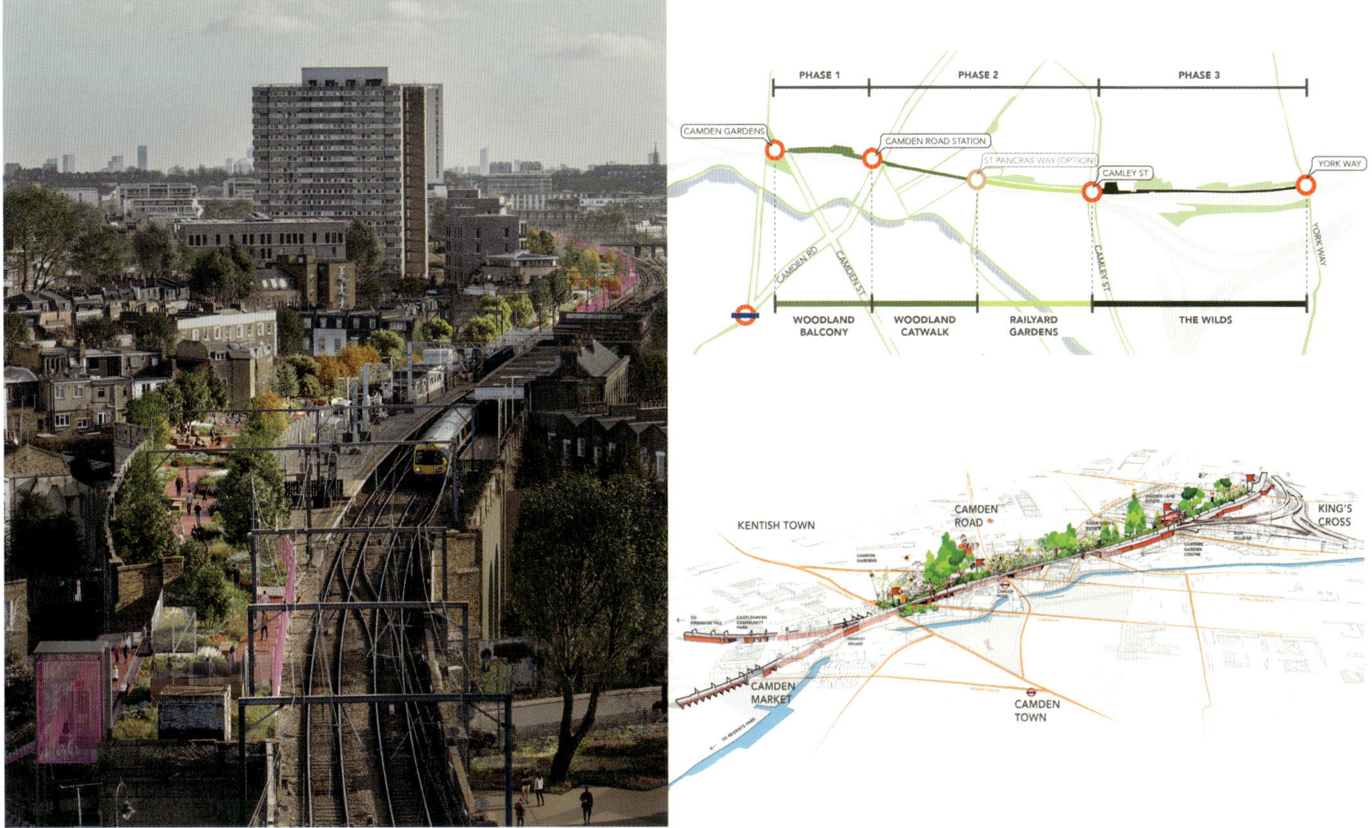

Upon reaching the elevated park, visitors will be immersed in a natural world that will offer different views to London's cityscape while fostering new connections between neighboring communities. A perforated pink fence will provide a rhythmic frame for passing trains on the adjacent line, while Oudolf's planting scheme will function as a living artwork for the community. This elevated sanctuary will be simultaneously removed from and deeply connected to Camden's urban fabric. Locke's artworks will reveal forgotten narratives of Camden's railway heritage and social history.

The Camden Highline is an example of how art and architecture can combine to transform urban infrastructure into a cultural catalyst, creating meaningful civic spaces that enrich urban life while preserving and reinterpreting historical fabric. Through a considered design language—from the theatrical pink stairs to the curated planting and integrated artworks—the project is set to create a new type of public space that celebrates both Camden's industrial heritage and its creative future, while dissolving divisions between the city and the park.

Blurring the Boundaries of Art and Architecture

The projects explored here illustrate the transformative potential of integrating art and architecture in different typologies. By investigating artworks as both conceptual foundations and literal interventions, vPPR Architects seek to create immersive environments that break down the boundaries between flatness and depth, inside and outside, culture and nature. This architectural approach dissolves oppositions and opens up spaces for provocation and play. The emotional potential of space—whether captured in the color progressions of the British Pavilion, the vertical inhabitation of a painting in Office Plus, or the dreamlike pink follies of the Camden Highline—allows architecture to slip beyond rational constraints and extend into the realm of collective imagination. The surreal and sensorial becomes a tool for defamiliarization, making the ordinary extraordinary and allowing users to see their environment with new perspectives. ⍉

Notes

1. See Lisson Gallery website: www.lissongallery.com/venice2024/venice-2024-john-akomfrah-british-pavilion.
2. See Janet C. Bishop and Mark Rothko, *Rothko: The Color Field Paintings*, Chronicle Books (San Francisco), illustrated edition, 2017.
3. See Bernd Becher and Hilla Becher, *Anonymous Sculptures: A Typography of Technical Constructions*, Schirmer/Mosel (Munich), 1970.

Adopting Alien Perspectives in the Performance of Fictional Speculation

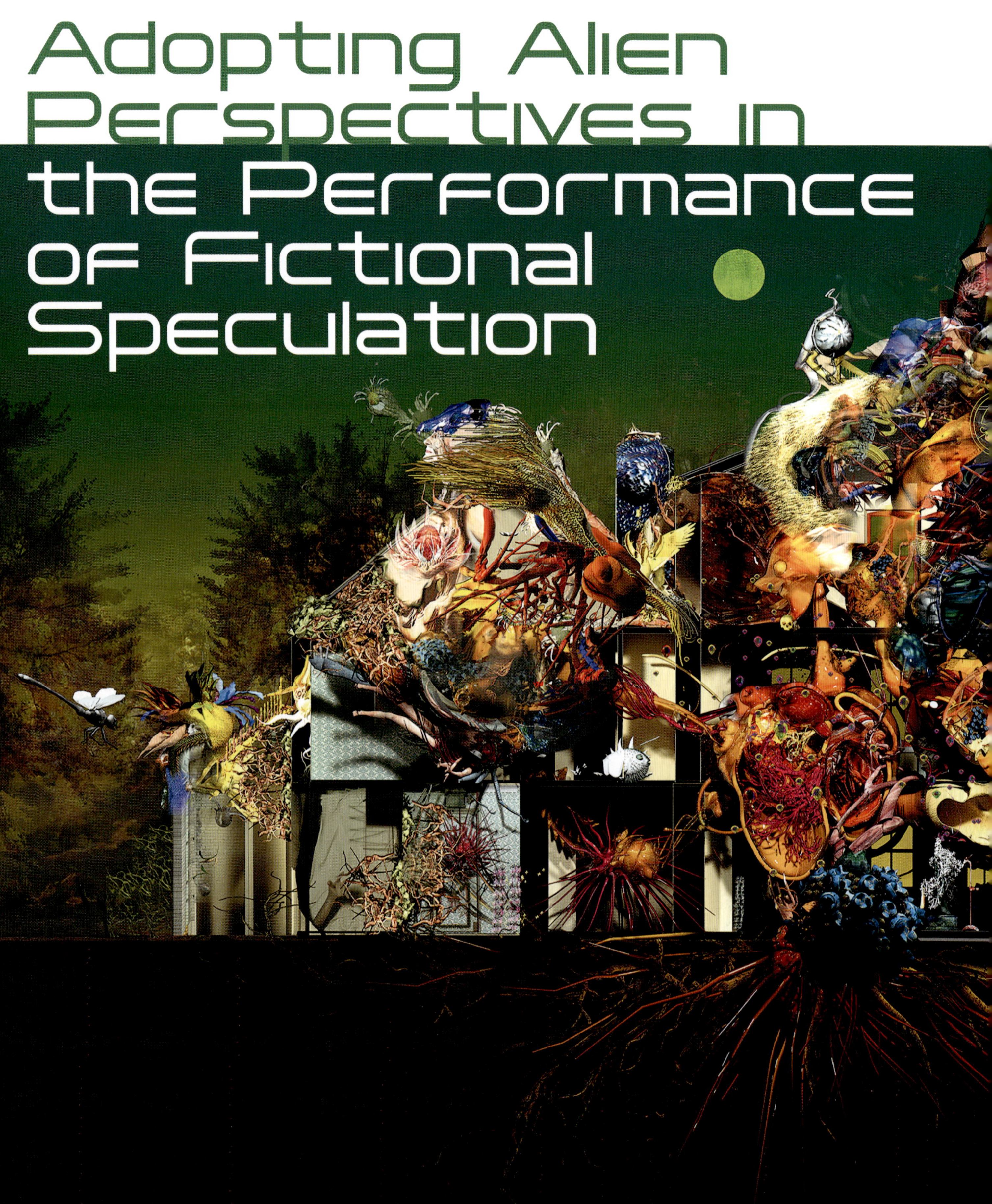

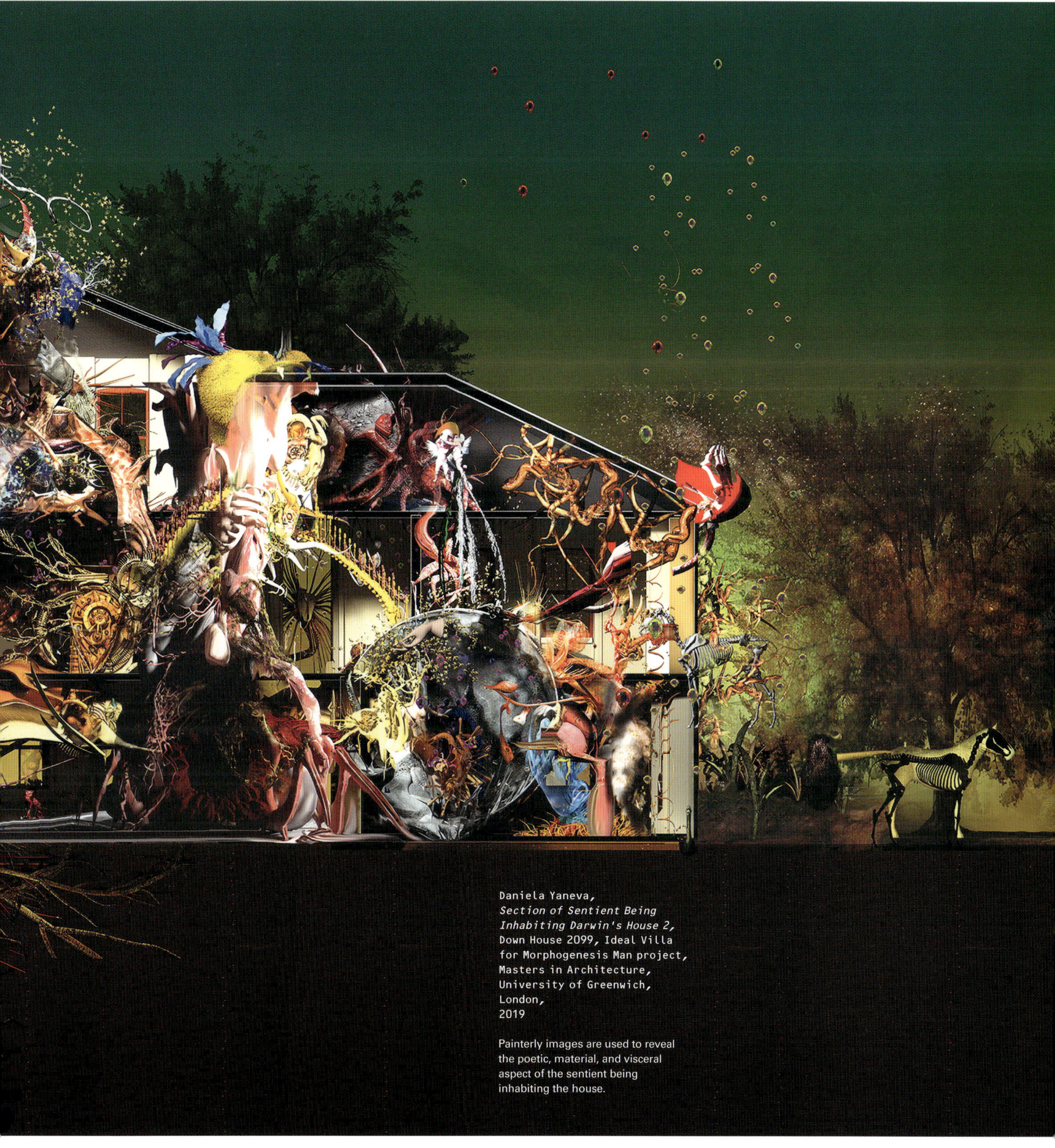

Daniela Yaneva,
Section of Sentient Being Inhabiting Darwin's House 2,
Down House 2099, Ideal Villa for Morphogenesis Man project,
Masters in Architecture,
University of Greenwich,
London,
2019

Painterly images are used to reveal the poetic, material, and visceral aspect of the sentient being inhabiting the house.

Architect and Head of Architecture at the University of Greenwich, London, **Rahesh Ram** encourages students to weave narratives into their designs to provoke architectural speculations which produces some extraordinary ideas and highly baroque renders. Here he calls on student Daniela Yaneva's project work to illustrate the web of associations and architectural intent that comes into being as she invents fictions about genetics, evolution, and sentient architecture.

Fiction is a constructed possible world. It can be seen as an imaginary experimental chamber where quasi-observational simulated experiments[1] can take place, allowing practitioners to construct possible worlds with their accompanying modal statements to enable them to speculate about what such worlds would be like. These constructions hypothesize how architecture—if architecture is the focus of the experiment—might perform in alternative future or alternative cultural, environmental, political, social, or technological contexts. The experiments aim to generate new knowledge or insights by relying on two key performances: the creators' act of formulating the fictional worlds in real-time while representing their world, and the audience's reading of the protagonists' (including architecture's) performance within these fictional environments. It is therefore important for creators to incorporate hermeneutic strategies to foster profound engagement, enabling observers to adopt alien perspectives and see the scenarios as plausible occurrences.[2]

Theory of Engagement in Architectural Fiction

Architectural fictions create scenarios that incorporate fictional elements into a real-world setting, resulting in the whole proposal becoming fictional. The creator decides which proportion of the world is real and which is fictional. The interpretation of the recalibrated world and what happens in that new world enables the audience to speculate about unknown and hypothetical situations. According to Czech literary theorist Lubomír Doležel, through logical deduction, the audience assesses the fiction to see if the world is possible, impossible, contingent, or even necessary.[3] However, when observing the fiction, "the concept is brought down from the logical pedestal and turned into a tool of empirical theorising."[4]

To enable the audience to engage and suspend belief, fictions are usually written as allegories and told as if they were true, even though fiction is an untrue poiesis. The construction of fictions is cultivated so that the audience can see the world as the creator intends it to be seen. Creators conjure up possible worlds with facts, notions, presumptions, suppositions, and flights of imagination, and ask the audience to accept their proposed world.

Initially, the possible world is created for the creators themselves, who want to conceptualize and advance their notions of the possible world. New insights and knowledge may appear at the initial research stages but, for the creator, it is in the performative act of representing the world that it comes into being. Once it is sufficiently crafted, the audience is allowed in to engage with image-based simulations, and it is left up to them and their imaginative and reasoning powers to decipher the fiction.

Architectural fictional worlds are produced and represented through textual and visual media, and together they articulate the fiction. As fictions are simulation-based speculations, the audience uses "quasi-observational" reasoning to gain understanding.[5] Representations of the fiction are critical as they are not only a framing device used to communicate an author's perspective, but they also, as Canadian professor of philosophy David Egan points out, satisfy "the human need for imaginative engagement, emotional excitement, and aesthetic pleasure,"[6] aspects of which are important in engaging with fiction.

As architectural fiction primarily uses drawings in its conjecture, this medium's inner hermeneutic qualities enable understanding. Drawings are semogenic instruments that transform perceptions of the world into artifacts that generate meaning. British linguist Michael Halliday states there are three main qualities in drawings that facilitate the creation of meaning.[7]

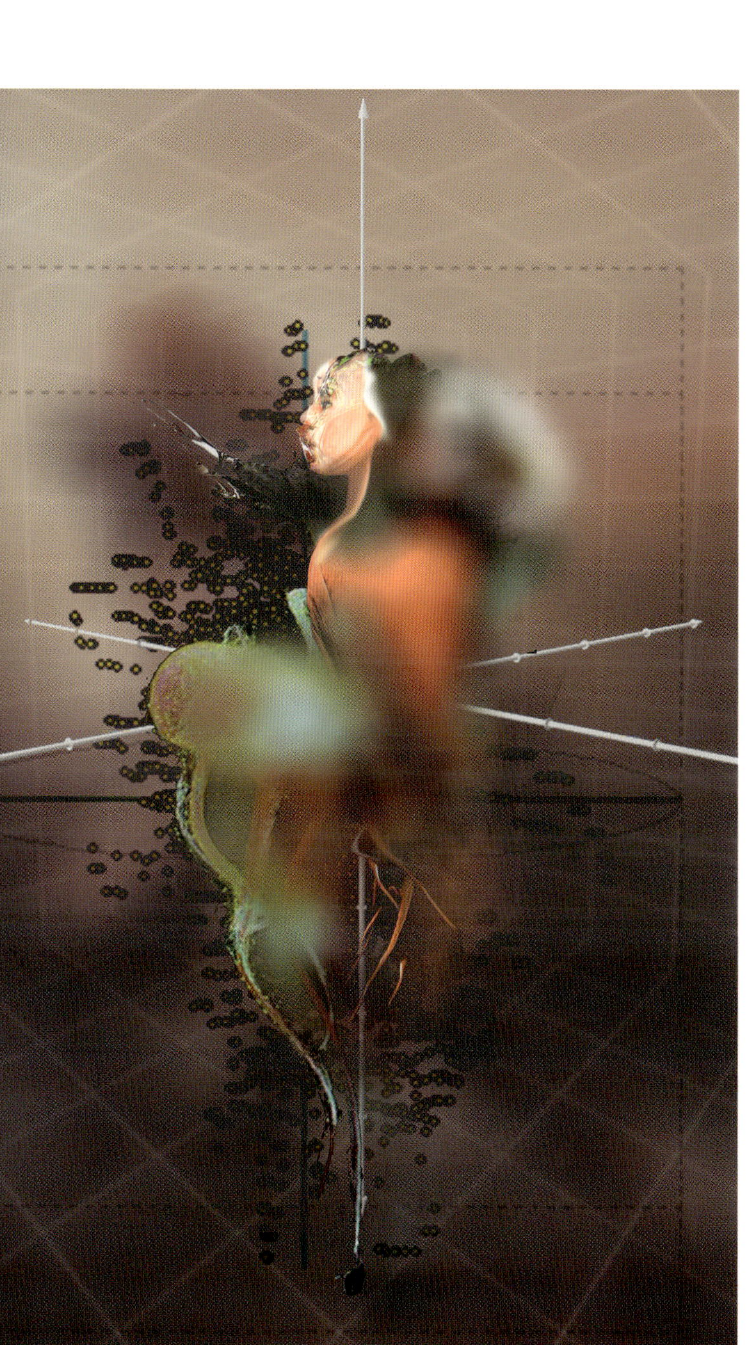

Daniela Yaneva,
Morphogenesis Man,
Down House 2099, Ideal Villa for Morphogenesis Man project, Masters in Architecture, University of Greenwich, London, 2019

Yaneva's MArch student project starts with the proclamation that the next evolution from Leonardo da Vinci's Vitruvian Man and Le Corbusier's Modulor Man is the Morphogenesis Man, a technologically augmented human. The scientist, in the fiction, sets out to design an Ideal Villa for this Morphogenesis Man.

Firstly, drawing reveals the narrative or subject matter; then, in the words of British professor emeritus Howard Riley, the drawing resets "the viewer's moods and attitudes and position[s] it to the creator's emotive drive";[8] and finally there is what Halliday calls the "poetic function,"[9] which relates to representation of the emotional experience through the media used. Creators use these elements along with a shared visual language of a knowing audience to communicate their ideas.

At first, drawings seem like representations of their creators' concepts. However, they not only communicate information but also facilitate subjective readings. The consequence of this is that audiences' insights may differ from what a drawing's creator intended. Drawing's ability to produce multifarious inner readings of the fiction, within the context of the creator's overall parameters, enables fiction to become an instrument to generate unique diverse insights.

For a creator to focus their fiction, there should be a number of features within it to facilitate audience understanding. Firstly, the creator must limit the fiction's scope, enabling the audience to effectively decipher a hypothesis so that it is specific and pertinent to the speculation.[10] Then there is the calibration of the fictional world with the actual world. Fiction has transworld identity;[11] the possible world created must be either approximate to the actual world, or very different from it; and worlds that "violate actual world laws" become "fantastical worlds."[12] It is up to the fiction writer to decide where their world sits in relation to the actual world. Thirdly, fictions cannot be too abstract, because they are usually allegorical, and audiences require symbolic direction in the representation if they are to extract meaning from them. If the fictions are too abstract, meaning cannot easily be attained. To enable abstract elements in fiction to be understood, concrete elements must be included so that the abstract ideas can be deciphered by contrasting them against solid elements.[13]

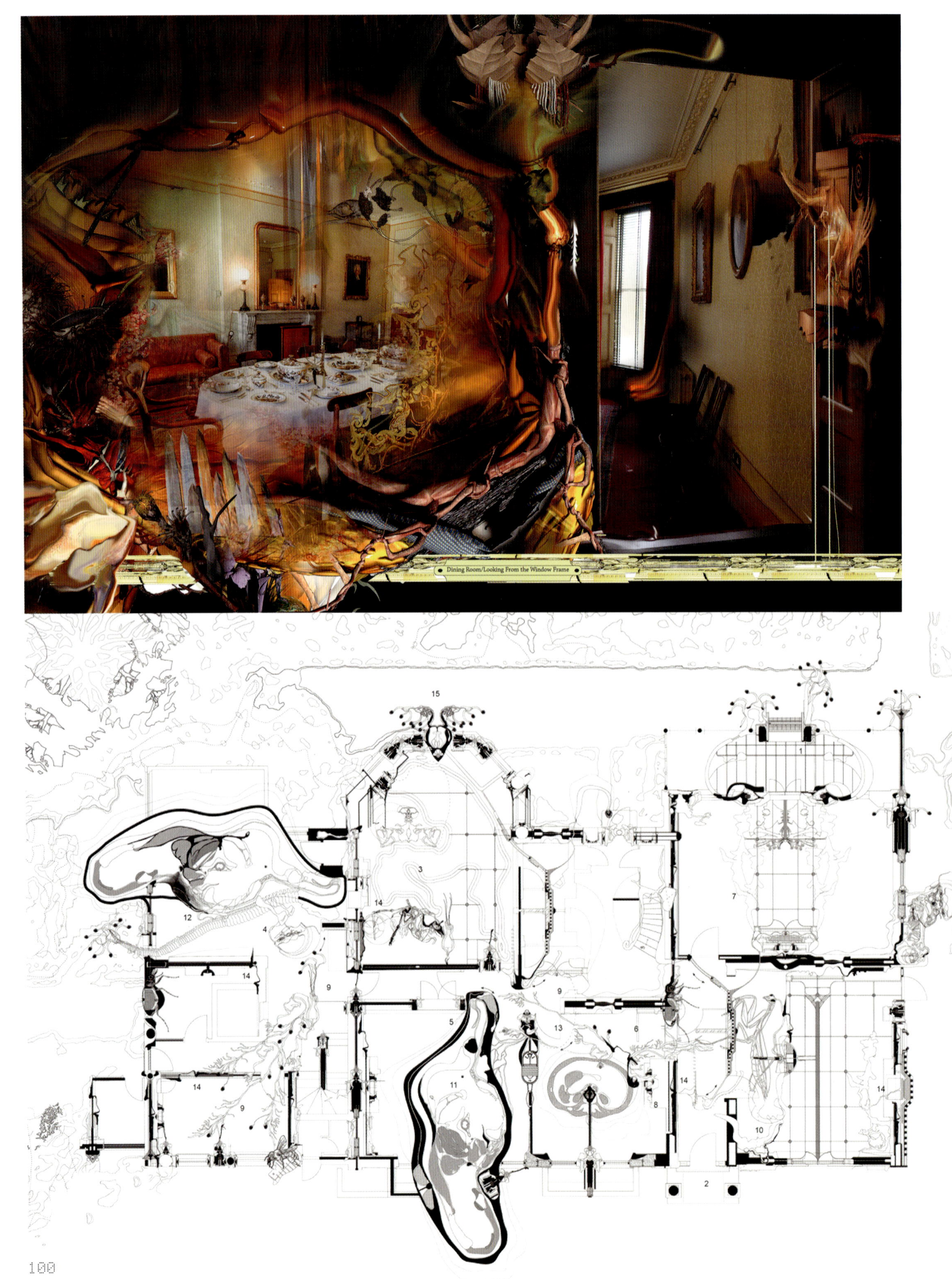
Dining Room/Looking From the Window Frame
15
1
3
7
14
12
4
14
9
9
5
13
6
14
11
14
9
8
14
10
2

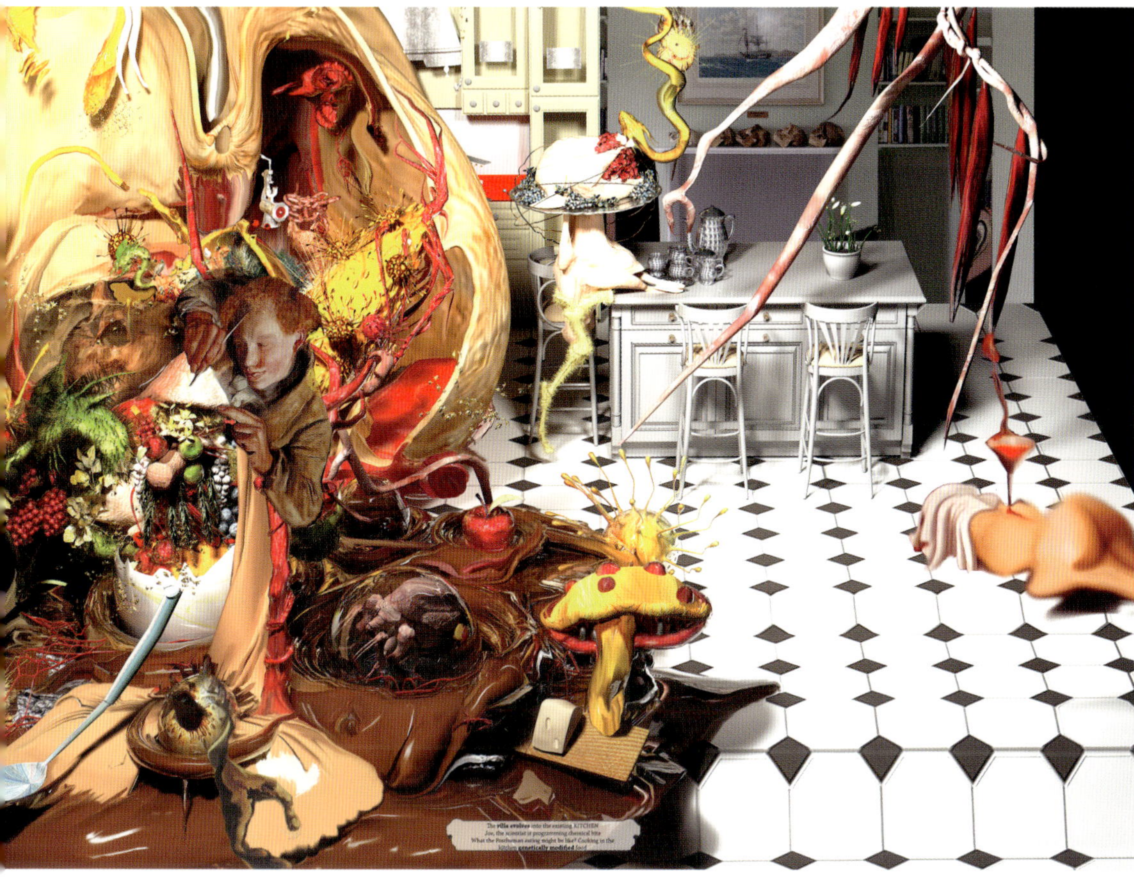

Daniela Yaneva, *Sentient Being Devouring Darwin's Kitchen*, Down House 2099, Ideal Villa for Morphogenesis Man project, Masters in Architecture, University of Greenwich, London, 2019

left: In this image the sentient being's inner world is revealed while it devours Darwin's kitchen.

When engaging with fiction, there is an innate conscious and subconscious deciphering of the truth, which depends on both the contingent facts within the fiction and counterfactual reasoning

KEY

1. Foldaway entrance ramp
2. Entrance seal pod
3. Dining room
4. Kitchen
5. Billiard room
6. Old study
7. Drawing room
8. Brain / Consciousness
9. Senso cells (The New Sensorium)—prosthetic detachments of the organism that peer into the occupant's brain, generating the emergence of consciousness from the actions of distinct neurons into a complex symphony of awareness
10. Signal skin: photosensitive pigment injected into the skin (wall) to allow the soft-living architectural entity to detect the inhabitant's movements
11. Sentient room
12. Foldaway staircase
13. Pivot joints allow a rotating or twisting motion
14. Fireplaces
15. Sensoring window

Daniela Yaneva, *Seen through the Eyes of the Sentient Being*, Down House 2099, Ideal Villa for Morphogenesis Man project, Masters in Architecture, University of Greenwich, London, 2019

opposite top: The fiction seeks to reveal the viewpoints of both the sentient being and the observer. In this image the viewer is asked to inhabit the sentient being's experience while it slithers through Darwin's house.

Daniela Yaneva, *Ground-Floor Plan of Darwin's House with Sentient Being*, Down House 2099, Ideal Villa for Morphogenesis Man project, Masters in Architecture, University of Greenwich, London, 2019

opposite bottom: The chosen location for the Ideal Villa experiment is Down House, Charles Darwin's former home, in the English county of Kent. As the scientist's experiment starts to go astray, the new sentient being begins to take over the house. The plan shows a moment in time as the sentient being starts to inhabit the building.

Daniela Yaneva,
Section of Sentient Being Inhabiting Darwin's House 1,
Down House 2099, Ideal Villa for Morphogenesis Man project,
Masters in Architecture,
University of Greenwich,
London,
2019

Using traditional architectural representation engages the knowing audience. Architectural detail drawings are employed to explain the pragmatic make-up of the sentient being while it inhabits Darwin's house.

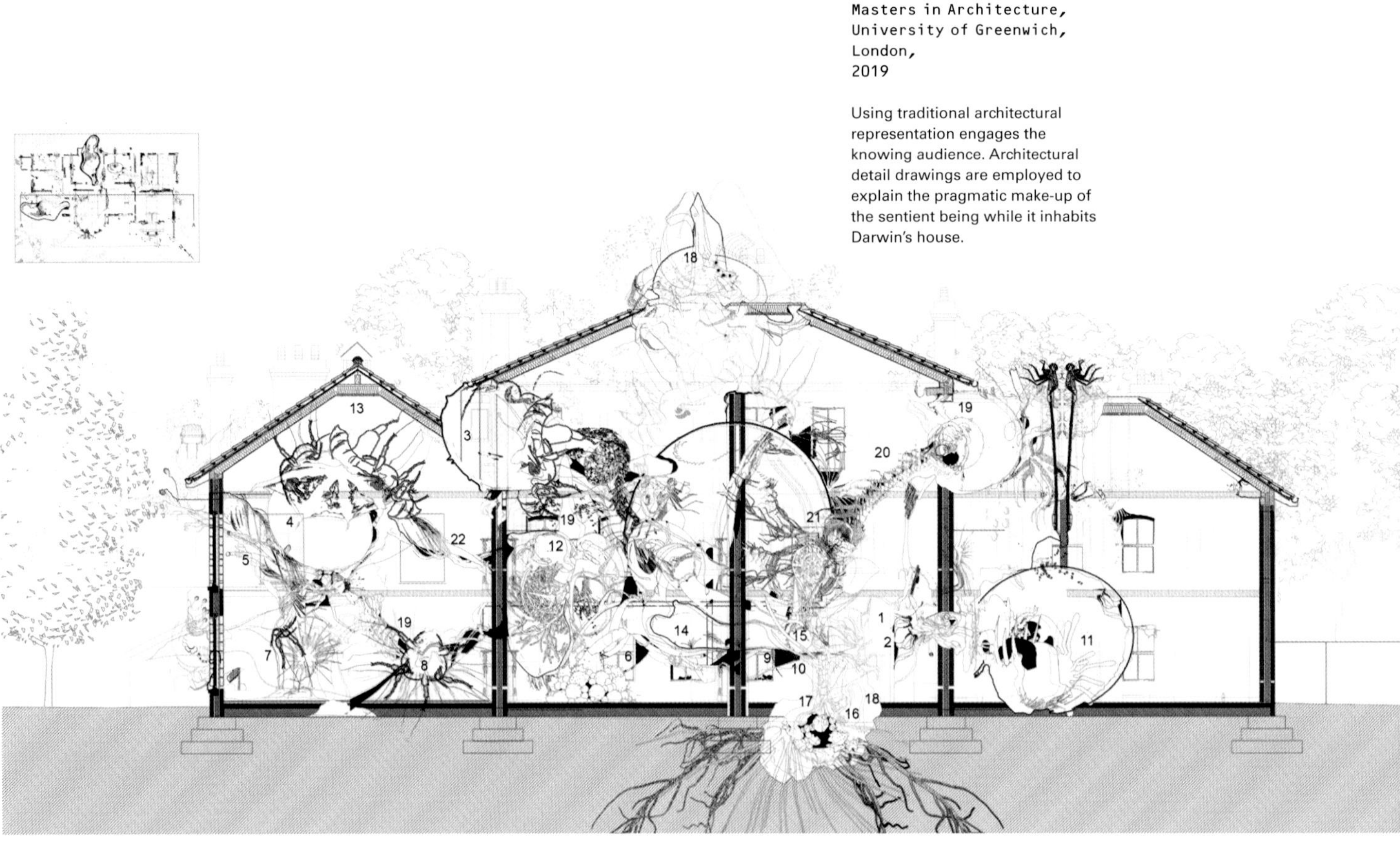

KEY
1. Foldaway entrance ramp
2. Entrance seal pod
3. Wash pods
4. Bedroom / Sleep pods
5. Clothing dispenser slip automatic
6. Dining room
7. Kitchen
8. Toilet
9. Billiard room
10. Old study
11. Drawing room
12. The digestive system links to the toilet and kitchen and creates a bioreactor which recycles and circulates food and waste
13. Muscles expand and create structure that holds the extensions of the body
14. Heart
15. The lungs fill with air that is used for ventilating the space
16. Brain / Consciousness
17. Senso cells (The New Sensorium)—prosthetic detachments of the organism that peer into the occupant's brain, generating the emergence of consciousness from the actions of distinct neurons into a complex symphony of awareness.
18. Signal skin: photosensitive pigment injected into the skin (wall) to allow the soft-living architectural entity to detect the inhabitant's movements
19. Sentient room
20. Foldaway staircase
21. Pivot joints allow a rotating or twisting motion
22. Muscles used when the organism bends to adjust to different size

Finally, there is the problem of how audiences engage with an untrue world. Even if they suspend belief until the end, the untrue nature of fiction can, as American philosopher Catherine Z. Elgin argues, "unsettle complacent convictions, calling into question what we take ourselves to know."[14] This, however, is what makes fiction engaging and exciting to audiences. Even though "the non-truths in fiction are cognitively valuable because they equip us to discern truths that we would not otherwise see or would not otherwise see so clearly,"[15] truth only plays a supporting role.

However, this supporting role is important, as without it, fiction does not work. When engaging with fiction, there is an innate conscious and subconscious deciphering of the truth, which depends on both the contingent facts within the fiction[16] and counterfactual reasoning. When these are combined with the suspension of disbelief, the audience usually accepts the fictional worlds, as they contain certain believable contingent facts. However, these contingent facts will be subject to the audience's evaluation as they determine what is true by their "tacit mastery of the very concept of truth in fiction."[17]

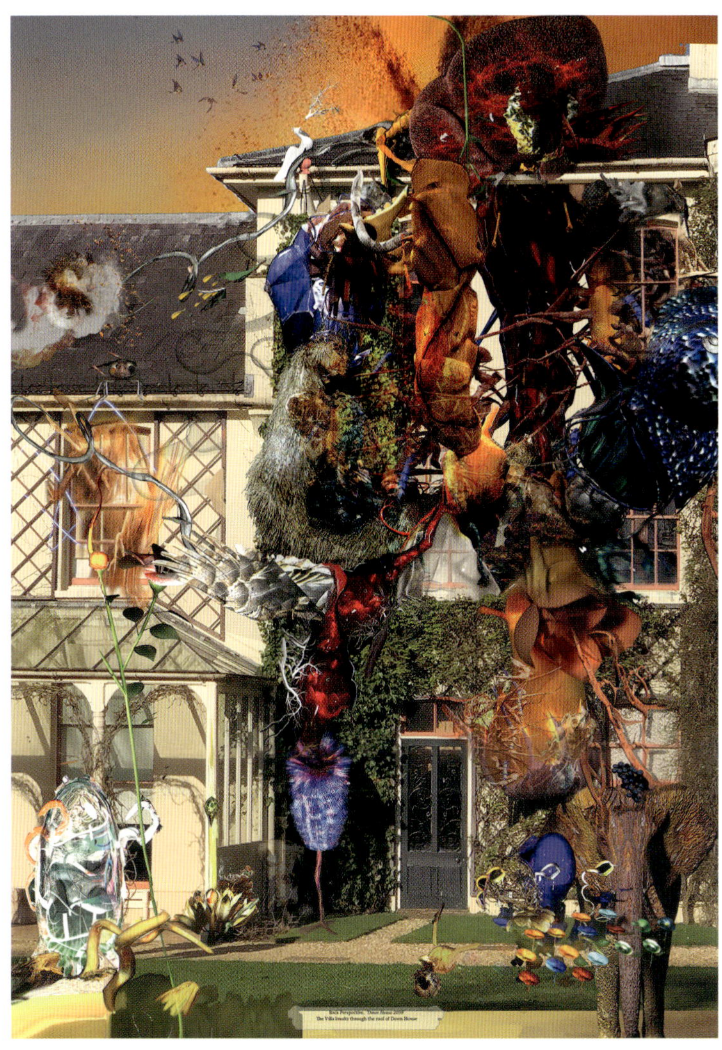

An Illustration of Architectural Fiction as Speculation

The work of Masters students in Unit 12 at the University of Greenwich instrumentalizes fiction as a tool for architectural speculation and pedagogic practice. The qualities needed to create a compelling architectural fiction are revealed, for example, in the drawings of MArch student Daniela Yaneva's project titled "Down House 2099, Ideal Villa for Morphogenesis Man" (2019), which functions as a set of quasi-observational simulations that can be interpreted, believed, extracted, and enjoyed. Her fictional project is a theoretical investigation into how modern scientific and technological advancement may impact the evolution of the human body and, in turn, architecture. Down House 2099 utilizes architects' preoccupation with ideal human proportions, as evidenced by examples ranging from the Vitruvian Man proposed by Leonardo da Vinci in the late 15th century,[18] to Le Corbusier's Modulor Man of the 1940s–50s[19]—both historical anthropometric scales of proportion used to improve the aesthetic and function of architecture. In speculating about what the next evolution of this concept might be, Yaneva conceives what she calls the "Morphogenesis Man": a hybrid, genetically modified, technologically augmented being. Her final project sought to design an Ideal Villa for this new entity.

Yaneva's hypothesis started by her investigating the concept of abiogenesis and the seminal scientific experiments of Russian biochemist Aleksandr Oparin (1924),[20] British scientist J.B.S. Haldane (1929),[21] and British professor of chemistry Lee Cronin (2012)[22] which speculated on the conditions and processes that led to life on earth gradually arising from inorganic matter. These investigations sparked the questions that initiated this project: what would happen if scientists found the methods and conditions to genetically modify inorganic material to enable it to become organic; and what would be the implications for architecture?

Beginning by genetically modifying an apartment in Le Corbusier's Unité d'Habitation in Marseille, France (1952)—a concrete structure grounded in rational design—Yaneva created a set of compelling speculative drawings that depict the architecture's evolution into a living being. It started growing cysts and tumors that emerged from the walls and ceilings, resulting in a challenge to the traditional spaces of human occupation. The representations were both unsettling and captivating.

Inspired by the initial proposal and by English novelist J.G. Ballard's short story "The Thousand Dreams of Stellavista" (1962),[23] the next hypothesis, in search of an appropriate "Ideal Villa for the new Morphogenesis Man," was to speculate whether it is possible to grow a technological hybrid house in a lab—a genetically modified, conscious being that can morph and modify itself to the user's requirements.

To explore and progress the idea, a fictional narrative was created. The story was set in Down House, Charles Darwin's home in Kent, where a scientist, while living in the building, undertakes an experiment to grow a sentient, conscious house. In this experiment, a bioreactor would be coded to generate a "being" with cardiovascular, nervous, respiratory, digestive, and reproductive systems, made of hybrid organic and digitally coded hardware technologies that would enable it to be kept alive.

The project however becomes a cautionary tale, as the sentient being evolves, grows, breaks through the experimental chamber, and starts inhabiting the house in oppressive and violent ways, ending in the complete colonization of the building. The black-and-white architectural drawings depict a moment in time as the "being" occupies Darwin's house; the colorful rendered images are representations of both how it sees the world and how it inhabits the house.

Daniela Yaneva, *Sentient Being Breaks Through Darwin's House*, Down House 2099, Ideal Villa for Morphogenesis Man project, Masters in Architecture, University of Greenwich, London, 2019

The penultimate moment in the fiction where the being finally breaks through the bricks and mortar of Darwin's house and escapes into the Kent countryside.

After a smaller infringement into the house, the entity's organic, slimy, tentacular forms eventually break and seep through the walls, ceilings, windows, and timber joists before smashing through the roof trusses and meandering down the external elevations to occupy Darwin's garden. The creature finally merges and cohabits with the Kent countryside, resulting not in the creation of an Ideal Villa for Morphogenesis Man, but a home for multi-species occupation.

Fiction's Inherent Componentry for Audience Engagement

Fictions are complex speculations that require their creators to be aware of specific principles, codes, and components that must be inherent in fiction for them and the audience to be able to create, decipher, adopt alien perspectives, and engage with an untrue scenario. If these elements are in place, the audience will suspend disbelief, accept the fiction as a true occurrence, and enjoy the simulated possible world for all its unique novel offerings.[24] ⌂

Notes

1. See Margherita Arcangeli, "Imagination in Thought Experimentation: Sketching a Cognitive Approach to Thought Experiments," in Lorenzo Magnani et al. (eds), *Model-Based Reasoning in Science and Technology*, Springer-Verlag (Berlin and Heidelberg), 2010, pp. 571–87.
2. See Catherine Z. Elgin, "The Laboratory of the Mind," in Wolfgang Huemer, John Gibson, and Luca Pocci (eds), *A Sense of the World: Essays on Fiction, Narrative and Knowledge*, Routledge (London), 2007, pp. 43–54.
3. See Lubomír Doležel, "Possible Worlds of Fiction and History," *New Literary History*, 29 (4), Autumn 1998, pp. 785–809.
4. Ibid., p. 787.
5. See Arcangeli, "Imagination in Thought Experimentation."
6. David Egan, "Literature and Thought Experiments," *The Journal of Aesthetics and Art Criticism*, 74 (2), Spring 2016, p. 148.
7. M.A.K. Halliday, "On Matter and Meaning: The Two Realms of Human Experience," *Linguistics and the Human Sciences*, 1 (1), 2005, pp. 59–82.
8. Howard Riley, "Drawing as Language: The Systemic-Functional Semiotic Argument," *Journal of Visual Art Practice*, 18 (2), 2019, p. 137.
9. Halliday, "On Matter and Meaning," p. 63.
10. See Doležel, "Possible Worlds."
11. See David Lewis, "Truth in Fiction," *American Philosophical Quarterly*, 15 (1), January 1978, pp. 37–46.
12. Doležel, "Possible Worlds," p. 788.
13. Ibid.
14. Elgin, "The Laboratory of the Mind," p. 54.
15. Ibid.
16. See Lewis, "Truth in Fiction."
17. Ibid., p. 39.
18. See Leonardo da Vinci, *Vitruvian Man* (drawing), *c.* 1490, Gallerie dell'Accademia, Venice, Italy.
19. See Le Corbusier, *The Modulor: A Harmonious Measure To The Human Scale Universally Applicable To Architecture and Mechanics* [1948], tr. Peter de Francia and Anna Bostock, Faber & Faber (London), 1954.
20. See A.I. Oparin, *Origin of Life*, Macmillan (New York), 1938.
21. See J.B.S. Haldane, "Origin of Life," *The Rationalist Annual*, 148, 1929, pp. 3–10.
22. See Lee Cronin, "Synthesizing Life: The 81st Joseph Henry Lecture," May 25, 2012, Powell Club, Washington, DC: https://pswscience.org/meeting/synthesizing-life/.
23. J.G. Ballard, "The Thousand Dreams of Stellavista" [1962], *Vermilion Sands*, Berkley Books (New York), 1971, pp. 30–60.
24. This article builds on concepts from a conference paper: Rahesh Ram, "Architecture, Fiction and Thought Experiment," in Danilo Di Mascio (ed.), *EAEA15: Monograph of the 15th Biennial Conference of European Architectural Envisioning Association*, University of Huddersfield (Huddersfield), 2021, pp. 235–45.

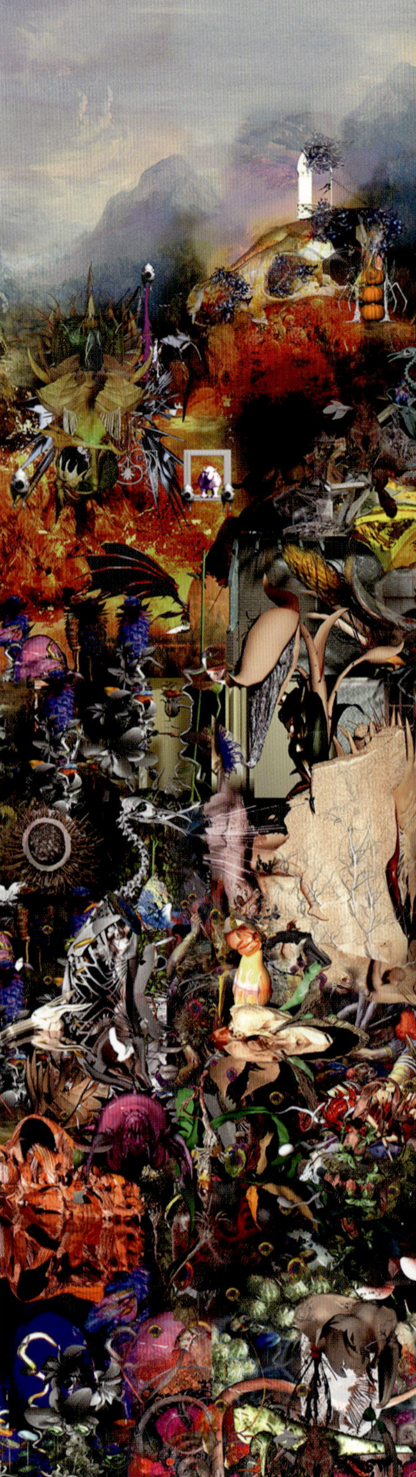

Daniela Yaneva, *Ideal "Villa" for Multispecies Occupation*, Down House 2099, Ideal Villa for Morphogenesis Man project, Masters in Architecture, University of Greenwich, London, 2019

The finale: the being has continued to evolve and grow, broken through Darwin's House, and started inhabiting the Kent countryside. Finally, the all-encompassing entity colonizes the landscape, allowing itself to become an ideal habitat for multispecies occupation.

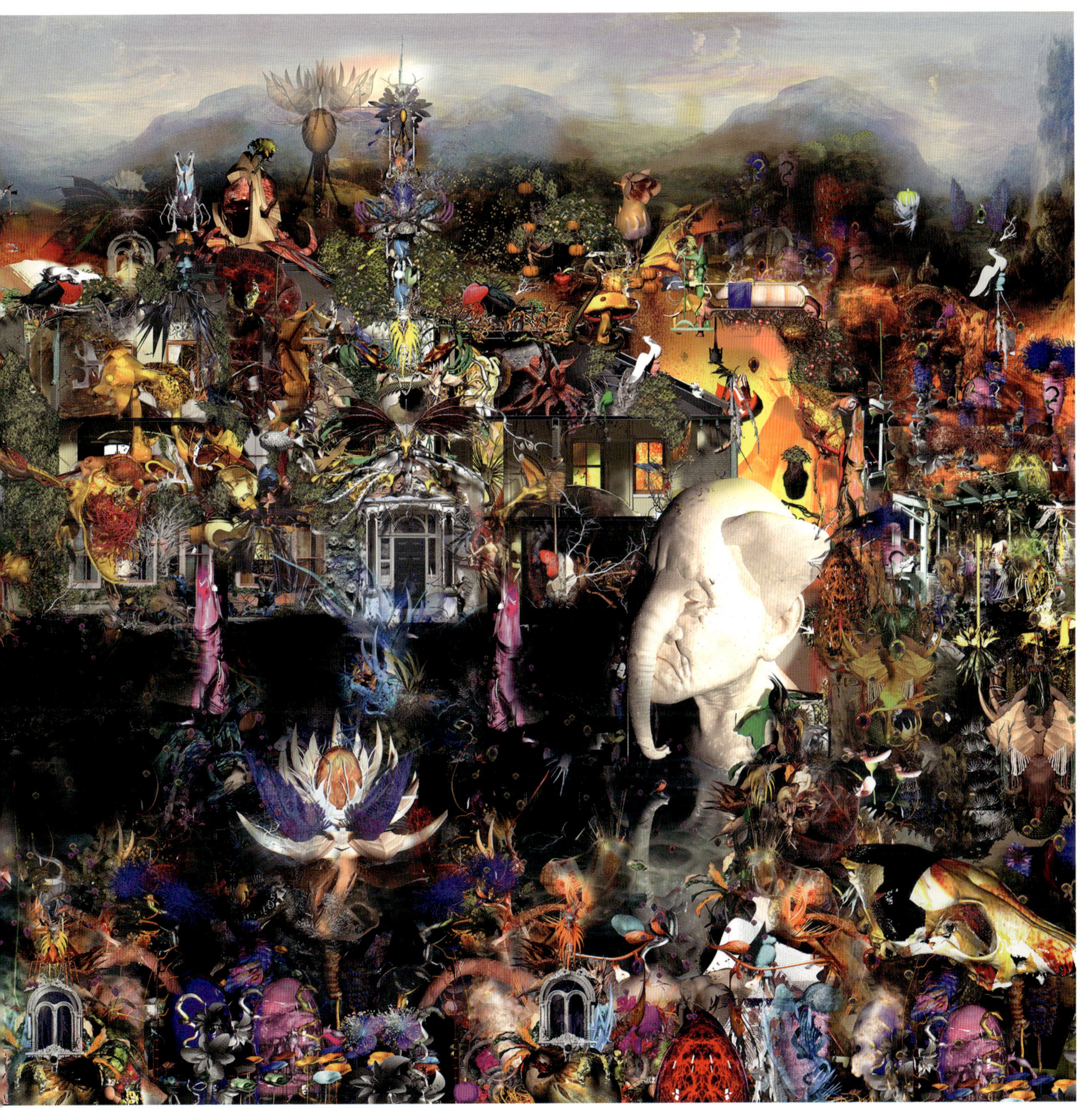

Heterotopia

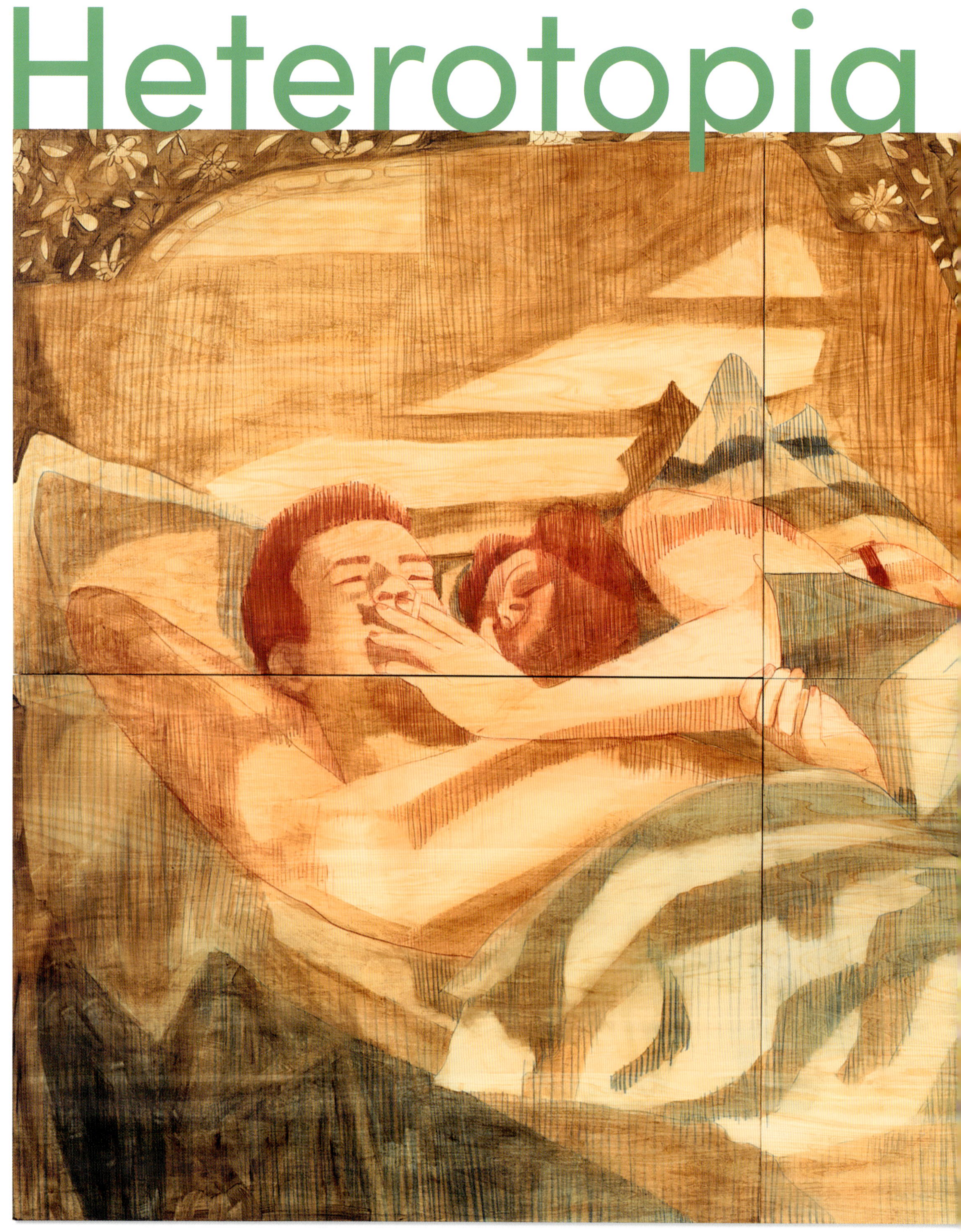

in Utopia

Ashley Simone

It Will End in Tears at the Barbican

Educator and Editorial Director of Axiomatic Editions **Ashley Simone** investigates an exhibition of the work of visual artist Pamela Phatsimo Sunstrum constructed in The Curve gallery at London's Barbican Centre in 2024–5. Entitled *It Will End in Tears*, the installation used artwork framed by timber constructions to choreograph visitors' journey around the space and the nature of when and how they perceived the work—all to augment and communicate its various narrative strands.

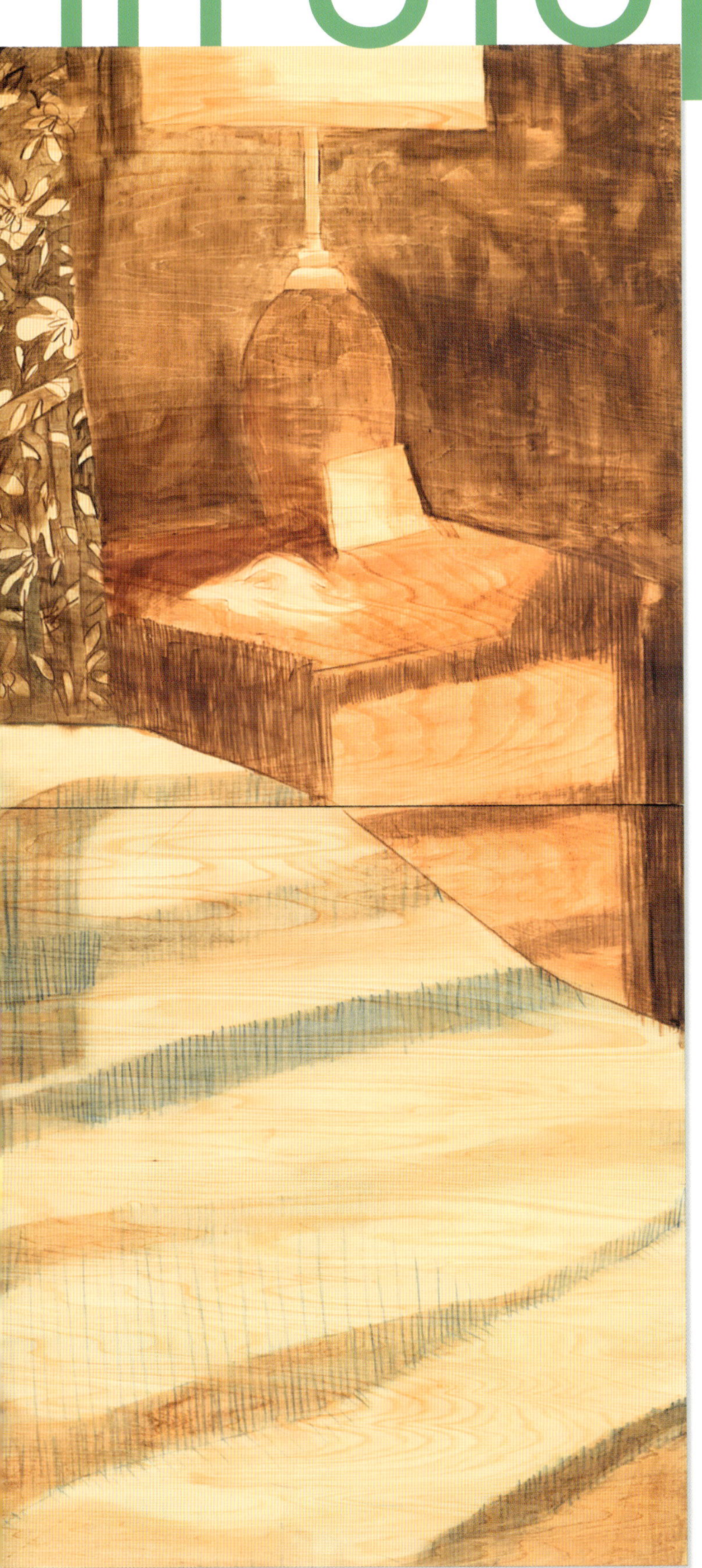

Pamela Phatsimo Sunstrum,
It Will End in Tears, Scene 31,
The Curve, Barbican Centre,
London,
2024-5

The artificial quality of the light, rendered in pencil and oil paint on wooden panels, enhances the impression that the scene is constructed. This generates a theatrical or surreal atmosphere, drawing the audience's attention to the staged aesthetic of the scene.

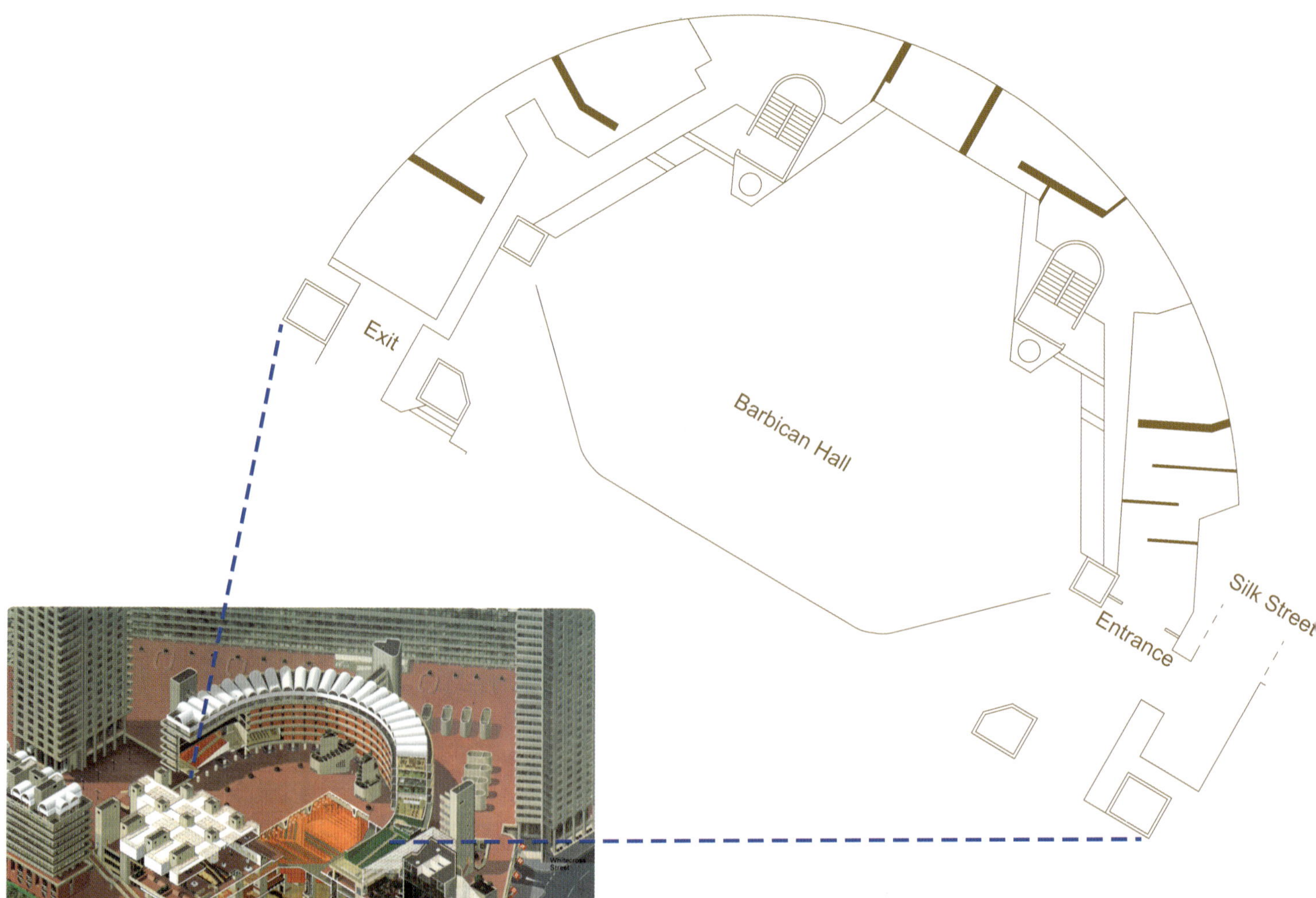

Composite drawing including an isometric view of the Barbican Centre and a plan of The Curve gallery

The plan shows The Curve as a cavity between the Barbican Hall theater and the lobby. The gallery, which hosts site-specific art installations, is embedded within the larger complex of the Barbican, a residential community made distinct by its cultural programming and its separation from the surrounding urban fabric of London. The integration of low- and high-rise residences, plus the absence of vehicular traffic and the presence of water and landscaped areas, signals the utopic ambition of the Barbican. The original colorized isometric drawing was 4 inches wide and was rendered by hand in the late 1970s by John Ronayne in advance of the opening of the Barbican Centre in 1982.

Streaks of light, contoured by a rumpled sheet that covers two lovers, fall obliquely across a four-paneled wood surface in an artwork within the site-specific installation *It Will End in Tears* (2024–5) by Netherlands-based artist Pamela Phatsimo Sunstrum. The composition's constructed, theatrical quality is heightened by the stark shadows, which lack penumbra and are underlined by the absence of a meandering puff of smoke lingering in the air above a cigarette held to one lover's mouth. Among 18 other compositions, the image of the lovers contributes to forming a narrative about Bettina—one of a cast of alter-egos invented by the artist—set in a generic 20th-century colonial outpost. In Sunstrum's UK debut, the work was mounted from September 2024 to January 2025 in London at The Curve, a bowed and cornerless gallery initially conceived as an acoustical barrier for the Barbican Centre's adjacent concert hall. Within this liminal space, Sunstrum, in collaboration with artist and designer Remco Osório Lobato, built a stage set made of unfinished plywood encompassing domestic and civic interiors, a porch, colonial offices, and a series of travel waiting rooms. In the gallery context, this set created a trajectory that guided visitors through an immersive installation that explored existential themes through analog means.

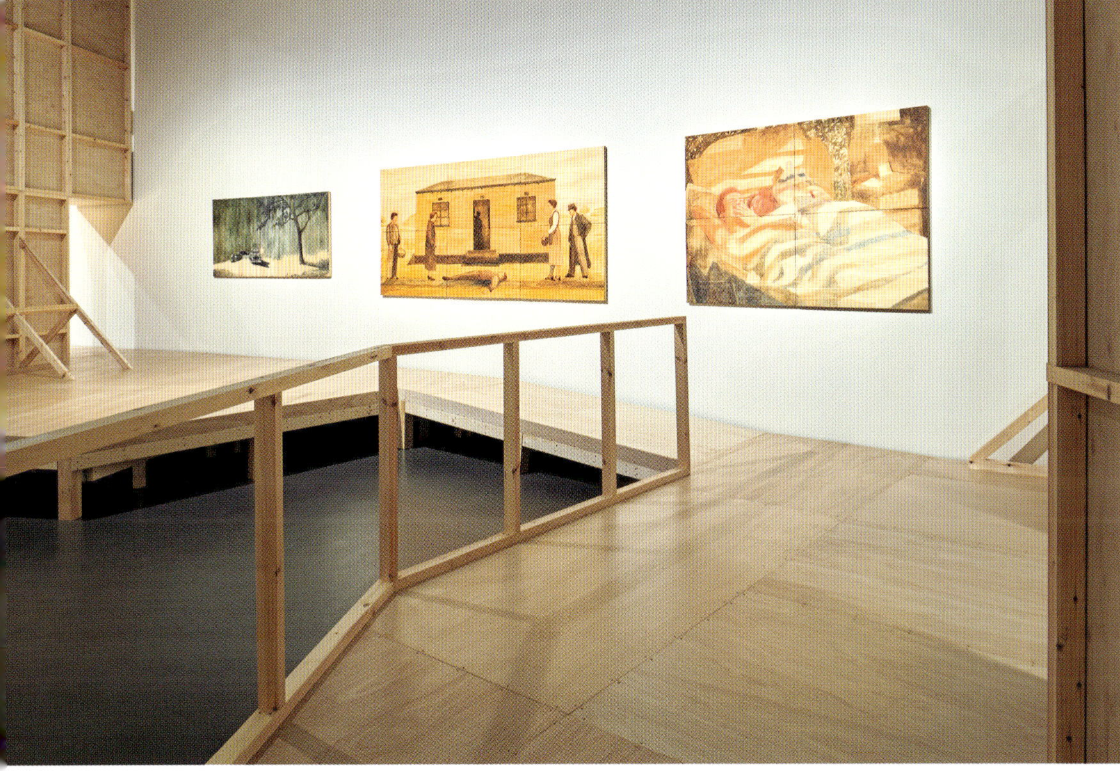

Pamela Phatsimo Sunstrum,
It Will End in Tears,
installation view,
The Curve, Barbican Centre,
London,
2024–5

Contributing to establishing the exhibition's film-noir aesthetic, these three works depict a police car that is seemingly lit by a spotlight in the dark of night (left), the splayed-out body at the threshold of a modest mid-century home, which alludes to a cynical narrative (middle), and the two lovers who are rendered morally ambiguous by their position in the gallery adjacent to an apparent crime (right). The rendered light has an artificial quality that heightens the drama of the visual narrative.

Sited and Sighted in Utopia

Upon entering the complex that comprises the Barbican Centre, visitors made their way around its elevated circulation platform, observing a present-day approximation of the utopian ideals for living advanced by Le Corbusier's rubric for modern architecture—geometric order, green space, fresh air, sunlight, verticality, and the separation of pedestrian and vehicular traffic.[1] This Brutalist-style construct opened in the 1950s to fulfill the ideal that architecture and urban planning could play an active role in social reform. Some 30 years later, in 1982, the Barbican Art Gallery held its first exhibition, signaling an expanded vision for social reform through the arts. In 2006, the space now known as The Curve was transformed from a utilitarian cavity into a space for avant-garde display, adding a new dimension to the Barbican arts program and establishing a venue for contemporary art that has been integral to advancing the careers of emerging and established artists.[2]

Heterotopia

Michel Foucault, in his 1967 lecture "Of Other Spaces: Utopias and Heterotopias," defines heterotopias as "counter-sites," real, physical spaces that reflect, contest, and invert other spaces while juxtaposing multiple, incompatible elements. These spaces embody transformation, serving as thresholds between different states of being where individuals can experience transitions and where the boundaries between the familiar and the unfamiliar, the real and the imaginary, become challenging to parse. He provides an example: "The mirror is, after all, a utopia, since it is a placeless place. In the mirror, I see myself there where I am not, in an unreal, virtual space that opens up behind the surface; I am over there, there where I am not, a sort of shadow that gives my own visibility to myself, that enables me to see myself there where I am absent: such is the utopia of the mirror. But it is also a heterotopia in so far as the mirror does exist in reality, where it exerts a sort of counteraction on the position that I occupy."[3]

A heterotopic condition is present in the biomorphic shape that forms The Curve gallery at the Barbican, where the mounting of *It Will End in Tears* embedded one sort of heterotopia within another.

Analog Immersion and the Viewer/Voyeur

Sunstrum's work utilizes reflective and projective aspects to construct narratives inhabited by a cast of invented characters, archetypal heroes whose fidelity to the African-Canadian artist, born in Botswana, remains fluid. They are simultaneously unreal and real, primordial and modern, named and anonymous. The characters allow the artist to explore the world unbounded, moving seamlessly through time and space, culture and history. Through *It Will End in Tears*, Sunstrum invites her audience on a journey with Bettina, whom she describes as a "kind of dangerous lady, ... this lady with a bit of an agenda ... of a particular time and born from an interest in a mid-century moment on the continent of Africa."[4] The story of Bettina played out inside The Curve, where viewers could experience a drama mediated by a stage set and drawings rendered with oil paint. The imagery produced for the installation announced inspiration from film noir through various means: the calibration of light (highly contrasted or moody), foreboding expressions of the depicted characters, and elements alluding to a murder—a body splayed out on the ground, the lovers, a knife, a police car dispatched in the night, a jury—that lead to a trial where the proceedings and verdict are unknown.

The set itself was a device that mediated visitors' experience within the gallery. They entered the story by moving along a switchback ramp that manipulated sightlines and created a montage-like experience: dressed in a dark coat, suitcase in hand, Bettina is glimpsed from behind; arriving on an airplane, she is hidden from view; behind the wheel of a car, she exchanges uneasy glances with a companion. The car's thin steering wheel and the bend at the edge of the windshield glass allude to a mid-century moment, as does Bettina's attire and the configuration of a teller window within the stage set. The constructed path transported audiences repeatedly back and forth before releasing them onto a counterclockwise trajectory along the curve of the gallery. Viewers became voyeurs immersed in Sunstrum's constructed world. The experience of the viewer/voyeur, much like the one Alfred Hitchcock constructs for L.B. Jeffries in the film *Rear Window* (1954), invited subjective association, suspicion, assumption, and, ultimately, a series of questions.[5] Is Bettina arriving at this colonial outpost or returning? Is the man in the car the same one to whose lips Bettina later holds a cigarette? Was a murder committed somewhere between the stage set's stripped-down porch and the courtroom a viewer encounters at the end of the exhibition's curve? Did Bettina go on trial for murdering her lover?

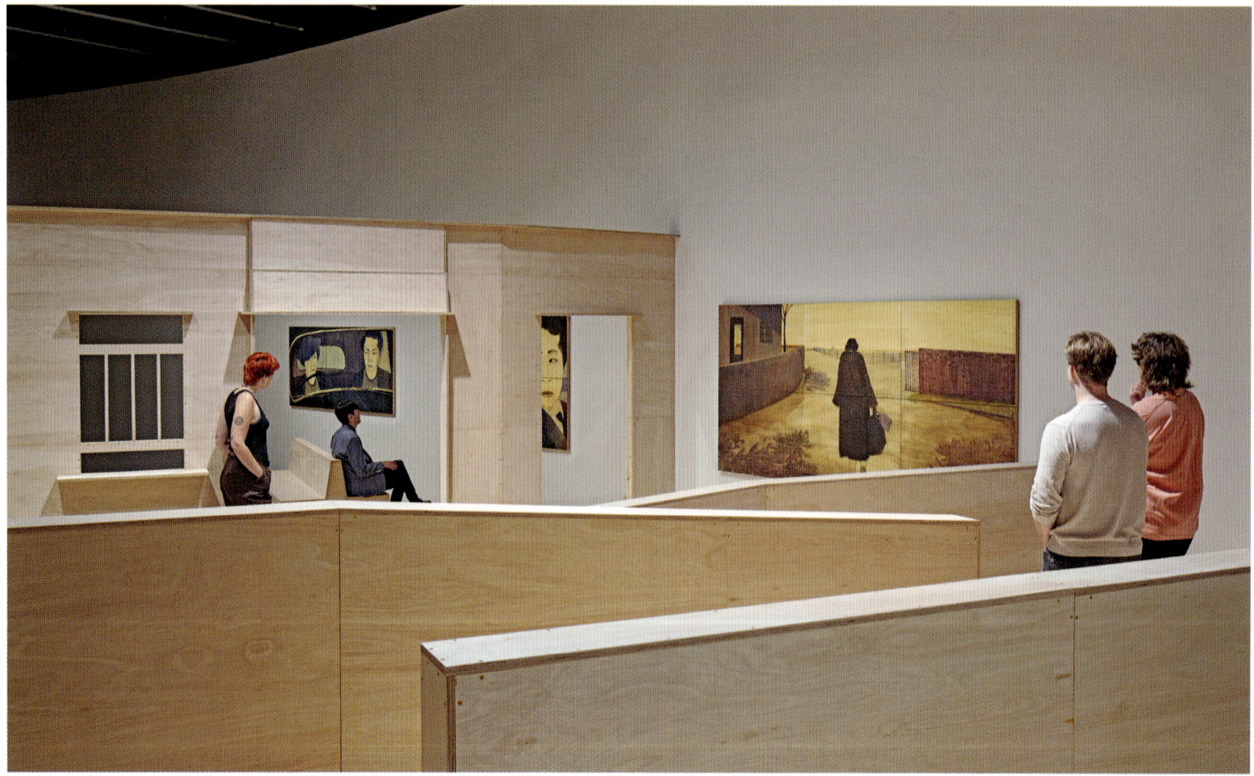

Identity and Place: Play and Performativity

The artist embraces play and performativity in her work. The male and female characters featured in *It Will End in Tears* reflect the artist's actual self while not explicitly mirroring it. They are conduits for exploration, offering, in her words, "a more complicated view of an idea of self." One might describe this view as pensive, sentimental, aspirational, even proud. Sunstrum projects her intentions and desires through Bettina, a "lady with some ideas about herself, which, for some reason, makes a woman very dangerous." Yet, the artist also sees herself in certain male characters, though she does not specify which ones. Sunstrum has expressed an intention to divorce her own physical characteristics from those of the jury in the courtroom scene, explicitly rejecting any affiliation with the harbingers of judgment.

Empire building is something Sunstrum associates with her childhood, which took place across disparate contexts, including Botswana, Canada, Sudan, Sri Lanka, Malawi, and South Africa. She has described experiences in "colonial outposts," where regional architectural traditions and objects were juxtaposed with Western aesthetics. The physical worlds in which she grew up were amalgamations of local and foreign symbols—a colonial aesthetic that she associates with progress and privilege and that she carried through the installation mounted in The Curve. There is dignity and formality to her characters' accoutrements: a triple-strand of pearls adorns Bettina's neck; her companion clasps in his hands a fedora. In a sense, Sunstrum exhibited her genealogy at the Barbican, memorializing and remixing identity and place while abstracting and transforming them into a fictional alter-world she drew, painted, built, and put on display. She allowed visitors to activate the work and participate in co-constituting it by bringing their memories and associations into play. In her words, "There's a lot that I leave dangling, and I think that it's important, not to be kind of purposely vague but to try to leave room for multiple readings … [This] creates longing and desire in the viewer … If you take the time to look, you'll get something out of it. This isn't a one-night stand … This is like an ongoing thing; if you give into it, it gives back."

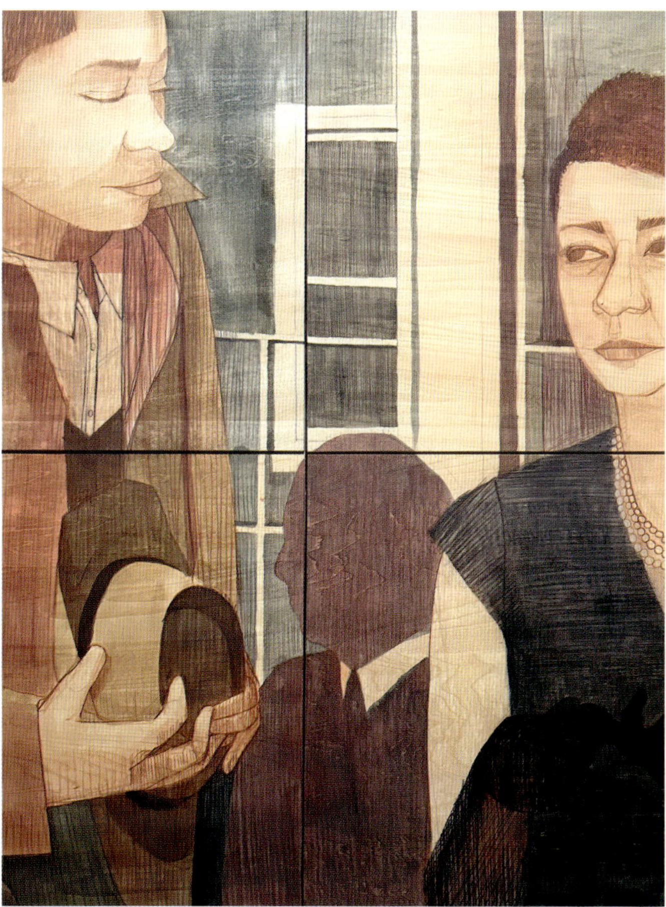

Pamela Phatsimo Sunstrum, *It Will End in Tears*, installation views, The Curve, Barbican Centre, London, 2024-5

opposite: At the entrance to The Curve gallery, a switchback ramp guided visitors into the installation. The story visualized by the artist commenced with a painting depicting Bettina leaving on a journey. The concept of a journey was complemented by a threshold that took form in a permeable wall, alluding to a ticket window at a train station, which ran perpendicular to the pathway through the gallery.

left: The artist built the images for the exhibition element by element, paying attention to how specificities such as attire relate to performativity and storytelling. Bettina, the main character of the show's plot, is shown here wearing a triple strand of beads while locked in a gaze of mutual acknowledgment with a male character. The two figures, appearing on the four-paneled wooden substrate, are backdropped by a faceless third figure in formal attire who contributes to the visual narrative's theatrical, film-noir quality.

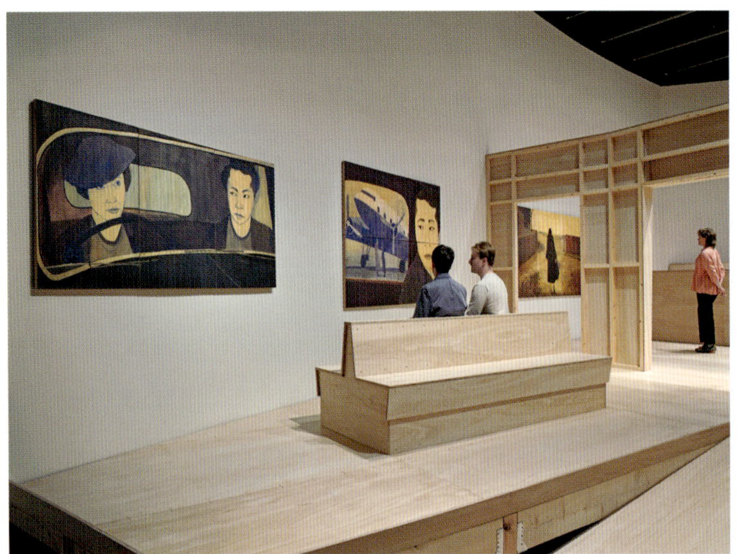

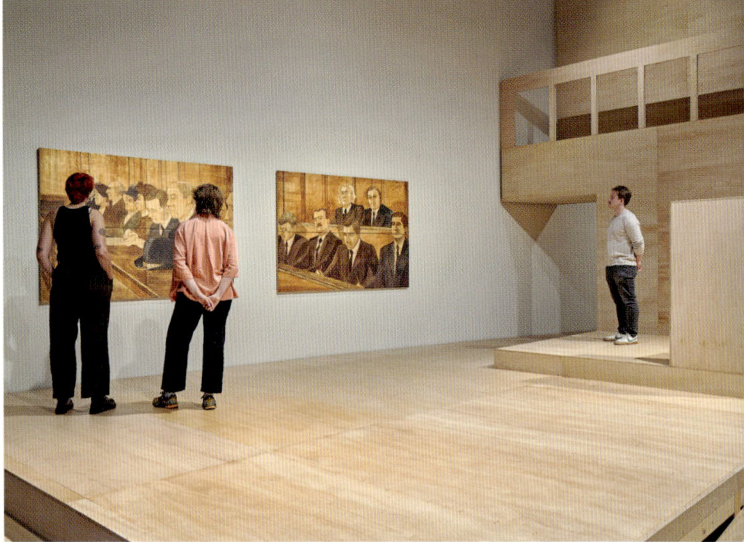

Body Schema

The body activates space, and space activates the body. As they moved across the stage, Sunstrum's audience became attuned to various cerebral and sensorial experiences. They saw the space's vanishing point recede westward and heard and felt footsteps on the stage's elevated platform. They may also have smelled the odor of wood or run their hands along the rough texture of the concrete aggregate enclosing the vertical circulation cores that pierce the gallery's southern wall.

In his book *The Eyes of the Skin: Architecture and the Senses*, Finnish architect Juhani Pallasmaa, building on philosopher Maurice Merleau-Ponty's concept of the embodied experience of perception, makes the following pertinent observations regarding the role of architecture in shaping one's self-identity: "The timeless task of architecture is to create embodied and lived existential metaphors that concretise and structure our being in the world. Architecture reflects, materialises and eternalises ideas and images of ideal life. Buildings and towns enable us to structure, understand and remember the shapeless flow of reality and, ultimately, to recognise and remember who we are. Architecture enables us to perceive and understand the dialectics of permanence and change, to settle ourselves in the world, and to place ourselves in the continuum of culture and time."[6]

The myriad domestic scenes in Sunstrum's exhibition signaled that she understood, while creating work for the exhibition, that our homes are bound up with our self-identity. The experiences the artist displayed at the Barbican—whether fictional or a mirrored reality of her life, or a combination thereof—resonate with Pallasmaa's words when he intimated that architecture engages with existential questions by structuring action, power, and identity. Further to the point, both the architect and Sunstrum have articulated that embodied memory plays a crucial role in remembering spaces and integrating places into our bodily experience.

Immersion and Embodied Experience

The stage set in *It Will End in Tears* provided an architectural armature to structure an embodied experience. This construct allowed Sunstrum to transport her audience through her world. She transformed architecture into another character capable of reflecting her lived experience while activating an experience for others. In her words, "I wanted to build these architectural elements in the space to offer these constantly moving, framing devices for looking at the work, so that the work has its own frame, and it does its own thing by itself ... [The exhibition] became an opportunity to do something along this epic curve and see how meaning changes, or how the story might change when you encounter these [images] one after the other or one painting with a fragment of the next one that's almost visible on the horizon."

It Will End in Tears is a sort of Foucauldian mirror for Sunstrum and the audience she invited into The Curve. Here, through tactile image media and built form, she immersed her audience, orchestrating a placeless physical and pictorial space in service of an indeterminate narrative. Her story was predicated on and built around elements that blur the boundary between the familiar and unfamiliar, the past and present. The exhibition can be read as a reflexive response to the heterotopic condition of the gallery—a space that began as a non-place, a buffer between two volumes, one programmed for performance and the other belonging to the public realm of the Barbican—a heterotopia inside of a heterotopia, inside of a utopia.

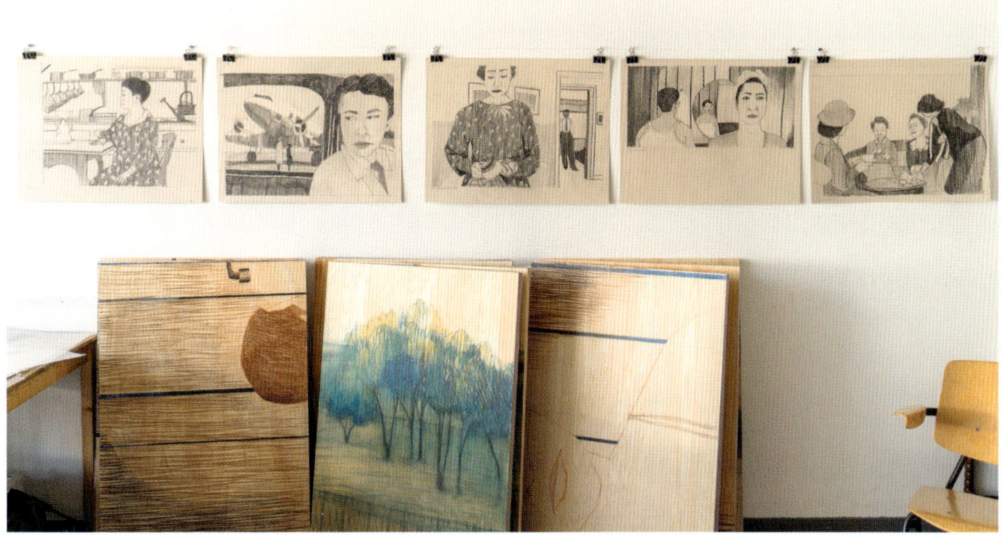

Pamela Phatsimo Sunstrum, *It Will End in Tears*, works in progress in Pamela Phatsimo Sunstrum's studio, The Hague, Netherlands, 2024

left: The drawings hanging on the wall are early iterations of images later transposed to wooden panels and rendered with oil paint, applied thinly to preserve the appearance of the wood grain. For the exhibition at the Barbican, the artist wanted the wood to be visible as a texture within the final images that could resonate with the architectural intervention, the stage set designed by her collaborator Remco Osório Lobato.

Pamela Phatsimo Sunstrum, *It Will End in Tears*, installation views, The Curve, Barbican Centre, London, 2024-5

opposite left: A provisional travel waiting room is shown here in the foreground. The stage set that formed a path to guide viewers through the exhibition comprised various domestic and public-space typologies. In the gallery context, the set took on a functional quality, wherein visitors appropriated it for seating and closer observation of the scenes that formed the visual narrative.

opposite right: The stage set ended with a double-height courtroom spanning nearly the entire width of the gallery. The artist has referred to the courtroom scene as an analogy to consequences in the reality of subversive activity. She worked with both the set designer and a lighting designer to calibrate the atmosphere of the exhibition's final scene. Visitors were left to draw their own conclusions about who was on trial for what, before leaving The Curve and being deposited back onto the red carpet of the Barbican Hall's lobby.

right: This view toward the gallery's entrance features a fragment of a concrete stair core at the right of the image and, in the foreground, a schematic porch made of plywood built into the stage set that guides viewers through the exhibition. The artist created an interdependent sequence of paintings to see how the story would be altered through the experience of the images one after the other or one painting with a fragment of the next one visible on the horizon.

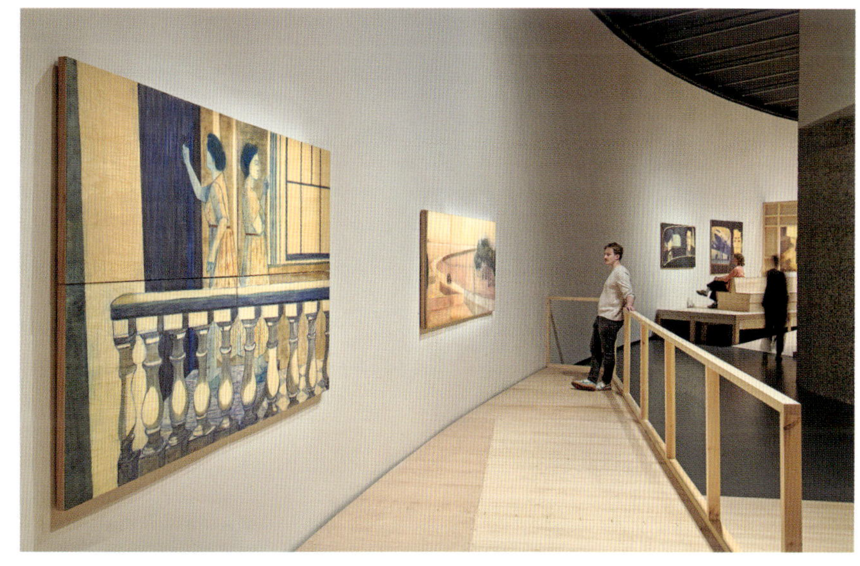

Notes

1. See Le Corbusier and Pierre Jeanneret, *Oeuvre Complète, Volume 1: 1910–1929*, ed. Willy Boesiger and Oscar Stonorov, reprint edition, Birkhäuser (Basel), 1995, p.128.
2. See Tony Chambers, "Art," in Nicholas Kenyon (ed.), *Building Utopia: The Barbican Centre*, Batsford (London), 2022, pp. 204–6, 209, and 217.
3. Michel Foucault, "Of Other Spaces: Utopias and Heterotopias," tr. Jay Miskowiec, *Architecture/Mouvement/Continuité*, October, 1984 (based on lecture "Des Espace Autres," March 1967).
4. All quotations of Pamela Phatsimo Sunstrum are from a video call with the author, December 11, 2024.
5. Alfred Hitchcock, director, *Rear Window*, Paramount Pictures, 1954.
6. Juhani Pallasmaa, *The Eyes of the Skin: Architecture and the Senses*, Wiley (Chichester), 2005, pp. 71–2.

Sandra Youkhana and Luke Caspar Pearson

An Architecture Studio in Game Space

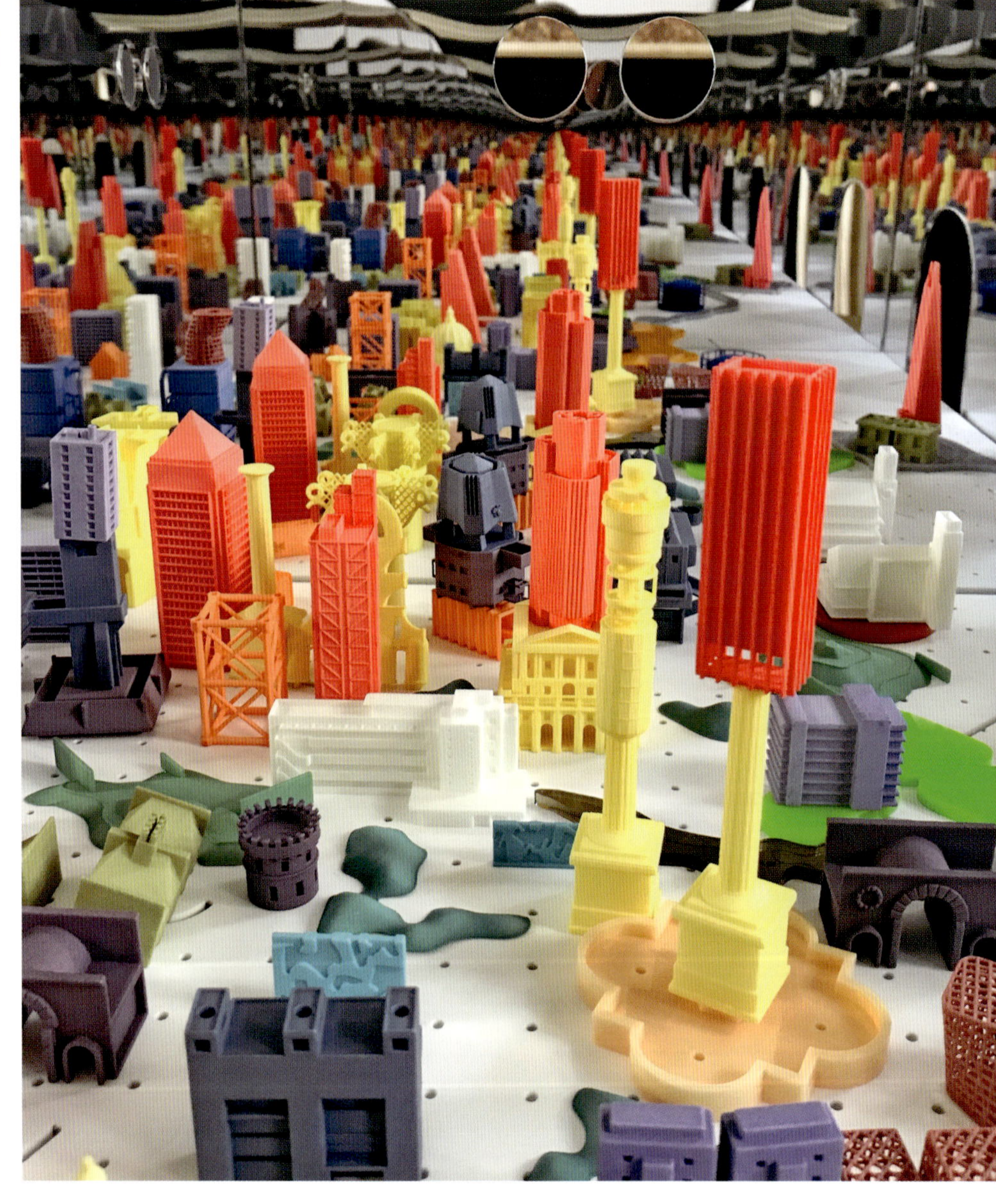

You+Pea,
Peep Pop City,
Now Play This games festival,
Somerset House,
London,
2018

A collaborative, tabletop city-building game, Peep Pop City encouraged creative solutions to London's urban planning logics.

Architecture is a whole different game than it was a decade ago, with gaming engines becoming widespread, cheaper, and hackable. Architects are using such visualization technologies to posit architectures within playful game-space, opening up architectural approaches to new, younger audiences. Cofounders of architectural design studio You+Pea, Sandra Youkhana and Luke Caspar Pearson are also Associate Professors at the Bartlett School of Architecture, University College London, where they teach the Cinematic and Videogame Architecture MArch program. Here they explain their explorations in these realms.

For over a decade, design studio You+Pea has been developing innovative and experimental ways of approaching architectural design through video-game technologies. Using a popular digital medium to try and reach new audiences, the work is presented in interactive and playful ways as a platform to create virtual spaces that provoke conversations about the physical world and to make these discussions more accessible. The research draws from architectural history and representation, using game-engine technologies as narrative tools to reframe architecture in new ways that are digestible for multiple audiences.

Through gaming methodologies, the studio questions what it means to realize architecture today. The work ranges from physical installations driven by game-based logic to hybrid experiments operating between the physical and digital, alongside those sited purely in the virtual that allow the studio to challenge and critique the physical world. In both practice and teaching, this involves the design of both games and game worlds, as well as the use of analytical methods to study existing commercial game worlds in order to outline their architectural agency. In this context, You+Pea no longer operates in the typical domains of architecture, but instead as an architecture studio in game space. Exactly where this work sits at the intersection of architecture and art varies project by project.

A Collaborative City

Peep Pop City (2018), a physical "city builder" game, was initially designed for the Now Play This games festival at Somerset House in London. As an architectural project commissioned by a gaming organisation, it aimed to challenge the possibilities of design dialogues using tabletop gaming logics. Inspired by Italian avant-garde design group Archizoom's *No Stop City* (1969), the game was contained within a mirrored box to allow the players to propose a city that repeats forever, as what the group's cofounder Andrea Branzi called a "quantitative utopia."[1]

Players collaborated to construct a city from a kit of over 500 3D-printed game pieces sourced from the past, present, and future of London's urban morphology. These were color-coded by typology, including green spaces, rooftops, and walls, and styles specific to London, such as Brutalist, Postmodern, and suburban architecture. The game was centered around two players, the "Administrator," responsible for pulling objective cards based on the history and legal frameworks of London, and the "Architect" who creatively interprets these instructions.

Placed in a public setting, the game engaged with additional players in its periphery by allowing them to peer into and above the growing city and participate in the dialogue between Administrator and Architect. The discrepant abilities of the players echo the capacities of different stakeholders in city planning processes, and how these perspectives inform design conversations in different ways. In the context of the Somerset House gallery, the game encouraged both structured play—following the architectural rules and procedures—and more freeform play (particularly by children), where a city emerged organically and creatively through gameplay. New players continued where others left off, creating an effect where the city became "temporarily filled and now waiting indefinitely to be stumbled on again."[2] Peep Pop City used game mechanics to explore urban design as collective play, instantiating a form of "virtual space" through the reflections of the mirrored box, as well as player negotiation and creativity. But unlike traditional city-builder games such as SimCity (Maxis, 1989) or Cities: Skylines (Colossal Order, 2017), no one player has total agency over the world, promoting a collaborative approach to city design.

You+Pea,
Playing the Picturesque,
Royal Institute of British Architects (RIBA),
London,
2019

right: Physical follies from a series of picturesque landscape design typologies collided with their virtual counterparts to be interacted with by visitors.

opposite left: The game space shed new light on the principles of picturesque design, comparing it to worldbuilding techniques used in contemporary digital media.

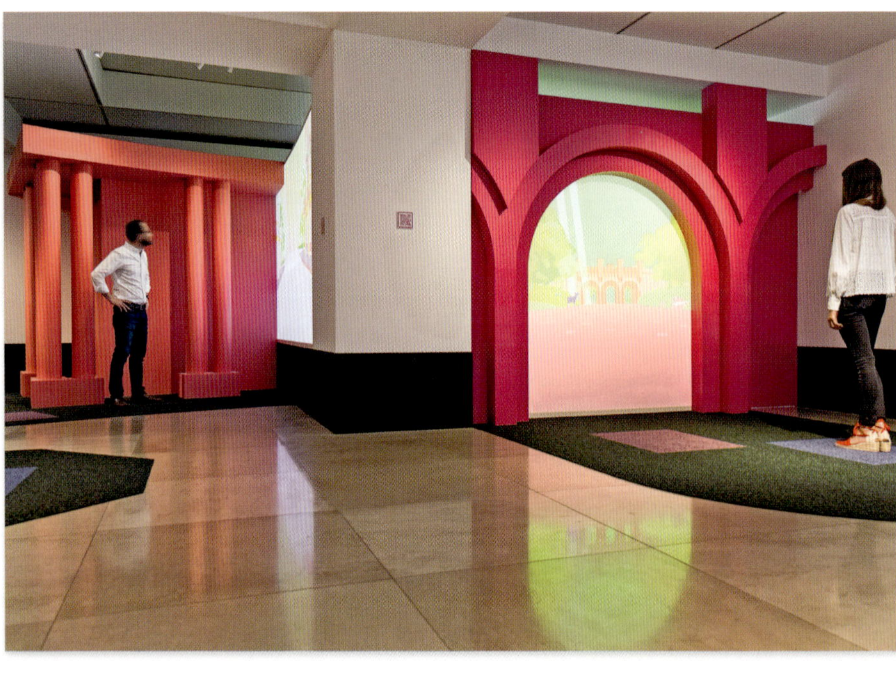

Virtual Picturesque

While Peep Pop City used the form of a dynamic physical architectural model for its game structure, You+Pea's practice proposes works at the intersection of the physical and virtual. Playing the Picturesque, a project exhibited at the Royal Institute of British Architects (RIBA) architecture gallery in 2019, investigated the symbiosis between historical picturesque architectural projects and the design of contemporary game worlds. By integrating video games into physical structures by means of projections and pressure pads, the gallery was extended into the realm of a virtual picturesque to demonstrate how contemporary game worlds often use similar design principles. The virtual interactions were triggered by the player's position and movement in the gallery, making them more accessible and mirroring how one would interact with a real picturesque landscape. Complementary strategies included routes that "never let the foot travel the path of the eye,"[3] an emphasis on the irregular and asymmetrical experience of space, and "sham" structures that appeared complete from one angle but were revealed as flat façades or fragments on closer inspection.

This work involved research using RIBA's drawings archive, historic paintings, and books as precedents for the design of a series of game environments that establish a one-to-one relationship between the viewer's body and the virtual space. As with previous projects, the familiarity and openness of gaming models encouraged playful experimentation into the idea of the picturesque as a prototype of modern virtuality, but also produced new collective experiences and reappraisals of historical architectural hierarchies.

Playing with Representations

You+Pea see game worlds as structured by a relationship between a represented world and the logics through which it can be engaged with. In this context the studio contrasts its approach to architects adopting game engines for visualization purposes, by using games to interrogate architectural representation and its

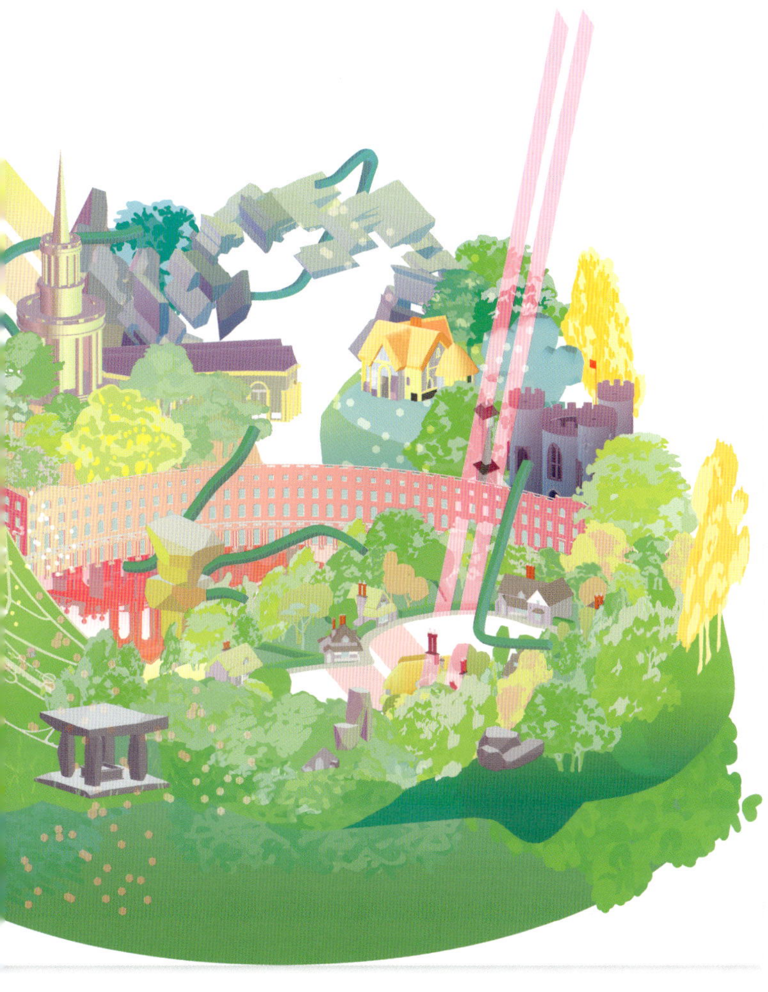

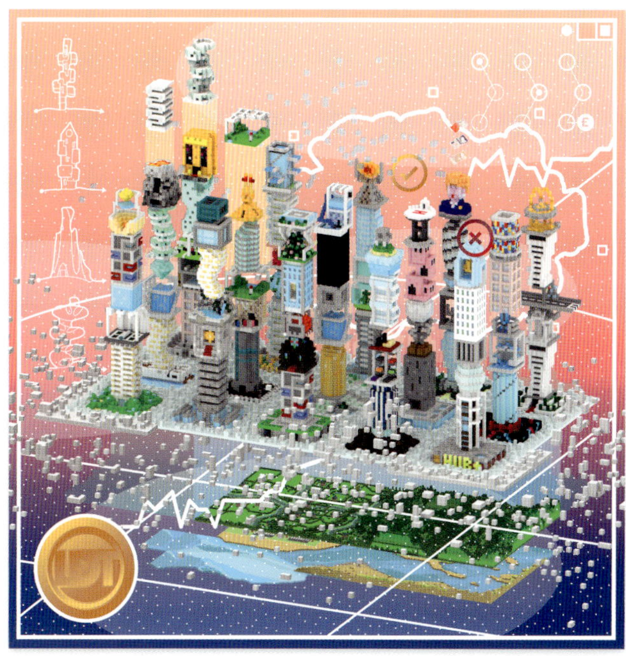

You+Pea,
London Developer's Toolkit 2.0,
"The Architecture Machine" exhibition,
Architekturmuseum der TUM,
Munich,
2020

above: A promotional drawing made to accompany the London Developer's Toolkit 2.0 game showed the range of architectural elements and gameplay systems players could engage with.

relationship to the building of cities. The London Developers Toolkit 2.0 game (2020) examined the relationship between architectural imagery and capital. Players took responsibility for designing and marketing a high-rise luxury development. The game took on the loose appearance of a "city-builder," but the mechanisms spoke more specifically about the architectural imagery that accompanies flows of capital in the city. The player notionally operates as an architect for a pair of property developers, undertaking several tasks involving the gesture recognition of architects' "napkin sketches" and performing parametric calculations. However, unknown to the player, these tasks have no effect on the design of the building, which is procedurally generated in-game. Following this, players used the in-game "crap Photoshop" to design advertising images for their tower, directly printing them in the gallery or posting them to a Twitter bot. Using Minecraft-style voxel modeling, the game maintained a blocky and childlike look. This cuteness held an architectural agency which challenged "from a position of playful vulnerability" and "light heartedly probe[s] the established ways in which we invoke power."[4]

You+Pea,
FusiForms,
"No Quarter 2023" exhibition,
New York University,
New York,
2023

right: Gaming as spectacle: using front and rear projections, two players operated their individual screens that were combined onto one surface, designed to generate a social space around the game.

You+Pea,
Katamari Damacy route analysis from the *Videogame Atlas*,
2022

opposite: A mapping of the complex route taken by the player in Namco's Katamari Damacy game (2004) demonstrates the player's relationship and interaction with both urban and natural forms.

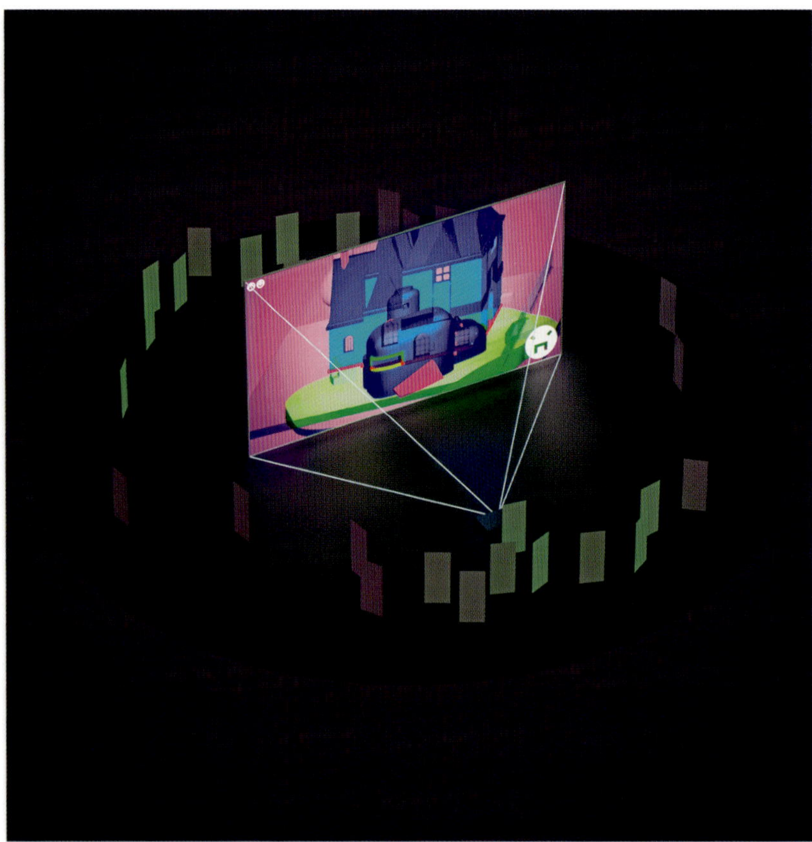

This reinforces the "gameness" of the architecture and American author and game designer Ian Bogost's claims about games and simulations as caricatures of reality,[5] because as Austrian-born art historian Ernst Gombrich argues, "caricature, showing more of the essential, is truer than reality itself."[6] While the game was intentionally ironic and grotesque in outlook, it is only one step away from the truth of the vast swathes of London under development. The Toolkit probed the relationship between design software, image making, and investment. The project could only be realized through the interplay of interactive and random game systems, allowing players to "try on the agency" of an architect[7] while ironically being offered little to no design agency at all. It fits into both the lineage of historical critical and satirical architectural designs, while connecting these conversations to platform and software cultures.

Volumetric Flatness

As You+Pea's work with architecture and games has developed, the studio increasingly operates between the two industries, questioning the orthodoxies of both. FusiForms was designed as an "ambient" architectural puzzle game about buildings that look like faces, extending prior interests in the architectural space of game playing by using large dual-facing projections. Taking its name from the part of the brain responsible for shape recognition, the game drew upon face-like architecture from around the world, both intentional and incidental. This can be most clearly seen in Japanese architect Kazumasa Yamashita's iconic Face House (1975) in Kyoto, a building humanized by its facial characteristics, and French architect François Blanciak's "Tokyoids" (2022) photographic survey and writing which connects Tokyo's architecture to Japan's culture of anthropomorphic robots.[8]

The game was structured around a series of architectural archetypes that embed facial features within their designs, a "roving typology"[9] that emphasizes how the face-like transcends architectural periods or styles. Random combinations of these buildings are then generated and visually overlaid on a two-way projection screen. Players move, rotate, and scale buildings on screen, finding common facial features and combining them, and merging them into new shapes that create a city of FusiForms. Each face can be found in multiple buildings at varying scales and orientations, and every playthrough of the game generates a unique city shaped through collaboration (or competition) and connected through shared expressions.

Installed in-situ at New York University's No Quarter 2023 gaming showcase, this created a social space around the game. The double-sided projection system meant that the two players, separated by the central screen, were both responsible for cooperating remotely. Three-dimensional game worlds became collapsed onto one surface, yet the relative strength of both projections interfered with the players' perception of space. Due to the properties of the central projection screen, the opposite player's viewpoint appeared more visibly than the other player's own view, creating an unexpected relationship in the image space of the participants.

The game operated on two architectural levels: through the structures that players could generate in it, and through the social space generated around it while it was being played. In an empty gallery, players could easily communicate, but as the space filled up the dialogue became more chaotic and the lines between collaborative and competitive play became blurred. FusiForms therefore situates design as a dialogue between different participants that may sometimes be fractious or difficult, and connected through smiles or grimaces.

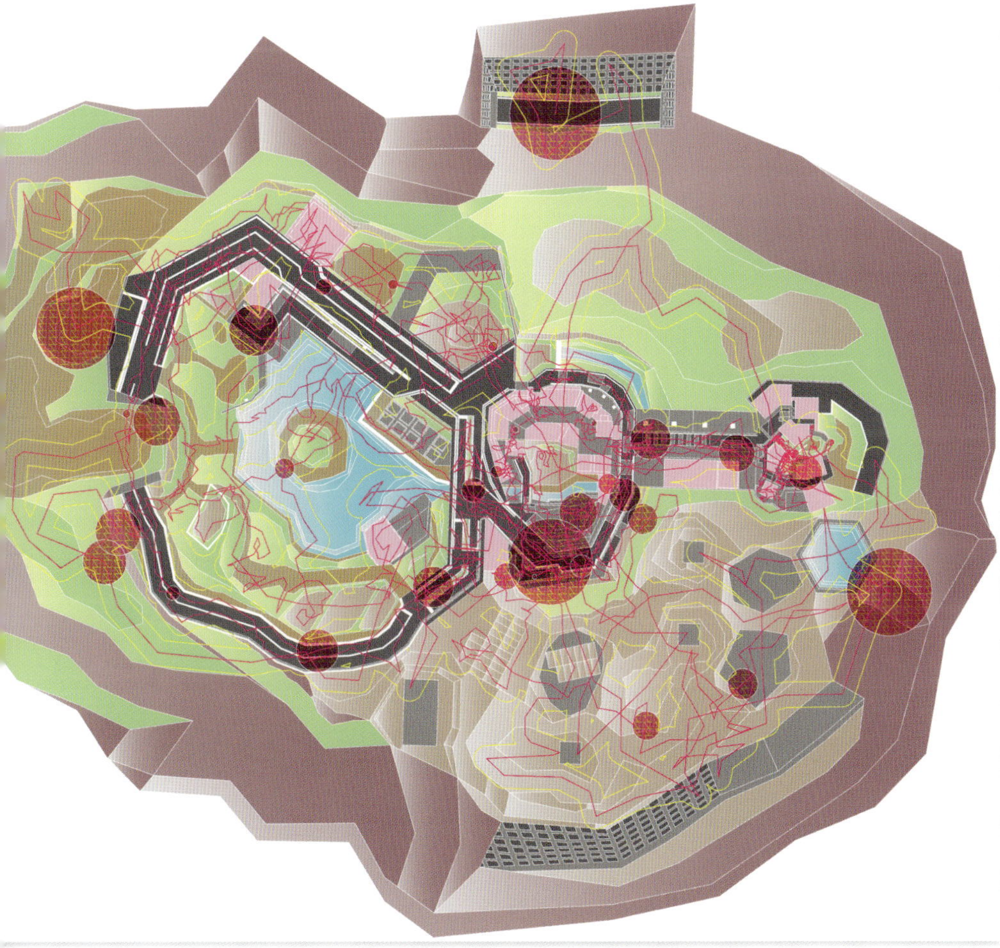

Fully Virtual Architecture

The studio's interests have culminated in a Videogame Atlas (2022) research project, which also became a book,[10] that frames the worlds of 12 popular video games in a new light by looking at them in relation to buildings, places, and cities from the physical world. The Atlas uses architectural surveys, mapping and visual analysis as ways of reframing and deeply examining what makes virtual game worlds so unique. In doing so, You+Pea demonstrate that many of the principles key to the design and experience of these modern game worlds connect to architectural ideas and concepts that are often hundreds of years old. This reinforces the value of game worlds as architectural sites in their own right, such as the notable worldbuilding of Dark Souls (FromSoftware, 2011), with the studio's own spatial innovations and design histories in challenging what it means to realize, or construct, a piece of architecture today.

You+Pea has grown around the many new ways in which we may realize architecture in today's media landscape, to become an architecture studio in game space

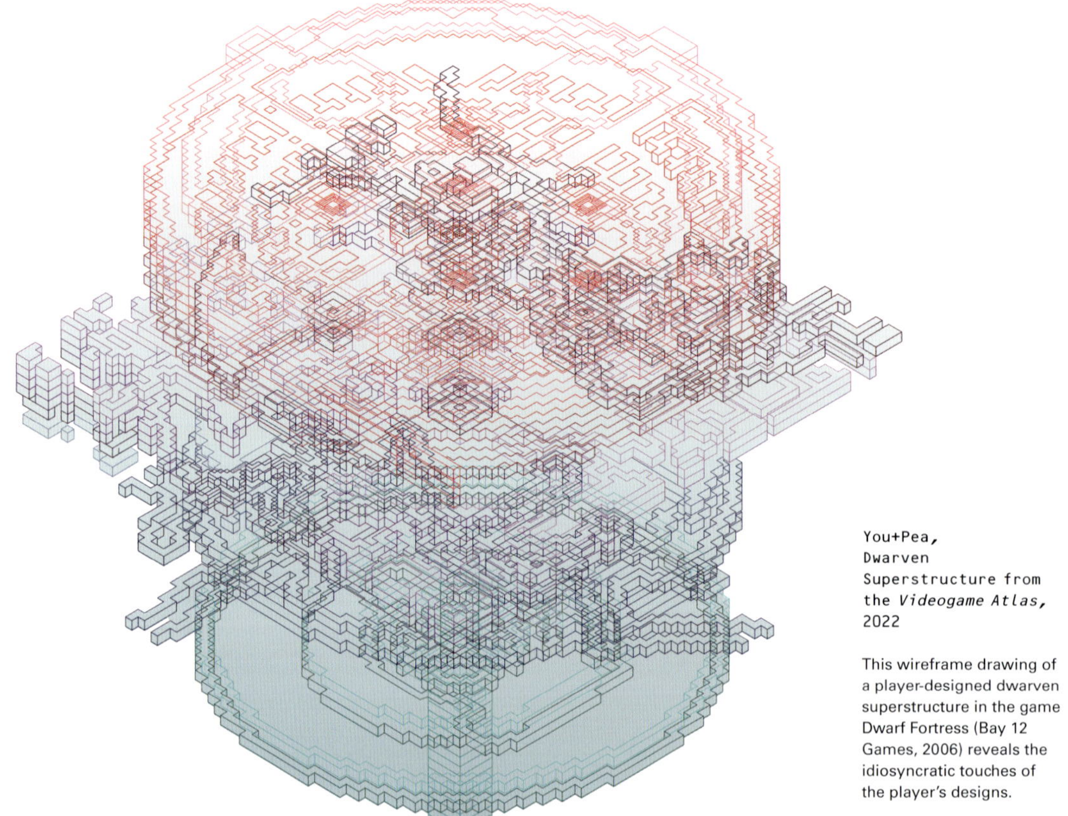

You+Pea, Dwarven Superstructure from the *Videogame Atlas*, 2022

This wireframe drawing of a player-designed dwarven superstructure in the game Dwarf Fortress (Bay 12 Games, 2006) reveals the idiosyncratic touches of the player's designs.

The Videogame Atlas project outlined the architectural significance of different types of interactive game worlds by unraveling all the many spatial messages a player receives from the moment they pick up the controller and start a new journey, even in an ostensibly domestic setting such as the game Persona 5 (Atlus, 2016). It led to an architectural commission from Ubisoft, developers of the Assassin's Creed game series, to create a carte blanche response to its games in the form of a model transcribing the city of Paris in Assassin's Creed Unity (2014). Following the architectural analysis in the Videogame Atlas, You+Pea used the relatively normative form of a 3D-printed and milled model to examine an architectural space only possible in the virtual. As the game relies on parkour techniques, and a rooftop landscape of architectural details, the model explored a journey through Paris that becomes progressively abstracted the further away the city is from the player's attention, demonstrating a city experienced at speed and through repeated interactions and multiple resolutions. This culminated at the Bourse de Commerce, at which the model was exhibited, representing a symbolic junction point between the contemporary city and the historic, virtual one.

Both the research and the model established a back-and-forth workflow between physical and virtual, revealing how architectural methodologies can be used to enhance the spatial understanding of game worlds while reflecting that pop-cultural worlds designed for the screen now represent part of the architectural canon.

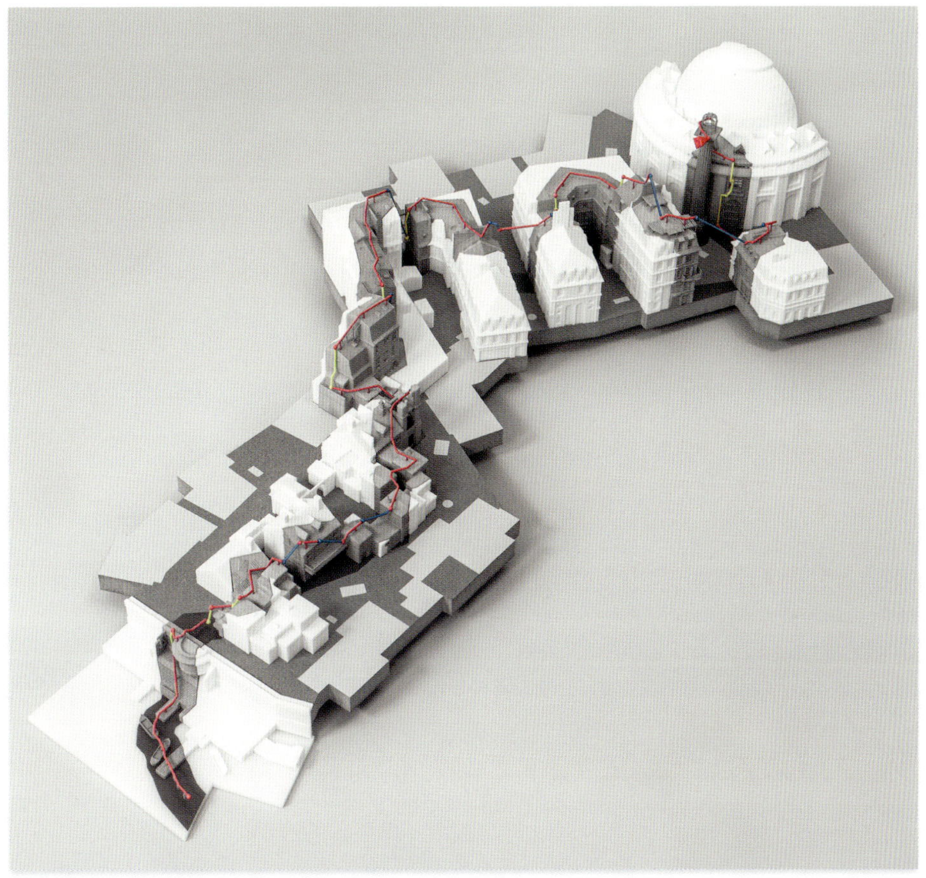

You+Pea,
Model for Ubisoft's
Assassin's Creed Unity,
Bourse de Commerce—Pinault Collection,
Paris,
2022

The architectural model follows the route of the player in Assassin's Creed Unity (2014), demonstrating a journey through Paris at speed that becomes progressively abstracted the further away the city is from the player's attention.

Architecture in Game Space

You+Pea choose to use games in their work not only because they are arguably the defining medium of our time—"allegories for our contemporary life under the protological network of continuous informatic control"[11]— but because video-game spatiality is inherently paradoxical, messy, and entangled. Rather than smoothing out all of these threads, the studio's work interrogates how the cultural and aesthetic properties of games and game-like experiences can reshape the way we design for and within cities, and looks towards a moment where the border between physical and software space is entirely eroded. As such, You+Pea has grown around the many new ways in which we may realize architecture in today's media landscape, to become an architecture studio in game space.

Notes

1. Andrea Branzi, *No-Stop City: Archizoom Associati*, HYX (Orléans), 2006, p. 179.
2. Everest Pipkin, "I Know a Place: Beauty and Solace in the Abandoned Worlds of Roblox," *Pioneer Works*, July 7, 2021: https://pioneerworks.org/broadcast/i-know-a-place-pipkin.
3. William Shenstone, "Unconnected Thoughts on Gardening," cited in John Macarthur, *The Picturesque: Architecture, Disgust and Other Irregularities*, Routledge (London), 2007, p. 157.
4. Simon May, *The Power of Cute*, Princeton University Press (Princeton, NJ), 2019, p. 47.
5. Ian Bogost, "The Cathedral of Computation," *The Atlantic*, January 15, 2015: www.theatlantic.com/technology/archive/2015/01/the-cathedral-of-computation/384300/.
6. E.H. Gombrich with Ernst Kris, "The Principles of Caricature," *British Journal of Medical Psychology*, 17, 1938, p. 319.
7. C. Thi Nguyen, *Games: Agency as Art*, Oxford University Press (Oxford), 2020, p. 90.
8. François Blanciak, *Tokyoids: The Robotic Face of Architecture*, MIT Press (Cambridge, MA), 2022.
9. Ibid., p. 76.
10. Luke Caspar Pearson and Sandra Youkhana, *Videogame Atlas: Mapping Interactive Worlds*, Thames & Hudson (London), 2022.
11. Alexander R. Galloway, "Playing the Code: Allegories of Control in *Civilization*," *Radical Philosophy*, 128, November/December 2004: www.radicalphilosophy.com/article/playing-the-code.

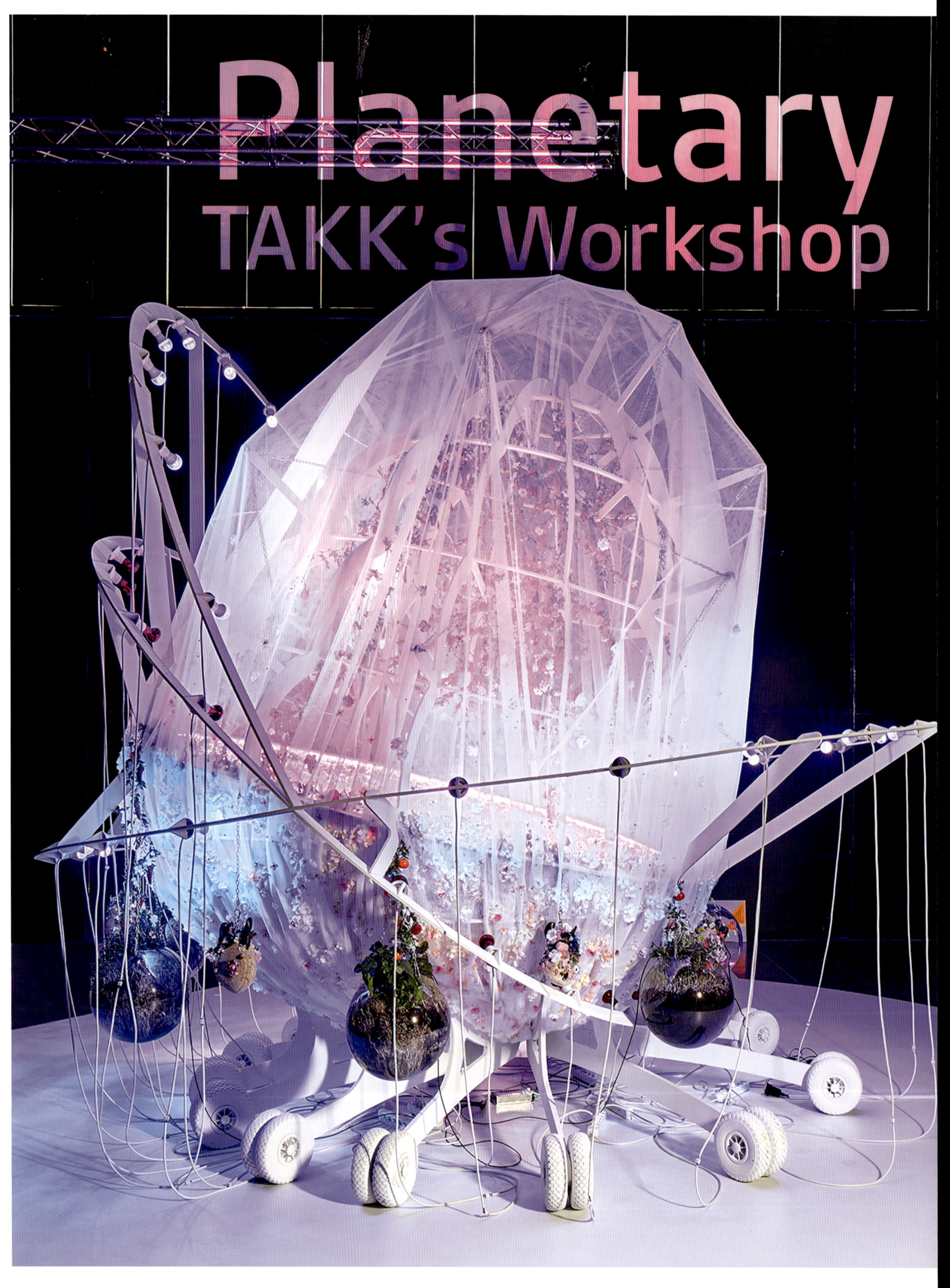
Planetary
TAKK's Workshop

Domesticity for *After*-modernity

Bart-Jan Polman

Within their home, a large warehouse and experimental workshop in Barcelona, architects Mireia Luzárraga and Alejandro Muiño of architectural practice TAKK have constructed a series of spaces that are of most use depending on the season and climatic conditions. Bart-Jan Polman, Director of Exhibitions and Public Programs, and Curator of the Arthur Ross Architecture Gallery, at Columbia University's Graduate School of Architecture, Planning and Preservation, explains TAKK's approach to the creation of this post-carbon domesticity, and their response to our contemporary unstable world.

How can domesticity be staged in an age of radical planetary instability? Instability itself would be a place to start. The instability of parts (growth, movement, scale, entropy). The instability of knowledge (scientific, spiritual, indigenous). Unstable ecologies (natural-artificial, pollution, climate, finance, labor). Or, perhaps more of a project than the realities that define the above, determining an instability for systems and institutions (patriarchy, heteronormativity, racism). Most of the above would mean little without decentering the human first: another act of destabilization challenging centuries of preconceived ideas.

An acknowledgement of these instabilities takes us to the core of TAKK's architectural practice, which consists of a combination of realized work and active pedagogical projects (Mireia Luzárraga, one half of TAKK, teaches at Columbia University's Graduate School of Architecture, Planning and Preservation in New York). The studio was founded by Mireia and Alejandro Muiño in Barcelona in the years after the 2008 financial crisis; yet another moment of radical instability that for many, including them, allowed for a rediscovery of the potential of politics at a time when austerity measures heavily accelerated the welfare state's destruction. Building on the ruins of this crisis, the associated real-estate crash allowed the two to take over an old factory building from which they not only develop their projects but also produce them. If the Bauhaus was a workshop for modernity, offering the space and tools to materially accommodate a project of societal transformation, then TAKK's is one of several workshops for *after*-modernity; one of a multitude of emerging practices ecologically shaping, testing, speculating, and crystallizing the social and political transformations needed for an exhausted world.

TAKK / Mireia Luzárraga and Alejandro Muiño, The Garden for Romantic Crossovers, Madrid, 2019

The Garden for Romantic Crossovers was designed for the Matadero Madrid cultural center, which stands at the heart of an urban heat island. To mitigate the effects of this, the nature-based design approach linked humans, non-human animals, biological entities, and technology to offer a microclimate that shields its occupants from excessive temperature swings.

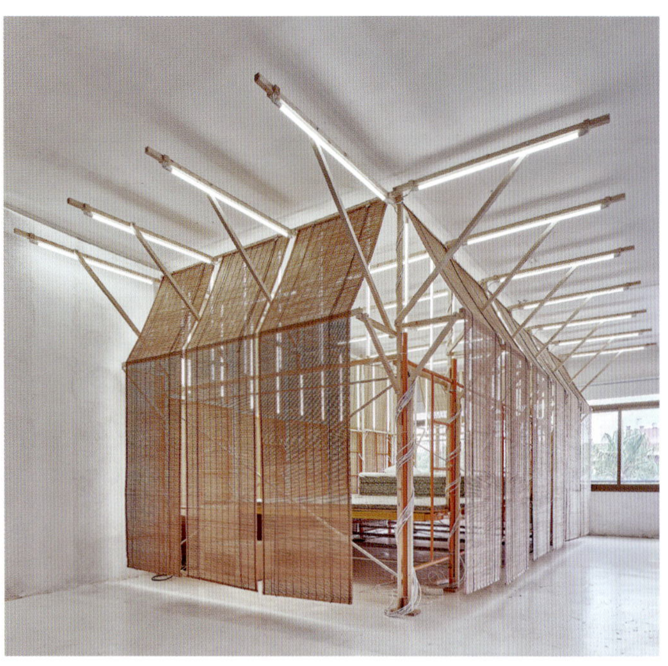

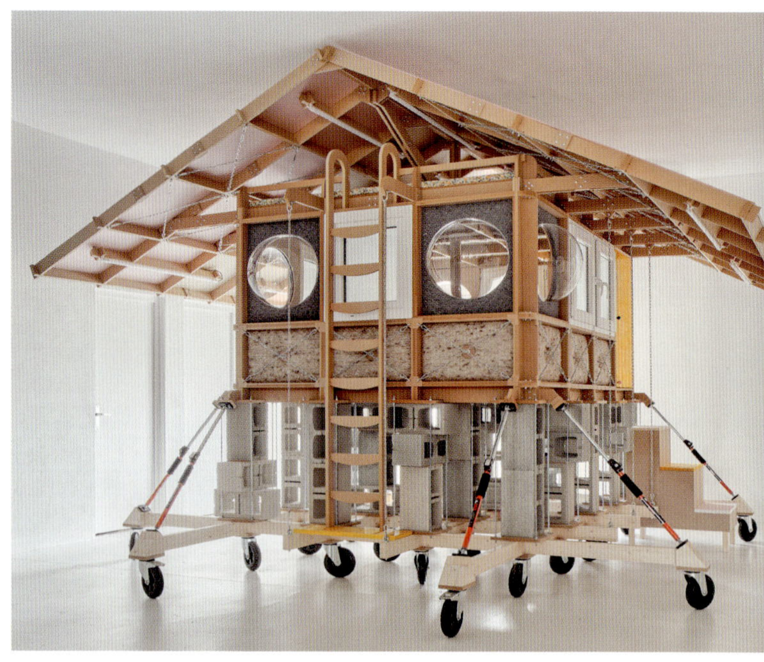

Domesticity as a Stage

The 400 square meters (4,300 square feet) that make up the workshop also make up the architects' home, and thereby offer a stage on which to design, build, and perform new forms of domesticity through their research-driven practice. TAKK calls this a post-carbon domesticity. The house they call the Seasonal House. It effectively functions as a large un-climatized space in which multiple objects are placed. These objects then offer spaces and conditions that are of most use during specific climatological bandwidths. There is a Winter Bedroom, for example, and a Summer Bedroom. If the house indeed serves as the stage on which to perform new forms of domesticity, then these objects function as their theatrical props.

The forms align with the four axes through which TAKK define their work: post-carbon, post-natural, postcolonial, and post-patriarchal. At the time of writing, in addition to the bedrooms, they consist of a Tropical Bathroom, Floor Lamp, Armchair, Winter Couch, Mobile Cinema, Vertical Sauna, and the more recent, spectacular, Roma's Bedroom. The Oxford English Dictionary defines theatrical props as "any portable object (now usually other than an article of costume) used in a play, film, etc." And indeed, like many of TAKK's projects, several of the props that make up the Seasonal House are on wheels. When not moveable or portable in the literal sense, their material lightness, adaptability, and transience offer another form of mobility.

The Language of Instability

The temporal instability of these structures is strengthened by the fact that many of them are made out of material from earlier TAKK projects. This engagement with a circular economy, possibly the key requisite for anything post-carbon, is variously defined. In one of the many diagrams TAKK has produced on their work, these processes are explained using the obvious term "recycling," but also "reviving," "upcycling," "re-using," "disclosing," "prolonging," "reprogramming," and "repurposing." This glossary of terms provides an extensive vocabulary through which one can start to engage within the material processes that separate traditional, carbon-intensive building methods from possible post-carbon ones. In other words, they are a necessary precondition that allows us to suppress and rethink questions of supply (chains) by fully acknowledging the scalar relationship between the architectural detail and the planetary effects caused by its production.

What makes TAKK's work so powerful is that this awareness also comes with the realization that such an architecture requires a new language altogether. While technology plays a pivotal role, its production is also fundamentally low-tech; a bricolage with a materiality consisting of concrete blocks, wooden slats, natural wool insulation, recycled cotton, scaffolding, or gypsum board. It is not fully free of precedents. The 1974 *Autoprogettazione* project by the Italian designer Enzo Mari immediately comes to mind.[1] By providing a set of blueprints with straightforward wooden furniture designs that could be self-assembled at home with simple materials, Mari sought a radical transformation of society by altering the modes of production for "design." This need to find a new language to accompany societal change, to build a language on your own, is an essential part of TAKK's worldmaking projects. Thus, while they are essentially low-tech, they rarely look that way.

TAKK / Mireia Luzárraga and Alejandro Muiño,
Summer Bedroom, Seasonal House,
Hospitalet del Llobregat,
Barcelona,
2023

opposite left: The 18-square-metre (194-square-foot) platformed Summer Bedroom combines six metal scaffolding elements with operable hemp blinds as well as pinewood slats that house the room's electrical system. The platform, 75 centimeters (0.75 feet) above the ground, is covered with recycled foam insulation.

TAKK / Mireia Luzárraga and Alejandro Muiño,
Roma's Bedroom, Seasonal House,
Hospitalet del Llobregat,
Barcelona,
2024

opposite right: Made entirely out of recycled materials, the two-story structure is fully mobile.

TAKK / Mireia Luzárraga and Alejandro Muiño,
Seasonal House, Hospitalet del Llobregat,
Barcelona,
2022–

right: Diagram showing several of the props in TAKK's Seasonal House in relation to the climatic bandwidths in which their functionality is optimal.

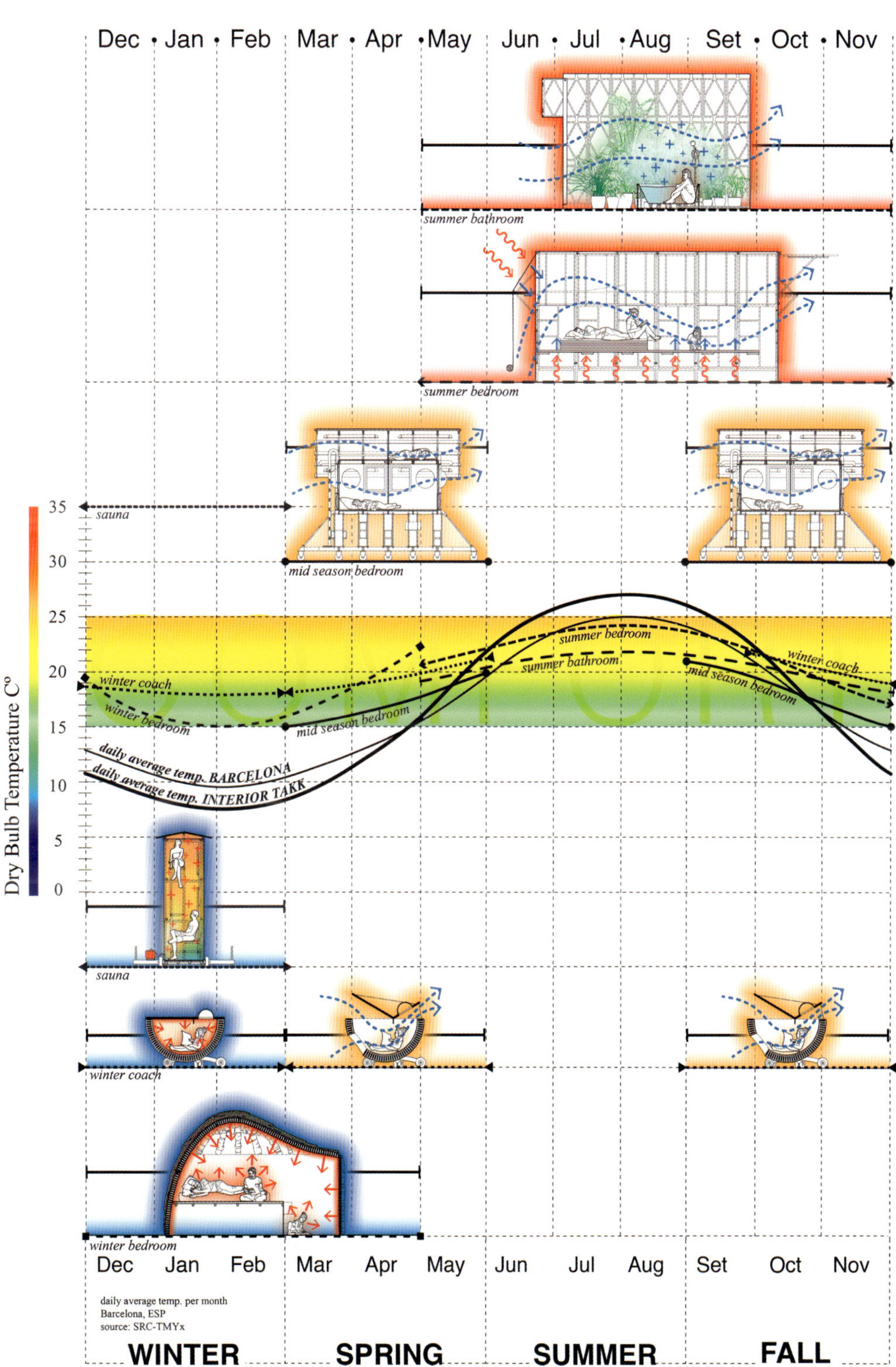

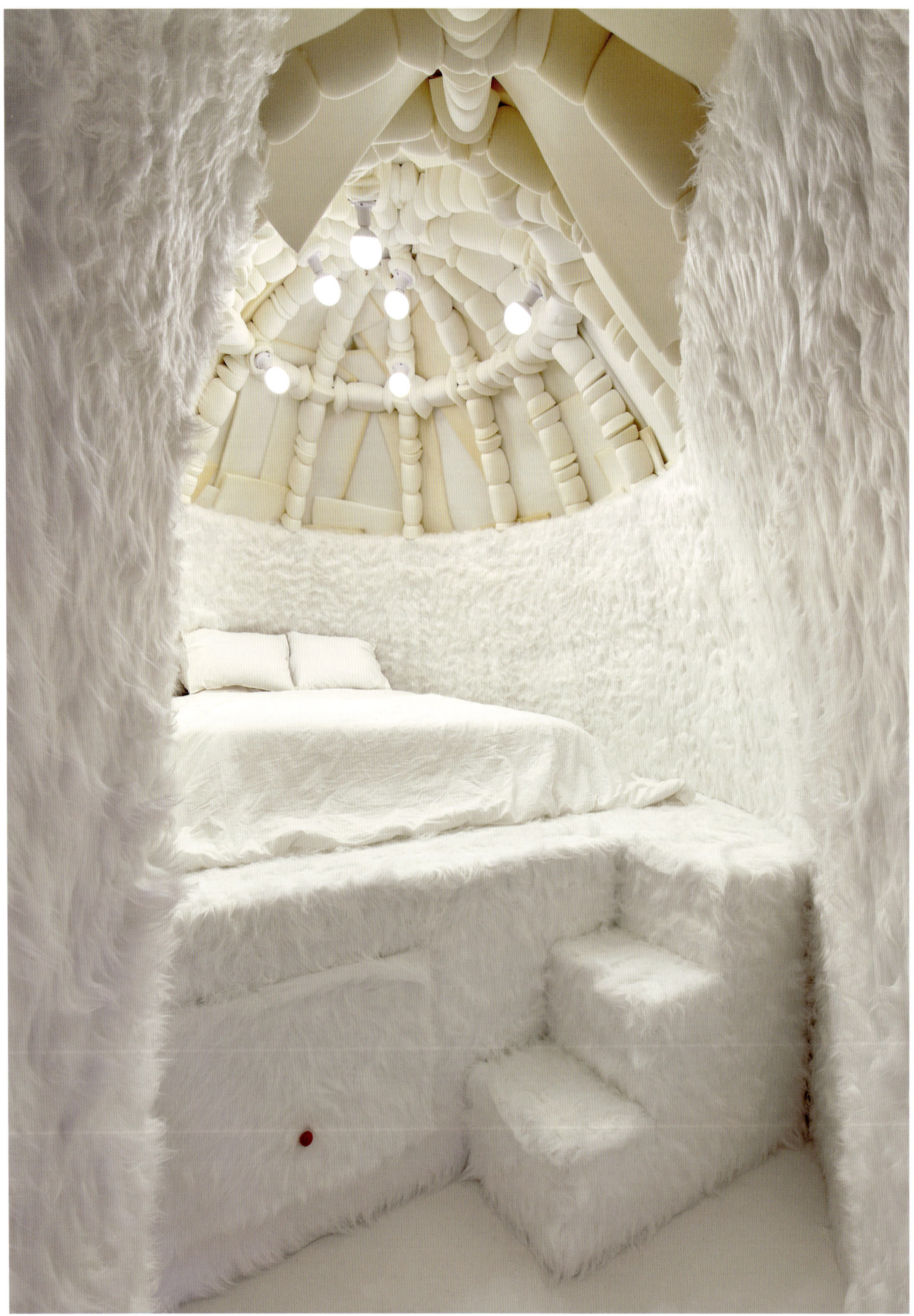

TAKK's exploration of domestic codes also entails a rethinking of domesticity itself as something that is opposed to a wilderness outside

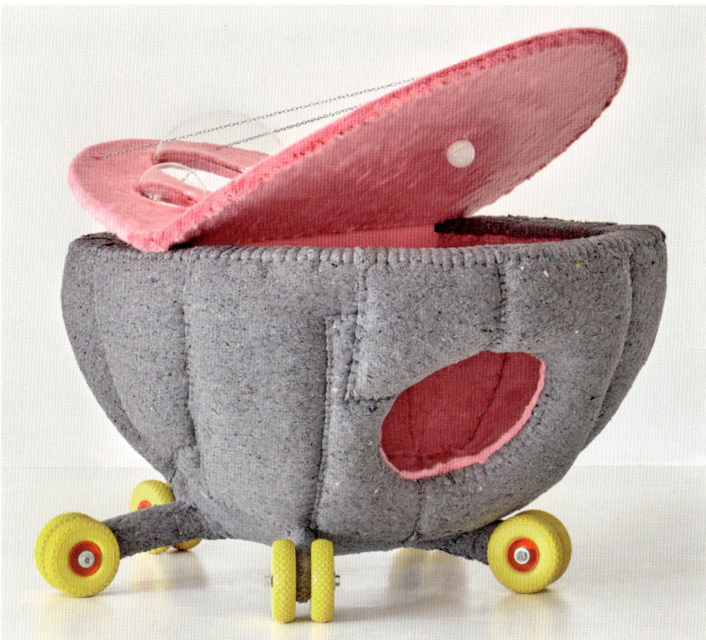

TAKK / Mireia Luzárraga and Alejandro Muiño,
Winter Couch, Seasonal House,
Hospitalet del Llobregat,
Barcelona,
2023

left: The most nest-like of the structures in the house, the Winter Couch can be used by the whole family during the cold winter months in a configuration that is either open or closed.

TAKK / Mireia Luzárraga and Alejandro Muiño,
Winter Bedroom, Seasonal House,
Hospitalet del Llobregat,
Barcelona,
2022

opposite: For use during the colder months, the Winter Bedroom reuses materials from *Eat Me*, a temporary installation TAKK designed for the 2021 Urvanity urban art festival in Madrid.

Feral Ecologies as Domestic Codes

TAKK's exploration of domestic codes also entails a rethinking of domesticity itself as something that is opposed to a wilderness outside. Instead of accepting a hard separation between the inside and the outside, rather, as what they call "Queer natures," the distinction between the natural and artificial is constantly contested. At the risk of a reduction to metaphors (TAKK's practice moves far beyond that), it is hard not to see many of the objects in the Seasonal House—such as the Winter Couch and Winter Bedroom—as nests, and the same goes for many of the other projects in TAKK's rapidly growing body of work. Human Nest (Domaine de Boisbuchet, France, 2023)—a summer workshop that experimented with weaving techniques based on observations of local birds' nests—is the most clear-cut example, but also the ELISAVA Fall Pavilion (Barcelona, 2023), Rosa Daybed and Lighthouse (Girona, 2019), and the Garden for Romantic Crossovers (Madrid, 2019).

Designed for an exhibition at the Matadero Madrid cultural center, the Garden for Romantic Crossovers served to illustrate how these nests are not simply symbolic, but are part of material and social compositions ranging from, say, the nano-spectrum of UV light to planetary heating. This included Madrid's heat-island effects, accelerated by climate change, for which the garden offered a stage on which the interaction between humans, non-human animals, biological entities, and technology was performed. TAKK calls it a "non-anthropocentric cohabitation infrastructural garden."[2] Like all of the practice's projects, it offered a narrative for possible futures, and in doing so situated it firmly within critiques of human-centeredness of the term "Anthropocene" to describe our current predicament. Indeed, for thinkers like Donna Haraway, the understanding of our times as the Anthropocene, by putting humans at its center, fails to grasp the ways in which humans and more-than-humans are inextricably linked, and thereby excludes the making-with that could define our possible futures.[3] Better would be to understand TAKK's exploration of possible futures as creating "feral" ecologies in which non-human entities become tangled up with human infrastructure projects.[4]

Such ecologies constitute the stages on which TAKK performs new forms of domesticity, with radical instability as one of many actors. Not quite wild and not quite domestic, the practice's entanglement of infrastructures offers the space for future human speculations that can then be socialized through various acts. This is the stage on which design can function as a tool for activism. In this future, nature is equally mobile as technology, simply because that distinction has fully collapsed.

Notes
1. Enzo Mari, *Proposta per un'autoprogettazione*, Galleria Milano (Milan), 1974.
2. See https://takksarchive.cargo.site/the-garden-for-romantic-crossovers.
3. Donna J. Haraway, *Staying with the Trouble: Making Kin in the Chthulucene*, Duke University Press (Durham, NC), 2016.
4. Anna L. Tsing et al., *Feral Atlas: The More-Than-Human Anthropocene*, Stanford University Press (Redwood City, CA), 2020.

BEEFY BABIES AND OTHER STAGING TECHNIQUES

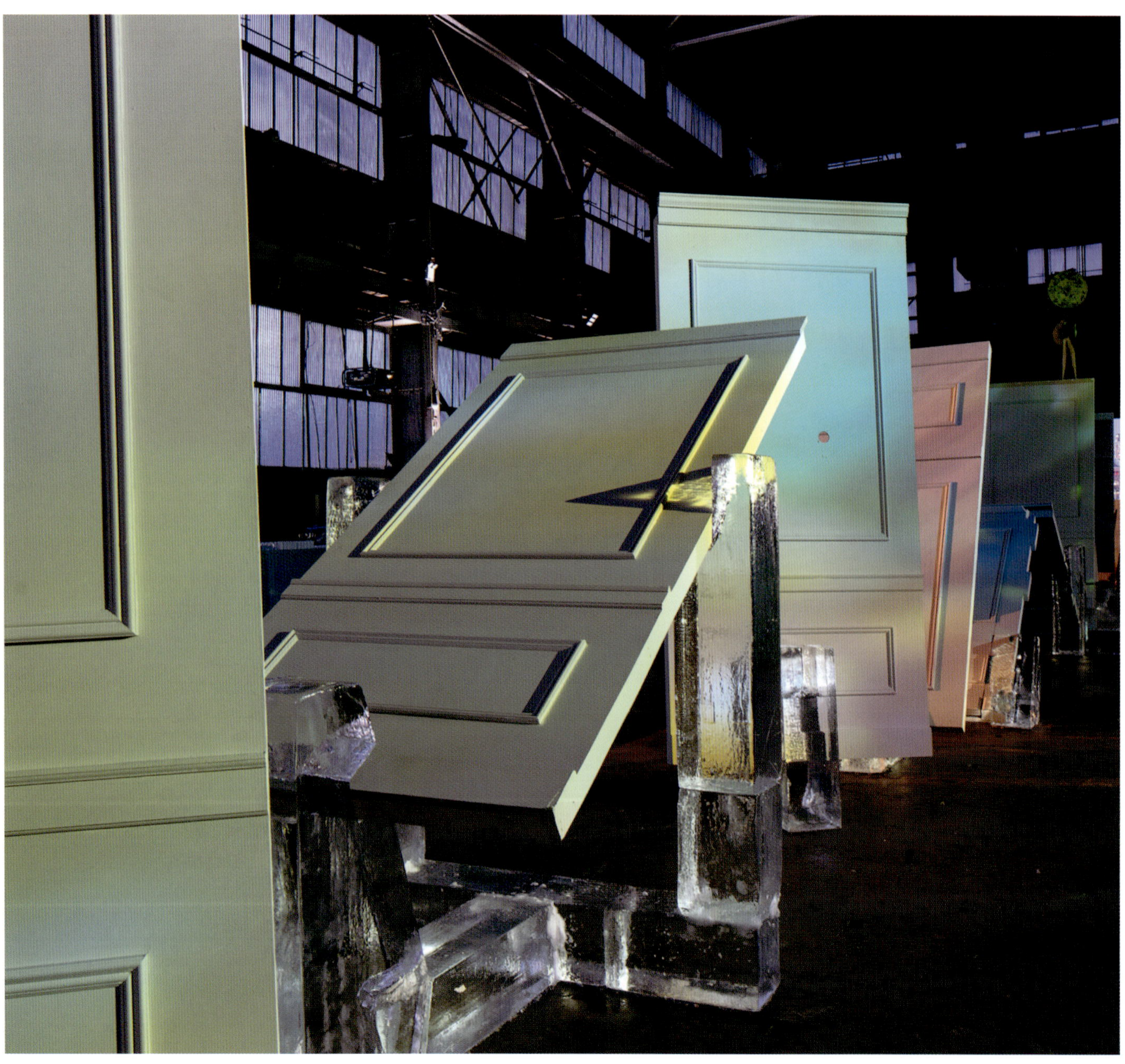

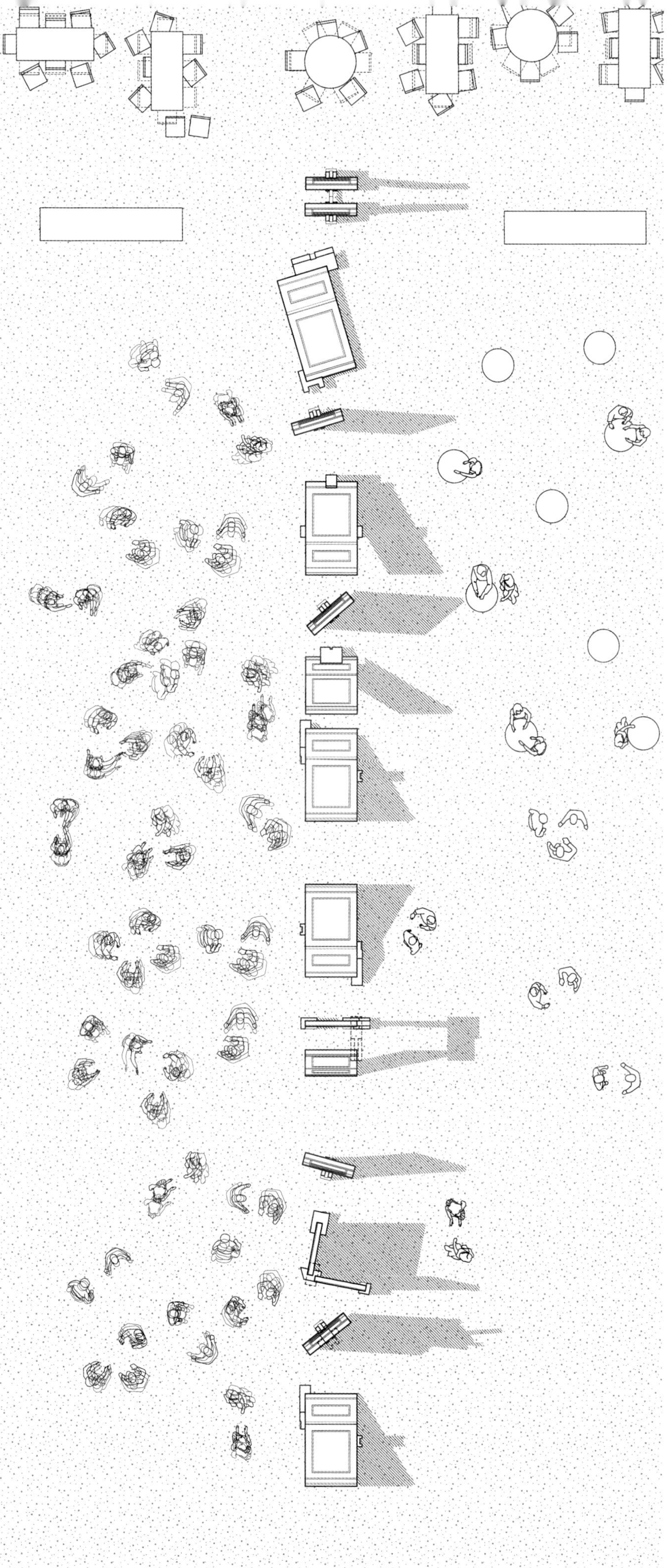

Jaffer Kolb

New Affiliates,
Beaux Arts Ball
installation,
Brooklyn Navy Yard,
New York,
2022

opposite: The architects focused on designing a series of ice-joints that ranged from small props to large sculptural armatures to hold the reclaimed panels in multiple orientations. Some leaned casually and slightly in a *contrapposto* stance while others were held in acrobatic suspension.

left: The custom-designed ice joints held 16 panels reclaimed from another set design in an animated sequence down the center of the large warehouse, which was once used to build military-grade submarines.

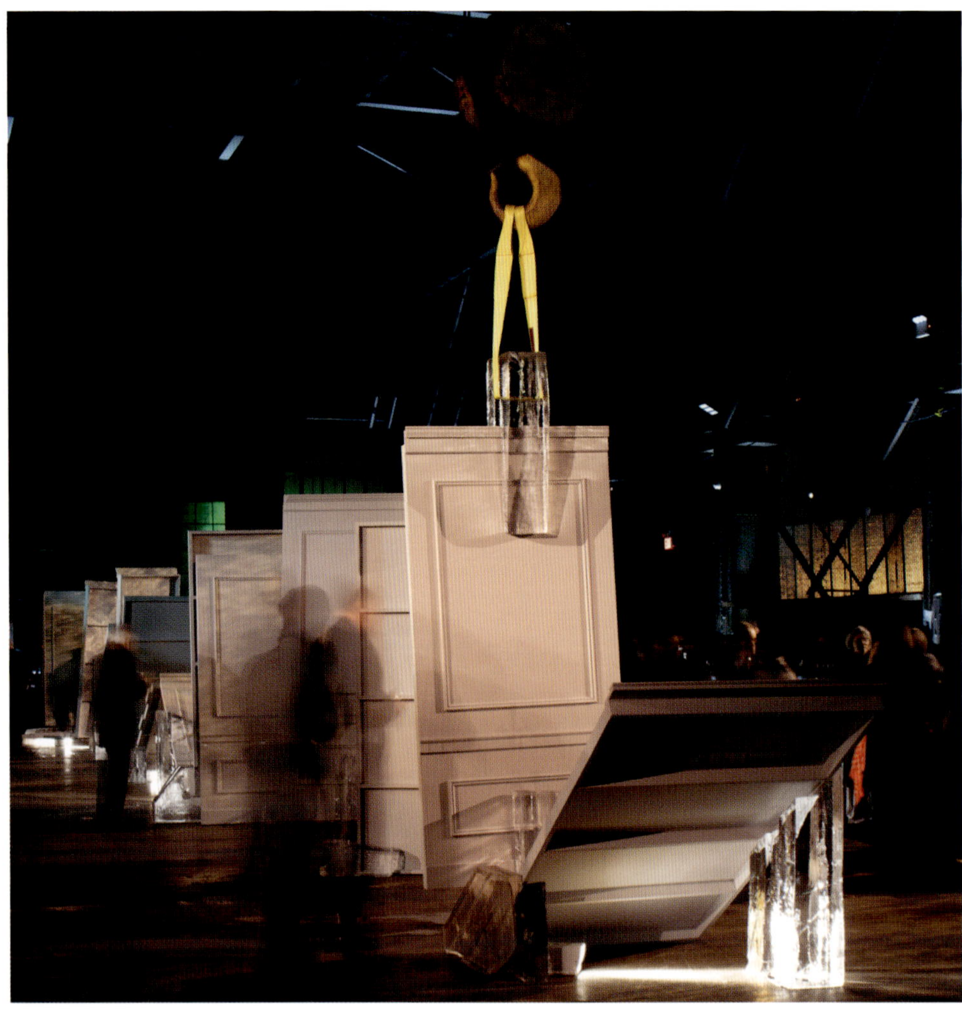

Included on the pages of *The Backstage Handbook*[1] are meat axes, turtles, knuckle-busters, cat's paw hitches, and beefy baby stands, among countless other delightful and strange rigging details commonly used in theatrical staging. The names are partly descriptive, partly anecdotal, and suggest how they are as much characters in the theatrical world as those played by the actors. Together, such details participate in a constellation of systems, connections, fast joints, clamps, and supports that produce a lexicon of temporary arrangements.

Staging produces its own architectural language, or vernacular, tasked to hold things together securely while transforming quickly. Assembly and disassembly may be required at a moment's notice. Rigging connections hold surfaces apart from structure to create seamless enclosures and interiors. Supported surfaces coalesce into specific environments (e.g. sets) complete with dedicated infrastructure (e.g. lighting) that may remain for a few weeks or just a few scenes.

Having worked on many temporary exhibitions and installations, at New Affiliates we have always been struck by the material ecologies produced by short-term architecture. Short-term, as in a six-month pavilion, a four-month exhibition, a two-week event, a one-night performance. Short-term, as in a way for a small office to get small projects, expand its client network, and to enter the market. Short-term, as in something disposable, but rarely designed with that consideration in mind.

Just in Time

We have a visceral memory from our first year in practice in 2017 of meeting a repeat museum client to discuss a new project and passing by our previous work dismantled and in dumpsters at the institution's service-entrance curb. A lifecycle, from fabrication to disposal, on immediate display—the walls and heavy tables used to produce interior organization all crumpled into a fragile pile. And this was just one exhibition.

Architecture is largely fueled by the desire to project an image of regeneration and novelty. New homeowners personalize through renovation. Public buildings are designed to reflect ideology and vision—all temporary conditions. Commercial buildings and stores communicate brand values. Where earlier generations may have been content to deploy superficial symbols (see: decorated shed), now we are expected to embed branding into less transferable media (form, material, space). Ironic, given the increased rates at which things change. Perhaps businesses know they may quickly become obsolete, so they commission heavier design strategies to portend longevity.

We find ourselves in an era of architecture in warp-speed, part of a constant cycle of perpetual newness that points to larger issues dealing with reuse and obsolescence. And this causes us to fantasize about permanence, both in its ego—the fantasy of leaving behind a 200-year trace of our work—and its ethos—what could be more sustainable than the pyramids?

COFOUNDER OF NEW YORK ARCHITECTURAL FIRM NEW AFFILIATES, **JAFFER KOLB** RECOUNTS THEIR TRANSIENT AND DISAPPEARING SETTING FOR THE CITY'S BEAUX ARTS BALL. AN INTERIOR STAGING PREDICATED ON USING DOORS FROM A DECOMMISSIONED INSTALLATION PERCHED IN PRECARIOUS POSITIONS AND SUPPORTED BY MELTING ICE CONNECTIONS AND STRUCTURES, AN ICY LEXICON OF JOINTING CONFIGURATIONS WERE EXPLOITED TO PRODUCE A MOMENTARY THEATRICAL SPACE OF IMPLIED JEOPARDY AND DRAMA.

Fantasy and reality collide, and we are left in a fragile balance: to produce lasting images while acknowledging shifting speeds of desire and fluid models of ownership.

Through this double-bind, staging techniques become increasingly germane, describing not just a particular temporality of design, but in the production of architecture itself. We might learn from these techniques to produce environments that shift quickly and envelop wholly, through ingenuity found in connection and assembly.

New Affiliates,
Beaux Arts Ball installation,
Brooklyn Navy Yard,
New York,
2022

The series of identical panels were held in various configurations to make the large-scale centerpiece, together forming a sequence recalling Eadweard Muybridge's stop-motion photographs.

Setting the Stage

Walking past that dumpster packed with our last exhibition design, we promised ourselves we would try to do better. We would try to figure out a way to participate in designing the same endless array of environments but with other timelines in mind. To consider circulating in boundless networks of exchange instead of thinking of histories as stretching from beginning to end.

In 2018 we partnered with New York City's Department of Sanitation to work across museums and galleries to share resources, minimize waste, and invent details oriented to future use: surfaces designed for easy removal and reinstallation, casework designed for transportation and adaptation. These details would allow shows to maintain their character—the network would remain largely imperceptible to maintain the appearance of perpetual newness.

New Affiliates,
Beaux Arts Ball installation,
Brooklyn Navy Yard,
New York,
2022

right: The supports for the large panels were made of ice to ensure there was no waste once the one-night installation concluded, and also to highlight the fragility of architectural connections.

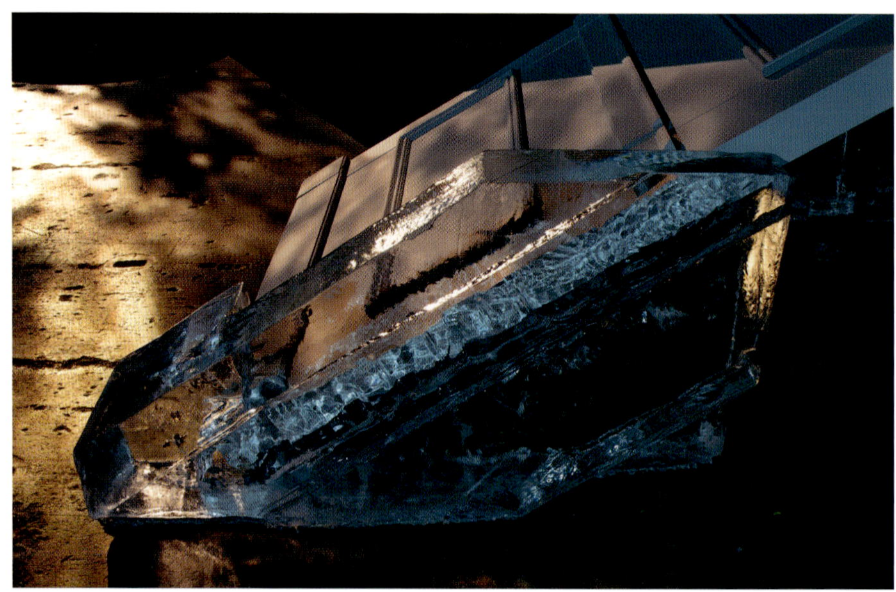

BEEFY BABY STANDS DO NOT SEEM QUITE SO BEEFY

At the same time we were invited to design the scenography for a large production at New York City's Park Avenue Armory by the contemporary artist Rashaad Newsome who realizes work on artificial intelligence and performance through sculpture and digital media. *Assembly*, his work for the Armory, demanded a 10,000-square-foot (930-square-meter) gallery, 350-seat auditorium, and additional exhibition space—all for a two-week run. From the outset we developed design options with concern hovering above us like a warning signal or a cloudy horizon.

The Armory's producers redirected such concerns to conversations about speed: the build-out would need to go up and come down in a matter of days. No time for drywall, for studs, and certainly no time for dumpsters and trash. We would need to use rentable set systems: trusses and modular frames and scrims, and raked seating, that would arrive on truck beds, perfectly sized for transportation, engineered for drop-off and pickup.

Throughout the project we witnessed the lean and practiced efficiency of staging. Installation schedules were so tight that crews were unable to pause for disposal: waste was minimized due more to speed than to do-gooderism. And because this speed is demanded by the market, it is remarkably effective. At the end of the run we watched as neatly packed rental trucks carted away the modular 40-foot (12-meter) walls and steel-framed platforms to their next destination. It was like a children's book where cats are mayors and everything seems to work in a frictionless circuit. There is no past or future, just the mechanics of cheerful repetition.

Scrounging Through a Microeconomy

In 2022 we were invited to design a one-night installation for the Architectural League of New York's annual Beaux Arts Ball. The event would take place in a 20,000-square-foot (1,860-square-meter) warehouse in Brooklyn Navy Yard—a 19th-century military boat-building complex turned into an incubator for small businesses and startups. Our site was Building 269, once a submarine-building facility that later became a fish distribution center and then an event space hosting film shoots, fashion shows, and political debates.

Today, the Navy Yard hosts fabrication shops pumping out the stage sets, commercial displays, and exhibition furniture that oxygenate the city's blood. It is full of startups that capture venture capital, opening and closing doors like gently lapping waves. It hosts specialized artisans from plaster experts to sand-blasters to garment manufacturers who all plug into various niches around the city's equally specialized production ecosystem. The Navy Yard is an engine for the city's own ephemeral stagings—where it manufactures the surfaces that reflect its shifting character.

We used the project to investigate its material networks, contacting businesses to learn about their processes and byproducts. Memorably, we stumbled into the shop that has been producing all of *Saturday Night Live*'s sets for the last 40 years. Most people we talked to were surprisingly sympathetic, giving us physical material (waste materials, set pieces) that we could carry away and for which we might invent second lives.

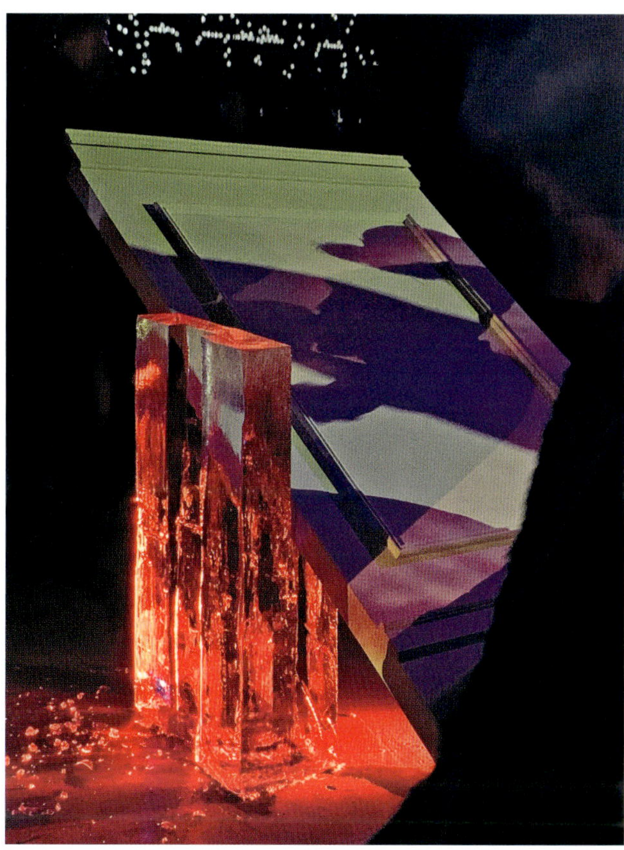

left: The custom-fabricated ice modules were held together using a technique based on Japanese wood joinery.

WHEN YOU CONSIDER MAKING THEM OUT OF ICE

Our largest haul came when we found ourselves talking to Thom De Jesu, founder of the scenographic fabrication shop Daddy-O Productions in Building 280. De Jesu gave us a tour of his shop, showing us recent projects and stored objects. In a back corner and covered in a thin layer of sawdust we spotted 16 identical 8-foot panels featuring minimal wainscoting, crown- and base-molding, and painted white. They were built for a New Year's Eve promotion by Airbnb, cladding the interior of a room hosting a lucky guest for one night in Times Square, for whom Mariah Carey performed a private concert on Zoom. De Jesu didn't want to discard the panels and agreed to lend them for the week.

We considered how to restage the 16 panels for the Architectural League's fundraising gala, first imagining the connections that would bring them back to life. Drawing from our recent experience at the Park Avenue Armory, we turned to the same joints that turn flats into scenes. These details—the beefy babies and knuckle-busters—hold everything together but are formally neglected, painted black, and covered in traces (scratches, gaff tape) of previous stagings. They are under pressure: should they fail, the entire set collapses—the fourth wall toppled, the fantasy dissolved.

We wanted to exaggerate these details: to bring them to life and treat them as scenographic protagonists. We wanted to play with their visibility and low-waste efficiency through standardization. We wanted to make them out of something solid that would disappear, something as ephemeral as the installation itself. We wanted something fit for a party but inherently structural.

So we settled on ice.

We thought of ice swans at weddings and those trendy ice hotels. At first it seemed impossible, given the connection details outlined in rigging manuals. Beefy baby stands do not seem quite so beefy when you consider making them out of ice. We turned to Japanese wood joinery, which is more solid and structural, and began to use that as the basis for designing a staging system of fittings and connections.

Weak Joints

The blocks would hold our panels in an animated sequence down the center of the room, recalling a sequence from photographer Eadweard Muybridge's pioneering, late 19th-century studies of movement, or an early Cubist painting. They would produce a range of positions to create varied arrangements: hoisting them overhead, hanging them from above, positioning them in various angles. We designed the connections to interlock. In the end, there were eight types producing 27 pieces fabricated by an ice sculptor in nearby Long Island who had only ever made freestanding displays.

On the day of the ball, the pieces were brought to the Navy Yard in wool blankets in the fabricator's insulated and refrigerated van and set up as late as possible to avoid melting. Once the panels were set, they were projection-mapped and used as a large-scale lighting feature that transformed over the course of the evening, which began as a 200-person sit-down dinner and turned into a 1,400-person party over six hours.

THE ICE DETAILS PRODUCED ENVIRONMENTS IN TWO REGISTERS: THE PRODUCTION OF SPACE THROUGH THE SUSPENDED PANELS, AND THE SUGGESTION OF THEIR PRECARITY

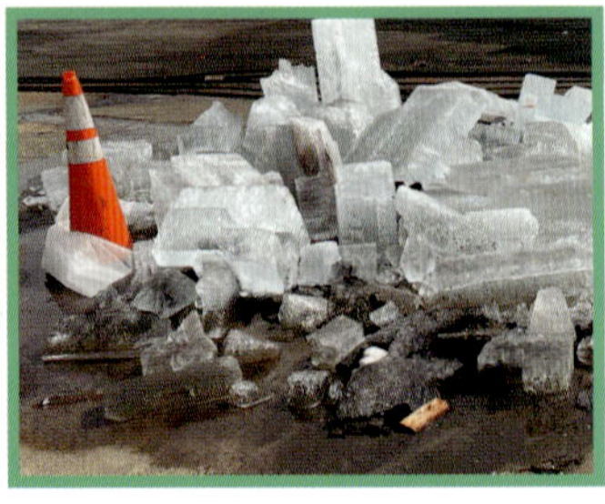

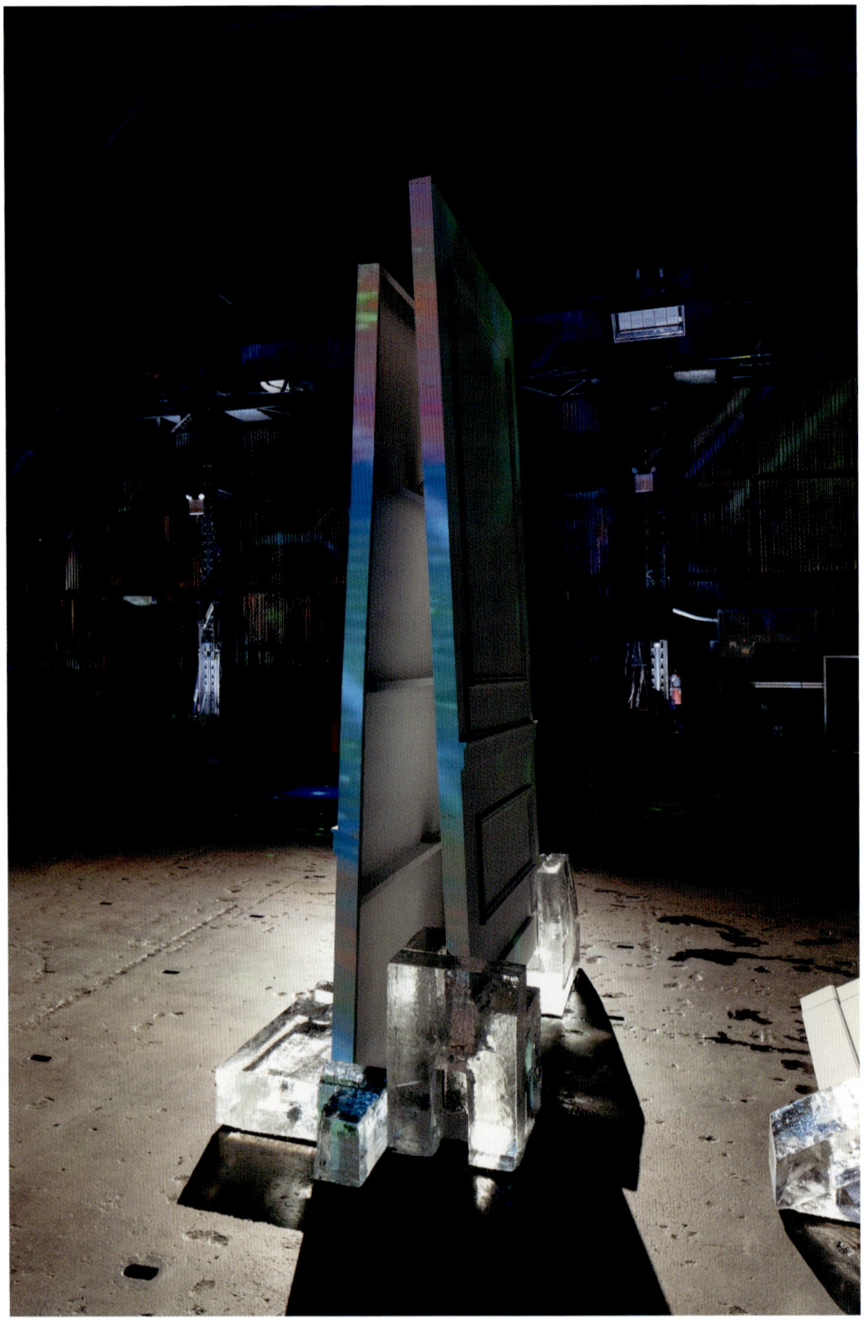

New Affiliates,
Beaux Arts Ball installation,
Brooklyn Navy Yard,
New York,
2022

left: The blocks of ice melted away the following day, resulting in no material waste.

above: Screen painting and projection-mapping of the panels created a custom lighting design element. The lights highlighted and activated the panels, refracting through the ice joints to produce a litany of effects that expanded their spatial impact within the large room.

opposite: Designing each connective ice-joint required structural calculations to determine how the individual wood panels would be propped up. The calculations included estimating the rate of melting and ensuing deflection to the orientation of the panels.

The event took place on a chilly evening in early March. The building was barely conditioned, but as more bodies pressed around the installation, the individual ice-blocks began to sweat and water started to pool at their bases. The joinery pieces, so carefully calibrated, began to shift and slacken. We initially considered the Cubist gesture a frozen moment in time, but it became instead a wobbly and unstable form.

As the ice sweated, so did we. It was melting faster than we thought. We nervously circled the installation like fretting parents but could do nothing. The party's organizers remained optimistic and confident. We counted down the minutes until the party's end, pools of water under each panel expanding until they touched. At the party's designated finish, we began prodding staff to usher out revelers, who themselves were becoming increasingly emboldened to touch, poke, and even caress the installation. When there were only 15 or 20 people left, scattered around the massive room, the first piece broke. We fled.

The next day, when we returned, the panels had been picked up by their fabricator and the ice had been taken out to an adjacent loading dock, warmed under the sun and melting into an amorphous whole. Inside was empty, save for a few traces of drying water on the ground and a crew unloading chairs and building a stage for a musical performance that evening. There was no other evidence of our labor, other than a relief so great it must have a physical form.

The ice details produced environments in two registers: the production of space through the suspended panels, and the suggestion of their precarity. The former ties back to the history of theater, of event, of spectacle, and of atmosphere; the latter ties to the ecology of material circulation and interwoven chronologies of use and value. Staging provides a framework to understand architecture itself, which is only ever just a combination of materials held together for fleeting moments, from millennia to microseconds. ᗡ

Note
1. Paul Carter and George Chiang, *The Backstage Handbook: An Illustrated Almanac of Technical Information*, Broadway Press (Louisville, KY), 3rd edn, 2010.

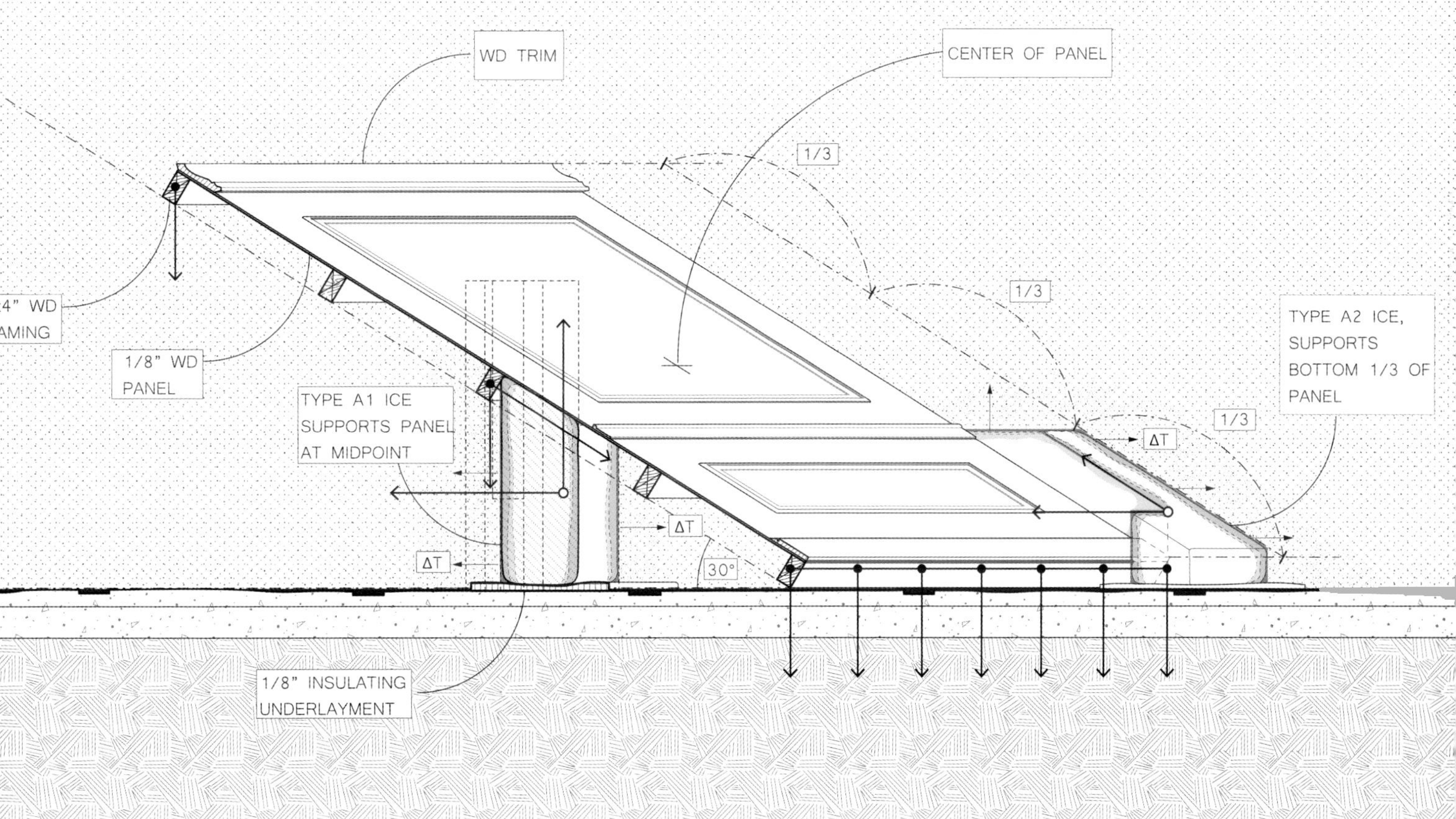

Re-**staging** the Glance

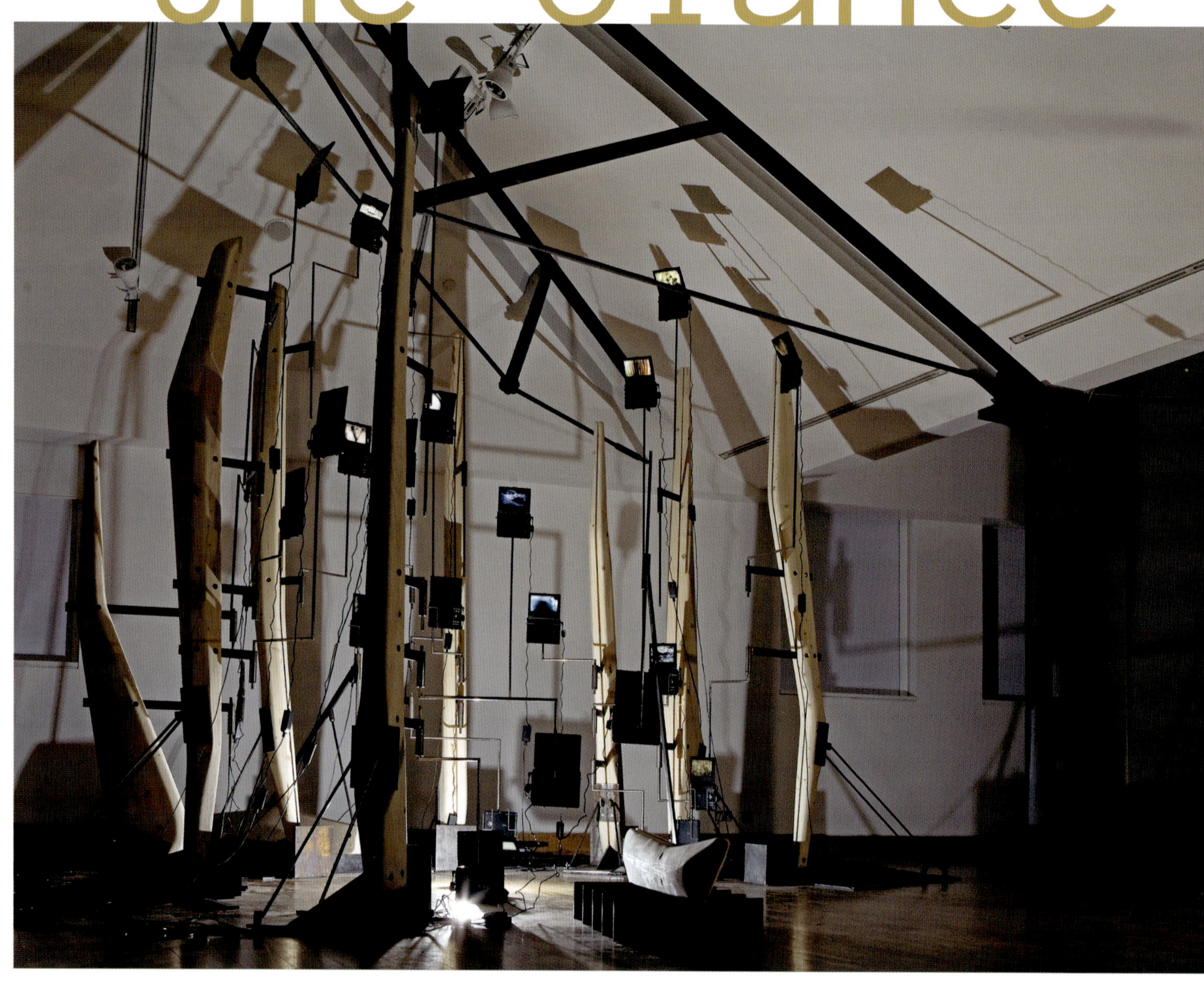

Metis (Mark Dorrian and Adrian Hawker)
with Victoria Clare Bernie,
Northroom installation,
The Lighthouse,
Glasgow, Scotland,
2006-7

The cinematic skin formed by the installation's 32 screens re-enacted the geometry of David Hume's mausoleum, the neoclassical monument on Edinburgh's Calton Hill designed for the Scottish Enlightenment philosopher by Robert Adam. The timber and steel figures were assembled as though in discussion. An outrider stood back as a witness and gatekeeper, inviting entrance.

Northroom— a Polyoptic Panorama

Adrian Hawker

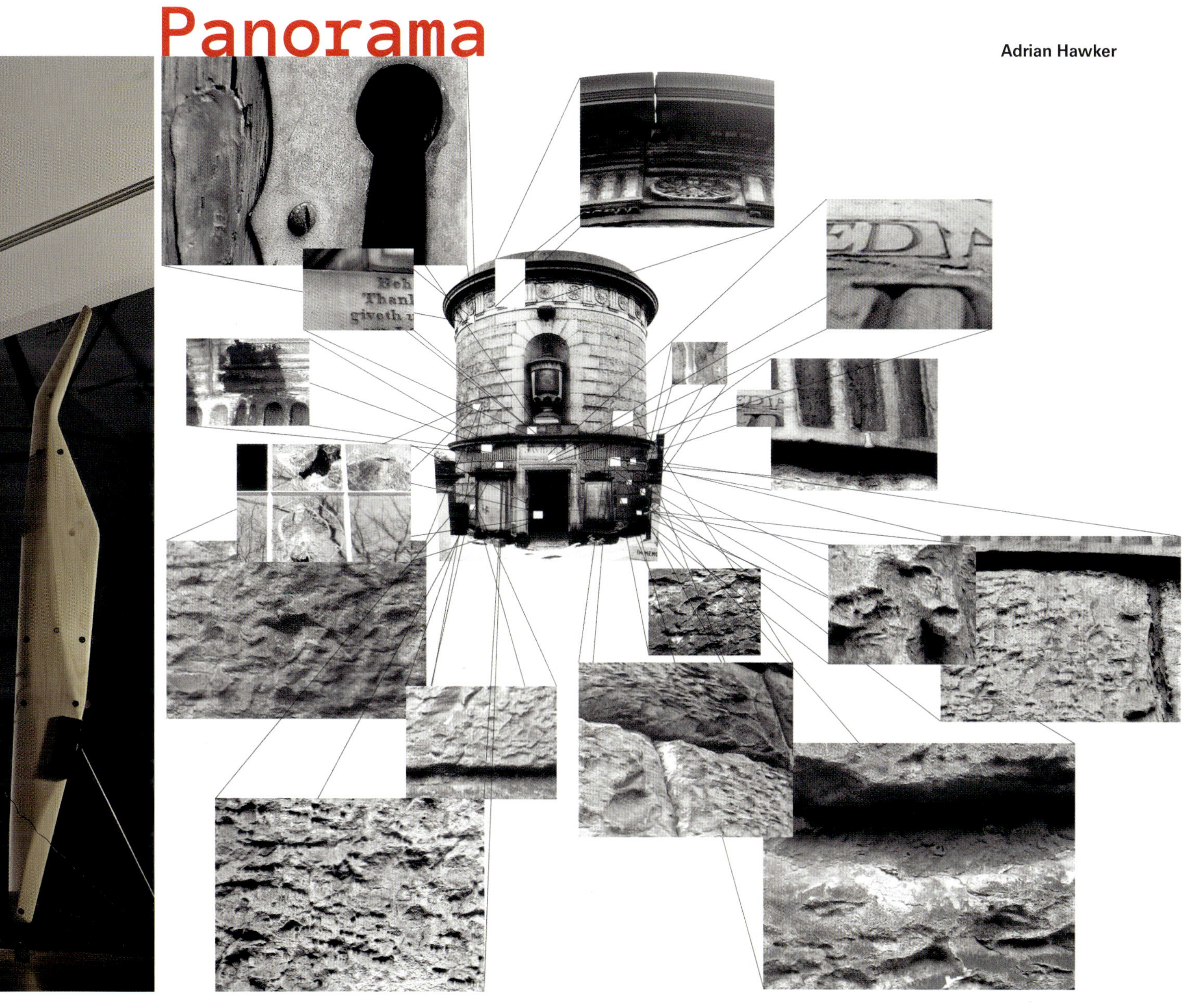

Metis (Mark Dorrian and Adrian Hawker) with Victoria Clare Bernie, *Northroom*, survey of David Hume's tomb, Edinburgh, Scotland, 2006

The gaze of the panorama was inverted and dispersed, allowing a close scrutiny of Hume's mausoleum. Marks of time, cracks, and inscription defined a polyoptic field, a micro-cartography, a map from which to situate the individual films.

Taking inspiration from Edinburgh's Robert Adam-designed memorial to Scottish Enlightenment philosopher David Hume, Metis (Mark Dorrian and Adrian Hawker) with artist Victoria Clare Bernie proposed *Northroom*—an architectural observatory dedicated to the close scrutiny and metaphoric transformation of the monument's surfaces. Mobile and discontinuous, using analog and digital means, it critically and playfully folds the logic of the panorama in on itself, proposing a kind of expansive thinking that is driven through the viewing of small things. **Adrian Hawker** describes its gestation.

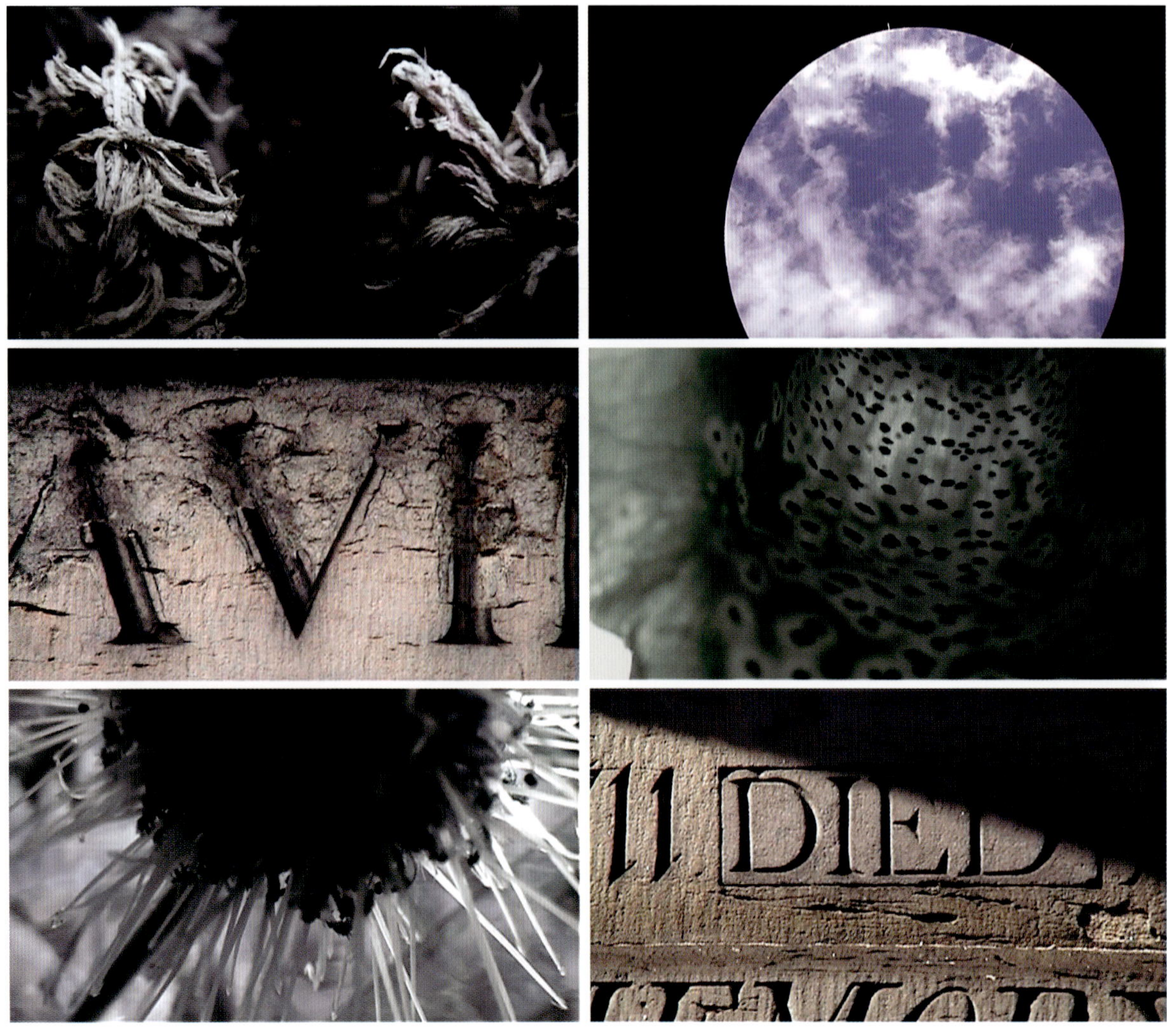

Northroom was conceived in relation to Edinburgh's Calton Hill, a locus of optical experimentation and the birthplace of the panorama. It was a re-staging of 18th-century British neoclassical architect Robert Adam's cylindrical monument to the Scottish Enlightenment philosopher David Hume. As a traveling installation, *Northroom* re-performed the panorama, switching its distant visuality to one that became about the close scrutiny of the monument's surface. Twelve timber and steel figures were gathered to array a suite of 32 films that depicted multiple landscapes, scales, and temporalities imagined through the weathered fissures in Adam's neoclassical enclosure and cast them onto new contexts as a drifting and polyoptic form of observatory.

Northroom was produced as part of a touring exhibition entitled "The Northern City: Between Light and Dark,"[1] organized by The Lighthouse architecture center in Glasgow. Their home was its first destination, the upper galleries of the Charles Rennie Mackintosh-designed former Glasgow Herald building (1895). From here it traveled to the Renaissance hall of the Palagio di Parte Guelfa in Florence, designed by Filippo Brunelleschi in 1418, before returning to Edinburgh to be installed below the undulating soffits of the entrance foyer to the Scottish Parliament Building (2004), the work of Enric Miralles Benedetta Tagliabue (EMBT). Finally, two figures and their associated films were, on invitation, exhibited at the Royal Academy of Arts' galleried extension (1873) to London's Burlington House, designed by Robert Banks and Charles Barry Jr.

The structure and cinematic skin of *Northroom* referenced the curious cylindrical "northern room" of Adam's mausoleum to Hume. Designed in 1777, the year following Hume's death, the tomb was constructed on the flanks of Calton Hill overlooking Scotland's capital. Hume's will, written the year prior to his death, detailed the conditions in which he wished to be interred: "if I shall dye any where in Scotland, I shall be bury'd in a private manner in Calton Church Yard, the South Side of it, and a Monument be built over my Body at the Expence not exceeding a hundred Pounds, with an Inscription containing only my Name with the year of my Birth and Death, leaving it to Posterity to add the Rest."[2] Adam conceived the monument as a singular, cylindrical stone chamber, open to the sky.

Optical Terrain

Hume's specification ensured that he would become part of the great monument to the Enlightenment itself, an Athenian Acropolis of the North elevated above the open and ordered vision of Edinburgh's First New Town. Constructed between 1766 and 1850, this civic plan offered an airy, formal alternative to the dense medieval cluster of the capital's Old Town. By the year of Hume's death, James Craig, its architect, had also initiated the construction of an observatory on the plateau of Calton Hill but, as Robert Adam witheringly observed, "here is a building, which the folly of its contrivers led them to begin but without considering that by their poverty, they were unable to finish it."[3] Craig instead shifted his attention to a more modest Gothic tower overlooking his nascent city. In doing so, he seeded what was to become an extraordinary terrain of optical experimentation.

The tower was utilized by Thomas Short, the celebrated Edinburgh optician who installed his astronomical telescopes as a form of public observatory. Following Short's death in 1788, the newly formed Edinburgh Astronomical Institution commissioned William Playfair to build a more scientifically orientated observatory on the site of Craig's incomplete "folly." By 1818, his Palladian rotunda had emerged alongside a curiously telescopic tower, a monument to Admiral Lord Nelson, later crowned with a nautical timeball whose one o'clock drop was synchronized to the Institution's astronomical observations and choreographed to cannon report from Edinburgh Castle.

In 1827, Maria Short claimed her father's "Large Gregorian Reflecting Telescope" for her inheritance and set up a Popular Observatory below the tower. As if in mockery of the elite austerity of the official Institution, a handbill advertisement from 1830, currently held in the Bill Douglas Cinema Museum in Exeter, England, revealed her building to be a timber miniature of Playfair's design. For the entrance price of one shilling, she demonstrated the "Finest and most Extensive Collection of Optical Instruments in Europe" including a "Superb Achromatic Telescope," a "Grand Solar Microscope," and a "Splendid Camera Obscura." Following forced eviction from the hill in 1851, she set the latter upon a more permanent support, a building on the foot of the Castle esplanade later adopted as the Outlook Tower by the sociologist and town planner Patrick Geddes.

Metis (Mark Dorrian and Adrian Hawker) with Victoria Clare Bernie, *Northroom*, film stills, 2006

The suite of films that formed the subject and inner surface of this polyoptic panorama engaged detailed studies of distant micro-landscapes of Scotland with the weather-beaten, scribed skin of the monument. Through temporality and soundscape, they alternately held the gaze through slow hypnotic repetitive movement or diverted it with a distracting flicker or aural intervention.

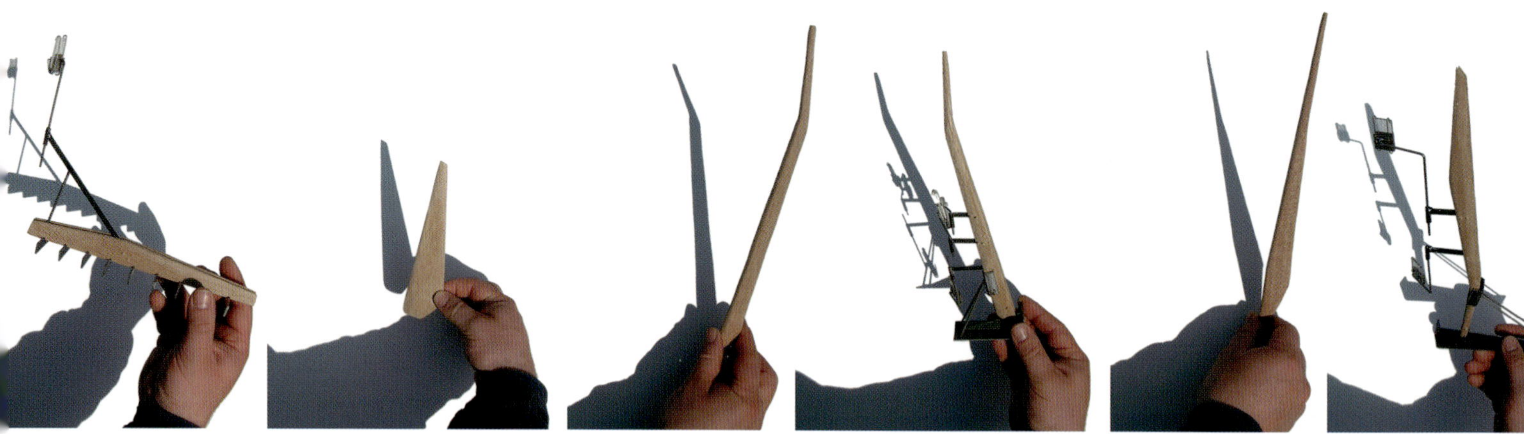

Metis (Mark Dorrian and Adrian Hawker)
with Victoria Clare Bernie,
Northroom, model studies at 1:10 scale,
Edinburgh, Scotland,
2006

above: Each of the 12 figures was formed from paired single sections of yellow pine set upon steel footings. Their forms, designed to realize the full reach of the tomb survey, were studied through models. While resembling one another, their poise and posture differed. Some maintained the verticality of the tomb, others were hunched, some reclined, almost horizontal.

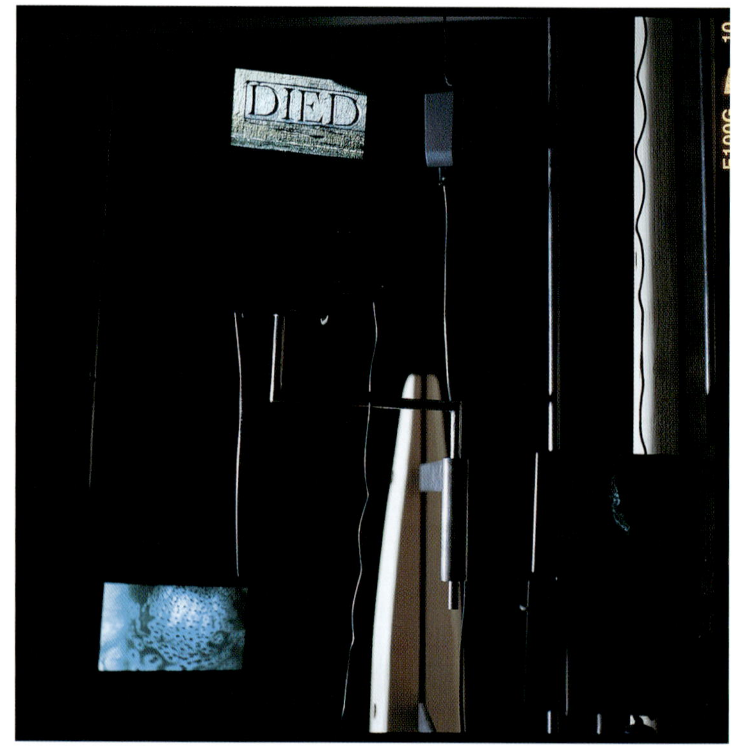

Metis (Mark Dorrian and Adrian Hawker)
with Victoria Clare Bernie,
Northroom installation, The Lighthouse,
Glasgow, Scotland,
2006-7

above: From inside *Northroom* the experience was always to do with the glance between subjects, attempting to form connection or calibrate scale and distance. The pan across the minute surface of a petal appeared vastly enlarged as though describing a greater landscape, the passage across a strange forest floor. Movement was a constant; the camera when stationary registered the slow passage of a shadow across inscribed stone or a breeze upon a cobweb.

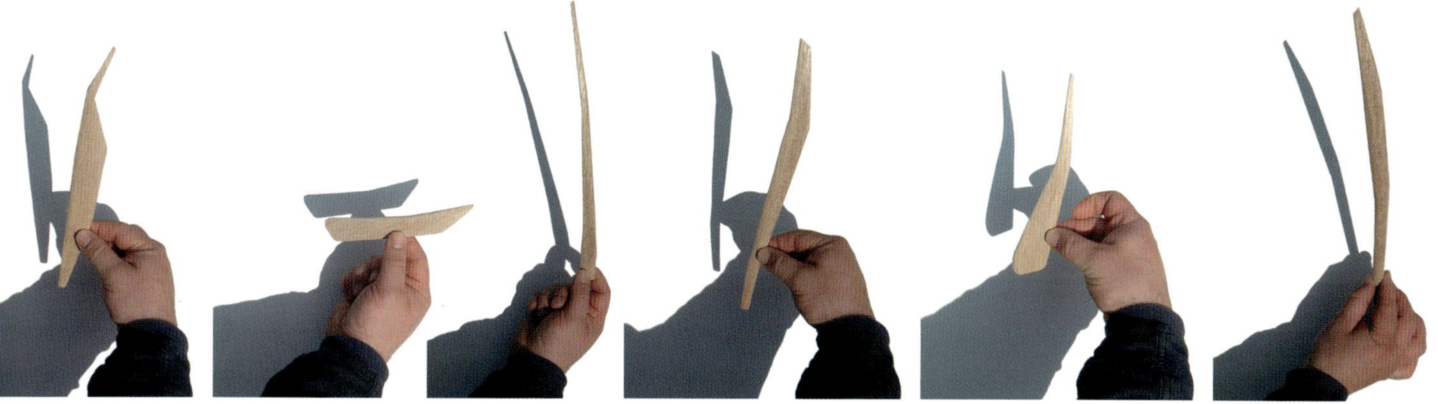

By 1791, Robert Adam's concerns had moved east of Hume's mausoleum with a commission for a new prison. The Bridewell, as it became known, was based on the philosopher Jeremy Bentham's project of surveillance. Bentham had just published the first of three volumes to promote proposals for a "Panopticon or Inspection House." Although demolished in the late 19th century, its figure is still evident in the ruins adjacent to the Old Calton Burial Ground and in detailed Ordnance Survey maps from the 1850s where exercise yards are shown enclosed by walls hinged with circular towers in a manner recalling Hume's tomb.

The following year, from the roof of Craig's tower, the painter Robert Barker prepared a continuous sequence of six engravings depicting a 360-degree view of Edinburgh. Through this work he introduced the term "panorama," from the Greek *pan* (all) and *horama* (view). Ironically, The Bridewell is obscured by raised ground but Hume's mausoleum is evident to the left of the third panel, with Craig's ordered streetscape emerging to the right. In the sixth, an incongruously foreshortened Craig chimney modestly obscures a fragment of his octagonal "folly" set in a strange astronomical garden of tree-like orreries.

Barker obtained a patent for "an entire new Contrivance or apparatus which he calls La Nature a coup d'œil for the purpose of displaying views of Nature at large by Oil Painting Fresco Water Colours Crayons or any other Mode of Painting or Drawing."[4] This "contrivance" involved a rotunda onto which a painted panorama, such as the one first devised on Craig's rooftop, would completely line the inner surface so that when viewed from the center it would provide an all-encompassing illusion of reality. The immersion required the image to be of such a scale that the visitor would necessarily rotate their gaze—"*à coup d'œil*" meaning "at a glance." Initially exhibited through temporary installations in Edinburgh, by 1793 Barker had commissioned the architect Robert Mitchell to form the first permanent, purpose-built Panorama building in London's Leicester Square, with variations touring Europe throughout the late 18th and 19th centuries in a precursor to the Lumière brothers' traveling cinematograph and the ultimate attraction of cinema.

In stark contrast to Barker's rotunda, the inner surface of Hume's drum-like mausoleum was found to be blank, devoid of even the restrained neoclassicism of its exterior. As with the astronomical observatories above, the Adam-designed tomb's sole gaze was to the sky, to the passing of clouds or arriving mist from the Forth estuary. The city around was screened off, blinkered. The interior was of rough stone, unpolished and unresponsive. Here, the city was only registered through audible hum and occasionally discernible sound—the Castle gun, the screech of brakes or the rumble of trains from Waverley station below.

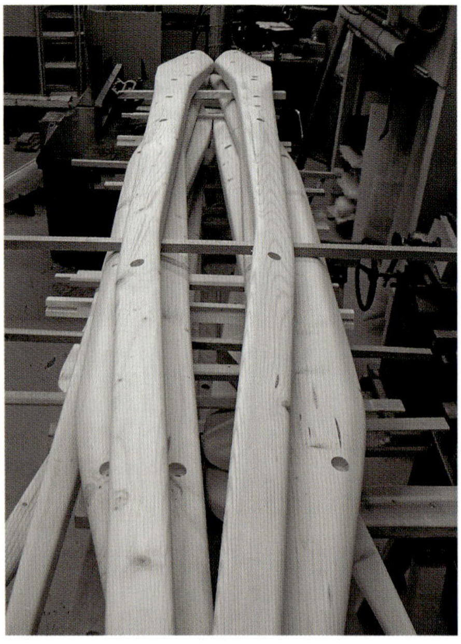

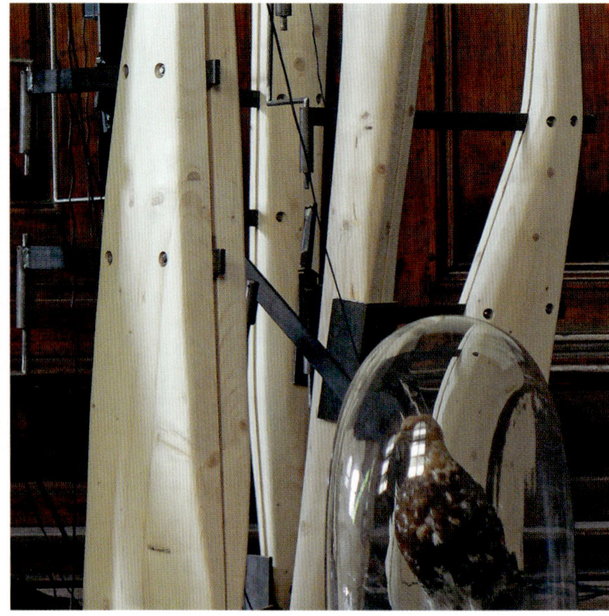

Weathered Skin

Adam prepared six ink and grey wash variations of the design for the mausoleum. While all show a cylindrical body, only the one selected for construction was devoid of apertures pierced into the upper section. It was noticeably plainer than the others, without such embellishments as a square or hexagonal plinth, a third tier, or spur walls surmounted by sphinx. Instead, a rusticated base rose to a fluted frieze and cornice from which an austere, upper section of smooth ashlar extended to a simple frieze of triglyphs and metopes finished with a dentiled cornice. The tomb was entered via an iron gate set below an entablature inscribed with Hume's name. Above, the sole ornament, an urn in an arched niche, was a later addition.

Adam was clearly aware of his close friend Giovanni Battista Piranesi's etchings of the Caecilia Metella tomb and Mausoleum of the Plautii, both near Rome, published just a few years prior to Hume's death. Here, Piranesi placed emphasis on the decay and ruin of the classical tombs. Adam's drawings—one of which is held by the National Galleries of Scotland in Edinburgh, the rest in Sir John Soane's Museum in London—similarly depicted his proposals for Hume's mausoleum to be ruinous as though they too were remnants of antiquity.

Polyoptic Panorama

Over two hundred years on, the tomb had begun to accrue true marks of time—a consequence of "leaving it to Posterity to add the Rest."[5] Inverting the distant gaze of Barker's panorama, the research for *Northroom* engaged a close scrutiny of the tomb's weathered outer fabric. As with Adam's romanticized depictions, the classical features were revealed to be blackened, pitted, and scarred—primarily the marks of weather, subsidence, and settlement, but occasionally they were cut with intent. At some point before 1813 the word "NATUS" was cut from the entablature above the gate and replaced with "Born"; "OBIT" with "Died." The inserts were loose in a manner that suggested the two words were now interchangeable, not as rebirth or resurrection, more as a recurring memory or thought.

Calibrated to these micro-cartographic observations, *Northroom* was conceived as an array of imagined views among and through the tomb's blemishes, an opportunistic seeping of visions into the solidity of Adam's masonry cylinder. Unlike Barker's encompassing vantage point upon Craig's observatory, this vision was fragmented as though the gaze through the monocular eye of the iron gate lock had become paired with the eight-fold vision of a spider nested on its outer surface. Each mark, scribing, or crack suggested a different level of resistance. Some would hold their gaze on the outer surface, transfixed by the almost imperceptible creep of shadow on stone, or become distracted by a fly momentarily alighting. Others would imagine more deeply, drawing visions from landscapes further afield.

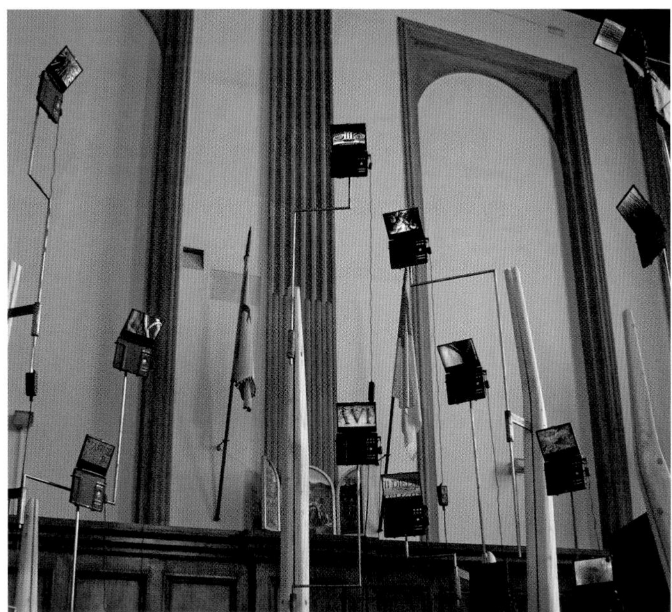

Metis (Mark Dorrian and Adrian Hawker) with Victoria Clare Bernie, *Northroom*, fabrication of timber figures, 2006

opposite left: The figures were bone-like, smooth as though worn by actions of movement. The remains of great leviathans or else the weathered remnants of Scots Pine, a choir of trees standing in a forest clearing. Ghost-like, stripped of bark, and exposed to time and wind.

Metis (Mark Dorrian and Adrian Hawker) with Victoria Clare Bernie, *Northroom* installation, Palagio di Parte Guelfa, Florence, Italy, 2007

opposite right: The timber figures leaned into blackened steel saddles or were restrained by ties tethering them to heavy steel footings. The paired timbers were bolted together, the whole assembly designed for dismantling, transit, and reassembly. Adjustable armatures extended from the timber's clasp, able to respond and recalibrate to new contexts and locations.

left: With each installation, *Northroom* re-staged the cartographic presence of Hume's inverted mausoleum. In the Brunelleschi-designed interior of the Palagio di Parte Guelfa, these calibrations measured off against 15th-century stained wooden dados and the intercolumniation of fluted stone pilasters. The timber stands and their armatures corresponded with heraldic flags, and the hinged form of the digital tablets formed a curious pairing with the religious scenes of a gilt triptych.

In all, the *Northroom* project surveyed and defined 32 such views as a choreographed suite of films mapped onto an unfurled survey of the tomb exterior. Detailed studies of distant micro-landscapes of Scotland were offered back to the neoclassical embellishments of the tomb's surface: bog cotton and foxgloves from the forests of Glen Affric in the Scottish Highlands mingled with spiders' webs and snails' trails. The resulting cinematic constellation, then turned outside-in, displayed the monument as a form of re-imagined polyoptic panorama.

Each film, looped on the screen of a small tablet, operated within its own timeframe, some lasting a few minutes, others an hour, so that when set in play, the chorus never repeated in the same way. To stand within this interior was to stimulate the "glance" through the fluctuations of peripheral vision. The flickering images were accompanied by respective low-level soundscapes, an aural overlay of insects and water, flight paths, and train announcements recalling the immediate city and the country beyond. The experience was of a visually and acoustically fragmented dreamscape in which what is seen and heard is always on the point of becoming something else.

The screens were held on steel armatures that reached out from 12 timber figures, with one pulled back as an invitation to enter. These bone-like figures and their assembled composition were initially studied through small timber models, then replicated at scale. Although equally spaced on heavy steel footings, their form varied as though offering the screens to the central space with individual attitude and gesture—some aloof and upright, others weary and reclined. They formed a gathering, an assembly. Each section was cut from a single length of yellow pine, then paired with a mirror image. They were formed through abrasion, weathered into shape through lengthy processes of planing and sanding.

With each installation of this polyoptic panorama, the posture of the timber figures, the reach of the steel armatures, the mane of black cables, the flicker, glow, murmur, and whisper of the digital screens recalibrated the close observations of Hume's tomb to the industrial loft space, the Renaissance hall, the vaulted landform, and the gallery enfilade. ⌂

Notes

1. Catalogue essay on *Northroom* by Paul Carter, *Agreeable Follies: Mental Geography and the Polyoptics of Place*, The Lighthouse (Glasgow), 2006: www.metis-architecture.com/wp-content/uploads/Paul-Carter-on-Northroom.pdf.
2. Iain Gordon Brown, "David Hume's Tomb: A Roman Mausoleum by Robert Adam," *Proceedings of the Society of Antiquaries of Scotland*, 121, 1992, p. 393.
3. Kitty Cruft and Andrew G. Fraser (eds), *James Craig, 1744–1795*, Mercat Press (Edinburgh), 1995, pp. 108–9.
4. Robert Barker's Royal Panorama Patent, 1787, University of Edinburgh Special Collections.
5. Brown, "David Hume's Tomb," p. 393.

"In Memoriam"

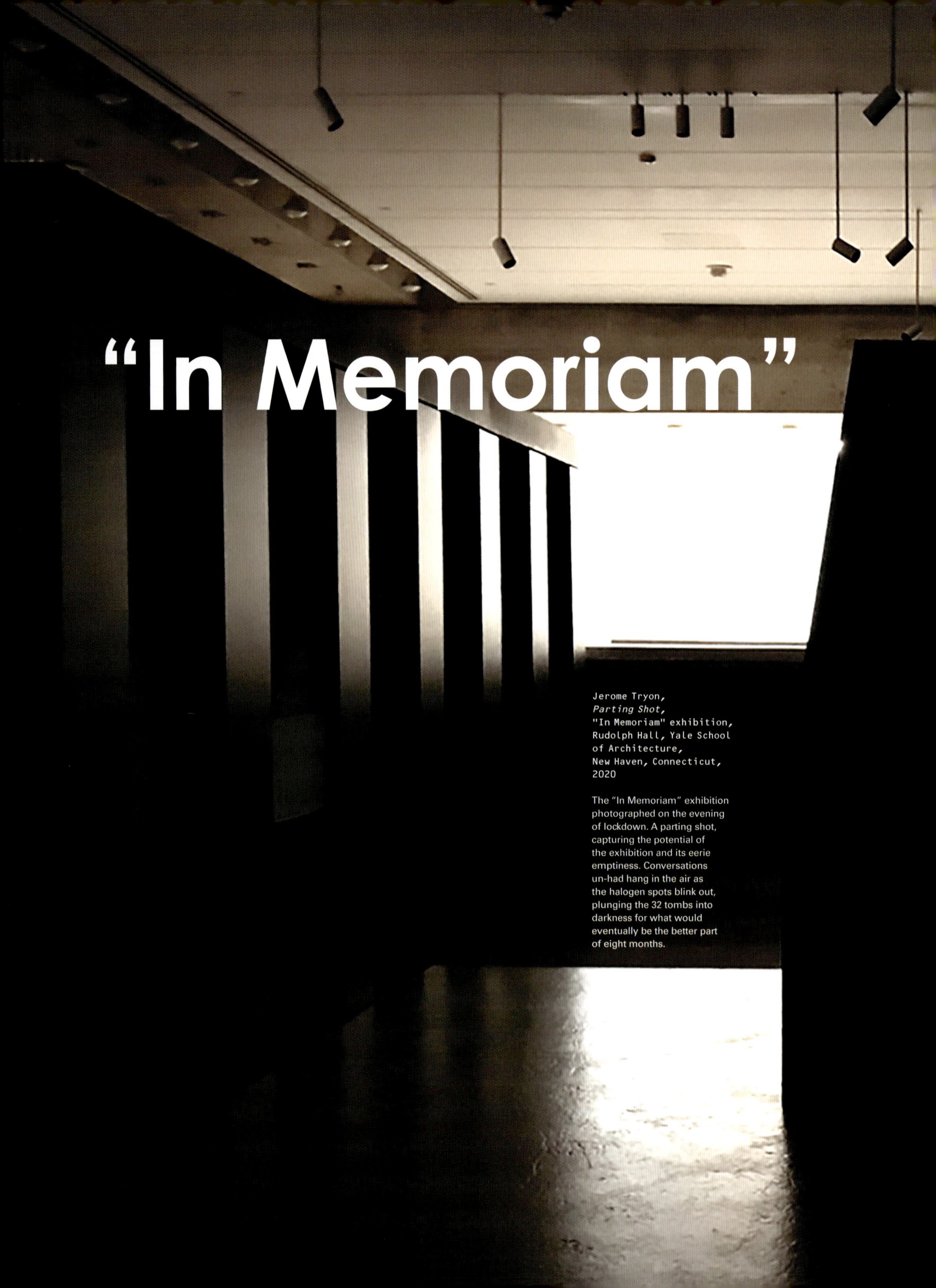

Jerome Tryon,
Parting Shot,
"In Memoriam" exhibition,
Rudolph Hall, Yale School of Architecture,
New Haven, Connecticut,
2020

The "In Memoriam" exhibition photographed on the evening of lockdown. A parting shot, capturing the potential of the exhibition and its eerie emptiness. Conversations un-had hang in the air as the halogen spots blink out, plunging the 32 tombs into darkness for what would eventually be the better part of eight months.

Concerning the Choreography of Knowledge

Peter J. Baldwin

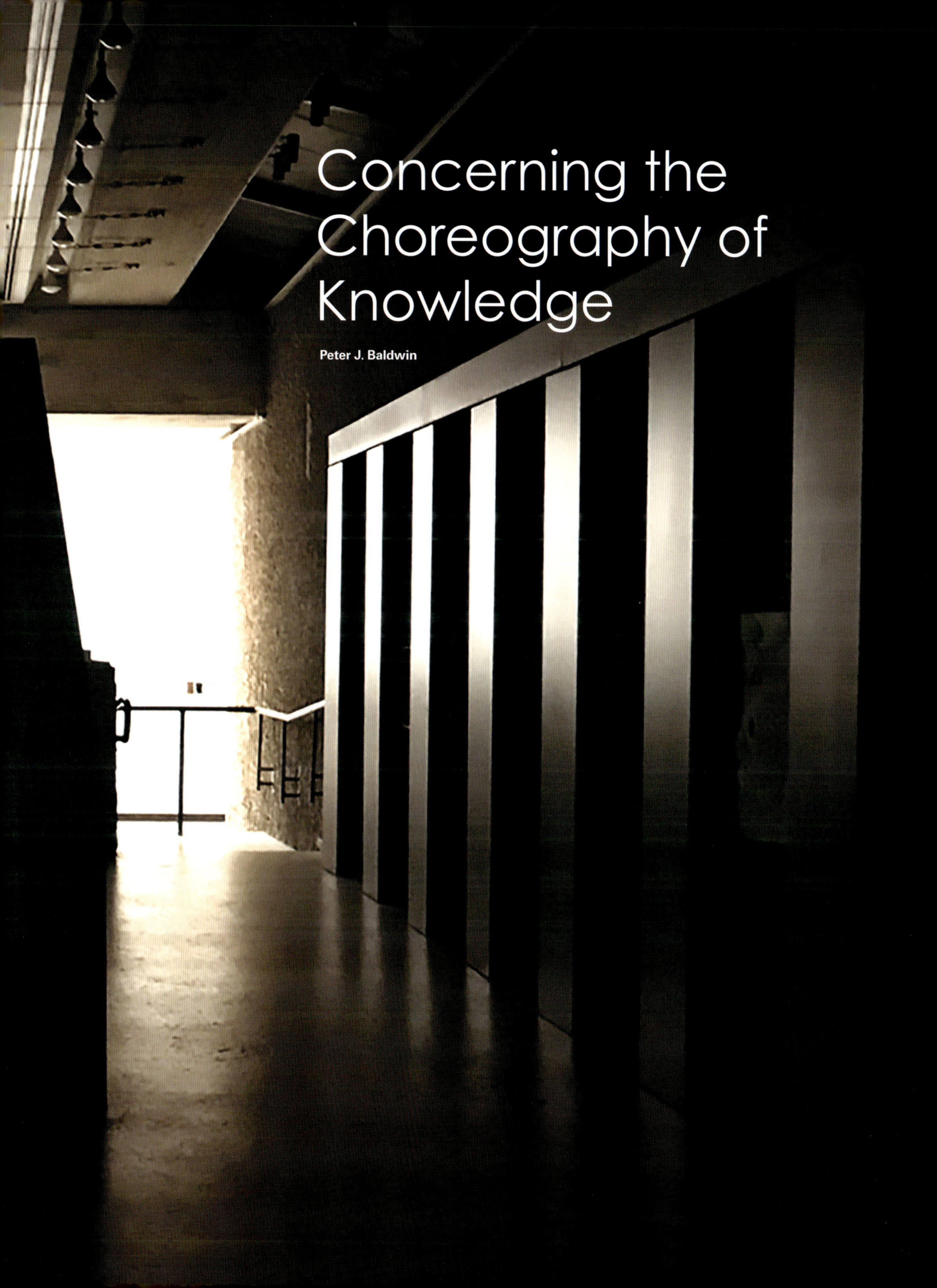

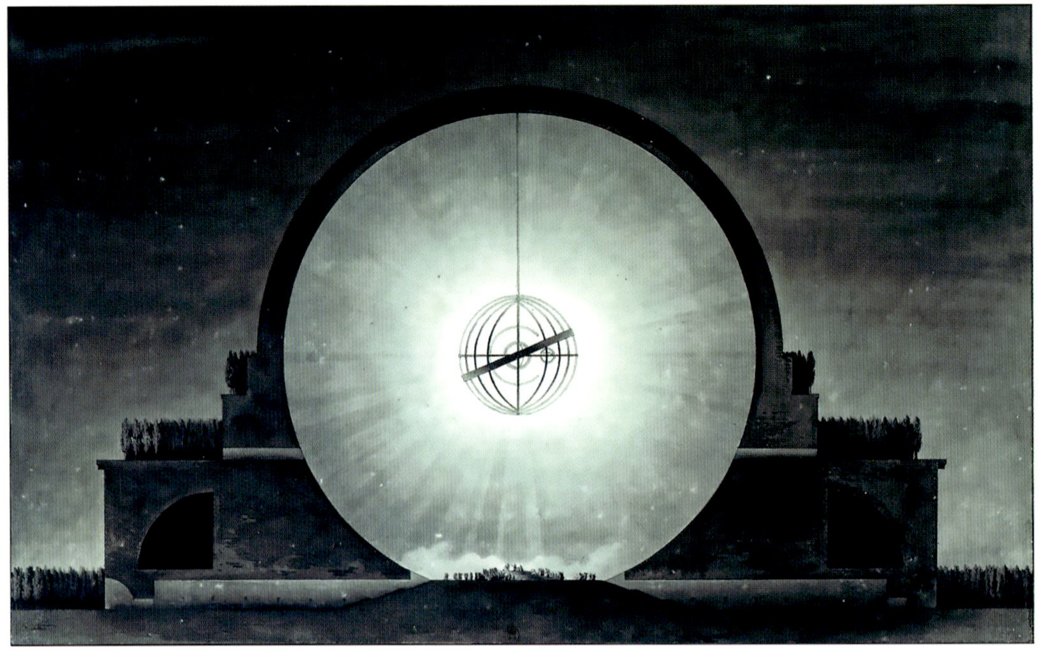

Étienne-Louis Boullée, *Cenotaph for Newton*, 1790–93

The notion of experiential exhibition as a way of enacting knowledge is not new. In the late 1700s the famed French architect Étienne-Louis Boullée proposed designs for a cenotaph for scientist Sir Isaac Newton. Embodying Enlightenment ideas and a symbolic formal language, the cenotaph would have been illuminated from within by the armillary sphere seen in this cross section hanging in the center of the spherical chamber. This light was intended to represent, both literally and metaphorically, the illumination of knowledge.

> I shall reconsider human knowledge by starting from the fact that we can know more than we can tell.
> — Michael Polanyi, *The Tacit Dimension*, 1967[1]

> The dance can reveal everything mysterious that is hidden in music, and it has the additional merit of being human and palpable.
> — Charles Baudelaire, *La Fanfarlo*, 1847[2]

For architecture, as with nearly every creative discipline, the exhibition is a critical part of our disciplinary pageantry. While historically exhibitions have often been seen as a celebratory staging, a gathering of collaborators and peers, frequently friends (although occasionally foes), around the works of our best and brightest, there has, in more recent decades, been a marked shift, with the emergence of a more thematic curatorial philosophy intended to stimulate disciplinary discourse, often as a call for action.

Yet for all their self-evident significance in (re)shaping our contemporary disciplinary discourses (would Postmodern Post-Structuralist thinking ever have arrived in architecture were it not for Mark Wigley and Philip Johnson's efforts in late 1980s New York to deconstruct the dominant dialectic dialogue?[3]), exhibitions are all too often seen as cataloguings, as curatorial affairs, rather than processual act(ion)s that generate new knowledge and understanding through performed proximities and choreographed correlations.

Indeed, it is somewhat incongruous to note that, while the performative has been a (re-)ascendant force for the generation of new knowledge and understanding within the creative and fine arts for many decades now, despite architecture's inherently embodied nature, and the recent resurgent scholarly interest in our primary praxis of tacit transference (the action of enaction that we, oh so reductively, refer to as drawing), the architectural canon has been silent on the subject of embodied knowledge.

Pondering this paradox, we recall the pandemically prolonged "In Memoriam" exhibition, hosted by the Yale School of Architecture, New Haven, Connecticut, in its Rudolph Hall exhibition space in 2020. Conceived and curated by a trio of architectural artist-academics—Jerome Tryon, David Schaengold, and Luke Pajovic—the exhibition invited 32 architects and designers from around the globe to envisage their own tombs and memorials, provoking considerations of professional persona and personal presence, while eliciting parallel mediations on the nature of embodiment, understanding, and memory in the (post-)digital age. Originally intended to open from February 20 to March 28, it remained installed yet unvisited until November 2020, owing to the various lockdown and social distancing protocols.

Act(ion)s of Embodiment

Of the many existential questions that have plagued western philosophy over the millennia, one of the most enduring is the question of the nature of knowledge, and by extension that of meaning itself. From Aristotelian notions of gnosis[4] to Roland

Architects of the past, and a very few of the present, have designed tombs for themselves or for other prominent individuals. Architect, artist, and educator Peter J. Baldwin examines the "In Memoriam" exhibition (of which he was part), curated at the Yale School of Architecture in 2020. The show was held in stasis by the months of pandemic inactivity—a strangely appropriate paradox for the subject of the work and its staging.

Barthes's postmodern post-mortem passing of author-itarian centrality,[5] debates on the nature and construction of memory and meaning have long waged as philosophers and theorists, shamans and charlatans have advanced, disputed, defended, and radically redacted their various theories and hypotheses throughout the centuries. Perhaps the most divisive of the many divisions that fuel these rhetorics and retorts is the notion of embodiment—the role that the body plays as a mediating mechanism, and the locus of our perceptions, in our experience of the world.

First formalized in his tragically fragmented treatise *De Anima* (*On the Soul*; *c*. 350 BC),[6] Aristotle describes our inextricable engagement with the world as a consequence of the irreducible form of the self that he names the "soul." Unlike later (often Christian) theories within Aristotelian metaphysics, this soul is not a distinct, divisible thing, but instead contingent upon the intimate entanglement between the body (or sensing organs), the mind, and the world around us. Guided by the twin(ed) motivators of intellect and desire, this soul is the unifying force that connects experience, memory, and understanding.

Yet with the dominance of the intellect, and the primacy of epistemological (scientific) thought that inevitably followed the 17th-century French philosopher René Descartes's conceptualization of a "Cartesian dualism"[7]—the separation of mind and body, that he saw as an inevitable consequence of the necessity of intellectual abstraction—notions of the subtle, the soul(ful), and the intangible were driven into the hinterlands of esoterica. Despite this marginalization and our subsequent struggles to reconcile tacit knowledge with an increasingly empirical worldview, such notions remain an enduring (counter)cultural agent, a shadow that haunts the dominant dictates of mainstream thought, disrupting epistemological and ontological models alike. Existing in performative potential, this latent state occupies a dialectical tension that blurs the boundaries of conception and perception, awaiting enaction and embodiment.

Building on these Aristotelian foundations, the 20th-century French philosopher Maurice Merleau-Ponty, in his seminal challenge to Cartesian cognition titled *Phenomenology of Perception* (1945),[8] posits the body reconceptualized as an incarnated subjectivity—the *corps propre* (body-subject), an irreducible (pre-)reflective agent in our engagement with the world around us. Redefining experience as an inextricable correlate of the intricate intwining of our cognitive faculties and our bodily sensory and motor functions, this vision inherently implicates performative enaction in the construction of knowledge and understanding. Extrapolating Merleau-Ponty's thesis, it would seem plausible to suggest that performances (of all kinds) are both ways of knowing, and ways of staking claims about the creation of (that) knowledge.[9]

Jerome Tryon,
Layout sketch for the
"In Memoriam" exhibition,
2019

right: Sketch showing refinements to the design for the exhibition stands. In this version, each of the sections would have held three of the contributors' memorials, in a manner similar to the way a columbarium contains the urns of those interred there.

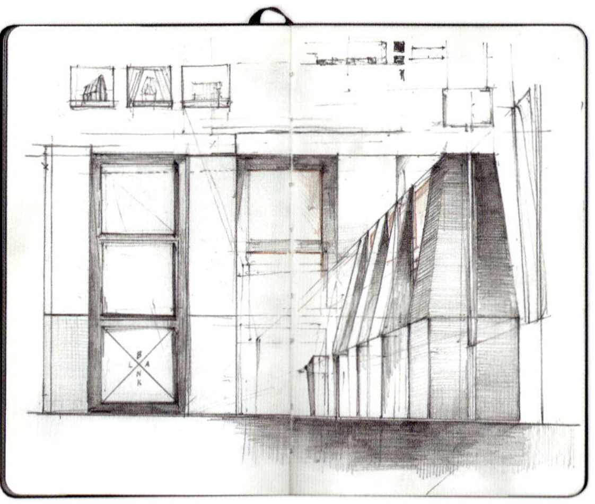

Inès Martinel / Flores &
Prats Architects,
Branches and Vault,
"In Memoriam" exhibition,
Rudolph Hall,
Yale School of Architecture,
New Haven, Connecticut,
2020

below: Originally developed for the Vatican Pavilion at the 2018 Venice Architecture Biennale in Italy, the Spanish architectural practice Flores & Prats Architects' design references both classical forms and more modern representational tropes as exemplified in the work of 20th-century Italian architect Carlo Scarpa, in a choreographed connotative ambiguity.

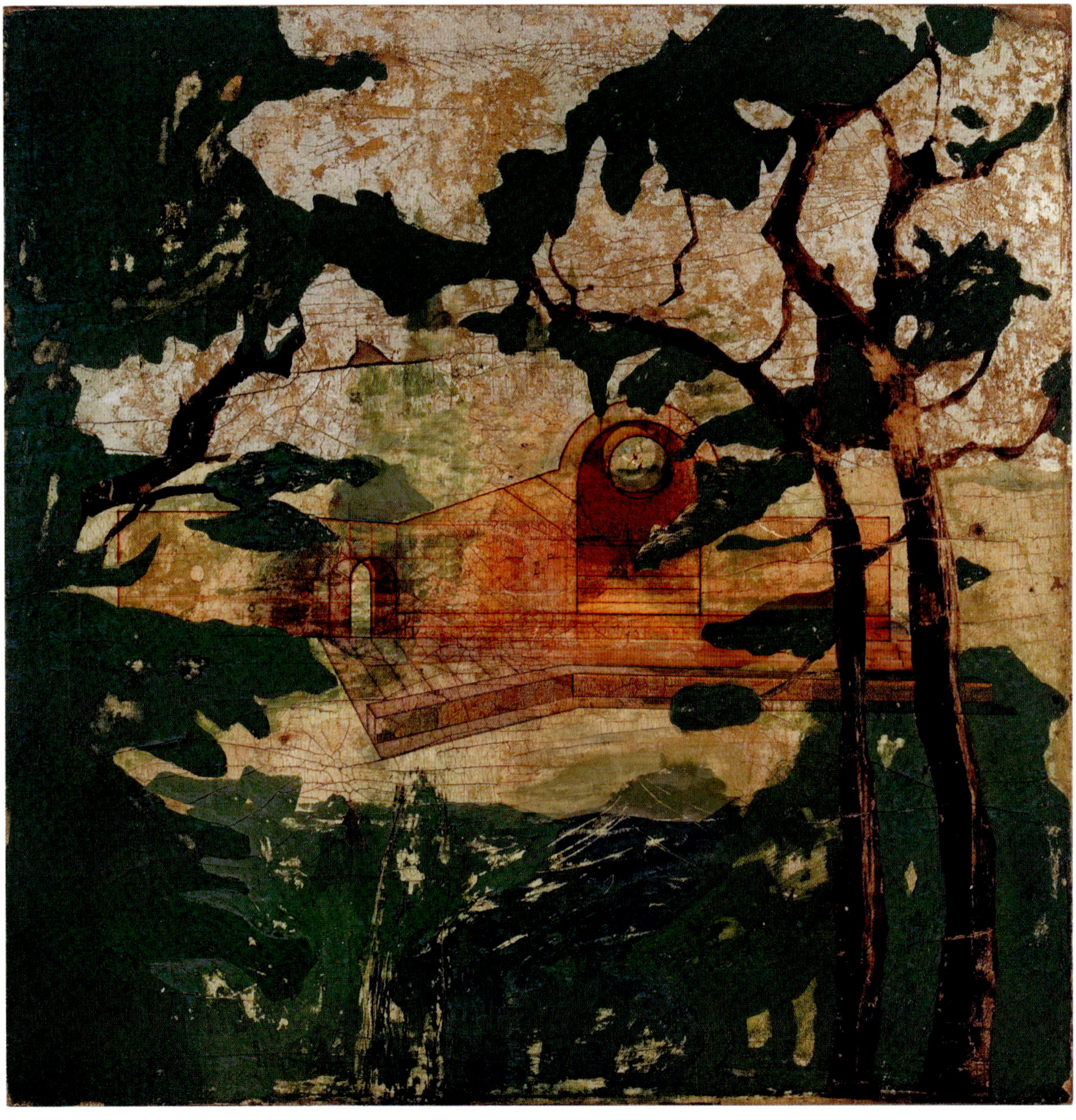

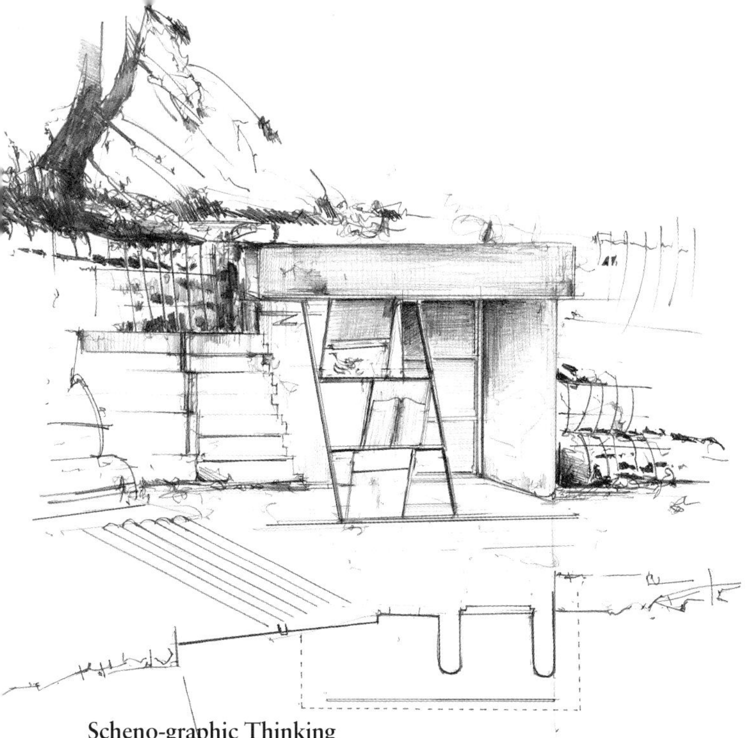

Jerome Tryon,
After Miralles,
"In Memoriam" exhibition,
Rudolph Hall, Yale School
of Architecture,
New Haven, Connecticut,
2020

A drawn study of the entrance to one of the private tombs located in Igualada Cemetery in Catalonia, Spain, designed by Spanish architects Enric Miralles and Carme Pinós and completed in 1994. The cemetery is intended to merge with the post-industrial landscape within which it is set.

Scheno-graphic Thinking

Returning then to our original contention, while processual thinking is not without prior precedent within our disciplinary discourses, unlike the tangible traces[10] that manifest as a consequence of the drawing process, tangibly evidencing the transformative enaction of understanding and projective intent, the liquid knowledge that inevitably condenses through performative praxes belongs to the orders of experience and embodiment.[11] Just as the architectural experience is the consequence of a staged and sequenced choreography of relational and spatial assemblies, so too are the insights and understandings that arise from the creation or exploration of an exhibition.

From the Mannerist mimesis of Francesco de' Medici's Studiolo (1572)[12]—a highly ornamented and decorated room located within the Palazzo Vecchio in Florence, Italy, that functioned as the Grand Duke's office, laboratory, and personal cabinet of curiosities—to the eclectic enclave established by famed British architect Sir John Soane in Lincoln's Inn Fields, London, to serve as his family home and the offices for his then fledgling architectural practice (a sprawling complex that would also serve as an informal space of education, where Soane would instruct his various students and apprentices), and their more modern counterparts, we are all too familiar with the notion of collection, and the associated act of gathering objects, and artifacts, for the purpose of study and private inquiry. From plaster casts to books, from paintings to more esoteric *objets d'art*, these antiquities are often the residues of earlier enaction(s). While these objects are, themselves, object signs saturated with meaning, within the choreographed concatenation of the exhibition they surpass their value as emblematic thing and totemic fragment transformed by the vitality and variability of the relational proximities, positions, and juxtapositions of those artifacts and "objects in space."[13]

Not unlike *maai*—a central philosophical concept within Japanese martial arts, translatable as "interval" and used to denote and describe the fluid interstitially between combatants as contingent arenas of latent creative, intuitive, and reflexive potential—exhibitions comprise multiple dynamic reciprocities, between the exhibition and its creator, the exhibition and its occupant, and between the objects themselves. Rendered simultaneously as sign signifier and soluble substitution value, by the performative paradox, the assemblage of the exhibition permits the manifestation of multiple, mutable, relational structuring(s).

Yet this production of knowledge is not only something gleaned through the compositional concatenation of curation: as readers, viewers, and visitors, we also become embroiled in this act of enaction. As we view the exhibition, synthesizing and sustaining the simultaneous, superimposed sets of information and multiple media types, we are required to suspend the rules of immediate resolution, becoming instead increasingly implicated co-conspirators in the co-construction of meaning.

Through our interaction, occupation, or inhabitation of this cosmology of informative fragments, we activate this potential, blurring the boundaries of observations, cognition, and being, opening new interstitial territories, and creating cognitive elbow room within which serendipitous insights can occur.[14] So fecund, bountiful, and varied are these new insights that they overspill, necessitating selection, juxtaposition, and critical curatorial omission.

What then of the exhibition without the audience? What happens if the normal expectations of communicative choreography are suspended, either by circumstance or design? If we take exhibitions as enacted, processual forms of knowing in which the audience is implicated in the creation of meaning and knowledge, the absence of audience raises some interesting questions.

Digital *De Anima*

In a tragic or perhaps triumphant twist of fate, this exact scenario of "an exhibition in absentia" played out in 2020 at the Yale School of Architecture. Just after the opening of "In Memoriam," the (Western) world was plunged into a lock[ed]-down condition by the tragic events of the Covid-19 pandemic. As social-distancing protocols radically redefined the parameters for spatial and bodily interaction(s), they indelibly influenced our enacted understandings as places, spaces, and surfaces became viewed with increasing suspicion; but perhaps we digress?

Mark Foster Gage,
Mausoleum,
"In Memoriam" exhibition,
Rudolph Hall, Yale School of Architecture,
New Haven, Connecticut,
2020

American architect Gage prepared this speculative design for his own tomb specifically for the exhibition. Featuring the Latin graffiti "Et in Arcadia ego" ("Even in Arcadia, there am I")—an inscription used in art since the 17th century to signify death's presence even in the most idyllic settings—the mausoleum can be seen as a reference to both the inorganic perfection of contemporary society and the natural splendor and harmony of the classical world. The hooded figure presumably represents Charon, the ferryman who transports the dead to the underworld in Greek mythology.

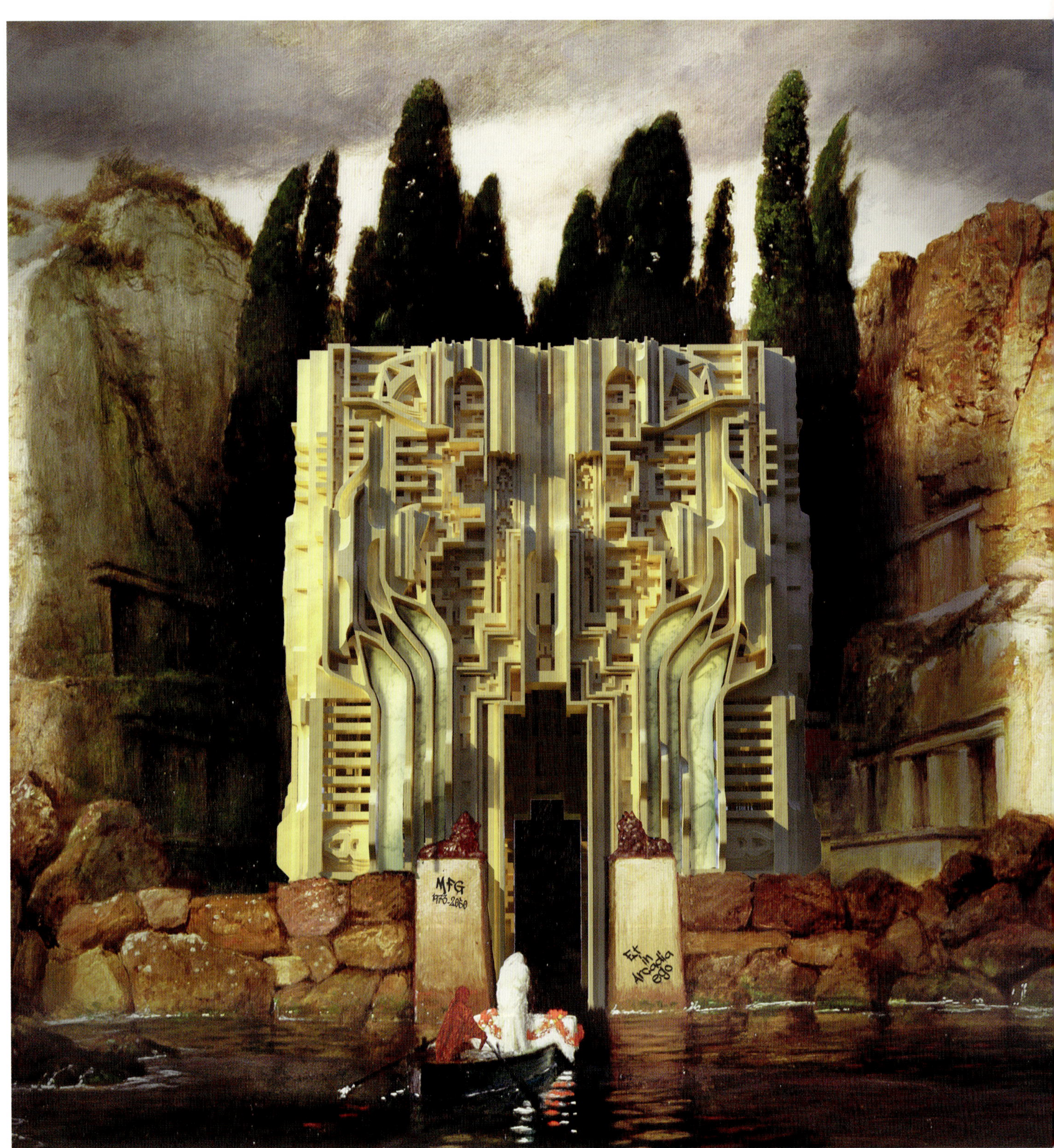

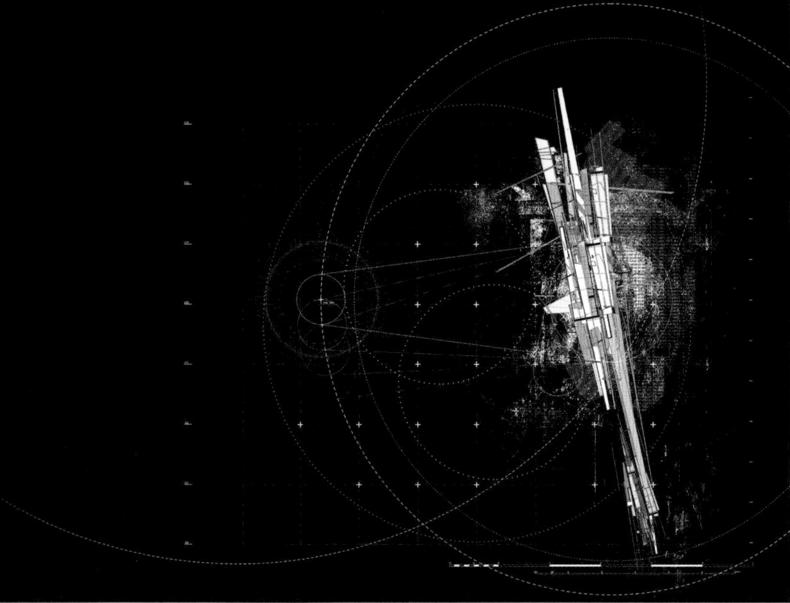

Peter J. Baldwin,
Soul B[u]oy,
"In Memoriam" exhibition,
Rudolph Hall, Yale School of Architecture,
New Haven, Connecticut,
2020

Conceived as a monument for an age of digitized perpetuity, the *Soul B[u]oy* is a cognizant machine that watches over our immortal data, an archive and guardian, a machine of loving grace.

Evoking notions of memory and death, the exhibition's call necessitated reflection and consideration of both personal and professional interests in the postmortem condition. It asked not only how we would wish to be remembered and thought of by those close to us but, more vitally for a profession and preoccupation in which performative enaction plays such a vital part in the palpability of our legacy, how we might wish to be known to have thought, perceived, and interacted with the world around us, and consequently where this might position our work and its contribution to disciplinary thinking and public perceptions. On a more personal, immediate, and (im)material level, the creation of a memorial or tomb compels introspection and with it a stark realization of the finitude and finiteness of the bodily medium as an Aristotelian vessel for experience and consequentially the embodied self.

Simultaneously, as the disconnect between symbolic meaning and the built environment grows ever greater, it seems incongruous that our funerary processes would be so familiar to our ancient ancestors, as we erect monuments to the departed and honor them with public displays of grief and anguish. Yet this is only one medium of manifestation. More fascinating is the ever-more-public act of digital mourning—an event which continues for years after the departure of the loved one, indeed often long after genuine emotive response has been lost, where mourning has reached a state of entropy, remembered only as the result of memory prompts rather than genuine emotion.

Conceived in response to these complex and contradictory connotations, my own offering, *Soul B[u]oy* (2020), forms a literal and metaphorical geo-synchronous satellite to my ongoing Null Island project (2017–), an exploration of the new territories that are the consequences of consumer cult(ure)s, socio-technological saturation, and emerging environ-mental trends.

Exploiting an algorithmic anomaly that assigns a default location of 0°, 0° to any untagged data, *Soul B[u]oy* is a speculation on the nature of mourning and remembrance in an age in which the digital dissolution of the body as the locus of experiential input(s) has resulted in a delirious dislocation of the (pre-)reflective self, gathering and broadcasting the art(ifacts) and traces that constitute one's digital footprint, in a cognitive columbarium of cyber-spatial residues.

Through this complex profusion of fragments, the *Soul B[u]oy* dances, a desirous, phantasma-allegorical engine, a memorial made manifest through the choreographic entanglement of structural, symbolic, and imagined orders, a ritual(ized) response to transformative recognition and digital datasets.

In Performative *Potentia*

As the post-digital age renders meaning ever more contingent, architecture must, as a discipline, begin to (re-)examine the (re)new(ed) relevance of the performative paradigm as a medium for the transmission of architectural ideas and the spatialized embodiment of architectonic intent. By engaging with the world on its own terms through revelatory relativity and relational structuring, we can ready ourselves for fluid future(s) and transformed states of being. AD

Notes

1. Michael Polanyi, *The Tacit Dimension*, Routledge & Kegan Paul (London), 1967, p. 4.
2. Charles Baudelaire, "La Fanfarlo" [*Bulletin de la Société des Gens de Lettres*, 1847], tr. Raymond MacKenzie, in *Baudelaire: Paris Spleen and La Fanfarlo*, Hackett Publishing Company (Indianapolis, IN), 2008.
3. See Philip Johnson and Mark Wigley, *Deconstructivist Architecture*, The Museum of Modern Art (New York), 1988.
4. Aristotle, *De Anima*, tr. Hugh Lawson-Tancred, Penguin (London), 1986, p. 168.
5. See Roland Barthes, "The Death of the Author," tr. Stephen Heath, in *Image Music Text*, Fontana Press (London), 1977, pp. 142–8.
6. See Aristotle, *De Anima*.
7. See René Descartes, *The Philosophical Writings of René Descartes*, vol. 2, tr. John Cottingham, Robert Stoothoff, and Dugald Murdoch, Cambridge University Press (Cambridge), 1986.
8. See Maurice Merleau-Ponty, *Phenomenology of Perception*, tr. Donald Landes, Routledge (London), 2012, pp. 100–101.
9. Elizabeth Bell, *Theories of Performance*, Sage Publishing (Thousand Oaks, CA), 2008, p. 18.
10. See Jacques Derrida, *Speech and Phenomena; And Other Essays on Husserl's Theory of Signs*, tr. David B. Allison, Northwestern University Press (Evanston, IL), 1973, p. 141.
11. Robin Nelson, *Practice as Research in the Arts: Principles, Protocols, Pedagogies, Resistances*, Palgrave Macmillan (New York), 2013, p. 52.
12. See Larry J. Feinberg, "The Studiolo of Francesco I Reconsidered," in *The Medici, Michelangelo, and the Art of Late Renaissance Florence*, Yale University Press (New Haven, CT), 2002, pp. 45–65.
13. Peter Bjerregaard, "Exhibition-Making as Aesthetic Inquiry," in Peter Bjerregaard (ed.), *Exhibitions as Research: Experimental Methods in Museums*, Routledge (New York), 2020, p. 4.
14. Neil Spiller (ed.), AD *Drawing Architecture*, September/October (no. 5), 2013, p. 7.

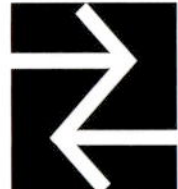

FROM ANOTHER PERSPECTIVE *A Word from AD Editor* ***Neil Spiller***

'Toons, Horror, and Dolls

Some architects and their offices are lucky enough to attract clients that rejoice in what they do. This is the case with Sam Jacob Studio (SJS). The London-based office has managed to create architecture, interiors, and objects with much humor and joy—for many established institutions—that playfully violate architectural protocols and dogmas yet still have a healthy respect for architecture itself.

Pow, Zap, and Boom

SJS's involvement with the Cartoon Museum was to design its interiors when it moved to its current location off London's Oxford Street in 2019.

We are all familiar with still cartoons often caricaturing political or entertainment figures, that bring a smile to our face. This form of drawing is a long-standing tradition that originated in the mid-18th century in both North America and Great Britain and was purposely conceived to poke fun at establishment figures. London became an epicenter for such barbed illustrations at the time. Today figures like Ralph Steadman and Gerald Scarfe, as well as other younger caricaturists, carry on this tradition. We are also familiar with comics and graphic novels. Comics originated in the US in the mid-19th century, and in the 20th century the British comic genre gave us Billy Bunter, Desperate Dan, Dennis the Menace, and the irreverent *Viz*, for example.

The first animated cartoon, called *Fantasmagorie*, was created in 1908 by Émile Cohl in France, depicting metamorphosing human figures, a door, and even a horse and elephant, plus the animator's hands. Likewise, we are familiar with many of the fictional characters created in British popular animated cartoon culture. Mr Benn, Danger Mouse, Peppa Pig, Roobarb and Custard, and many others have populated our television sets over time. This particularly British smorgasbord of animated humor, slapstick violence, and satire is curated, collected, and exhibited by the Cartoon Museum in London.

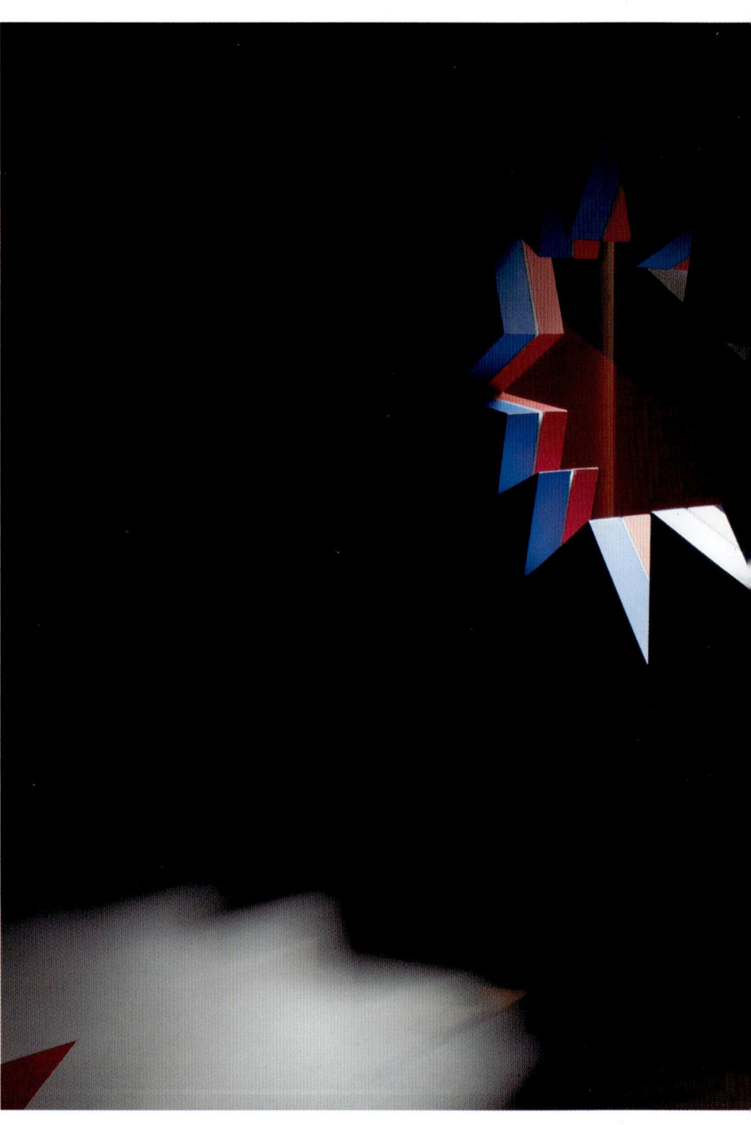

Sam Jacob Studio, Cartoon Museum interior design, London, 2019

above: Sam Jacob Studio is renowned for its theatrical staging of exhibitions, urban interventions, and buildings, taking cues from their programs and context and exploiting these to considerable effect.

Dispensing With the White Box

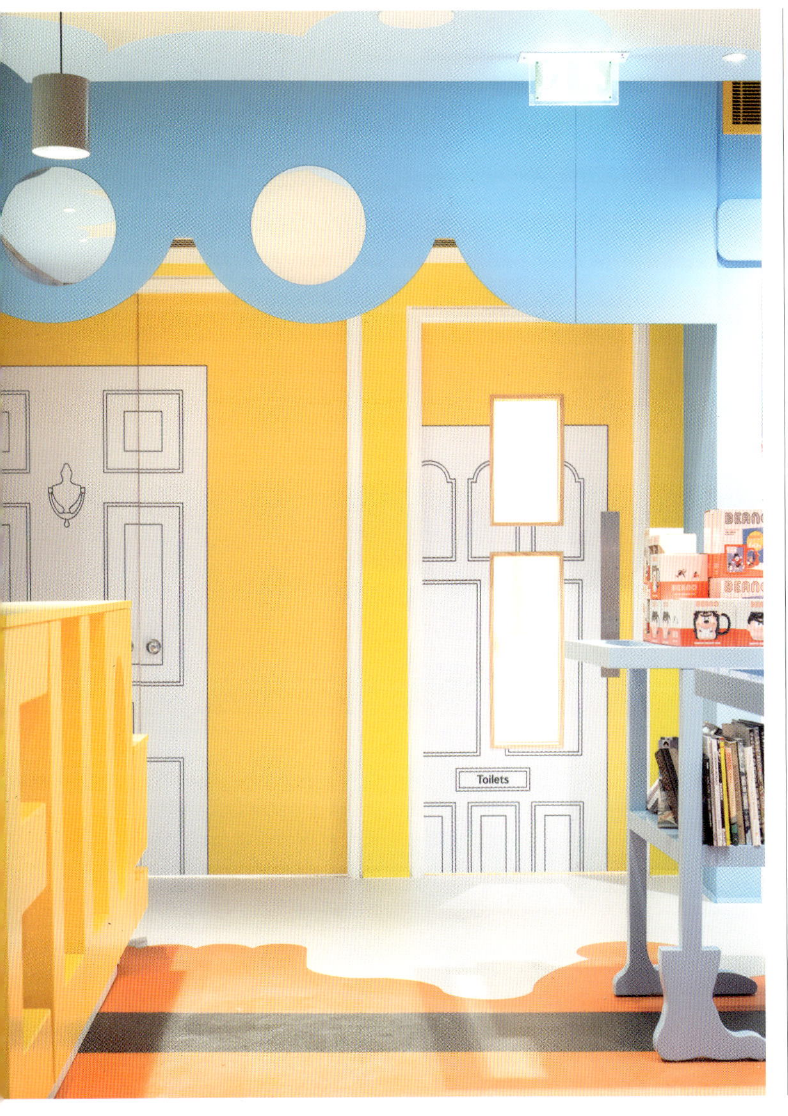

above: Cartoon colors and cartoon lifework characterize the space and added to a healthy wit. A yellow desk shouts "Hello" to the visitor.

The Cartoon Museum houses over 6,000 original cartoons and comics as well as a library of 8,000 comics and books that spans from the 18th century to the present day. Its activities range from events, exhibitions, and educational outreach to competitions, all encouraging fuller public awareness of these important art forms but also encouraging active public participation in the creation of such art. The Museum aims to be a happy place bubbling with humor, enthusiasm, and dexterous draftsmanship. SJS has captured these ambiences and aspirations perfectly. Previous to founding his own studio, Jacob was a director of internationally renowned architects FAT (Fashion Architecture Taste). His design preoccupations have been honed over the past thirty years or more. He has always had a maverick take on the architectural profession and a post-postmodernist design language where visual jokes and warped perspectives, both physical and conceptual, abound.

The interior of the Cartoon Museum is, naturally, inspired by the magical world depicted in cartoons. The strangely surreal pictorial space of cartoons, particularly those that are animated, is one where objects and animals are anthropomorphized, where pain lasts just momentarily, where gravity is an animator's joke, and where form and materiality of all sorts are morphable and elastic. SJS has used these tactics in their design, particularly around the entrances of the museum and shop. The wall and door treatments, the furniture, and the wall and partition articulations are not as they should be. All is a cacophony of bright colors. A neon speech bubble signifies the presence of the museum in the street. The interior is initially seen via a smashed window, and a 3D explosion choreographs the visitor's arrival. Graphic tricks such as stylized clouds, trees, and even paint drips are present. Doors play the "When is a door not a door?" game, sometimes masquerading as bookcases, sometimes too big or too small, and sometimes out of place. Table legs sprout feet—or are they socks?—and rest on a "tiger skin" rug. Much creative fun has been had.

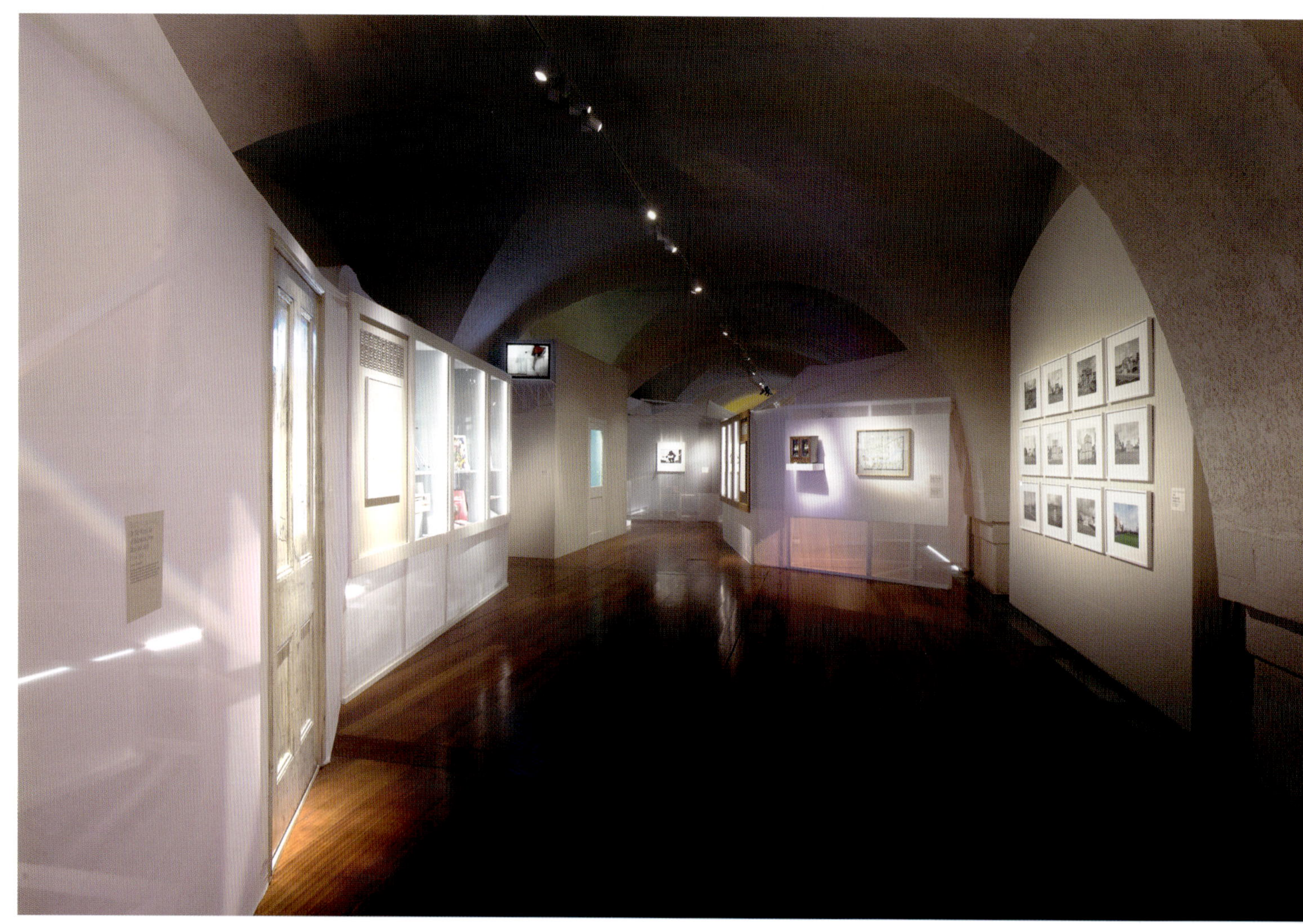

Sam Jacob Studio,
"The Horror Show!" exhibition,
Embankment Galleries,
Somerset House,
London,
2022

above: Graphics, dark colors and dim lighting came together to create an ambience at once spooky yet also contemporary, which facilitated the juxtaposition of a diverse collection of items from the last 50 years of British cultural history.

Monster, Ghost, and Witch

In 2022 SJS added a darker string to their bow as the Somerset House Embankment Galleries staged "The Horror Show!," for which they were the spatial designers. The exhibition was conceived as a romp through the seamier side of British provocative art practices of the last fifty years. The show was ordered around three acts or themes—Monster, Ghost, and Witch. To say the exhibition was eclectic was an understatement. Again SJS managed to create an appropriate entrance sequence for "The Horror Show!" to powerfully announce itself to passersby. The façade of the gallery's entrance was temporarily enhanced with teeth and fangs, a pig's snout, and a wonky pair of Surrealist-like eyes. Once inside, the interior—co-curated by Iain Forsyth & Jane Pollard and Claire Catterall, who also conceived the idea—was modulated by dark colors and signposted with internationally notable graphic-design practice Barnbrook's gothic and occult runic fonts. Over 200 objects and other artifacts were presented from the seedier side of recent art history, as the visitor was guided through often dim spaces

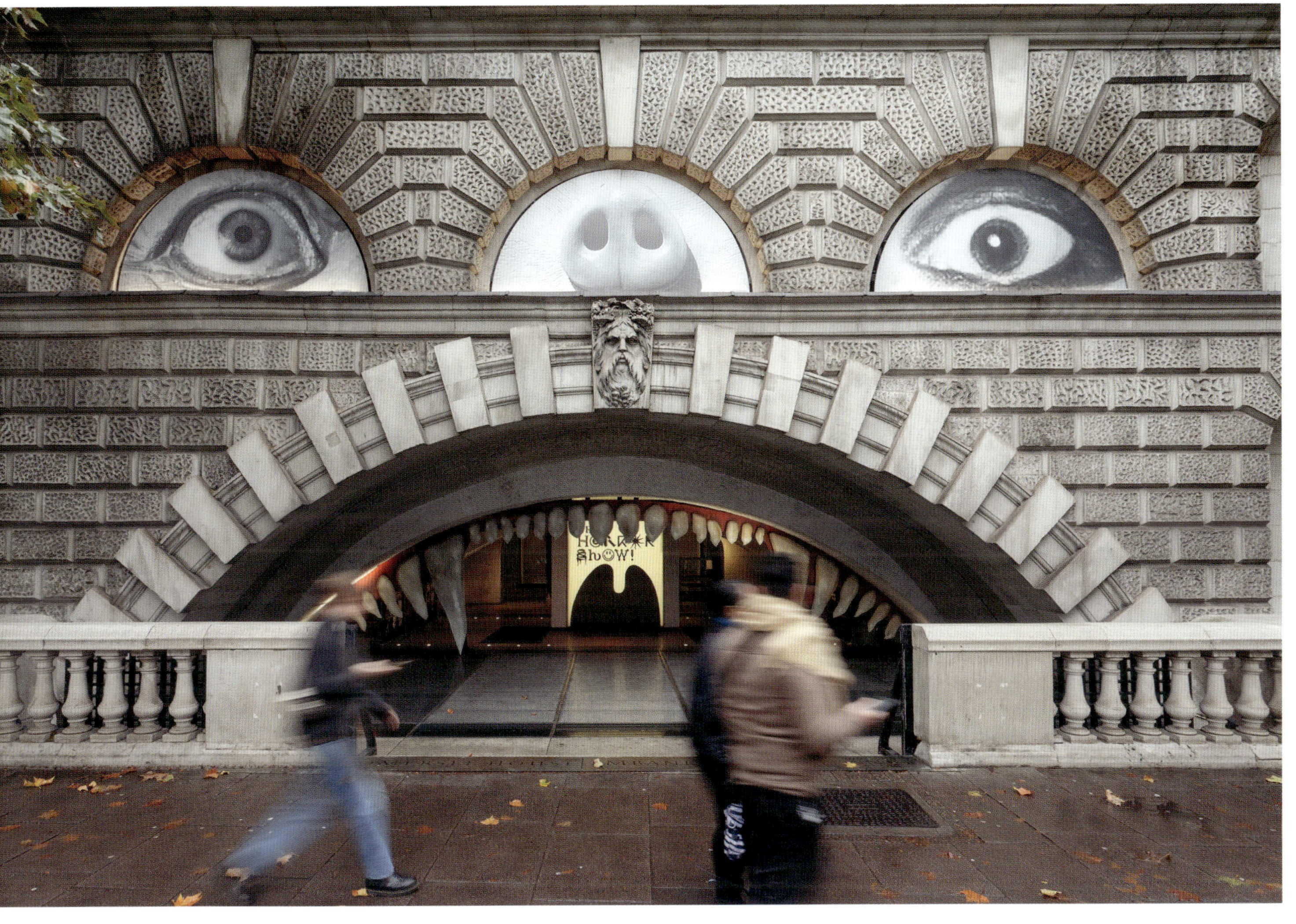

with particular spotlit items seeking attention, giving the whole ensemble a spooky ambience. The variety of the collection had the air of a three- and four-dimensional collage, and indeed collage was an important aspect of the show—bringing together as it did disparate, culturally different materials and aesthetic codes in a search for something new. Punk was featured highly in the journey as it has been such a powerful force in British fashion, music, design, and art in the last half century. So too were many objects, images, and clothes announcing the broad spectrum of human sexuality and the search for individual identity. Magic and the Tarot were explored, a scold's bridle (an iron muzzle historically used to literally hold women's tongues in place so they could not speak) made an appearance, as did an original puppet of former British Prime Minister Margaret Thatcher from the satirical 1980s–90s television series *Spitting Image*, which was spotlit in its own case, as well as some contemporary corn dollies and much, much more. Subversion and transgression, indeed, are ideally suited to SJS's talents.

above: "The Horror Show!" announced itself to the world by subverting the Classical facade of Somerset House, anthropomorphizing it into a chimeric face with a pig's snout.

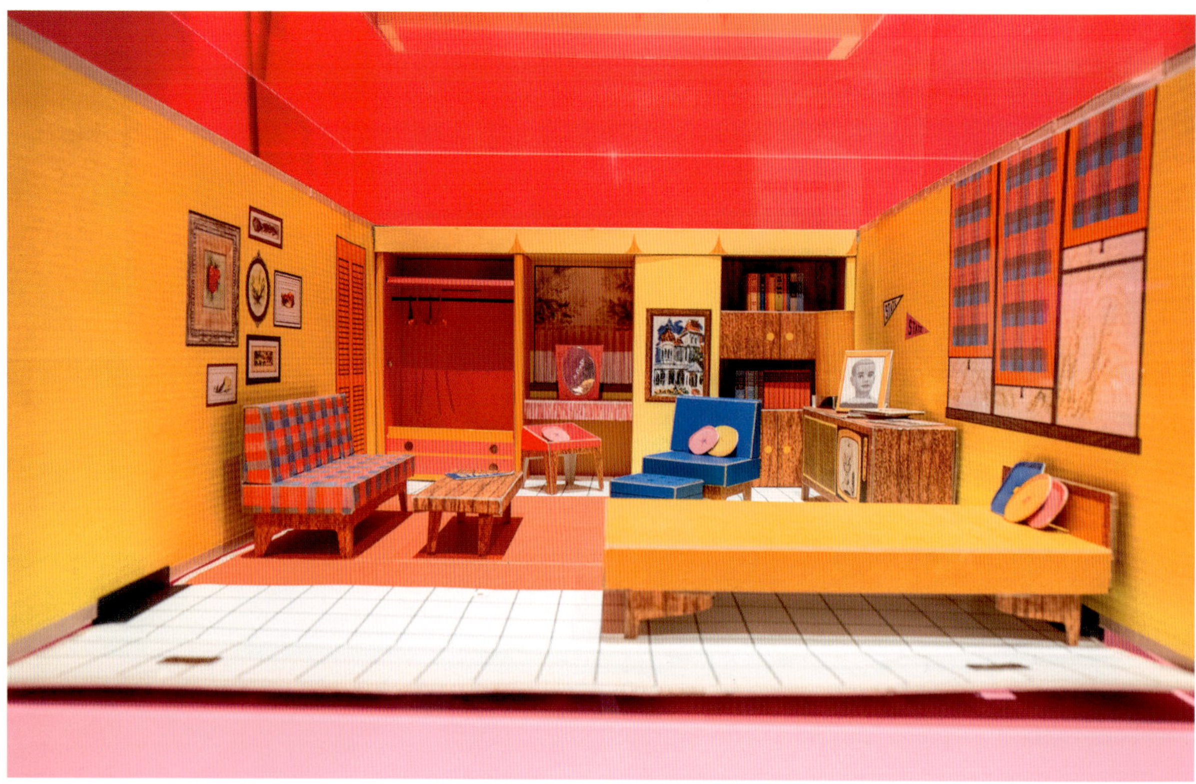

Barbietecture

In 2024–5, "Barbie®: The Exhibition" at the Design Museum, London, was another opportunity for SJS to return to their bubblegum and Bertie Bassett color swatches (Bertie is a primary-colored mascot figure made from Bassett's Liquorice Allsorts sweets) in order to provide the exuberance required for the design of an interior staging in which to exhibit the world-famous iconic doll, her various manifestations and ethnicities, her chattels and houses, and her friends. Exceedingly vibrant and very popular with the public, the show was programmed to mark the 65th anniversary of her first appearance in 1959. It illustrated also how Barbie and her creators engaged with the prevalent wider social, cultural, spatial, and fashionable ideas of their days, and how they changed over the years and vicariously changed her and her world over time. Barbie is, and continues to be, a microcosm of certain aspects of the American dream; so the SJS-designed exhibition was a comprehensive overview of her at a pensionable age, although her health and looks have remained purely in her twenties—something Hollywood actors aspire to even more today than ever. The show was permeated by Barbie's trademark pink, yet augmented by other mainly primary colors. Lit colored vitrines were mounted on walls or perched on bespoke tables displaying single or grouped Barbies from her various eras.

One part of the show was dedicated to Barbie's Dreamhouses—miniature sets created for Barbie to act out her domestic life—which, like the doll itself, have changed over time, engaging with trends. The ingeniously designed first Barbie Dreamhouse, marketed in 1962, was bought as a cardboard case with a plastic carrying handle. Its contents comprised a flat-packed kit of carboard parts that allowed the owner to construct furniture from further pre-printed elements. The box itself unfolded to become the walls and floor of a one-story house. The accommodation was a microcosm of early 1960s aspirations, fashion, and style: open-plan and with no kitchen, but equipped with a bed, sofa, and coffee table, a hi-fi and television unit, a clothes closet, a chair, and a footstool. The whole ensemble was designed in a mid-century modern idiom. While this initial version of the Barbie Dreamhouse still had some of the trappings of commercial vernacular style on its external walls, such as timber cladding, its interior was much more intentionally "modern."

As the museum's publicity blurb said: "Together these items show how Barbie's homes, vehicles and other products have all helped to design the universe in which she exists and has always reflected the tastes and trends of day [sic], engaging with modern design in an aspirational but accessible way."[1] SJS designed a series of episodic spaces that choreographed the viewer's journey through the history of Barbie, reflecting her frequently featured colors and her plastic but sleek material palette. Like the toy and its accessories themselves, the whole ensemble had a wonderful make-believe aura—truly bringing us into Barbie's world.

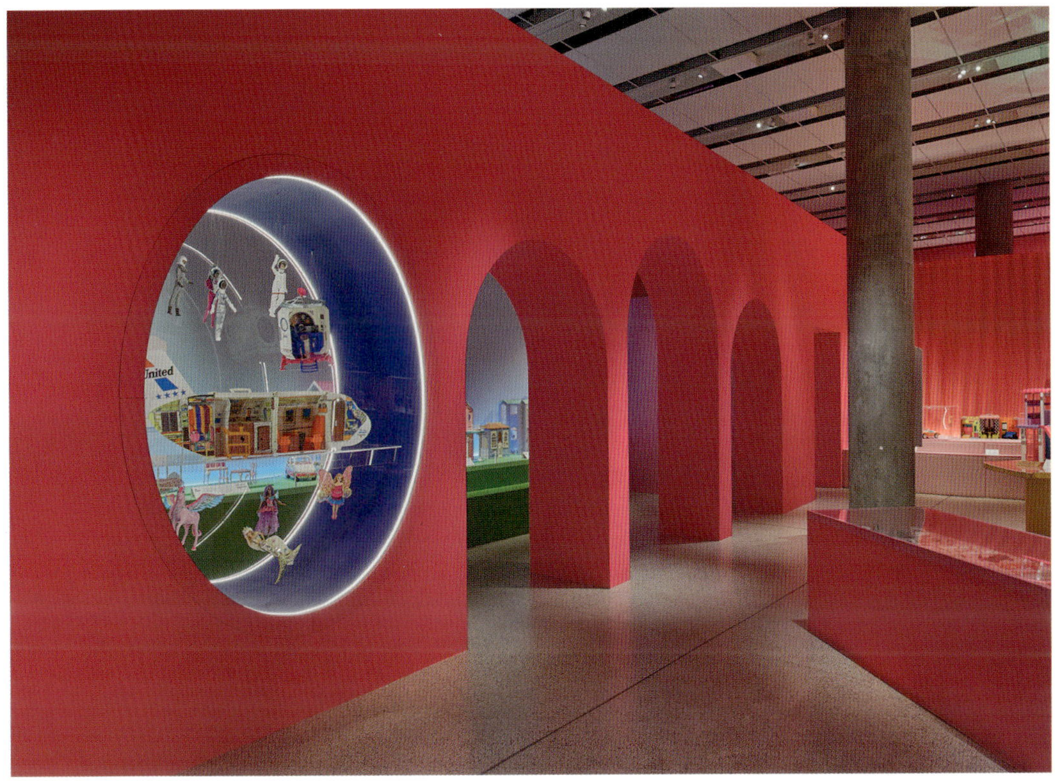

Pedagogic Play

Recently Sam Jacob has been appointed to head one of the three architectural design studios at the Institute of Architecture (I oA) at the University of Applied Arts Vienna / die Angewandte. Here he succinctly describes his design ethos: "Studio Jacob explores architecture as representation. For architecture, representation is simultaneously a technical, cultural and political question. It raises questions about: 1. Who is represented (publics, communities, civicness etc.) 2. What is represented (narratives, symbolism, histories, content etc) and 3. How things are represented (techniques, material, construction methods etc)."[2] SJS has created a multi-scalar cornucopia of color and form with each of these three exhibition designs, but with sense and rigor as well as fun. The same concepts also play out in the studio's buildings and placemaking, its street installations, and its objects—in everything it does. The normally dour architectural landscape is much enhanced by SJS's presence and the wit of its founder.

Notes

1. Exhibition website: https://designmuseum.org/exhibitions/barbie-the-exhibition.
2. I oA website: https://ioa.angewandte.at/studios.

Sam Jacob Studio,
"Barbie®: The Exhibition,"
Design Museum,
London,
2024-5

above: Barbie's signature hot pink pervaded and choreographed the exhibition design, binding it together yet allowing other Barbie colors to maintain their identity.

Mattel,
Barbie Dreamhouse,
1962

opposite: The first Dreamhouse was bought as a cardboard case and opened out to form the house's walls, with flat-pack furniture inside to fit out the interior. It could then be packed away for storage.

CONTRIBUTORS

Peter J. Baldwin is an architect, artist, and educator known for his experimental drawings and critical commentary on contemporary representational practices. Charting a largely unmapped disciplinary territory between the documentation of spatial effect and artistic arti[fact], his work exploits the generative potential of non-traditional modes of architectural representation in an attempt to initiate a conversation between process, image, and representation. His research has been widely published, including in the AD issues *A Sublime Synthesis: Architecture and Art* (September/October 2023) and *The Allegorical Architectural Machine* (November/December 2024). He is also the guest-editor of AD *Ghost Stories: Architecture and the Intangible* (July/August 2024).

Lorna Burn has worked as a curator in national and regional museums, galleries, and development agencies, and is currently an Assistant Curator at the Farrell Centre at Newcastle University. She previously held the position of Exhibition Manager at the Royal Academy of Arts, London, and was a Collection and Exhibitions Curator at both the Crafts Council and Museums Sheffield.

Mark Burry is an architect and leads Swinburne University of Technology's development of a whole-of-university research approach to "urban futures," helping to ensure that our future cities and regions anticipate and meet the needs of all through novel strategies for citizens to participate in the development of their own communities. He has been Senior Architect to the Sagrada Família Basilica Foundation, pioneering the digitalization of all aspects of architectural practice through a Gaudí lens, a collaboration with his colleagues based in Barcelona, spanning 37 years and concluding in late 2016. He also contributes to the Institute for Advanced Architecture of Catalonia (IAAC) as a Senior Faculty member to the Master in Advanced Architecture program, and as a PhD Supervisor. He was previously Professor of Urban Futures at the Faculty of Architecture, Building and Planning at Melbourne University.

Adrian Hawker is a graduate of the Mackintosh School of Architecture, Glasgow, and the Architectural Association (AA) in London. His architectural designs, drawings, and constructs have been awarded, exhibited, and published internationally. He is a co-director of Metis, an atelier for art, architecture, and urbanism founded with Mark Dorrian in 1997. He is Senior Lecturer in Architecture and Contemporary Practice at Edinburgh School of Architecture and Landscape Architecture (ESALA) at the University of Edinburgh.

Charles Holland is an architect, teacher, and writer. He is the principal of Charles Holland Architects, a design and research practice based in the UK, and Professor of Architecture at the University for the Creative Arts in Canterbury. Prior to starting his own practice, he was a director of FAT Architecture, where he was responsible for a number of the practice's key projects, including A House for Essex, a collaboration with the artist Grayson Perry. He writes regularly for both academic and industry publications, and is the author of *How To Enjoy Architecture* (Yale University Press, 2024). His work has been published and exhibited extensively and combines design practice and academic research.

Owen Hopkins is a curator, writer, and historian. He is the founding Director of the Farrell Centre in Newcastle, UK—a public venue for the built environment which opened in April 2023. He was previously Senior Curator at Sir John Soane's Museum, London, and Architecture Programme Curator at the Royal Academy of Arts. He was also part of the curatorial team that developed the exhibition for the British Pavilion at the 2025 Venice Architecture Biennale.

Leah Kelly is a neuroscientist at Rockefeller University in New York. Her scientific research has been published in *Nature*, *Nature Neuroscience*, and *Cell Metabolism*. She consults and writes for artists and architects, and co-taught a neuroscience seminar—"building sense"—at Columbia University's Graduate School of Architecture, Planning and Preservation (GSAPP). Her essay "Sense of Self" was published in *Experience: Culture, Cognition, and the Common Sense* (MIT Press, 2016).

Jaffer Kolb is a co-founder of the New York-based practice New Affiliates, and is faculty at the Massachusetts Institute of Technology (MIT) School of Architecture. New Affiliates has been recognized with a Design Excellence award from New York City's Public Design Commission, a Bessie Award for Outstanding Visual Design, and the Architectural League Prize, in addition to numerous other accolades and profiles for its work in the arts and innovations in reuse and public space.

Elena Manferdini is principal of Atelier Manferdini. She has over 20 years of experience in design, placemaking, and education. In 2019 she received the ICON Award at the LA Design Festival for her impact on Los Angeles and society. She serves as Graduate Programs Chair at the Southern California Institute of Architecture (SCI-Arc), and has taught at Cornell University in Ithaca, New York, at the University of California, Berkeley, University of Pennsylvania (UPENN) in Philadelphia, and Kyoto Seika University, Japan. Her work has been exhibited internationally, and she holds engineering and architecture licenses in Italy and Switzerland, with a Master's from the University of California, Los Angeles (UCLA).

Eva Menuhin is a London-based writer, editor, copy-editor, and translator specializing in architecture and art. Her experience includes collaborating with individuals and institutions such as the late Sir Philip Dowson, Ian Ritchie, the AA School of Architecture, and STUFISH Entertainment Architects. She regularly contributes to Ɗ. A graduate of Stanford University, California, she combines her professional expertise with a love of travel and the outdoors whenever she can escape from her computer.

Mark Morris is Senior Curator of Architecture and Design at the Victoria and Albert Museum, London, as well as the Lead Curator of the V&A+RIBA Architecture Partnership. His research focuses on architectural representations in drawings, models, set design, and in literature. For the last decade he has looked at architectural novels, organizing seminars on the topic at Cornell University and at the Architectural Association (AA) where he was previously Head of Teaching and Learning. He is the author of *Models: Architecture and the Miniature* (Academy Press, 2006) and numerous essays featured in anthologies and journals.

Luke Caspar Pearson is an Associate Professor at the Bartlett School of Architecture, University College London (UCL). He is a co-founder of You+Pea and a co-director of the Cinematic and Videogame Architecture MArch at UCL. He has written widely on the relationship between architecture and games, and was a guest producer for the Serpentine Galleries' *Future Art Ecosystems 2: Art x Metaverse* (2021). He is the guest-editor of Ɗ *Re-Imagining the Avant-Garde* (July/August 2019), and editor of *Drawing Futures* (UCL Press, 2016).

Bart-Jan Polman is Director of Exhibitions and Public Programs, and Curator of the Arthur Ross Architecture Gallery, at Columbia University's GSAPP. He is a trained architect whose writings have been widely published, and he has taught at Columbia, Delft University of Technology in the Netherlands, Princeton University in New Jersey, and Barnard College and Pratt Institute in New York. He was a consulting curatorial research specialist for the Museum of Modern Art (MoMA), New York, and has developed exhibitions for the Centre Pompidou in Paris, Swiss Architecture Museum in Basel, the Power Station of Art in Shanghai, and Princeton University.

Rahesh Ram is an Associate Professor in Architecture. He is Head of Architecture at the School of Design, and Programme Lead for the Master's in Architecture, at the University of Greenwich, London. He also leads the Master's Unit 12 at Greenwich, which places speculation at the center of pedagogic practice, with a particular interest in fiction and identity. He previously ran NAAU Ltd, a collaborative practice that worked with architects, artists, and filmmakers.

Jessica Reynolds is a director at vPPR Architects, which she co-founded in 2009 with Tatiana von Preussen and Catherine Pease. She teaches a unit at the Architectural Association (AA) School of Architecture, researching the role of museums in the climate emergency. She studied at the University of Cambridge and Princeton University, and is currently an external examiner for Cambridge. From its studios in London, Liverpool, and Hamburg, vPPR collaborates with private clients and public institutions to create cultural, commercial, and residential projects with an emphasis on the crossover of art and architecture.

Stephen Rustow is an architect, educator, and the founding principal of Museoplan, a design consultancy working with cultural collections. He previously directed the Kohn Pedersen Fox architectural team on the MoMA expansion (with Taniguchi Associates), and worked for 12 years with I. M. Pei on the Grand Louvre project in Paris as architect, gallery designer, and Director of the Paris office. A member of the proportional faculty at Cooper Union for 20 years, he retired as a Distinguished Professor. He has written extensively on museum design and is completing a book on the museum as an architectural typology.

Michael Szivos is the founder of SOFTlab, a design studio based in New York City. The studio combines a research-based design practice with an interest in how technology, craft, and materials come together in ways that explore the boundaries between art, architecture, interaction design, other disciplines, and the public. In addition to directing SOFTlab, he is a Senior Critic at the Yale School of Architecture in New Haven, Connecticut, where he teaches core design studios and computational design seminars.

Sandra Youkhana is an Associate Professor at the Bartlett School of Architecture, UCL, where she is Director of Short Courses, and is a registered architect. She is a co-founder of You+Pea and teaches the Cinematic and Videogame Architecture MArch at UCL. She has consulted for game developers, technology companies, and city planners, and is undertaking a PhD at UCL, creating experimental video-game works that challenge Iraq's representation through video-game media.

AD WHAT IS ARCHITECTURAL DESIGN?

Founded in 1930, *Architectural Design* (AD) is an influential and prestigious publication. It combines the currency and topicality of a newsstand journal with the rigor and production qualities of a book. With an almost unrivaled reputation worldwide, it is consistently at the forefront of cultural thought and design.

Issues of AD are edited either by the journal's Editorial Director, Ashley Simone, and Editor, Neil Spiller, or by an invited Guest-Editor. Renowned for being at the leading edge of design and new technologies, AD also covers themes as diverse as architectural history, the environment, interior design, landscape architecture, and urban design.

Provocative and pioneering, AD inspires theoretical, creative and technological advances. It questions the outcome of technical innovations as well as the far-reaching social, cultural, and environmental challenges that present themselves today.

For further information on AD, subscriptions and purchasing single issues see: www.archdesignjournal.com

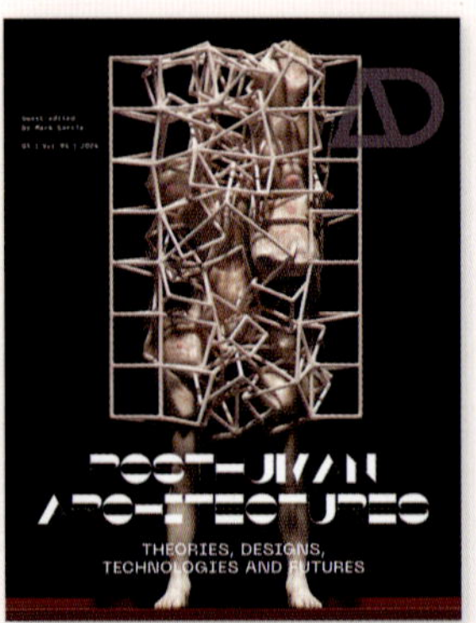

Volume 94 No 1
ISBN 978-1-394-17003-6

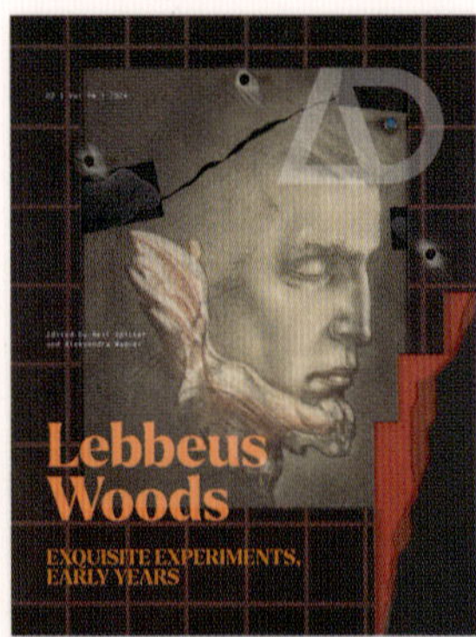

Volume 94 No 2
ISBN 978-1-119-98430-6

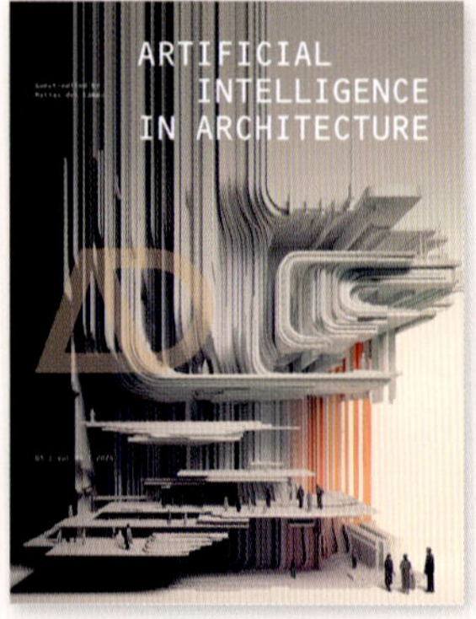

Volume 94 No 3
ISBN 978-1-394-19121-5

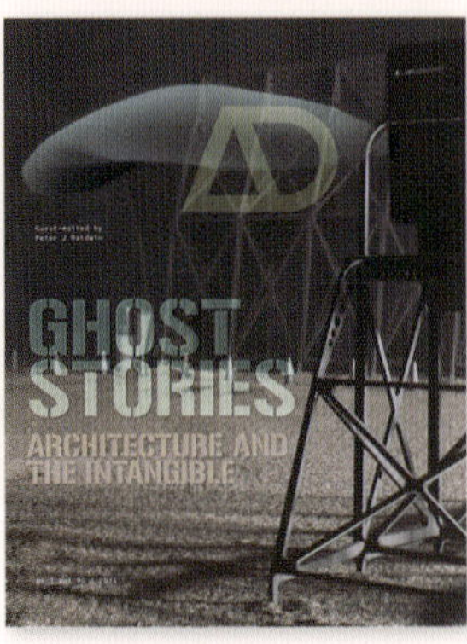

Volume 94 No 4
ISBN 978-1-394-18508-5

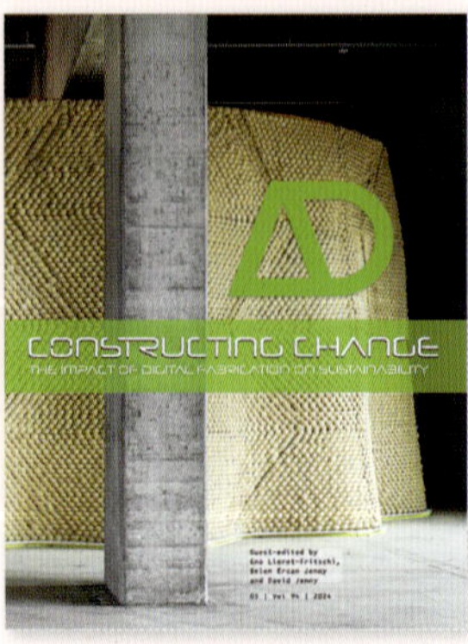

Volume 94 No 5
ISBN 978-1-394-23216-1

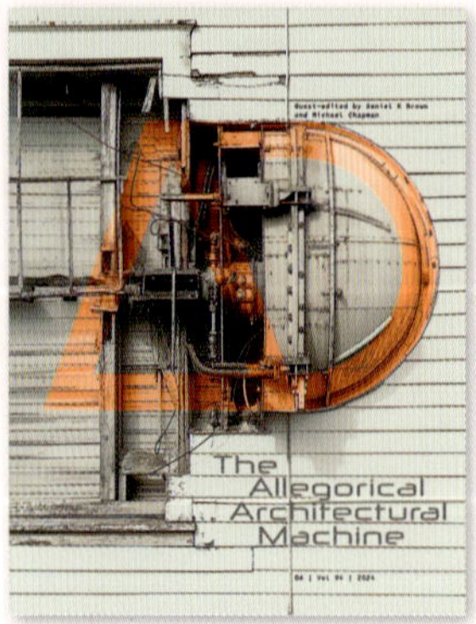

Volume 94 No 6
ISBN 978-1-394-20417-5

HOW TO SUBSCRIBE

Individual backlist issues of AD are available as books for purchase starting at US$45

www.archdesignjournal.com

With 4 issues a year, you can subscribe to AD either print or online.

Institutional subscription

$950
print and online

$850
print only

$850
online only

Individual subscription

$190
print and online

$160
print only

$120
online only

Individual issues

$40

To subscribe to (print or online)
E: subscriptions@archdesignjournal.com
W: www.archdesignjournal.com

General queries
E: hello@archdesignjournal.com

Visit our Online Customer Help
www.archdesignjournal.com